Sarah Buschfeld · Patricia Ronan · Manuela Vida-Mannl

Multilingualism

A Sociolinguistic and Acquisitional Approach

Sarah Buschfeld
Faculty of Cultural Studies
TU Dortmund University
Dortmund, Germany

Patricia Ronan
Faculty of Cultural Studies
TU Dortmund University
Dortmund, Germany

Manuela Vida-Mannl
Faculty of Cultural Studies
TU Dortmund University
Dortmund, Germany

ISBN 978-3-031-28404-5   ISBN 978-3-031-28405-2 (eBook)
https://doi.org/10.1007/978-3-031-28405-2

© The Editor(s) (if applicable) and The Author(s), under exclusive licence to Springer Nature Switzerland AG 2023

This work is subject to copyright. All rights are solely and exclusively licensed by the Publisher, whether the whole or part of the material is concerned, specifically the rights of translation, reprinting, reuse of illustrations, recitation, broadcasting, reproduction on microfilms or in any other physical way, and transmission or information storage and retrieval, electronic adaptation, computer software, or by similar or dissimilar methodology now known or hereafter developed.

The use of general descriptive names, registered names, trademarks, service marks, etc. in this publication does not imply, even in the absence of a specific statement, that such names are exempt from the relevant protective laws and regulations and therefore free for general use.

The publisher, the authors, and the editors are safe to assume that the advice and information in this book are believed to be true and accurate at the date of publication. Neither the publisher nor the authors or the editors give a warranty, expressed or implied, with respect to the material contained herein or for any errors or omissions that may have been made. The publisher remains neutral with regard to jurisdictional claims in published maps and institutional affiliations.

This Palgrave Macmillan imprint is published by the registered company Springer Nature Switzerland AG

The registered company address is: Gewerbestrasse 11, 6330 Cham, Switzerland

Paper in this product is recyclable.

Preface

This textbook assesses the complex and multifaceted phenomenon of multilingualism from a wide angle of different viewpoints, focusing on both sociolinguistic and acquisitional phenomena and perspectives. While the focus is on the English language as one of the major players in many multilingual scenarios, the book also provides insights into select examples of multilingual societies or communities of practice involving languages other than English and in which English plays only a minor role, if at all.

In the course of this book, the more traditional aspects of multilingualism, such as its historical dimensions, societal and individual multilingualism, aspects of identities, ideologies, education, and language policies, are introduced and scrutinised, if necessary (Parts I and II). Subsequently, the authors turn towards the newer manifestations of multilingualism, that is, multilingualism at the grassroots, in migrant and refugee contexts, in new media and pop music, as well as in linguistic landscapes (Part III). These new manifestations are recent issues of multilingual communities and language use and largely emerged as a result of globalisation, the fluid, global mobilities of our modern age, and the emergence of the digital era. This book is, to the authors' knowledge, the first textbook to include all of these issues in a systematic and comprehensive way. The final chapters are devoted to introducing research methods and tools to interested readers, novice researchers, and students who would like to pursue multilingualism research themselves.

The textbook uses evocative examples from a broad range of contexts from around the world, which allows the authors to regularly depart from the frequently pursued traditional Anglo-centred perspectives and include contexts and constellations where English is not the major player in the multilingual scenario. Germany, for example, is one of the countries that, from a traditional and in particular the lay perspective, is still often considered one of the last strongholds of monolingualism. This, however, is no longer true; with migration and globalisation, multilingualism has become an important aspect of German society as well, especially in the metropolitan areas. Most importantly, this textbook takes an integrated approach, combining sociolinguistic, cognitive, and acquisitional perspectives on multilingualism. Its inclusiveness, broad scope, and organisation into 14 chapters, which corresponds to the teaching weeks per university semester, make this textbook an ideal basis for readers, students, and teachers to immerse into the field of multilingualism.

We have worked on the textbook as a team of linguists who have brought their own individual perspectives and research experiences into the book during the last two and a half years. It has been a time of fruitful and intense collaboration. At the end of this journey, we are more convinced than ever that such collaboration, which has united different viewpoints and, at times, negotiated diverging opinions, has been extremely valuable for the structure and contents of the book and has sometimes been an eye-opener for the parties involved. Finally, we would like to thank, Brian Hess, Emily Weidle, and Lisa Westermayer for their invaluable support in creating this book.

Sarah Buschfeld

Patricia Ronan

Dortmund, Germany

Manuela Vida-Mannl

Contents

I Contextualising Multilingualism

1 Welcome to a Multilingual World 3
1.1 Introduction 4
1.2 Some Facts and Figures 7
1.3 Some Basic Concepts and Terminology Related to Multilingualism 9
1.4 Let's Get Started 13
References 20

2 Multilingualism Then and Now 23
2.1 Introduction 24
2.2 The Historical Dimensions of Multilingualism 24
2.2.1 How Does Multilingualism Arise? 24
2.2.2 How Do Multilingual Countries Arise? 26
2.3 Some Myths About Multilingualism 32
2.3.1 Myth #1: Multilingualism Is a Recent Phenomenon 33
2.3.2 Myth #2: Monolingualism Is the Norm 35
2.3.3 Myth #3: Multilingualism Is Disadvantageous 35
2.3.4 Myth #4: A Bilingual Person Is Two Monolinguals in One 37
2.3.5 Myth #5: Multilingualism Causes Identity Problems 38
References 40

II Conceptualising Multilingualism

3 The Multilingual Individual: Who Is Multilingual and What Is Special? 45
3.1 Introduction 46
3.2 Who Is Multilingual? 47
3.3 Acquiring Two or More Languages from Birth: What Is Different? 50
3.3.1 Acquiring Sound System(s) 53
3.3.2 Acquiring Words: The Lexicon 55
3.3.3 Acquiring Morphosyntax 59
3.4 Language Choice and Cross-Linguistic Influence 60
References 66

4 Linguistic Mechanisms, Processes, and Results 73
4.1 Introduction 74
4.2 Language Contact 74
4.3 Language Change and Its Mechanisms 77
4.3.1 First vs. Second Language Acquisition and Language Change 78

4.3.2	Factors of Language Change	81
4.3.3	Mechanisms of Language Change	87
4.4	**Linguistic Effects of Language Change on the Recipient Language**	**91**
4.5	**Language Change or Temporary Variation?**	**94**
	References	97

5	**Linguistic Manifestations in a Multilingual World: Focus on English**	**101**
5.1	**Introduction**	**102**
5.2	**Types of English Around the World**	**102**
5.2.1	The English as a Native, Second and Foreign Language Distinction	103
5.2.2	Pidgin and Creole Languages	104
5.2.3	English as a Lingua Franca, English for Specific Purposes, and Grassroots Englishes	106
5.3	**Hybrid or Mixed Languages in Multilingual Settings**	**109**
5.4	**But What's in a Name?**	**113**
	References	117

6	**Societal Multilingualism**	**121**
6.1	**Introduction**	**123**
6.2	**What Makes a Country or Society Multilingual?**	**124**
6.2.1	Measuring Linguistic Diversity	124
6.2.2	Typologies and Frameworks of Societal Multilingualism	128
6.2.3	Terms and Labels Expressing Language Status and Power Relations Amongst Speakers	131
6.2.4	Contemporary Social Trends	132
6.2.5	Language Policies and Attitudes	134
6.3	**Patterns of Multilingual Organisation**	**135**
6.3.1	Type I: Territorial Multilingualism Type A	135
6.3.2	Type II: Territorial Multilingualism Type B	137
6.3.3	Type III: Territorial Monolingualism	138
6.3.4	Type IV: Predominantly Territorial Monolingualism with Urban Multilingualism	139
6.3.5	Type V: Diglossia	140
6.4	**Determinants of Multilingual Patterns**	**141**
	References	145

7	**Multilingualism Between Identities, Ideologies, and Language Policies**	**149**
7.1	**Introduction**	**150**
7.2	**Identities**	**150**
7.2.1	Defining Identities	150
7.2.2	Language and Identity	152
7.3	**Attitudes and Ideologies**	**157**
7.3.1	Defining Language Attitudes	157
7.3.2	Defining Language Ideologies	158

7.3.3	Effects of Language Ideologies	161
7.4	**Policies**	164
	References	171

8	**Multilingual Education and Teaching**	**175**
8.1	**Introduction**	176
8.2	**Why and When are Schools Monolingual or Multilingual?**	176
8.3	**Multilingual Approaches in Schools**	180
8.3.1	Weak Multilingual Approaches	180
8.3.2	Strong Multilingual Approaches	182
8.4	**Multilingual Third-Level Education**	188
	References	190

III Multilingualism in the Modern Age: Emergent Contexts and Current Perspectives

9	**Multilingualism in Migrant and Refugee Contexts**	**195**
9.1	**Introduction**	196
9.2	**Migration Contexts**	196
9.3	**Modes of Communication in Migration Contexts**	198
9.3.1	Super-Diverse Settings	198
9.3.2	Communication in Super-Diverse Settings	203
9.4	**Multiethnolects**	204
9.4.1	Introduction to Multiethnolects	205
9.4.2	Linguistic Features of Multiethnolects	206
9.4.3	Why Are Multiethnolects Used?	209
9.5	**International Diasporas**	210
	References	214

10	**Multilingualism in New Media**	**217**
10.1	**Introduction**	218
10.2	**The History of Multilingual New Media**	218
10.3	**Practices of Multilingualism in New Media**	220
10.3.1	Multilingual Sites	220
10.3.2	Multilingual Language Use on the Internet	220
10.4	**Benefits and Pitfalls of Multilingual New Media**	224
10.5	**Two Case Studies**	226
10.5.1	Multilingual Exchanges in YouTube Comments	226
10.5.2	Appropriating your Idol: Instagram	230
10.5.3	What the Sample Studies Show Us	233
	References	234

11	**Multilingual Pop Music**	**235**
11.1	**Introduction**	236

11.2	The History of Multilingualism in Music	236
11.3	Multilingualism and Language Use and Choice in (Pop) Music	237
11.4	Reasons for Employing a Particular Singing Style or Multiple Languages or Dialects	241
11.5	A Short Resumé	243
11.6	Manifestations of Multilingual Pop Music in the Twenty-First Century	243
	References	249
12	**Linguistic Landscapes**	**253**
12.1	Introduction	254
12.2	The Background to Linguistic Landscapes	254
12.3	Types of Signs	256
12.4	What Counts as a Sign?	260
12.5	The Study of Linguistic Landscapes in the Context of Multilingualism and English	261
	References	273

IV Methodological Perspectives

13	**Investigating Multilingualism**	**277**
13.1	Introduction	278
13.2	Multilingual Data Types and Approaches to Studying Them	278
13.3	Before Data Collection: Getting Started on the Project	282
13.4	Data Collection Methods	284
13.4.1	Questionnaire Studies	284
13.4.2	Interviews	288
13.4.3	Ethnographic Observations	291
13.4.4	Linguistic Landscapes	292
13.5	Ethical Aspects of Data Collection	293
	References	298
14	**Using Existing Data Repositories and Data Analysis**	**301**
14.1	Introduction	302
14.2	Making Use of Existing Data Repositories	302
14.2.1	Collecting Data in the Multilingual Social Media Space	302
14.2.2	Corpus Linguistics	304
14.3	Processing and Analysing Linguistic Data	307
	References	312

Supplementary Information

References	316
Index	339

About the Authors

Sarah Buschfeld is a full professor of English Linguistics (Multilingualism) at TU Dortmund University (Germany), after previous appointments at the universities of Regensburg and Cologne. She has worked on postcolonial and non-postcolonial varieties of English (e.g. English in Cyprus, Greece, Namibia, Singapore, and St. Maarten) and in the field of language acquisition and multilingualism. She has written and edited several articles and books on these topics and explores the interfaces of such disciplines and their concepts.

Patricia Ronan is a full professor of English Linguistics at TU Dortmund University (Germany). She has held previous positions in Maynooth, Vitoria-Gasteiz, Bonn, St. Gall, Uppsala, and Lausanne. Her main research interests are language variation, language contact and change, and multilingual societies with a focus on English and Celtic in contact. Other recent publications include joint edited volumes on language, migration, and identity, societal inclusion, corpus linguistics, and corpora in language teaching.

Manuela Vida-Mannl is a post-doctoral researcher at TU Dortmund University (Germany) who specialises in conceptualising multilingualism and the global use and value of English. During her appointment at the University of Cologne, she has developed a framework of the value of English, focusing especially on individual speakers and institutional stakeholders. Furthermore, she works on multilingual contexts such as higher education and tourism (Croatia, Cuba, and Cyprus) and investigates the role, use, and value of individual languages in these contexts.

Abbreviations

AJT	Acceptability Judgement Task
AmE	American English
BFLA	Bilingual first language acquisition
BrE	British English
BSLA	Bilingual second language acquisition
CFA	Camfranglais
CG	Cypriot Greek
CLIL	Content and Language Integrated Learning
COCA	Corpus of Contemporary American English
EAP	English for Academic Purposes
EFL	English as a Foreign Language
EIF	Extra- and Intra-territorial Forces
ENL	English as a Native Language
EOP	English for Occupational Purposes
ESL	English as a Second Language
ESP	English for Specific Purposes
EST	English for Science and Technology
GJT	Grammaticality Judgement Task
GloWbE	Corpus of Global Web-based English
ICE	International Corpus of English
KWIC	Key-Word-In-Context
L1	First language
L2	Second language
L3	Third language
LFC	Lingua Franca Core
MLE	Multicultural London English
MLU	Mean Length of Utterance
MPF	Multicultural Paris French
RoC	Republic of Cyprus
SLA	Second language acquisition
SMG	Standard Modern Greek
TESOL	Teaching English to Speakers of Other Languages
TRNC	Turkish Republic of Northern Cyprus
UNESCO	United Nations Educational, Scientific and Cultural Organization
USSR	Union of Soviet Socialist Republics

List of Figures

Fig. 1.1	Living languages as of 2022 (Eberhard et al., *2022*)	4
Fig. 1.2	Regulatory sign in Nice, Southern France	14
Fig. 1.3	A restroom door at a German university	15
Fig. 1.4	Advertisement from Split, Croatia	16
Fig. 1.5	A welcome sign at a German university café	17
Fig. 1.6	A thank-you note from a Polish female to a German female	18
Fig. 1.7	Regulatory sign of a Corsican/Sardinian ferries company	18
Fig. 1.8	Writing sample of a 9-year-old German boy in English immersion education	19
Fig. 1.9	Multilingual signage in Singapore	19
Fig. 12.1	Multilingual infrastructural discourse: entrance sign in Vrsi, Croatia	257
Fig. 12.2	Multilingual commercial discourse: pseudo-Asian/English/Spanish discourse	258
Fig. 12.3	Multilingual transgressive sign in English and German in Tübingen	258
Fig. 12.4	The market place: Irish language signage on a taxi in Dublin, Ireland	259
Fig. 12.5	Language use in Dortmund Hörde	263
Fig. 12.6	The use of English and Irish in Galway City commercial signage	265
Fig. 12.7	(**a**, **b**) Health shop with both English and Irish signage	266
Fig. 12.8	Pub with English and Irish signage	267
Fig. 12.9	Jewelers with English and Irish signage	267
Fig. 12.10	Irish fonts used for English language pub name	268
Fig. 12.11	Effect of Irish language use versus Irish-style letters on likelihood of tourists entering a business	269
Fig. 12.12	Distribution of languages in St. Martin signage	271
Fig. 12.13	Extent of multilingualism on St. Martin signage	272
Fig. 13.1	Sample consent form for the project "Modeling English and multilingualism in St. Maarten", PIs: Buschfeld & Weihs	295
Fig. 14.1	Excerpt from an Excel file	308
Fig. 14.2	AntConc screenshot on a search query for "Singapore"	310

List of Tables

Table 1.1	Types and definitions of bilingualism (adapted from Gass & Selinker, *2008*, pp. 27–28; original source: Valdés, *2001*, p. 41)	10
Table 5.1	Some examples of pidgin and creole languages	105
Table 6.1	The ten most multilingual countries (Simplified and adapted from Eberhard et al., *2019*)	124
Table 6.2	The five least multilingual countries (Simplified and adapted from Eberhard et al., *2019*)	125
Table 6.3	Linguistic diversity of countries in the world (highest to lowest; simplified from Eberhard et al. *2019*)	127
Table 6.4	Rating of degree of use. (From Stewart, *1968*, p. 542)	130
Table 6.5	Five types of multilingual organisations of nations	136
Table 10.1	Language choices in the comment section	228
Table 10.2	Overview of languages used in comments on @saorseronan post	231

Contextualising Multilingualism

The first part of the textbook aims to contextualise the phenomenon of multilingualism. We introduce readers to the multilingual world by providing and discussing different definitions of the phenomenon, presenting the historical background and different dimensions of multilingualism, as well as relevant facts and figures related to the topic. We discuss a whole range of social, psychological, and linguistic facets and aspects shaping the manifold manifestations of multilingualism to showcase its complexity.

Contents

Chapter 1   Welcome to a Multilingual World – 3

Chapter 2   Multilingualism Then and Now – 23

Welcome to a Multilingual World

Contents

1.1 Introduction – 4

1.2 Some Facts and Figures – 7

1.3 Some Basic Concepts and Terminology Related to Multilingualism – 9

1.4 Let's Get Started – 13

References – 20

© The Author(s), under exclusive license to Springer Nature Switzerland AG 2023
S. Buschfeld et al., *Multilingualism*,
https://doi.org/10.1007/978-3-031-28405-2_1

1.1 Introduction

According to Ethnologue, an annual reference publication that provides statistics and other information on languages and linguistic matters worldwide, 7151 living languages are currently spoken around the world (Eberhard et al., 2022). Of course, this number is always in flux because we constantly update and expand our linguistic knowledge and most importantly, languages themselves constantly evolve. They are spoken and shaped by communities of practice which are shaped by our constantly and rapidly changing world. This makes languages dynamic, living, and fluent systems. However, not all languages have the same impact, for example, in terms of speaker numbers, worldwide spread, attachment, and association with economically and politically powerful nations and prestige speaker groups. At the far end of the continuum of power and influence of languages, approximately 40% of the living languages around the world are endangered and might have less than 1000 remaining speakers. At the other end of the continuum, only about 23 languages are distributed across more than half the world's population (Eberhard et al., 2022). ◘ Figure 1.1 illustrates the recent distribution of languages across the world.

As indicated, this illustration is taken from the Ethnologue website. On the Ethnologue webpage, this map is an interactive tool that provides the names of all languages depicted. Readers are encouraged to visit the website and try out this tool to explore the diversity of languages and their geographical locations.

The introductory chapter to this book introduces the reader to this international linguistic diversity and issues relating to multilingualism as a product of linguistic diversity and language contact. It prepares the ground for deeper engagement with the subject matter. The book is organised into three major parts. The

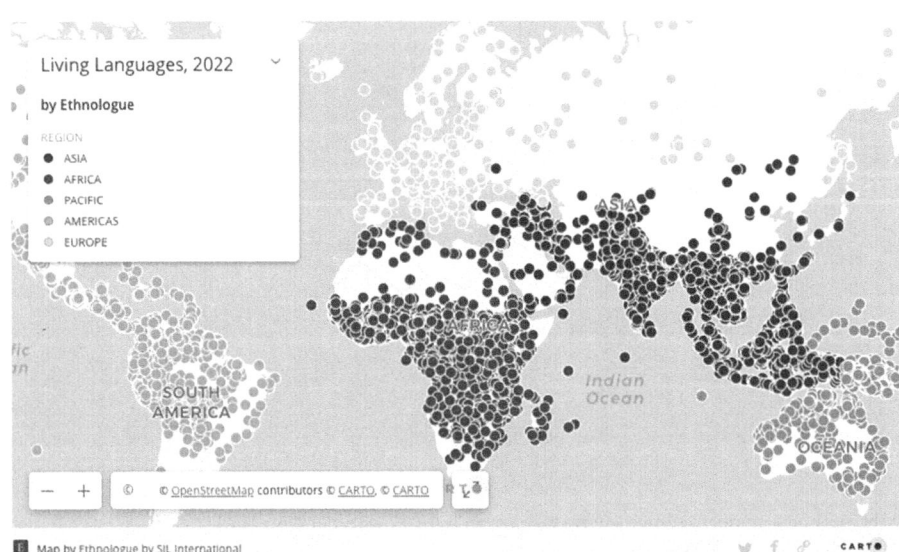

◘ Fig. 1.1 Living languages as of 2022 (Eberhard et al., 2022)

introductory part (Part I) is meant to briefly contextualise multilingualism and contains the present introductory chapter (▶ Chap. 1) as well as ▶ Chap. 2, which explores the origins and historical dimensions of multilingualism. ▶ Chapter 2 further presents and discusses some facts and figures as well as language myths revolving around the notion of multilingualism and challenges many of them.

Part II of the book is devoted towards conceptualising multilingualism, that is, establishing the conceptual and theoretical framework for the topic. ▶ Chapter 3 focuses on the multilingual individual and addresses questions such as "Who is multilingual and what is special about multilingual language acquisition?". Furthermore, we address the process of acquiring more than one language and discuss the social and acquisitional differences and similarities between monolingual and multilingual language acquisition to highlight the benefits and advantages of being multilingual and further rebut myths about monolingual defaults and standards; we still aim to avoid the traditionally employed comparisons of the two modes of language acquisition. We end ▶ Chap. 3 with an assessment of language dominance, specifically focussing on language choice and the notion of *cross-linguistic influence*. ▶ Chapter 4 deals with linguistic mechanisms, processes, and results of multilingualism. We discuss notions, processes, and facets of phenomena such as language contact and language change, code-mixing, and related concepts. We discuss the effect of language contact on various levels of the recipient language and offer an excursus into the field of first and second language acquisition. ▶ Chapter 5 zooms in on the products of such language contact and its underlying processes and mechanisms. We include more traditional and widely-researched cases of language contact such as those to be found in former colonies of the British Empire, that is first- and second-language varieties of English, as well as varieties of English that have emerged in more recent times, in particular non-postcolonial second-language varieties. The focus, however, is on mixed languages, hybrid codes, and the notion of grassroots multilingualism. These linguistic manifestations show even stronger traces of their origin in individual and societal multilingualism than postcolonial and non-postcolonial second-language varieties in that they are often more distant from what has been referred to as *superstrate languages* (e.g. English or French) and have a strong tendency to truly integrate multiple linguistic systems, hence the term *mixed/hybrid codes*. Subsequently, ▶ Chap. 6 deals with societal multilingualism, presents the most multilingual nations of the world, and discusses ways to measure linguistic diversity. It further introduces different frameworks and typologies which have been developed for categorising and describing multilingual nations, drawing on a number of case studies and examples. The question of who is multilingual, which we address in ▶ Chap. 3, is not only difficult to answer scientifically. Answers to this question also strongly depend on the societal and political contexts that speakers and speaker groups experience. ▶ Chapter 7, therefore, addresses three factors that determine which languages speakers may prefer to use within their habitats: identities, ideologies and attitudes, and language policies. As we explore in this chapter, these factors are located on a continuum from personal choice to societal pressure. Also, to some extent related to societal and political contexts of language use and speaker choice, ▶ Chap. 8 focuses on multilingual education and teaching. This is an important facet of multilingualism, as language and educational policies as well as speaker attitudes often have a strong impact on the general linguistic setup of multilingual nations and societies (as partly already mentioned in ▶ Sect. 6.2.4). ▶ Chapter 8, first, introduces socio-political contexts and their impact on mainstream (mostly monolingual) education. Second, it offers a survey of different possible approaches to multilingual teaching and their potential implications.

Part III of the book deals with the phenomenon of multilingualism in the modern age and focuses on emergent contexts and current perspectives. In ▶ Chap. 9, we look into multilingualism in migrant and refugee contexts, and focus on the topic of immigration, which has been identified as one of the major current trends which have promoted the spread of multilingualism worldwide, in ▶ Sect. 6.3.1. ▶ Chapter 9 focuses on different types of migration and discusses their linguistic effects on society in these often super-diverse settings. Subsequently, ▶ Chap. 10 is devoted to a comparatively new area of linguistic research, namely multilingualism and language use in new media. We here focus on the history of multilingual new media, practices of multilingualism in new media, and the benefits and pitfalls of multilingual new media. The chapter concludes with two case studies of multilingual new media language use. Another sparsely researched topic of multilingualism is that of multilingual music. This topic is addressed in ▶ Chap. 11, which, to our best knowledge, is the first time a textbook includes this topic at chapter length. We will briefly sketch out the background of linguistic analysis of (pop) music and discuss different manifestations of multilingualism in pop-music, that is the use of multiple languages in musical pieces but also less obvious effects such as transfer and transliteration effects. We therefore apply the concepts discussed and introduced in ▶ Chap. 4 to different songs and discuss the differences between, for example, *code-mixing*, *code-switching*, *borrowing*, and *translanguaging* again. The chapter further addresses potential reasons for and effects of multilingualism and language contact in songs.

In ▶ Chap. 12, we deal with another rather underexplored topic in multilingualism research, namely linguistic landscapes. Often found in larger metropolitan areas, multilingual linguistic landscapes are a form of visual multilingualism and, as such, at least partly coincide with or are part of the manifestations of multilingual societies and speech communities. We introduce contexts of linguistic landscapes as well as structural properties and different types and functions of multilingual signage. Since language choices in signage not only tell us what their creators consider to be most effective to reach their audiences but also which languages they want to be associated with themselves or which they want to dissociate from, this chapter also takes up aspects of identity and language attitudes again, which were discussed in some detail in ▶ Chap. 7. We conclude Chapter 12 with reference to three case studies of our own: first, a study of landscapes in a culturally diverse town in the German Ruhr Valley, Dortmund; second, a study of how language users react to the visual multilingualism in a multilingual environment in Ireland; and third, a study on multilingual signage in the two capitals of the divided Caribbean island of St. Martin.

Part IV of the book focuses on methodological perspectives and explores different methods and procedures to investigate multilingualism. The first chapter of this final part, ▶ Chap. 13, is devoted to the preparatory steps when aiming to research multilingualism. It explains how (novice) researchers may collect their own data in that it introduces different types of linguistic data, elaborates on important ethical considerations, and presents four commonly used data collection methods (i.e. questionnaires, interviews, ethnographic observations, and linguistic landscaping). Subsequently, ► Chap. 14 turns to how existing data repositories can be used to research multilingualism and addresses potential ways to analyse and interpret multilingual data.

1.2 Some Facts and Figures

Even though multilingualism is by no means a recent phenomenon (to be explored in more detail in ► Chap. 2), a number of current trends, mostly related to globalisation and immigration (to be further explored in ► Chap. 6), have strongly increased the number of bilingual or even multilingual speakers. Grosjean (2010), for example, assumes that around half of the world's children grow up in multilingual homes or communities; Crystal states that "[s]ome two-thirds of the children on earth grow up in a bilingual environment, and develop competence in it" (2004, p. 17). As the trends of globalisation and migration have kept increasing rather than going down during the more than 15 years since Crystal's estimate (be it realistic or slightly overestimated), these numbers can be expected to be even higher today. Bi- and multilingual language acquisition and use have thus clearly turned into a majority phenomenon (cf. Crystal, 2004, p. 17; De Houwer, 1995, p. 220; Paradis, 2007, p. 15; Pearson, 2009, p. 379). This has created much-needed competition for the once-predominant model of the monolingual language learner and has attracted much scientific attention, especially since the late 1990s (cf. Pearson, 2009, p. 379; see also De Houwer, 1995, p. 219). From a scientific perspective, these developments have resulted in the emergence and wide dissemination of journals such as *The International Journal of Bilingualism* or *Bilingualism: Language and Cognition* (both founded in the late 1990s), conferences such as the *International Conference on Bilingualism*, and language corpora. Hundreds of book chapters and articles and many monographs and handbooks, all of which deal with issues to be discussed in the different chapters of this textbook, have been published since then (Serratrice, 2013, p. 87). It is the aim of this book to bring together this knowledge and add more recent insights, as we believe that understanding the concept of multilingualism is crucial for understanding our modern ways of life and for implementing successful language teaching.

According to some rough estimates (Ilanguages, 2018), about 40% of the world's population are monolingual, this means they know one language only. Forty-three percent of the world's population are bilingual and thus able to use two languages with equal fluency (note that this equal-fluency account is not the definition of bilingualism we follow in this book; for further discussion, see ► Sect. 3.2); another 13% of the population worldwide are trilingual and speak three languages fluently. Approximately 3% of the worldwide population speak four languages and less than 1% of the world's population speak five languages fluently. These figures roughly correspond to what has been claimed by Grosjean (2010), but, of course, they need to be treated with some caution for two main reasons. First of all, they are rough estimates only as it is close to impossible to capture the linguistic background of the worldwide population in statistical terms. To our best knowledge, no such worldwide census exists. Related to this methodological problem is the second problem that a number of partly competing terms relating to similar phenomena exist. Commonly, we differentiate between people who speak only one language (monolinguals), people who speak two languages (bilinguals) and people speaking more than two languages (multilinguals). The term *polyglot* is sometimes used synonymously with the term *multilingual* and refers to speakers with a high degree of proficiency in several languages. Furthermore, in more recent years the terms *bilingual* and *multilingual* have also been generalised and used interchangeably for speakers of more than one language. In addition to overlapping terms and concepts, no clear-cut definition exists of who really is bi- or multilingual. The latter point is discussed in some detail in ▶ Chap. 3 on the multilingual individual.

Differences and similarities between bi- and multilingual speakers have been discussed extensively in the literature. Aronin (2019, p. 10), for example, points out that

> [t]here is no doubt that bilingualism and multilingualism have much in common. Both are defined as the ability in an individual to use at least one language in addition to the mother tongue or, in a community or a country, the use or existence of more than one language. But similarity does not mean identity.

She further argues that "the distinction between the two is becoming increasingly apparent" (Aronin, 2019, p.10; see also, e.g., Aronin & Hufeisen, 2009; Cenoz et al., 2001; and a number of chapters in Singleton and Aronin, 2019). For one thing, even though bi- and multilingualism are both complex phenomena (as will become clear in the course of the textbook and in particular in ▶ Chap. 3), multilingualism is yet more complex than bilingualism. This manifests itself in a number of ways. For example, the number of words and grammar options are higher and/or more complex for multilingual speakers speaking three (or more) languages than for bilingual speakers. An additional language system (or even two, or three, etc.) has yet another lexicon, grammar, and pronunciation system as well as an additional accompanying culture. It also requires additional metalinguistic awareness how the third, fourth, etc. system relates to the others, which, of course, offers great opportunities but also poses higher cognitive demands. Cross-linguistic interactions are naturally more complex between three or more languages than between just two (Aronin, 2019, p. 10). What is more, systemic differences have been identified, which refute the earlier assumption "that processing, acquiring and using three and more languages are essentially the same as processing, acquiring and using only two languages" (Aronin, 2019, p. 11). In addition to that, linguists have identified a number of aspects in which multilinguals clearly differ from bilinguals. Higby et al. (2013, p. 68), for example, point out differences in early language representation, lexical retrieval, and grey matter density, that is, the exact composition of grey matter, a central component of the human central nervous system. In general, various studies have shown that the additional language experience language learners receive when acquiring a third language – opposed to the initial learning experience when acquiring another language for the first time – leads to the development of mechanisms that would not have emerged if the person had not learnt the third language (L3) (e.g. Flynn et al., 2004). Other studies have identified, for example, an enhancement of learners' syntactical knowledge due to multilingual experience (Berkes & Flynn, 2012) or differences in the use of politeness strategies in the L3 (Safont-Jordà, 2013). Kemp (2007) found that the more languages a speaker has acquired, the more grammar learning strategies they have at their disposal and the more frequently these are being used. While we cannot list the full set of existing studies on this topic (see Aronin, 2019, pp. 10–12; Aronin & Jessner, 2015; Gabryś-Barker, 2019, pp. 36–38 for further details), we should be aware of the fact that bilingualism cannot necessarily be equated with multilingualism and that such and similar research findings have a number of practical implications, in particular for language education.

Still, since most of the aspects treated in the following chapters of the textbook are general phenomena which apply to both bi- and multilingual speakers, we use the term *multilingual* as a cover term for the acquisition and use of two (or more) languages, following the traditional habit of conflating the two terms (e.g., Meisel, 2001, p. 11; Unsworth, 2013, p. 21). We use the term *bilingual* whenever exactly two languages are involved and point out aspects that are influenced by the more complex state of more than two languages being involved, wherever necessary.

1.3 Some Basic Concepts and Terminology Related to Multilingualism

In ▶ Sect. 1.2, we have already presented basic definitions and speaker numbers for such terms as *monolingual*, *bilingual*, *multilingual*, and *polyglot* and have noted the complexity of defining who exactly can be considered a bi- or multilingual language user. We discuss this in more detail in ▶ Sect. 3.1. As multilingualism and, in particular, bilingualism are widely researched topics of language acquisition and use, concepts and terminology abound. In the following, we give an overview of basic concepts and terms that are commonly found in the literature. Although these terms often include the term *bilingual*, they are easily transferable and also relevant when assessing multilingualism. Keep in mind, however, that it is ultimately impossible to account for all types of multilingualism as many different situations and contexts exist in which people acquire language(s). These reach from growing up with two (or more) languages resulting in adult multilingualism to acquiring two languages but losing the language first acquired and becoming a speaker of the second language 'only' (language attrition, cf. Sect. 4.3). Furthermore, different language reception and production abilities exist, which also play into the existing sets of concepts and terms. Some people have native-like proficiency in all four skills, that is, speaking, listening, reading, and writing, while some are not literate in a language they speak perfectly well otherwise, while yet other people may have receptive skills (i.e. listening and reading) but lack productive skills (i.e. speaking and writing). While not being comprehensive, ◘ Table 1.1 provides some basic types and definitions of bilingualism.

◘ **Table 1.1** Types and definitions of bilingualism (adapted from Gass & Selinker, 2008, pp. 27–28; original source: Valdés, 2001, p. 41)

Label	Definition
Achieved bilingual	See *late bilingual*
Additive bilingual	Someone whose two languages combine in a complementary and enriching fashion
Ambilingual	See *balanced bilingual*
Ascendant bilingual	Someone whose ability to function in a second language is developing due to increased use
Ascribed bilingual	See *early bilingual*
Asymmetrical bilingual	See *receptive bilingual*
Balanced bilingual	Someone whose mastery of two languages is roughly equivalent
Compound bilingual	Someone whose two languages are learnt at the same time, often in the same context
Consecutive bilingual	See *successive bilingual*
Coordinate bilingual	Someone whose two languages are learnt in indistinctively separate contexts
Covert bilingual	Someone who conceals their knowledge of a given language due to an attitudinal disposition
Diagonal bilingual	Someone who is bilingual in a nonstandard language or a dialect and an unrelated standard language
Dominant bilingual	Someone with greater proficiency in one of their languages and uses it significantly more than the other language(s)
Dormant bilingual	Someone who has emigrated to a foreign country for a considerable period of time and has little opportunity to keep the first language actively in use
Early bilingual	Someone who has acquired two languages early in childhood
Emergent bilingual	See *ascendant bilingual*
Equilingual	See *balanced bilingual*
Functional bilingual	Someone who can operate in two languages for the specific task, irrespectively of the fluency level
Horizontal bilingual	Someone who is bilingual in two distinct languages which have a similar or equal status

1.3 · Some Basic Concepts and Terminology Related...

Table 1.1 (continued)

Label	Definition
Incipient bilingual	Someone at the early stages of bilingualism where one language is not fully developed
Late bilingual	Someone who has become a bilingual later than childhood
Maximal bilingual	Someone with near-native control of two or more languages
Minimal bilingual	Someone with only a few words and phrases in a second language
Natural bilingual	Someone who has not undergone any specific training and who is often not in a position to translate or interpret with facility between two languages
Passive bilingual	See *receptive bilingual*
Primary bilingual	See *natural bilingual*
Productive bilingual	Someone who not only understands but also speaks and possibly writes in two or more languages
Receptive bilingual	Someone who understands a second language, in either its spoken or written form, or both, but does not necessarily speak or write it
Recessive bilingual	Someone who begins to feel some difficulty in either understanding or expressing themselves with ease, due to a lack of use
Secondary bilingual	Someone whose second language has been added to a first language via instruction
Semibilingual	See *receptive bilingual*
Semilingual	Someone with insufficient knowledge of either language
Simultaneous bilingual	Someone whose two languages are present from the onset of speech
Subordinate bilingual	Someone who exhibits interference in their language usage by reducing the patterns of the second language to those of the first
Subtractive bilingual	Someone whose second language is acquired at the expense of the aptitudes already acquired in the first language
Successive bilingual	Someone whose second language is added at some stage after the first has begun to develop
Symmetrical bilingual	See *balanced bilingual*
Vertical bilingual	Someone who is bilingual in a standard language and a distinct but related language or dialect

As we can see, a long list of terms exists that all address somewhat different manifestations of bilingualism related to acquisitional patterns, such as age of onset of acquisition, language constellations, different production and reception abilities, etc. Some of these terms overlap, such as the terms *asymmetrical bilingual*, *passive bilingual*, *semibilingual* all being alternative terms for *receptive bilingual*, few are uncontested and clear-cut, and all are in close relation to one another.

Next to these mainly acquisition-related terms and concepts, further modes of multilingualism exist. *Individual multilingualism* describes multilingual language acquisition and use in individuals as well as their linguistic attitudes and is often distinguished from *societal multilingualism*. Societal multilingualism deals with multilingual language acquisition and language use by whole speaker groups, communities, and societies, and their attitudes as well as language policies and practices in particular countries or regions and the resulting multilingual patterns and organisation. However, these domains are not clear-cut but closely interwoven phenomena. As Aronin (2019, p. 4) states: "[I]t is impossible to study individual multilingualism without considering its societal dimensions." Still, the existence of multilingualism in a country or society does not automatically imply that all community members are equally multilingual. Differences exist in multilingual patterns and organisation, for example, in how many speakers are multilingual and in what specific constellations of languages, in what regions of the country multilingualism is strongest or does not exist at all, etc. These patterns and types of societal multilingualism will be addressed in ▶ Chap. 6.

Multilingualism as a language practice adds another perspective to our understanding of multilingualism while overlapping with the concepts of individual and societal multilingualism. Multilingualism as language practice does not focus on specific, individual speakers or geographically defined speaker groups or societies but on the communicative aspect of multi-language use and results in concepts such as, for example, *grassroots multilingualism*. In addition, the usage domains and learning contexts of multilingual language users may differ. Some people acquire additional languages as part of their home language repertoire, others mainly through formal instruction in school or afternoon classes (home vs. school multilingualism). We can further differentiate between *elite/elective multilingualism* and *heritage/folk/immigrant multilingualism*. Blommaert (2011, p. 11), for example, discusses such differences as "multilingualism of the elite" versus "multilingualism of the poor". These terms are certainly politically questionable but they still exist in peoples' minds and reflect the value, and often stigma, attached to specific forms of being multilingual as well as the complex nature of the phenomenon. The difference between these two concepts relates to choosing to become a bilingual for prestigious or academic reasons and being able to afford linguistic education versus becoming bilingual due to one's family situation. While the former is nowadays standard in many countries of the Global North, the latter might be a result of forced migration or of being multilingual due to having historical or ethnic roots in a specific region of, for example, the Global South.

Multilingualism may also be fuelled by different motivations. We can differentiate between *intrinsic* and *extrinsic motivation*, for example in case one decides to learn an additional language because they want to learn the language of their partner versus learning a language since it is part of the educational curriculum. Multilingualism can therefore be anchored in school-based education, migration, mixed marriages, the wish or necessity to trade with foreign nations, and many more reasons. Another crucial aspect that should be considered when dealing with multilingualism is identity. On the one hand, speakers' identity constructions may influence their linguistic choices and attitudes while, at the same time, these constructions are shaped by their multilingual experiences. Many of these and similar aspects will be dealt with in the individual chapters of the textbook (and see, e.g., Bialystok, 2001, pp. 56–89; Paradis, 2007, pp. 15–16; Pearson, 2009, pp. 380–384 for further details and summaries of these aspects, esp. types of bilingualism), in particular since they all play a major role in how we define and conceptualise multilingualism (see ▶ Sect. 3.2 for a more detailed discussion of this). However, before we move on to such more detailed treatments, let us get started with some hands-on activities.

1.4 Let's Get Started

Take a look at the multilingual signs and other examples of multilingual language use and discuss the different manifestations of multilingualism. The examples come from different continents and countries (indicated in the title of the example) and are real-life pictures and photographs, text excerpts, and other examples of multilingual language use. They come from different registers of communication, involving different languages and modes of communication, situations, and purposes, and were all collected by the authors of this textbook. If you use this book in a classroom setting, you can get together in groups, if possible, choose one of the examples you find most interesting or you are most familiar with, and discuss them with your group members. You can lead this discussion along the following guiding questions:

1. Describe what you see in the example.
2. What type of multilingual language use does the example constitute (e.g. a public sign, an example of electronic communication, lyrics, etc.)?
3. How many languages are used and which ones? What is the most prominent language in the example?
4. Describe what you think is remarkable about the language use in the example.
5. Explain and comment on at least one specific linguistic characteristic in the example that catches your attention.
6. What is the probable reason for the multilingual language use in the example?
7. What is the effect of the multilingual language use on the reader, viewer, or observer?

▶ Example 1.1

Regulatory sign in Nice, Southern France (◻ Fig. 1.2). ◀

◻ **Fig. 1.2** Regulatory sign in Nice, Southern France

▶ Example 1.2

Lyrics excerpt from "Meine Gang (Bang Bang)" (Cro, 2014) (English translations of the German material in single quotation marks and brackets; from: Buschfeld, 2021, pp. 37–38).

Ich bi-bi-bin nicht Drake, doch hab' Love für die Crew, meine Dawgs
('I'm not Drake but I have love for the crew, my dawgs')
Alle Boos sind im Club, but I don't give a fuck
('All the uncool guys are in the club, . . .')
Und alle Babes sagen, ‚Boah, du bist straight hier der Boss.'
('And all babes say, "Wow, you're clearly the boss here."')
Egal wie viele Tapes ich record'
('No matter how many tapes I record')
Und ich sag', "Bitch, get off, keine Zeit für dich, Hoe."
('And I say, "Bitch get off, no time for you, hoe"')
Bin unterwegs mit meinen Doggys, also scheiß mal auf Cro
('I'm on tour with my doggies (a German youth language variant of dawgs, indicating submissiveness), so don't give a shit about Cro')
G-G-Gangsterattitüde, Motherfucker (ah!), life is a hoe
('Gangster attitude, motherfucker . . .')
Und meine Gang ist eigentlich broke, aber immer wieder high von dem Dope, oh, oh
('And my gang is actually broke, but again and again high on dope')
Digga, Digga, meine Gang ist voller Chicks oder Atzen
('Dude, dude, my gang is full of chicks and fellas')

1.4 Let's Get Started

Die bis Mitternacht ratzen, aufsteh'n, obwohl sie noch nicht wach sind
('Who sleep until midnight and get up even though they are not awake yet')
Lieber ficken statt quatschen (ah!), Jimmys lieber spliffen statt klatschen
('Who rather fuck than chat (ah!), Jimmies who rather smoke spliffs than drink (alcohol)')
Kein bisschen erwachsen, but ain't nobody fuckin' with my motherfucking gang
('Not a bit grown-up, but . . .'). ◄

▶ **Example 1.3**

A restroom door at a German university (◘ Fig. 1.3). ◄

◘ **Fig. 1.3** A restroom door at a German university

▶ Example 1.4

A multilingual Facebook conversation between two Singaporean women (example first presented and discussed in Buschfeld et al., 2018, p. 35).

Female, 36: nice? no frog porridge this time? next time must jio me
Female, 38: Hahhaah u not in your hood mah. Yes. Ate up already 😊
Female, 36: Wah u 2 ate so much. U had the kung bao spicy one or spring onion?
Female, 38: Just 1 frog kungpao

Key: *jio* ('invite'); *mah, wah*: Chinese (and Singapore English) particles (*mah* indicates information as obvious; *wah* is an expression of surprise). ◄

▶ Example 1.5

Advertisement from Split, Croatia (◘ Fig. 1.4). ◄

◘ Fig. 1.4 Advertisement from Split, Croatia

1.4 Let's Get Started

▶ **Example 1.6**

Lyrics excerpt from "Amach anocht" (Kneecap, 2018, ▶ https://www.youtube.com/watch?v=L9TJMrKpe0k). English translations of the Gaelic material in single quotation marks and square brackets (from: ▶ https://lyricstranslate.com/de/amach-anocht--out-tonight.html).

Goodfellas yes ag ithe mar ríthe
Ag an self-checkout ach ní íocann muid daofa Suas chuig an foodbank, munchies, lethal Cúpla punt sa bhreis do na leaids in Ibiza Buidéal Whitelighting le cuidiú leis an tart Deoirín beag bucky, cocktail ceart Na leaids ar bís táimid ag dul ar an drabhlás Suas ta foc cúpla bump in sa leithreas.

('Goodfellas yes eating like kings
At the self-checkout but we didn't pay for them. Up to the foodbank, munchies, lethal. A couple of pounds extra for the lads in Ibiza. A bottle of Whitelighning helping with the thirst. Bucky's little tears, a right cocktail. The lads are excited we're going on a binge. Up to-fuck a couple of bumps in the toilets.') ◀

▶ **Example 1.7**

A welcome sign at a German university café (◘ Fig. 1.5). ◀

◘ **Fig. 1.5** A welcome sign at a German university café

▶ **Example 1.8**

A thank-you note from a Polish female to a German female (◘ Fig. 1.6). ◀

◘ Fig. 1.6 A thank-you note from a Polish female to a German female

▶ **Example 1.9**

Regulatory sign of a Corsican/Sardinian ferries company (◘ Fig. 1.7). ◀

◘ Fig. 1.7 Regulatory sign of a Corsican/Sardinian ferries company

1.4 Let's Get Started

▶ **Example 1.10**

Writing sample of a 9-year-old German boy in English immersion education (◘ Fig. 1.8). ◀

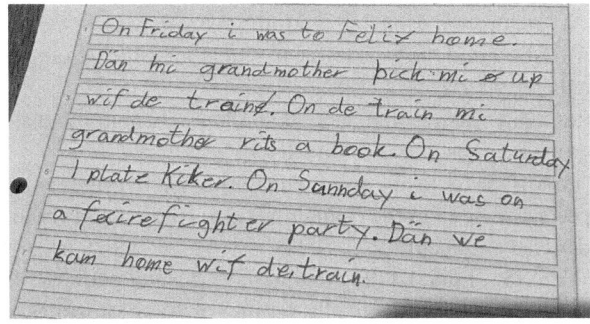

◘ **Fig. 1.8** Writing sample of a 9-year-old German boy in English immersion education

▶ **Example 1.11**

Multilingual signage in Singapore (picture taken by Edgar Schneider, printed with permission) (◘ Fig. 1.9). ◀

◘ **Fig. 1.9** Multilingual signage in Singapore

❓ Exercises

1. Now it is your turn. Collect examples of multilingual language use from the area you live in or from your daily (conversational) encounters and bring them to class for discussion.
2. What is an endangered language and approximately how many endangered languages exist around the world? Try to find at least three examples of endangered languages.
3. Outline the main reasons and facts that show that multilingualism is not a minority phenomenon.
4. Why is it important to distinguish bilingualism and multilingualism? Go back to the aspects presented in the chapter but also read on and try to find further or more detailed arguments.
5. Have a look at ◘ Table 1.1. Try to find more general patterns of being bilingual by grouping the more detailed types into broader categories. What are the general factors that have an impact on the different types of bilingualism?
6. Reflect on the modes of multilingualism presented in this chapter. In case you use more than one language, what type of multilingual are you?

References

Aronin, L. (2019). Lecture 1: What is multilingualism? In D. Singleton & L. Aronin (Eds.), *Twelve lectures on multilingualism* (pp. 3–34). Multilingual Matters.

Aronin, L., & Hufeisen, B. (Eds.). (2009). *The exploration of multilingualism: development of research on L3, multilingualism and multiple language acquisition.* John Benjamins.

Aronin, L., & Jessner, U. (2015). Understanding current multilingualism: What can the butterfly tell us? In C. Kramsch & U. Jessner (Eds.), *The multilingual challenge* (pp. 271–291). De Gruyter.

Berkes, E., & Flynn, S. (2012). Enhanced L3…Ln acquisition and its implications for language teaching. In D. Gabryś-Barker (Ed.), *Cross-linguistic influences in multilingual language acquisition* (pp. 1–22). Springer.

Bialystok, E. (2001). *Bilingualism in development. language, literacy, & cognition.* Cambridge University Press.

Blommaert, J. (2011). The long language-ideological debate in Belgium. *Journal of Multicultural Discourses, 6*(3), 241–256.

Buschfeld, S. (2021). Grassroots English, learner English, second-language English, English as a lingua franca…: What's in a name? In C. Meierkord & E. W. Schneider (Eds.), *The growth and spread of English at the grassroots* (pp. 23–46). Edinburgh University Press.

Buschfeld, S., Kautzsch, A., & Schneider, E. W. (2018). From colonial dynamism to current transnationalism: A unified view on postcolonial and non-postcolonial Englishes. In S. C. Deshors (Ed.), *Modelling World Englishes in the 21st century: Assessing the interplay of emancipation and globalization of ESL varieties* (pp. 15–44). John Benjamins.

Cenoz, J., Hufeisen, B., & Jessner, U. (Eds.). (2001). *Looking beyond second language acquisition: Studies in tri- and multilingualism.* Stauffenburg.

Cro (feat. Danju). (2014). Meine Gang (Bang Bang) [Song]. Retrieved June 6, 2021, from https://genius.com/Cro-meine-gang-bang-bang-lyrics

Crystal, D. (2004). *English as a global language.* Cambridge University Press.

De Houwer, A. (1995). Bilingual language acquisition. In P. Fletcher & B. MacWhinney (Eds.), *The handbook of child language* (pp. 219–250). Basil Blackwell.

Eberhard, D. M., Simons, G. F., & Fennig, C. D. (Eds.) (2022). *Ethnologue: Languages of the world* (25th ed.). SIL International. [Online version]. Retrieved from March 09, 2022, https://www.ethnologue.com/guides/how-many-languages.

References

Flynn, S., Foley, C., & Vinnitskaya, I. (2004). The cumulative-enhancement model for language acquisition: Comparing adults' and children's patterns of development in first, second and third language acquisition of relative clauses. *International Journal of Multilingualism, 1*(1), 3–16.

Gabryś-Barker, D. (2019). Lecture 2: Applied linguistics and multilingualism. In D. Singleton & L. Aronin (Eds.), *Twelve lectures on multilingualism* (pp. 35–64). Multilingual Matters.

Gass, S. M., & Selinker, L. (2008). *Second language acquisition: An introductory course* (3rd ed.). Routledge.

Grosjean, F. (2010). *Bilingual: Life and reality*. Harvard University Press.

Higby, E., Kim, J., & Obler, L. K. (2013). Multilingualism in the brain. *Annual Review of Applied Linguistics, 33*, 68–101.

Ilanguages. (2018). Retrieved February 2, 2022, from http://ilanguages.org/bilingual.php

Kemp, C. (2007). Strategic processing in grammar learning: Do multilinguals use more strategies? *International Journal of Multilingualism, 4*(4), 241–261.

Meisel, J. M. (2001). The simultaneous acquisition of two first languages: Early differentiation and subsequent development of grammars. In J. Cenoz & F. Genesee (Eds.), *Trends in bilingual acquisition* (pp. 11–41). John Benjamins.

Paradis, J. (2007). Early bilingual and multilingual acquisition. In P. Auer & L. Wei (Eds.), *Handbook of multilingualism and multilingual communication* (pp. 15–44). Mouton de Gruyter.

Pearson, B. Z. (2009). Children with two languages. In E. L. Bavin (Ed.), *The Cambridge handbook of child language* (pp. 379–397). Cambridge University Press.

Safont-Jordà, P. (2013). Early stages of trilingual pragmatic development: A longitudinal study of requests in Catalan, Spanish and English. *Journal of Pragmatics, 59*, 68–80.

Serratrice, L. (2013). The bilingual child. In T. K. Bhatia & W. C. Ritchie (Eds.), *The handbook of bilingualism and multilingualism* (2nd ed., pp. 87–108). Wiley-Blackwell.

Singleton, D., & Aronin, L. (Eds.). (2019). *Twelve lectures on multilingualism*. Multilingual Matters.

Unsworth, S. (2013). Current issues in multilingual first language acquisition. *Annual Review of Applied Linguistics, 33*, 21–50.

Valdés, G. (2001). Heritage language students: Profiles and possibilities. In J. K. Peyton, D. A. Ranard, & S. McGinnis (Eds.), *Heritage languages in America: Preserving a national resource*. Center for Applied Linguistics.

Key Readings

De Houwer, A. (1995). Bilingual language acquisition. In P. Fletcher & B. MacWhinney (Eds.), *The handbook of child language* (pp. 219–250). Basil Blackwell.

Gass, S. M., & Selinker, L. (2008). *Second language acquisition: An introductory course* (3rd ed.). Routledge.

Grosjean, F. (2010). *Bilingual: Life and reality*. Harvard University Press.

Further Readings

Aronin, L., & Singleton, D. (2019). Introduction. In D. Singleton & L. Aronin (Eds.), *Twelve lectures on multilingualism*. Multilingual Matters.

Aronin, L., & Singleton, D. (2012). Introduction. In L. Aronin & D. Singleton (Eds.), *Multilingualism* (pp. 1–9) John Benjamins.

Horner, K., & Weber, J.-J. (2018). Introduction. In K. Horner & J.-J. Weber (Eds.), *Introducing multilingualism. A social approach* (2nd ed., pp. 3–13). Routledge.

Multilingualism Then and Now

Contents

2.1 Introduction – 24

2.2 The Historical Dimensions of Multilingualism – 24
2.2.1 How Does Multilingualism Arise? – 24
2.2.2 How Do Multilingual Countries Arise? – 26

2.3 Some Myths About Multilingualism – 32
2.3.1 Myth #1: Multilingualism Is a Recent Phenomenon – 33
2.3.2 Myth #2: Monolingualism Is the Norm – 35
2.3.3 Myth #3: Multilingualism Is Disadvantageous – 35
2.3.4 Myth #4: A Bilingual Person Is Two Monolinguals in One – 37
2.3.5 Myth #5: Multilingualism Causes Identity Problems – 38

References – 40

© The Author(s), under exclusive license to Springer Nature Switzerland AG 2023
S. Buschfeld et al., *Multilingualism*,
https://doi.org/10.1007/978-3-031-28405-2_2

2.1 Introduction

In ▶ Chap. 1, we have learnt about various types of multilingualism, the fact that it is far more widely spread than people may assume, and, therefore, increasingly relevant to understanding social structures and the prerequisites of contemporary language learning and teaching. In this chapter, we go back in time and assess reasons for multilingualism to arise and become the norm—or rather to become normal. In the first part of this chapter, we assess various mobility trajectories that have caused contact between different social groups and, consequently, their languages. These language contact scenarios occur as part of various types of colonisation, voluntary and involuntary migration, or mere geographical proximity and often result in multilingualism. For (parts of) societies to become or remain multilingual, for example during or after colonial rule, certain social structures, administrative prerequisites, and state-internal policies have to be in place. These are presented and discussed to see who is more or less likely to become a multilingual speaker in these contexts and why. In the second part of this chapter, we further focus on multilingual individuals when turning towards commonly shared beliefs and myths about multilingualism. We try to understand how they came to exist, explain their core statements, and, finally, discuss whether and under which circumstances parts of these myths might be true but why they are incorrect or at least inaccurate most of the time.

2.2 The Historical Dimensions of Multilingualism

Multilingualism is a common phenomenon and many could not imagine a world without it. But how does multilingualism arise? Let us start at the very beginning and find out about how speaker groups have become multilingual, how multilingualism (can) be institutionalised as a means of power, and how multilingual states deal with it politically.

2.2.1 How Does Multilingualism Arise?

Historically, a number of situations have led to language contact. Thomason (2001, pp. 17–21) gives a good overview of the processes by which this can happen. Theoretically, language contact can take place when settler groups meet in formerly uninhabited territory. While Thomason mentions the historical examples of the settlement of Mauritius and the Seychelles by colonisers and their slaves during the eighteenth century, unsettled territories have been rarely encountered in more recent times.

More frequently, languages come into contact if groups of settlers move into territories that are already inhabited by population groups that use another language (or other languages). This is a scenario that we can observe repeatedly throughout history and often the situation is referred to as colonisation. One example of this is the arrival of Anglo-Saxon tribes in England during the fifth century AD. Eventually, these new settlers partly drove out indigenous Celtic population groups and partly led to their acculturation, during which the original population groups adopted the Anglo-Saxon language and culture. A parallel development took place in seventeenth-century Ireland. There, an increased influx of British settlers forced the Gaelic-speaking population into socially inferior positions and partly led to their displacement to the less fertile western parts of the country. As a result of the British settlement process, we find an increase in Gaelic and English bilingualism, followed by an increasing loss of the Gaelic language over time (cf. Thomason, 2001; Beal & Faulkner, 2020).

Further, language contact can ensue if individuals or small groups of people move to another country where they join existing minority groups. Such migration is often caused by the search for better living conditions, the hope to obtain better jobs and a better future. In this context, Thomason refers to large immigrant communities in the United States, such as the Pennsylvania Dutch, the communities of Swedes in Wisconsin, or the Japanese in Hawaii and California, as well as to more recent immigrants from Latin America and Asia. In contemporary Britain, recent immigrants often hail from former colonies. Some countries in northern Europe, such as Germany, have encouraged immigration from southern European countries during the second part of the nineteenth century in order to overcome labour shortages. The term often used for these migrants, *guest workers*, is a calque of the German word *Gastarbeiter*, with the same meaning. It was used because the original intention of the host country and the countries of origin was that these migrant workers would eventually return to their home countries. In reality, however, they very often remained in their new countries permanently and retained their original languages and cultures to varying degrees.

A different kind of migration and resulting linguistic contact is the involuntary migration of forced labourers, especially slaves or transported convicts, to new countries. Often, involuntary migrants are not given the opportunity to learn the language of their new environment comprehensively. As a result, mixed languages, so-called pidgins and creoles, can arise (cf. ▶ Chap. 5).

A further type of language contact can be found in the case of neighbouring groups of people, who are in contact due to their close proximity and interact in contexts like trade and marriage. This might, for example, be found if people living close to borders shop regularly in a neighbouring country because the price levels are lower there. This kind of neighbourly contact does not only take place across country borders but can also happen across different linguistic areas within one country, such as a citizen of German-speaking Switzerland shopping in French-speaking Switzerland. Another possible scenario here is that minority population groups who live within a majority population, guest-workers for example, interact with other linguistic minority groups or speakers of the majority language.

As a specific case of meeting in unsettled territories, Thomason (2001, p. 20) also makes the point that language contact can also take place if people who speak different languages meet in No-Man's Land. She gives an example of neighbouring tribes meeting in unclaimed land to gather food. Further, she mentions the dedicated trade zones that were created in coastal countries during the age of exploration. In areas like Canton or Macao, local population groups met European traders to exchange goods, and settlements developed. We suggest that we may also extend this concept of No-Man's Land and trade zones to contemporary marketplaces, especially in tourist destinations, where traders' command of the languages of the tourists may be very restricted and the command of the local languages by the tourists often non-existent. We could, for example, imagine a street seller in Bangkok interacting with tourists wanting to buy clothing or watches. Here, a way of interaction also needs to be found, most likely this would be one involving a global language like English (see ▶ Chap. 5 for a discussion of terms such as *grassroots Englishes* and *grassroots multilingualism*).

Finally, Thomason mentions as a possible language contact scenario the use of languages for educational and religious purposes. Language contact in educational contexts might occur, for example, if students learn a language because it is either a curricular language or a language of instruction. The former holds for the English language in many countries worldwide today, where English is learnt as a foreign language. The latter was the case with Latin in medieval and early modern Europe, and may also be the case with English, which is used as a language of instruction in many contexts in different countries. Latin can also be mentioned as an example of a religious language since it was the language of Christian teaching until early modern times and partly still is today. Similarly, Arabic has long been used to read and recite the Quran (Thomason, 2001; Stavans & Hoffmann, 2015).

2.2.2 How Do Multilingual Countries Arise?

If we consider the question of how multilingual countries arise from a historical perspective, we find many examples of mass migration and forceful acquisition of foreign territory and the expansion of empires. For example, we can think of antique empires like the Babylonian, Persian, Greek, Egyptian, Roman, or Ottoman ones (cf. Stavans & Hoffmann, 2015). Similarly, in early modern times, we find that colonial empires spread around the world and introduced their languages into the territories under their control. Here, especially England, France, or Spain come to mind, but the Portuguese, Dutch, and German empires also controlled overseas territories. For the population in the controlled territories, speaking the language of the conquerors brought social and economic advantages: being able to trade with the socially powerful group in their language, being able to interact with their administration, and having the power to translate between the local languages and the language of the conquerors were strong motivators to acquire their language. The use of the languages of the former conquerors repeatedly persisted also after the empires of the conquerors had collapsed and the territories had gained back their independence. Often the language of the empire became a *lingua franca*, the commonly used language, for communication between various population groups. Cases in point here are the continued use of Spanish, French, and English as official languages in multiple countries across the globe. The sociolin-

2.2 · The Historical Dimensions of Multilingualism

guistic results of the rise of English to world language and lingua franca status are discussed in ▶ Chap. 5 as an example for these developments.

Evidence of early multilingualism is provided for example by sixth century BC bilingual Greek and Punic inscriptions on Malta and by the famous Rosetta Stone. The Rosetta Stone is a bilingual stone found in the Nile delta, dating back to 196 BC. It offers the same inscriptions in both the local hieroglyphic and demotic Egyptian scripts as well as in Greek, the language of the empire which had conquered Egypt one and a half centuries earlier. The stone carries information on the then king of Egypt and on privileges for priests. Each language that was used on the stone fulfils specific functions: the Greek part of the inscription symbolises the language of the Greek administration; hieroglyphic Egyptian was used because it was typical of religious literature and thus appropriate for the priestly context, and demotic Egyptian script, the earlier language of local administration, was typically used for document writing. This stone is an illustration of how different languages and language varieties are used in their appropriate contexts. Incidentally, it was the Rosetta Stone, whose Greek inscriptions proved to be very helpful for later scholars learning to decipher Egyptian hieroglyphic and demotic writing (Thomason, 2001; Stavans & Hoffmann, 2015). The multilingual Rosetta Stone with its different languages and writing systems also illustrates the point made by Stavans and Hoffmann (2015) that the language which is the main administrative language, here Greek, need not necessarily be that of the majority of the population, but may be that of the most powerful subgroup, and the language for which a writing system exists.

These points already illustrate important social factors in language contact: the sociolinguistic situation in which language contact occurs has always been a key determinant for the outcome of the contact scenario. The socio-political situation often tells us which languages are valued or less-valued and therefore which languages are likely to be retained by a population group or given up. Language prestige and economic and political power tend to strongly correlate with each other (for further details on the influence and interaction of these and related aspects on multilingual societies, see ▶ Chap. 6).

We have seen above that regions or countries may become multilingual because they are conquered by foreign linguistic groups. In many cases, the influence of colonial powers united different ethnicities under their colonial rule. When the formerly colonised territories gained independence from the colonial powers, multi-ethnic and multilingual states were left behind, often also with diverse religions. A case in point is India, which gained independence from the British Empire in 1947. A new union state was formed which, in addition to containing multiple linguistic and social groups, also showed huge religious diversity. The former colonial language of English was to be replaced by the North Indian majority language, Hindi. However, there was widespread opposition to the use of Hindi by speakers of other local languages and English was reintroduced as the second official language in 1967 in order to serve as an alternative common language. As a result, children nowadays have to study both English and Hindi in school, and, if they live in a state which has a different official language than Hindi, they also study this third official language. As colonisation is an important factor for the rise of multilingual societies, we will now go into further detail (for further ways of how countries may have become multilingual over time, see Thomason, 2001, pp. 42–46; Stavans & Hoffmann, 2015, pp. 11–36).

2.2.2.1 The Role of Colonisation

The examples given above show that colonisation has played an important role in the rise of multilingualism. Mufwene (2001), followed by Schneider (2007), describes three types of colonisation patterns which differ in various respects, such as the manner of linguistic contacts, the relative social power of the population groups, or the amount of integration or segregation of the population groups involved.

One type of colonial relationship is that of trade colonisation: here we find contact between a foreign power and the local population groups for trade purposes, usually centred around trade forts or trade routes. The local population came in contact with the language of the foreign power only sporadically or to a restricted degree: words and expressions were used or taken over from the foreign language, and often a pidgin arose from the contact. This type of contact resembles Thomason's (2001, p. 20) trade contacts; however, in contrast to trade zones or market places, the colonisers are one foreign power and usually speak only one foreign language, which comes into contact with the sometimes multiple languages of the local population. Mufwene (2001, p. 8) argues that the European traders often spoke non-standard varieties of their languages and contacts between the traders and the locals resulted in structurally reduced varieties of language, which expanded structurally and in terms of communicative force over time. Historically, trade colonies often developed into exploitation or settlement colonies over time as the colonisers gained more and more power over the local population.

Whenever trade colonies developed into exploitation colonies, the position of the foreign powers became more formal: they typically provided the social or administrative elite in the colonised country. In exploitation colonies, contact with the local population took place through the help of some bilingual individuals who translated between the two population groups. For the local population, learning scholastic versions of the language of the colonisers was useful and important in order to gain a higher social status. Over time, as more local speakers acquired the colonisers' language, more and more features from the local language(s) were introduced into the language of the colonisers. Examples of such exploitation colonies can be found in South America, where many areas were colonised by Spain during the Early Modern period and in Africa, where a number of European powers established exploitation colonies during the Early and Late Modern periods and exported raw materials and even local population groups (Mufwene, 2001).

In settlement colonies, which saw the strongest type of contact between the foreign power and the local population, increasing numbers of colonisers settled in the colony. The colonisers often came from different backgrounds, were recent immigrants or already second- or third-generation settlers, and had different social status and different levels of contact with the local population groups. Still, contact between the local population and the colonisers was extensive in settlement colonies and thus, language contact was strong. While the settlers took over some concepts and expressions from the local languages, typically the local population groups had to learn the language of the settlers in order to reap the social benefits of mastering the colonisers' language. European examples for this development are the arrival of Anglo-Saxon settlers in England from the fifth century, later the arrival of Norman French settlers in England from the eleventh century, or the arrival of Anglo-Norman and later on, especially from the seventeenth century onwards, the settlement of mainly British population groups in Ireland. In these cases, we can observe that language shift to the language of the colonisers happened in either the most powerful population groups (as in medieval England and Ireland) or took place at all social levels of the population. Further examples include the colonisation of Australia and New Zealand, which was part of the British colonial overseas expansion.

Schneider (2007, p. 66) adds a further conceptual category of colony, namely that of plantation colony. In those cases, foreign settlers settled in new geographic areas and also (forcefully) imported workers from other regions (for further details on the geographical and demographic expansion of English around the world, e.g. Schneider & Buschfeld, 2022).

2.2.2.2 Internal Developments to Multilingual States

Above we have seen that countries have often become multilingual during their history because they have been conquered or colonised by external population groups. Alternatively, countries may also have become multilingual not due to external forces but to internal developments. Multilingual states have evolved because different regions have been joined in spite of linguistic differences and formed a federation, a political union of different linguistic and political entities. Such a union may be voluntary as is the case in Switzerland. In 1291, the three central German-speaking areas of Uri, Schwyz, and Unterwalden formed a federation. Over time, further German-speaking areas joined the confederation. The French-German bilingual area of Fribourg joined at the turn of the sixteenth century and the trilingual Graubünden, which comprises German-, Italian- and Romansh-speaking population groups, became an ally and finally joined the confederation at the beginning of the nineteenth century. In 1798, Napoleon invaded the Swiss Confederation's territory. In the years after these events, French-speaking Vaud, Geneva, and Neuchâtel joined, as well as the bilingual Valais. However, German remained the official language of this confederation. In 1848 a new constitution was introduced and German, French, and Italian were announced as the official languages of Switzerland. It was only in 1938 that Switzerland gave the status of a national language to Romansh, an offspring of the Vulgar Latin that had been brought to Switzerland by Roman soldiers. It has been spoken mainly in the mountain valleys of southern Graubünden ever since. In recent years, Romansh has lost ground and in 2020, it is only spoken by about 0.5% of the population of Switzerland. By contrast, German is the first language of more than 60% of the Swiss population, French of about 23%, and Italian of about 8% (Federal Statistical Office, 2022).

Even though Switzerland is a multilingual nation, it is not a nation where everyone is multilingual. Instead, we find a situation of territorial multilingualism: the country is divided into different linguistic regions and depending on which region Swiss citizens grow up in, they will be predominantly German-, French-, or Italian-speaking. Of the 26 Cantons of Switzerland, 17 are officially monolingual German, while four are French-speaking (Geneva, Vaud, Neuchâtel, and Jura), and one is Italian-speaking (Ticino). Only the Cantons of Valais, Fribourg, and Berne are French-German bilingual, while Graubünden is trilingual German-Italian-Romansh. It is mainly in the regions between the linguistic borders where strong functional bilingualism (see ▶ Table 1.1, ▶ Chap. 1, for a definition) is found. However, in Graubünden, speakers of the minority language Romansh need to be proficient in German, and, due to the close proximity to the Italian linguistic region, often are proficient in Italian as well (cf. Ronan, 2016).

A comparable situation to the one in Switzerland can also be found in Belgium and is described by Stavans and Hoffmann (2015). In the foundation of Belgium, the French-, Flemish-, and German-speaking parts joined in a federation in 1830. The Belgian constitution of 1831 allows its citizens free choice of their spoken languages, even though administrative language borders existed. A constitutional reform in 1960 fixed linguistic boundaries and decentralised the state. Linguistic tensions do, however, persist, especially concerning the language use in the capital Brussels, which, even though situated in the Flemish part, is becoming increasingly French-speaking (for further details and examples of multilingual societies, see ▶ Chap. 6).

A largely involuntary restructuring of nation-states was, for example, the result of what historians commonly refer to as the "scramble for Africa," that is, the colonisation and division of most of Africa by several Western European powers (e.g. Pakenham, 1991). Since traditional and naturally grown state boundaries were disregarded in the European allocation of Africa, people and languages that formerly formed units were split up and mixed with people and languages of separate, formerly independent units. The formation and current shape of Namibia, with its shapeless Caprivi Strip appendix, is a case in point for European power struggles and Euro-centred deals over the African continent.

2.2.2.3 Evolution of Multilingual States

We have seen in ▶ Sect. 2.2 above that multilingualism is historically entrenched. As a number of recent social trends have further increased global multilingualism (to be discussed in ▶ Sect. 6.2.4), we might think that for a country to be multilingual is, or should be, the norm. Yet many of us can probably think of countries that are virtually or factually monolingual. Why is this still the case?

If a country is officially monolingual, a frequent reason for this is a restrictive language policy of centralist governments, which is often based on false believes about the socio-political consequences of multilingualism. As an illustration of how a centralist state can feel threatened by multilingualism, Maher (2017) adduces the example of the tradition of Babylon and the tower of Babel, which is also recounted in *Genesis*. In the monolingual world after the Flood, the ruler Nimrod built a kingdom which defied God and the Tower of Babel was built to reach up to

Heaven. In order to spread confusion amongst this people, God caused them to speak in a multitude of languages so that they would not understand each other anymore and could not continue to build the tower and scattered them all over the earth. This myth of the Tower of Babel can be taken as an origin myth to explain multilingualism. Maher (2017) argues that multilingualism, a natural state, prevails over homogeneity and monolingualism and points out that on the one hand in this myth multilingualism can be viewed as a divine penance. On the other hand, it can symbolise humanity's desire for intimacy, secrecy, and cultural isolation: people who speak separate languages use a code which others do not understand. In this way, they exclude strangers and the uninitiated from their communication. This myth further illustrates, however, how speaking diverse languages—without being able to communicate in the languages of other citizens—can threaten a centralist state: information and administrative rules may not reach every citizen anymore; as a result, the government loses power.

Historically, multilingualism in a state has been a common phenomenon until premodern times. Thus, Coulmas (2018) argues that in premodern times, it was not unusual that a ruler was addressed by members of the population either in the ruler's language or through an intermediary who spoke both languages. In Europe, developments towards monolingual national ideologies (see ▶ Chap. 7 on language ideologies and policies) were particularly strong during the eighteenth and nineteenth centuries (cf. Stavans & Hoffmann, 2015, pp. 45–47). At the time, philosophical thinking about language considered the role of language for society and for national identity; the use of only one language was seen to enable the formation of a national identity. This view was taken up eagerly by the administrations of various states, presumably due to the assumption that speakers of different languages were more difficult to control by centralised governments than monolingual population groups. The idea behind this line of thinking was that speaking a language different from the language of the major population group may cause the creation of an additional community identity, which might cause these groups to look for self-government. A case in point is the linguistic development in France during and after the French Revolution in the late eighteenth century. The Jacobins were striving for national unity in France and considered this possible only if everyone could communicate in one language; one nation should have one language, *une langue, une nation*. Maher (2017) shows that before the revolution, France had strong regional languages and the knowledge of French was not widespread. The revolutionaries viewed the regional languages as part of the old order, as an obstacle to a unified nation, and thus something to be overcome. The resulting—monolingual—nation-state was to be modern and fraternal. However, this central focus also led to strong nationalism and devaluation of non-centralised languages and cultures.

Similar situations can be observed in the United Kingdom, where the Celtic languages not only lacked political support, but their use by children in schools also led to widespread punishment, as well as in Spain under Bourbon rule, where regional languages such as Basque, Catalan, and Galician were suppressed. Coulmas (2018, p. 62) quotes a senior officer of the Council of Castile in 1716, José Rodrigo Villaplando, who argues that unifying languages is of great importance and that it is a sign of superiority of princes or nations to do so. It was only during the middle of the twentieth century that linguistic rights of minorities largely came to be increasingly respected in a number of countries, such as Canada, the United States, and Wales. Even if the minority languages may not be recognised as national languages, that is, languages that represent the whole nation, they often fulfil functions as official languages, which are recognised and supported means of communication in specific regions: nowadays, this holds for languages like Welsh, Scots Gaelic, Scots, or Irish Gaelic in Wales, Scotland, and Northern Ireland respectively (see ▶ Sect. 6.2.4 for further details on language revitalisation and related aspects).

Thus, multilingual states may come into being by various different means. We have seen that small or larger-scale population movements can introduce new languages into a territory. Colonial powers can introduce their own language into territories under their control, where the colonial language then takes on functions of official or national language. Further, without population movement, states may be formed, voluntarily or involuntarily, which consist of different population groups who speak different languages. We will discuss whether speaking different languages automatically means being multilingual in ▶ Chap. 3. First, we turn towards what people commonly assume about bilinguals and multilinguals and debunk some widespread myths.

2.3 Some Myths About Multilingualism

As we have seen in ▶ Chap. 1, multilingual language use is the worldwide default case. Consequently, many people around the globe are in contact with multilingualism or live multilingually but only a few are experts in the study of multilingualism. Just as in any other area of life and concerning any other phenomenon, this has caused myths to emerge. Whether people believe that "monolingualism is the norm" or that "multilingualism is disadvantageous", these myths often lead to parents deciding to raise their children monolingually although they live in a multilingual environment. Often, the language these children are exposed to is the community language rather than their home language, for example in migration contexts such as the US, the UK, or Germany. Sometimes, even governments counteract multilingual development as in the following example. In her blog "5 Myths Surrounding Multilingualism" Roxane Maar (2021), a young mother, writer, and serial tech entrepreneur describes her own experience of growing up with more than one language:

>> It [multilingualism] is a topic that I find immensely important and at the same time difficult—much of my social identity has been shaped by the biases our society has towards multilingualism. When I arrived in Denmark my only means of communicating with the other children and pedagogues was, in the beginning, English—learning perfectly Danish became a number one priority for me to ensure that I fitted in. I actually even refused to speak Russian for many years (which I later have figured out is quite normal for children that are trying to adapt and feel that their mother tongue doesn't help them in that). When I became older we received a letter

from the municipality that they forbade my mother to speak Russian at home as they feared it would limit my Danish-speaking abilities and integration. Thankfully my mother was not a good listener back then and continued speaking with me in Russian—which has enabled me to be completely fluent in both Danish and Russian this day today.

However, not all parents are such 'bad listeners' and not all children are that lucky. Ill-advised and misconceived governmental or parental decisions have deprived many children of the option to grow up multilingually and to continue using their heritage language—or at least having the choice of doing so or not.

> **Think Tank**
>
> In the following, we present some more or less persistent myths about bi-/multilingualism. Some of these we have already indirectly touched on in ▶ Chap. 1 and ▶ Sect. 2.2. Before we go into more detail, discuss the following myths in small groups of two to four people. Try to identify the factual misconceptions as well as potentially valid aspects of the assumptions. Talk about their potential origin, that is, why has such a myth come into existence at all.
> — Myth #1: Multilingualism is a recent phenomenon.
> — Myth #2: Monolingualism is the norm.
> — Myth #3: Multilingualism is disadvantageous.
> — Myth #4: A bilingual person is two monolinguals in one.
> — Myth #5: Multilingualism causes identity problems.

We will now assess these myths in some more detail, see how they came into existence, and discuss their accuracy (for further details on language myths and related phenomena, see, e.g., Watts, 2011).

2.3.1 Myth #1: Multilingualism Is a Recent Phenomenon

This myth can be refuted easily: multilingualism is not a recent phenomenon. As we have just seen in ▶ Sect. 2.2, multilingualism, as well as multilingual states, have been around for quite some time already. For multilingualism to arise, speakers of different languages have to come in contact. While this can, of course, be contact-by-choice, from a historical perspective, colonisation has often been the reason for speakers and languages getting into contact (cf. ▶ Sect. 2.2). So, if multilingualism has already existed for millennia, why do some people believe it is a new phenomenon? There are several reasons for this myth coming into existence.

First, peoples' place of origin and residence might be an influential factor. While people in rural areas traditionally have had little contact with speakers of other languages, residents of urban areas have been more likely to experience multilingualism frequently. Cities have been magnets for immigration, multilingualism, and language and dialect contact from the earliest times of humankind (e.g.

Mackey, 2005 for an overview). Gupta (2000) lists Bombay, Dar es Salaam, Alexandria, and Constantinople as well-known historic examples of highly multilingual cities which have kept their multicultural and multilingual profiles throughout the centuries. In fact, it seems that multilingual cities line the history of humankind. The Levant accommodated some large multilingual trading cities, such as Alexandria, Smyrna, and Beirut, which linked the economies of Europe and Asia (Strauss, 2011; Mansel, 2014). The Early Modern Mediterranean in general, that is, not only the Ottoman but also the Habsburg and Venetian empires, were characterised by multiculturalism and multilingualism (Dursteler, 2012).

Second, multilingualism is believed to be a recent phenomenon because the term has only become more popular in- and outside academia around the middle of the twentieth century (Lin & Lei, 2020). So, multilingualism is a relatively recent term for an old phenomenon. Multilingualism is the result of (historical) language learning, as those people who were the first to be in contact with another language chose to learn this other language—although not everybody has had the freedom to 'not choose'.

Speakers, past and present, most often decide to learn another language because they want to be able to communicate with a (socially, ideologically, or economically) more powerful group than the group they belong to (see elaborations in ▶ Sect. 2.2). In colonial times, this meant that the educated population would learn the coloniser groups' language to be able to communicate with them and maybe even carry out an official function within the (new) power structures. Nowadays, multilingualism is still initialised and spread through migration, but this migration is more often (although not always) voluntary and amicable. In cases of work migration (cf. ▶ Chap. 9), the migrants decide to move to another country to have access to better or different job opportunities and most often also learn the local language(s) of their destination. For the next generation, the conscious learning effort is not necessary as children who grow up with a home language that differs from the societal language automatically become multilingual—that is in case they are exposed to both languages sufficiently (cf. ▶ Chap. 3).

Furthermore, multilingualism has not been spread equally across social classes. Multilingualism is based on language learning and languages are learnt upwards (cf. De Swaan, 2001). Consequently, educated people of the middle class would learn or maintain languages of higher social classes to enable upward social mobility—to climb the social ladder—and people of higher social classes would speak foreign languages, that is, languages that have a high prestige value, such as Greek, and those of literature and intellectual power, such as French or English. Some social groups, such as those of lower social class or those who interact within a monolingual environment, have had little contact with languages other than their own, especially in their everyday lives. These factors might have contributed to the origin of such a myth.

2.3.2 Myth #2: Monolingualism Is the Norm

In addition to multilingualism being a phenomenon that has been around for a long time already, it also is not rare (see ▶ Chap. 1 for numbers of multilinguals). Still, most people think being monolingual was 'normal' and being multilingual was 'special'. However, as Wiese (2020) argues, "[t]he strong dominance of a single national language and the related monolingual perspectives we see in Europe today" are "a historically comparably recent phenomenon" (261). We learnt in ▶ Sect. 2.2.2.3 that developments towards monolingualism only started during the eighteenth and nineteenth centuries in Europe (cf. Stavans & Hoffmann, 2015, pp. 45–47). The *one nation-one language* ideology, that is, the belief that each language belongs to one people and that one people would speak only one language, resulted from this tendency and became the dominant ideology—especially in societies of the so-called Global North (see Hymes, 1968 for elaboration, ▶ Chap. 7 this volume). This ideology has successfully but wrongfully served as a fruitful substrate for the related belief that monolingualism is the 'norm' (see Gramling, 2016 for an extensive discussion). Although the majority of the world's population speaks more than one language and multilingualism has been practised for centuries, many people still believe that the French speak French, the Germans German, and the British English. However, entering a café in any bigger city in these countries will refute this belief in no time at all. While the assumption that monolingualism is 'normal' is wrong and increasingly labelled as incorrect and unfair, it is still commonly believed. Consequently, monolingualism is indeed often taken as the 'norm' and its influence can be detected, for example, in school curricula and other educational testing or evaluation schemata, in immigration requirements, language policies, in the vast majority of language data collection practices as well as in the evaluation and interpretation of language data; here the focus is often on 'only' one (official or target) language rather than on all languages involved (cf., e.g., Gramling, 2009; Leeman, 2018; May, 2001; Pavlenko, 2002; Tollefson & Tsui, 2014; Wiley, 2014). While this myth #2 is, unfortunately, only half wrong, as monolingualism is often artificially made the norm, myth #3 clearly lacks any factual basis.

2.3.3 Myth #3: Multilingualism Is Disadvantageous

Despite being wrong (cf. Meisel, 2019, pp. 59–60), this myth is widely shared and reproduced and is especially discouraging for parents who think about raising their child bi- or even multilingually. Two main disadvantages of multilingualism are commonly believed and referred to: (1) multilingualism is assumed to cause delays in language development and (2) acquiring multiple languages is believed to hinder the complete acquisition of any of the involved languages which, in turn, would cause language mixing and potential problems during multilinguals' (school) education. As the first disadvantage is concerned with earlier phases of language development, it mostly refers to simultaneous multilinguals, that is, children who start learning more than one language early on. The second disadvantage is believed to occur during a later phase and is often also applied to sequential bilinguals, that is, children that start learning another language later in life (see ► Chap. 1 for definitions and ► Chap. 3 for details).

For quite some time, people believed that children can only learn one language at a time and that having to acquire more than one sound system and grammar simultaneously would result in delays, such as the first word to be produced later than by monolingual children. While the process of language acquisition does show some degree of variability, research has shown that the important milestones, such as sound and word recognition, babbling, production of first words, and grammatical development, are met at approximately the same age in multilingual and monolingual children (e.g. Byers-Heinlein & Lew-Williams, 2017; Conboy & Montanari, 2016; Grosjean, 2010, pp. 179–180, Pearson, 2013; Werker, 2012). Children who are exposed to more than one language neither need longer to understand these languages than monolingually raised children need to understand their language nor do they need longer to start to produce language than their monolingual peers. This is very much worth noticing as bilingual children appear to be able to achieve considerably more than monolingual children in the same period of time. This, of course, is an exaggeration as some mechanisms of understanding and using language are acquired only once. Furthermore, one might think that learning similar languages, such as Catalan and Spanish, might facilitate the process and reduce the extent of language characteristics that have to be learnt for bilingual children. However, it has been shown that, somewhat counter-intuitively, a high level of similarity of the languages that are to be acquired does not make the bilingual acquisition process easier or faster but exacerbates the acquisitional process: bilingual Spanish-Catalan-speaking children need longer to discriminate the very similar sounds of these two languages than bilingual children who acquire less similar languages (cf. Bosch & Sebastián-Gallés, 2003). While there is a certain level of individuality and variability in the language acquisition processes within and across monolingual and bilingual speaker groups, language acquisition generally takes the same path, that is, from easier features and rules to more complex and difficult ones, in approximately the same time, provided that the children are sufficiently exposed to each of the languages they are to acquire. Neither a delay in language acquisition nor an increased likelihood of language impairment have been found for multilinguals (cf. ► Chap. 3).

The second disadvantage often referred to, namely that children can only learn one language 'properly' and that acquiring multiple languages hinders full acquisition of any of the involved languages, is commonly based on the fact that multilingual children tend to mix their languages. This, in turn, has sometimes been understood as proof of a lack of knowledge in each respective language and led to the idea that multilingual children develop only one (unitary) language system. This theory (cf. Volterra & Taeschner, 1978) is, for example, supported by children using a linguistic feature or rule that is based on one of their languages for communication in all languages or by the fact that some multilinguals appear to have only few translation equivalents in their mental lexicon, that is, they tend to have only one word (in any of the involved languages) for a certain concept rather than one word in each language (cf. Grosjean, 2010, pp. 180–182). However, involuntary mixing of language (see ▶ Sect. 4.3.2 for a discussion of *code-switching* and intentional mixing of languages) decreases with age—typically by the age of four children can separate their languages quite well—and scholars like De Houwer (2021) have found that most bilinguals do have numerous translation equivalents in their mental lexicon. Since the late 1980s, such findings have caused the theory of individual but connected systems (sometimes called dual system hypothesis) to be considered more accurate (see Meisel, 2019, pp. 69–83, for a more detailed discussion). Evidence for children developing individual systems for each language that they acquire is in the fact that they can differentiate the sounds and grammatical systems of each of the involved languages (cf., e.g., De Houwer, 2021, pp. 10 & 29, Weikum et al., 2007). All in all, research has clearly shown that children can easily acquire more than one language comprehensively, but the myth of multilingualism causing language delay still perseveres.

Above, we have introduced that the idea of 'incomplete' acquisition can occur in simultaneous as well as sequential multilinguals. Regarding sequentially acquiring bilinguals, incomplete learning occurs especially in cases in which the language learnt later is the language of the society and formal instruction. When a child, for example, grows up in a monolingual home environment and starts acquiring the societal language only after the age of 2 years, for example when entering kindergarten, they might be more fluent in their home language than they are in the societal language once they reach school age. This, however, is not caused by a potential inability to fully acquire only one language but rooted in the fact that these children often have less exposure to the societal language than to their home language. In these cases, parents used to be—and unfortunately sometimes still are—advised to no longer use their home language with their child to 'not confuse them' and to support the acquisition of the sequentially learnt additional language. However, research has shown that growing up bilingually does not hinder complete acquisition or influence the likelihood of language delays, so, as Ibrahim argues, "let's hold on to those mother tongues!" (Ibrahim, 2015, "Myth: Multilingualism causes language delay", para. 2).

2.3.4 Myth #4: A Bilingual Person Is Two Monolinguals in One

This myth can be related to the previous one but conveys the contrary message: while myth #3 postulates that a multilingual person can only learn one language 'properly' and that acquiring multiple languages hinders the full acquisition of any of the involved languages, myth #4 states that a multilingual speaker equals multiple monolingual speakers. For easier understanding, we will refer to bilingual speakers and the myth that they equal two monolingual speakers for the remains of this section.

In our discussion of the previous myth, we have learnt that research suggests that children develop different language systems for each of their languages. While this means bilinguals develop two phonological systems, two syntactic systems, and two lexicons, they access the same conceptual knowledge when using either language and the two languages frequently interact with one another (Meisel, 2019). This interaction is called cross-linguistic influence or interference (see ▶ Sect. 3.3 for more details and Francis (2012, p. 128)) for a representation). The dominant or 'stronger' language predominantly influences the less dominant or 'weaker' language. In addition to being the linguistic reality of language acquisition and processing, the existence of interference debunks another aspect that is included in the idea of a bilingual speaker representing two monolingual speakers: the assumption that bilinguals are 'perfect' speakers of each of their languages. The fact that the vast majority of bilingual speakers have a dominant first language (which, in turn, interferes with the non-dominant language), contradicts this belief. In fact, how well bilinguals speak each of their languages depends on their needs. As Grosjean (2010, p. 21) argues, "many bilinguals are dominant in one language, some do not know how to read and write in one of their languages, and others have only passive knowledge of a language. Perhaps a sprinkling of bilinguals may have equal and perfect fluency in their languages". Consequently, it is important to realise that, while linguistic similarities between monolingual and bilingual speakers exist, there is also variability between and amongst these two speaker groups. Bilinguals can be as fluent and proficient as monolingual language users in one or all languages and in any or all of the four language skills (i.e. speaking, writing, reading, listening)—or not. Most importantly, debunking myth #4 teaches us that comparing monolingual and bilingual speakers on a linguistic level is not helpful but reproduces our assumption of monolingualism as the norm. The next myth is also concerned with bilinguals to be two speakers in one, but on a more personal level.

2.3.5 Myth #5: Multilingualism Causes Identity Problems

Being multilingual does not necessarily only concern speaking different languages. Being multilingual often also means belonging to more than one community and identifying with more than one culture. Consequently, people assume that multilinguals have several language-related personalities. They might be more talkative when speaking Greek and stricter when speaking German. While this sounds enriching at first, it might also result in a multilingual feeling like an incomplete member in all of these groups. Before we go into more detail, we would like to point out that these issues do only concern multilinguals that are also multicultural (cf. Grosjean, 2010, p. 125). Multilinguals who grow up in a multilingual society in which individual languages are not assigned to different user groups are considered monocultural and will not experience a feeling of incomplete membership—at least not because of their multilingualism.

Although there is some truth to the observation that multilinguals behave differently depending on which of their languages they use, multilingualism does not cause emotional instability or personality problems. Language use always depends on its context. Consequently, multilinguals, just like monolinguals, alter their linguistic behaviour depending on the situations or contexts they are in and on the people they talk to. Some people or some contexts are closely linked to a specific

2.3 · Some Myths About Multilingualism

language for a multilingual; they might speak Greek to their parents but German to their siblings and Greek during Sunday's family dinner. Other contexts are open to negotiation or can involve more than one language, that is, code-switching (cf. ▶ Sect. 4.3.2). In addition to switching or choosing between languages, multilinguals also have to consider pragmatic aspects: while in some languages, for example, asking for something politely must include a subjunctive construction, in other languages indicative mood is an option, too. Furthermore, certain domains and contexts of use demand certain linguistic behaviour, such as formal and thought-through communication with a teacher or just letting everything out when talking to a friend. Adhering to these varying pragmatic requirements can lead to very different language-dependent behaviour of a speaker. This difference in behaviour, in turn, might seem like different speaker-personalities at play. However, these differences in behaviour do not have anything to do with being bilingual in the first place; monolingual speakers show the same level of register variation. Grosjean (2010, p. 126) gives the example of a monolingual speaker who shifts linguistic behaviour depending on the situation or social/cultural group they are in. Consequently, different domains of use, different attitudes, and different people trigger the use of one or the other language, dialect, or register in multilinguals and monolinguals alike. On a side note: certain contexts or people might also trigger a bilingual to dream in one or the other language.

❓ Exercises

Student group work:

Consider the examples and take notes on the following tasks:

(one example per group; 5–10 min)

1. Find one example each for countries which are in the following linguistic situations:
   (a) They are multilingual because they have once been colonised by a power which introduced its administrative language, which later on became one of the official languages of the country.
   (b) They are multilingual because they have formed voluntary federations of different linguistic areas.
   (c) They are multilingual because their borders were (re-)drawn to create states.
2. Find examples of countries that are officially monolingual.
   (a) Try and find information on whether there are linguistic minorities, either from original population groups or from recently migrated population groups, or both.
   (b) Try and find out whether and how the linguistic rights of these minority groups have changed over time.
3. Consider the use of the English language in different English-speaking countries, taking into consideration the categories by Thomason (2001) and/or Mufwene (2001).
   (a) How was the English language introduced into that specific country?
   (b) What function does the English language currently have in that country?

4. Roxane Maar's mother has decided to not obey to the government's advice and continued to use Russian with her daughter. Why do you think authorities (governments, educators, etc.) advise against the acquisition and use of languages other than the societal language? What is the origin of such misconceptions? Get together in groups or discuss this in class.
5. Try to find further commonly shared beliefs/myths about multilingualism. Why are they (not) accurate? Compare and discuss.

Summary

In this chapter, we have assessed multilingualism from a historical perspective. We have introduced various scenarios of how multilingualism has developed and have discussed the level of language contact that commonly occurred in these scenarios. Specifically, they include voluntary migration to increase the quality of life or occupation, involuntary migration, for example as part of forced labour, contact for trade purposes, and different types of colonisation. Furthermore, we have learnt how and why states or governments might decide to become multilingual, this means to declare more than one official language. Unsurprisingly, many currently multilingual states have a history of colonisation, however also linguistic and cultural diversity rooted in other historical reasons can motivate official multilingualism in states. Likely due to the fact that multilingualism is quite common in a global perspective (cf. ▶ Chap. 1), myths about its nature, its causes, and its effects have arisen. In the second part of this chapter (▶ Sect. 2.3), the following five myths about multilingualism have been presented, briefly discussed, and (mostly) debunked: (1) Multilingualism is a recent phenomenon; (2) Monolingualism is the norm; (3) Multilingualism is disadvantageous; (4) A bilingual person is two monolinguals in one; and (5) Multilingualism causes identity problems. We have aimed at understanding why these myths arose and explained their core statements. As a result, we have found that, given certain contexts and scenarios, there might be some truth to some of them. However, most of the time they are simplifying reality or even scientifically refutable.

References

Beal, J. C., & Faulkner, M. (2020). Language contact in the history of English. In A. P. Grant (Ed.), *The Oxford handbook of language contact* (Online ed.). Oxford Academic.

Bosch, L., & Sebastián-Gallés, N. (2003). Simultaneous bilingualism and the perception of a language-specific vowel contrast in the first year of life. *Language and Speech, 46*(2–3), 217–243.

Byers-Heinlein, K., & Lew-Williams, C. (2017). Language comprehension in monolingual and bilingual children. In E. M. Fernández, & H. S. Cairns (Eds.), *The handbook of psycholinguistics* (pp. 516–535).

Conboy, B., & Montanari, S. (2016). Early lexical development in bilingual infants and toddlers. In E. Nicoladis & S. Montanari (Eds.), *Bilingualism across the lifespan: Factors moderating language proficiency* (pp. 63–80). De Gruyter Mouton. https://doi.org/10.1515/9783110341249-006

Coulmas, F. (2018). *An introduction to multilingualism: Language in a changing world*. Oxford University Press.

De Houwer, A. (2021). *Bilingual development in childhood*. Cambridge University Press.

De Swaan, A. (2001). *The world of words: The global language system*. Polity Press.

References

Dursteler, E. R. (2012). Speaking in tongues: language and communication in the early modern Mediterranean. *Past and Present, 217*, 47–77.

Federal Statistical Office. (2022). *Languages*. Retrieved January 29, 2021, from https://www.bfs.admin.ch/bfs/en/home/statistics/population/languages-religions/languages.html

Francis, N. (2012). *Bilingual competence and bilingual proficiency in child development*. MIT Press.

Gramling, D. (2009). The new cosmopolitan monolingualism: On linguistic citizenship in twenty-first century Germany. *Die Unterrichtspraxis/Teaching German, 42*, 130–140.

Gramling, D. (2016). *The invention of monolingualism*. Bloomsbury.

Grosjean, F. (2010). *Bilingual: Life and reality*. Harvard University Press.

Gupta, A. F. (2000). Bilingualism in the cosmopolis. *International Journal of the Sociology of Language, 143*, 107–119.

Hymes, D. (1968). Linguistic problems in defining the concept of tribe. In J. Helm (Ed.), *Essays on the problem of tribe* (pp. 23–48). Washington Press for the American Ethnological Society.

Ibrahim, N. (2015). *A few more myths about speakers of multiple languages*. British Council. Retrieved April 15, 2022, from https://www.britishcouncil.org/voices-magazine/few-more-myths-about-speakers-multiple-languages

Leeman, J. (2018). It's all about English: The interplay of monolingual ideologies, language policies and the U.S. census bureau's statistics on multilingualism. *International Journal of the Sociology of Language, 252*, 21–43.

Lin, Z., & Lei, L. (2020). The research trends of multilingualism in applied linguistics and education (2000–2019): A bibliometric analysis. *Sustainability, 12*(15), 6058. https://doi.org/10.3390/su12156058

Maar, R. (2021). *5 myths surrounding multilingualism*. Medium. Retrieved August 18, 2022, from https://roxanemaar.medium.com/5-myths-surrounding-multilingualism-5fcea034f01a

Mackey, W. F. (2005). Multilingual cities. In U. Ammon, N. Dittmar, K. J. Mattheier, & P. Trudgill (Eds.), *Sociolinguistics. An international handbook of the science of language and society* (Vol. 2/1, pp. 1304–1312). De Gruyter.

Maher, J. C. (2017). *Multilingualism. A very short introduction*. Oxford University Press.

Mansel, P. (2014). Cities of the Levant—the past for the future? *Asian Affairs, 45*(2), 220–242.

May, S. (2001). *Language and minority rights: Ethnicity, nationalism, and the politics of language*. Pearson Education.

Meisel, J. M. (2019). *Bilingual children: A guide for parents*. Cambridge University Press.

Mufwene, S. S. (2001). *The ecology of language evolution*. Cambridge University Press.

Pakenham, T. (1991). *The scramble for Africa: White man's conquest of the dark continent from 1876 to 1912*. Avon Books.

Pavlenko, A. (2002). 'We have room but for one language here': Language and national identity at the turn of the twentieth century. *Multilingua, 21*, 163–196.

Pearson, B. Z. (2013). Distinguishing the bilingual as a late talker from the late talker who is bilingual. In L. A. Rescorla & P. S. Dale (Eds.), *Late talkers: language development, interventions, and outcomes* (pp. 67–87). Brookes.

Ronan, P. (2016). Perspectives on English in Switzerland. *Cahiers de l'ILSL, 48*, 9–26.

Schneider, E. W. (2007). *Postcolonial English. Varieties around the World*. Cambridge University Press.

Schneider, E. W., & Buschfeld, S. (2022). The geographical and demographic expansion of English. In S. S. Mufwene & A. M. Escobar (Eds.), *The Cambridge handbook of language contact* (Population movement and language change) (Vol. 1, pp. 583–610). Cambridge University Press.

Stavans, A., & Hoffmann, C. (2015). *Multilingualism*. Cambridge University Press.

Strauss, J. (2011). Linguistic diversity and everyday life in the Ottoman cities of the Eastern Mediterranean and the Balkans (late 19th–early 20th century). *The History of the Family, 16*(2), 126–141.

Thomason, S. G. (2001). *Language contact. An introduction*. Edinburgh University Press.

Tollefson, J. W., & Tsui, A. B. (2014). Language diversity and language policy in educational access and equity. *Review of Research in Education, 38*, 189–214.

Volterra, V., & Taeschner, T. (1978). The acquisition and development of language by bilingual children. *Journal of Child Language, 5*(2), 311–326.

Watts, R. J. (2011). *Language myths and the history of English*. Oxford University Press.
Weikum, W. M., Vouloumanos, A., Navarra, J., Soto-Faraco, S., Sebastián-Gallés, N., & Werker, J. F. (2007). Visual language discrimination in infancy. *Science, 316*(5828), 1159. https://doi.org/10.1126/science.1137686
Werker, J. (2012). Perceptual foundations of bilingual acquisition in infancy. *Annals of the New York Academy of Sciences, 1251*(1), 50–61. https://doi.org/10.1111/j.1749-6632.2012.06484.x
Wiese, H. (2020). Contact in the city. In R. Hickey (Ed.), *Wiley handbook of language contact* (pp. 261–279). Wiley-Blackwell.
Wiley, T. G. (2014). Diversity, super-diversity, and monolingual language ideology in the United States: Tolerance or intolerance? *Review of Research in Education, 38*, 1–32.

Key Readings

Grosjean, F. (2010). *Bilingual: Life and reality*. Harvard University Press.
Stavans, A., & Hoffmann, C. (2015). *Multilingualism*. Cambridge University Press.
Thomason, S. G. (2001). *Language contact. An introduction*. Edinburgh University Press.

Further Readings

Bailey, A., Osipova, A., & Genesee, F. (2015). Debunking myths about multilingualism. In A. Bailey, A. Osipova, & F. Genese (Eds.), *Children's multilingual development and education: Fostering linguistic resources in home and school contexts* (pp. 24–73). Cambridge University Press.
Schneider, E. W., & Buschfeld, S. (2022). The geographical and demographic expansion of English. In S. S. Mufwene & A. M. Escobar (Eds.), *The Cambridge handbook of language contact* (Population movement and language change) (Vol. 1, pp. 583–610). Cambridge University Press.
Watts, R. J. (2011). *Language myths and the history of English*. Oxford University Press.

Conceptualising Multilingualism

In the second part of the textbook, we conceptualise the notion of multilingualism by approaching the topic from the many different perspectives it combines, viz. psycholinguistic, acquisitional, as well as sociolinguistic perspectives and approaches; individual versus societal bi-/multilingualism; educational dimensions and issues, and results of language policies; identity conceptions; as well as linguistic mechanisms, processes, and results of multilingualism and multilingual language acquisition. Once more, this illustrates the diverse and complex character of the phenomenon.

Contents

Chapter 3   The Multilingual Individual: Who Is Multilingual and What Is Special? – 45

Chapter 4   Linguistic Mechanisms, Processes, and Results – 73

Chapter 5   Linguistic Manifestations in a Multilingual World: Focus on English – 101

Chapter 6   Societal Multilingualism – 121

Chapter 7   Multilingualism Between Identities, Ideologies, and Language Policies – 149

Chapter 8   Multilingual Education and Teaching – 175

The Multilingual Individual: Who Is Multilingual and What Is Special?

Contents

3.1   Introduction – 46

3.2   Who Is Multilingual? – 47

3.3   Acquiring Two or More Languages from Birth: What Is Different? – 50
3.3.1   Acquiring Sound System(s) – 53
3.3.2   Acquiring Words: The Lexicon – 55
3.3.3   Acquiring Morphosyntax – 59

3.4   Language Choice and Cross-Linguistic Influence – 60

          References – 66

© The Author(s), under exclusive license to Springer Nature Switzerland AG 2023
S. Buschfeld et al., *Multilingualism*,
https://doi.org/10.1007/978-3-031-28405-2_3

3.1 Introduction

As we have seen in the previous chapters, multilingualism is neither a rare phenomenon nor a development of recent times. Famous examples of multilinguals across the last centuries are Elizabeth I (1533–1603, Queen of England), Friedrich Engels (1820–1895, social scientist and journalist), J.R.R. Tolkien (1892–1973, writer), Vladimir Nabokov (1899–1977, novelist and translator), Arthur Koestler (1905–1983, writer and journalist), or Elias Canetti (1905–1994, author) (see Bollnow, 1959; Coulmas, 2018, pp. 81–85; Doughan, 2021; Morrill & Greenblatt, n.d., for an overview and more details). More recent examples of famous multilinguals are Natalie Portman (1981-, actress) and Tom Hiddleston (1981-, actor). Currently, approximately 60% of the world's population speak two or more languages and the numbers are increasing (ilanguages, 2018).

The chapter at hand focuses on the multilingual individual and enquires into two central aspects. Firstly, we address the crucial but complex question of who is multilingual. We present and discuss widely diverging views, from Bloomfield's (1933) full fluency account to Grosjean's (1989) more pragmatic assertion, which assumes basic functionality in two (or more) languages. These positions, however, should be considered as the extreme poles on a continuum of proficiencies on which the various other manifestations and aspects of multilingualism, introduced in ▶ Sect. 2.2 and discussed throughout the textbook, operate and can be identified. As early as 1967, Macnamara noted that "we consider bilingualism to be a continuum, or rather a whole series of continua, which vary amongst individuals along a whole variety of dimensions" (1967, p. 60). Secondly, we discuss whether and in how far multilingual language acquisition differs from monolingual language acquisition. We will show that this is another complex endeavour in itself since the answers to such questions again depend on a variety of factors, such as age of onset of language acquisition, language dominance, input, and experience, and also the level of linguistic description, namely whether one considers the phonological, morphosyntactic, or lexical domain. To reduce the level of complexity, in this chapter, we will focus primarily on simultaneous multilinguals. Simultaneous multilinguals differ from successive multilinguals in their age of onset of language acquisition. Simultaneous multilinguals acquire multiple languages simultaneously from a very young age, while successive multilinguals acquire one language after they have already started learning another language. Several benchmarks have been suggested as possible dividing lines between simultaneous and successive bilingual acquisition. Some approaches suggest age three as such a benchmark (e.g., Paradis et al., 2010; McLaughlin, 1978). Others such as De Houwer (1995, p. 223) employ a much stricter definition of simultaneous bilingualism or bilingual first language acquisition. She distinguishes between *bilingual first* (BFLA) and *bilingual second language acquisition* (BSLA). In this strict definition, BFLA includes children who start both (or all) their languages within 1 month after birth. BSLA includes children who start the acquisition of their other language(s) after the age of 1 month but before age two. We here do not employ such a strict differentiation, but we follow De Houwer's later (2021) definition of bilingual first language acquisition and assume 2 years of age as a benchmark to distinguish simultaneous from successive bilingual language acquisition and 6 years as a benchmark to distinguish successive bilingual from second language acquisition (see ▶ Chap. 1, also De Houwer, 2021, p. 1; Nicoladis et al., 2012, p. 463 & Meisel, 2004 for a more detailed discussion). While the age of onset of acquisition is a factor which is easy to measure and define, it is not the only factor that influences whether or not someone can (or should?) be considered a multilingual.

3.2 Who Is Multilingual?

As presented in ▶ Chap. 1, different estimates exist of how many people are multilingual, but rough approximations seem to suggest that between half and two-thirds of the world's current population use two or more languages in their daily lives (Baker & Wright, 2021, p. 10; Grosjean, 2020). But why is it so difficult to make more precise estimates of how many people around the world are multilingual? The answer to this question is as simple as it is fundamental: there is no agreed-upon definition of who is to be considered a multilingual.

The question of what makes a speaker multilingual has been discussed ever since researchers have started looking into the phenomenon. In an early approach, Bloomfield (1933, p. 56) defines bilingualism as "native-like control of two languages" but also acknowledges that "[o]f course, one cannot define a degree of perfection at which a good foreign speaker becomes a bilingual: the distinction is relative" (1933, p. 56). Later, Grosjean (1989) suggests a more pragmatic definition which assumes only basic functionality in both languages. He states that

> [i]n many ways, the bilingual is like the high hurdler: an integrated whole, a unique and specific speaker-hearer, and not the sum of two monolinguals. He or she has developed competencies (in the two languages and possibly in a third system that is a combination of the first two) to the extent required by his or her needs and those of the environment. (1989, p. 6)

Later, he sums up that "bilinguals are those who use two or more languages (or dialects) in their everyday lives" (Grosjean, 2010, p. 4). Of course, Bloomfield's and Grosjean's positions should be considered as the extremes of a continuum of proficiency on which various other factors operate and interrelate. In addition to proficiency, multilingualism is commonly assessed based on, for example:
- modes of multilingualism (individual multilingualism vs. societal multilingualism vs. multilingualism as language practice, see ▶ Chaps. 5 and 6);
- age of onset of acquisition of one language in relation to the other language(s) acquired (i.e. simultaneous vs. successive/sequential multilingualism, cf. ▶ Sect. 3.3);
- language proficiency and dominance (balanced vs. unbalanced multilingualism, c.f. ▶ Sect. 3.4);
- use, usage domains, and learning contexts (home vs. school multilingualism (cf. ▶ Chap. 8);

- elite/elective multilinguals vs. heritage/folk/immigrant multilinguals (see ▶ Chap. 8 on educational contexts, ▶ Chap. 9 on migration contexts);
- registers (spoken vs. written vs. computer-mediated-communication, see ▶ Chap. 10 on language in new media; ▶ Chap. 12 on multilingual written signs);
- different origins and motivations (intrinsic vs. extrinsic; school-based, migrant or grassroots multilingualism; cf. Han 2013; ▶ Chaps. 5 and 8);
- different results (additive, balanced bi-/multilingualism vs. language attrition);
- and also issues of identity (cf. ▶ Sect. 2.3, ▶ Chap. 7).

We will deal with all these factors in the course of the book in some more detail, but let us start with some basic definitions first, and see how these reflect one or the other issue from this long list of factors, which influence our understanding of multilingualism.

In line with Bloomfield's (1933) full-fluency account, Merrim-Webster's dictionary (1961) defines bilingualism as "[h]aving or using two languages especially as spoken with the fluency characteristic of a native speaker; a person using two languages especially habitually and with control like that of a native speaker; the constant oral use of two languages." These, however, are clearly older accounts and have given way to more functional definitions in line with Grosjean's (1989) approach. The Oxford Dictionary (2023), for example, simply defines bilingualism as the "[a]bility to speak two languages" or "the habitual use of two languages colloquially" and Mohanty (2019, p. 17) understands multilingualism as "the ability of communities or persons to meet the communicative requirements of themselves and their society in normal day life in two or more languages in their interactions with the speakers of any of these languages". Hamers and Blanc (2000, p. 6) focus on communities rather than individual speakers when defining bilingualism as "the state of a linguistic community in which two languages are in contact with the result that two codes can be used in the same interaction and that a number of individuals are bilingual" (see ▶ Chap. 6 for a more detailed assessment of societal multilingualism). While the latter definitions are clearly more inclusive, they still leave room for interpretation. When is a speaker fluent in a specific language? When are specific communicative requirements met? Does using a language refer equally to all four language skills, namely language reception (reading and listening comprehension) and production (speaking and writing)? Is bilingualism context-dependent, meaning that a speaker with a medium level of proficiency in one of their languages is considered to be bilingual in a context in which this language is not used but considered to not be bilingual in a context in which it is used? Although the more recent definitions of bilingualism no longer refer to the 'native speaker' as a benchmark, it seems like multilingual language use still needs to be measured. However, which variety of a language would be our standard of comparison to measure language use, fluency and, often linked to fluency, linguistic proficiency? In the case of English, would British (and maybe American) English be the only standard(s)? Or all traditional first language (L1) varieties of English, including, for example, Scottish, Irish, Australian, New Zealand, and Canadian English? Even newly emerging L1s such as L1 Singaporean English?

Comparing a multilingual speaker of a language such as English to a monolingual English speaker suggests that multilingualism and monolingualism are essentially similar concepts. This, however, is not the case as the language system of a monolingual differs fundamentally from the one of a multilingual (cf. Delucchi Danhier & Mertins, 2018, p. 167). Although researchers have claimed that bilinguals are not two monolinguals in one (see ▶ Sect. 2.3) and that multi-language use differs from single language use, the details of these differences have not been included when defining multilingualism. Whatever definition we adopt, the one thing that seems to be clear is that "defining exactly who is or is not bilingual is essentially elusive and ultimately impossible" (Baker, 2006, p. 16)—and the same holds for defining who is multilingual. Like other researchers, we consider multilingualism to be a continuum rather than a category into which speakers do or do not fit. Such a categorisation would need to account for the complexity and variability of contexts of use, of speakers' levels of proficiency, and for other factors influencing multilingualism (cf. Baker & Wright, 2021, pp. 7–10).

Another aspect which is often not prominently considered in the debate but adds to the complexity of the issue is the unclear relationship between languages and dialects. The differentiation between a dialect and a language affects individual speakers as well as societies in being considered mono- or bilingual. Societies that use more than one language, such as the Quebecers (or Québécois) in Canada speaking French and English, are commonly considered to be multilingual while social groups that use various dialects are not. Mutual intelligibility is one of the traditional linguistic criteria considered for differentiating languages from dialects. It is traditionally expected that dialects of a language are mutually intelligible for speakers whereas languages are not.

However, a number of counter-examples exist. For example, it is commonly assumed that dialects of Chinese are mutually unintelligible to each other (Wardhaugh, 2002) or variably intelligible to speakers of other dialects (Chaojua & Van Heuven, 2009) at best, despite their status as dialects. This is due to typological factors and historical relatedness between the dialects that we cannot discuss within the framework of this textbook (for details, see Chaojua & Van Heuven, 2009). Still, speakers of Chinese feel united linguistically through a common writing system, which is an iconic system based on concepts and not on direct sound-symbol relations. Hindi and Urdu, both spoken in India, on the other hand, are almost identical when it comes to their grammar (Gumperz, 1982, p. 20) and intelligible to each other's speakers (Wardhaugh, 2002, p. 29). Still, they are considered to be two separate languages due to socio-historical factors and some linguistic differences: they use different alphabets and scripts and Hindi is written from left to right whereas Urdu from right to left (Stavans and Hoffmann 2015, pp. 37–39). The notion of *language* and the question of what distinguishes languages from dialects are thus complex issues. In particular, they relate to defining multilingual individuals since, depending on the status of a speech system as a language or 'just' a dialect, speakers would be classified as either multilingual or multidialectal. Still, they are also tightly connected to societal multilingualism since defining languages and dialects not only involves linguistic criteria but also social ones. Two languages, for example, can be very similar but perceived as and considered different linguistic entities by their speakers due to ideological, historical, or political reasons (see also Stavans and Hoffmann 2015, pp. 37–39).

The question of what is a language and what is a dialect is also relevant for the question of who is a bi- or multilingual speaker in that it can be discussed whether speakers of two dialects, say high German and the Bavarian dialect, should be considered bilingual. For this example, the answer seems to be straightforward. We would consider such speakers *bidialectal*. For speakers of, for example, Bavarian German and dialects of Austrian German, one of the other standard varieties of German, the answer would probably not be as straightforward since Austrian German is considered a language in its own right and not simply a dialect of German as spoken in Germany, even though it is linguistically much closer to Bavarian German than Bavarian German to some northern dialects of Germany. However, how informative is such a classification at all if the language-dialect divide is not always clear-cut? Furthermore, the cognitive advantages for *bidialectal*—or *bilectal* as Grohmann and colleagues call them for reasons of greater conceptual flexibility of the term—and bilingual speakers have actually been reported to be quite similar, especially concerning the development of (productive) vocabulary (e.g. Antoniou et al., 2014, 2016; Rowe & Grohmann, 2013; Taxitari et al., 2017). A whole body of partially contradictory findings exist on this issue and we can neither discuss nor answer this and similar questions conclusively in this textbook. Our aim, however, is to raise awareness of the complex nature of defining and identifying multilinguals. To reduce the level of complexity, we assess different manifestations of multilingualism separately in this book. For the remainder of this chapter, we mainly focus on the process of *simultaneous multilingual language acquisition*, starting between age 0–2, and tap into *sequential multilingual language acquisition*, which starts between ages 2–6 only in ▶ Sect. 3.4. In ▶ Chap. 4, we further elaborate on the process of *sequential multilinguals* and also include the process of *second language acquisition* (SLA; see ▶ Chap. 1 for a definition of this and similar notions of bilingualism).

3.3 Acquiring Two or More Languages from Birth: What Is Different?

Before we start to point out differences and similarities between monolingual and multilingual language acquisition, we would like to introduce an ideology that has long functioned as one of the foundations of research in multilingualism and is still commonly present whenever (lay) people talk about multilingualism: *the monolingual bias* (see De Houwer and Ortega 2018a, 2018b; Ortega, 2014 on the monolingual bias in bilingualism research). *The monolingual bias* refers to the belief that monolingualism is the norm (cf. ▶ Sect. 2.3) and that monolingual language use, proficiency, and abilities should be the desired outcome of any language acquisition process. While one could argue that full fluency, which monolingual speakers are commonly assumed to have as they will become *native speakers* of their language, can very well be a desirable outcome of language acquisition, the monolingual bias implicitly leads to the assumption that multilingual language users are inferior to monolingual language users whenever they use a language differently from the idealised monolingual speaker group. This bias suggests that multilingualism should be considered an odd, or at least a 'non-standard', form of language acquisition which potentially leads to inferior and imperfect language users. As we aim to avoid such incorrect and unhelpful beliefs, whenever we compare monolingual and multilingual language use, acquisitional processes, or levels of proficiency, we do not want to imply that monolingualism represents the norm or is the more desirable or more valuable outcome of language acquisition.

> **Think Tank**
>
> Imagine two multilingual speakers of the same number of languages. One is a literate multilingual adult who is competent in all four commonly posited language skills, i.e., reading, writing, listening comprehension, and speaking, on a level approximately the same as for their peer group of monolingual literate adults. The other multilingual speaker has full competence in the receptive skills in all their languages but is not used to formal oral conversations in one of the languages. Is the second multilingual speaker *less* multilingual than the first one?
>
> For a long time, scholars have focused on identifying to what extent the proficiency of multilinguals differs from that of monolingual speakers in one or each of their languages and in one or more of the four language skills (cf. Baker & Wright, 2021, pp. 8–9; Grosjean & Li, 2013, p. 12; Macnamara, 1967, pp. 59–60). This difference has often been called the *bilingual deficit* (cf. Treffers-Daller, 2018, p. 290). Discuss this notion avoiding *the monolingual bias*. Furthermore, try to conceptualise possible realities of bilingual speakers starting with the example of the two multilinguals at the beginning of the think tank.

Some people believe that acquiring more than one language might be problematic or even detrimental to children (see ▶ Sect. 2.3 on myths about multilingualism). Research of the last decades, however, has shown that the opposite is true: early bi- and multilingualism comes with a number of advantages, such as cognitive advantages such as increased metalinguistic awareness (on the lexical, syntactic, and phonological levels), advantages in problem-solving capacities, literacy development, conversational skills, and advantages for learning further languages (e.g. Bialystok, 2001; see also Clark, 2016, pp. 394, 400; De Houwer, 1995, p. 220; Pearson, 2009, pp. 392–393; Serratrice, 2013a, pp. 99–102) as well as advantages in communicative strategies (cf. Bialystok, 2001, p. 62). Furthermore, it has been found that children seem to be biologically equipped to acquire more than one language at a time (cf. Baker & Wright, 2021, p. 6; Serratrice, 2013a). Among the research on multilingual first language acquisition, most studies have focused on bilingualism. Studies on children acquiring three or even more languages from birth are much rarer (De Houwer, 1995, p. 222; Paradis, 2007, p. 16; Chevalier, 2015). The majority of such studies focus on aspects similar to those treated in bilingual first language acquisition research, such as early language differentiation of the two (or more) languages acquired, the differences between monolingual and bilingual children (which is not necessarily useful, as we argued earlier), effects of reduced input, etc. The latter aspect is, of course, of heightened importance for children acquiring even more than two languages, and studies have revealed that in trilingual environments, the language for which the child receives the least amount of input may be marked by incomplete acquisition or develop into a rather passive language in the child's linguistic repertoire (e.g., Maneva, 2004; see also Paradis, 2007, p. 17). Chevalier (2015) investigates environmental and contextual factors that support trilingual language acquisition. In particular, she examines the roles of minority versus majority languages, in which context the languages are spoken by caregivers, and the impact of their conversation styles. While in some accounts the term *bilingualism* covers the acquisition of more than two languages (e.g., Meisel, 2001, p. 11), in other accounts, the term *multilingual first language acquisition* is used as a cover term for both scenarios and describes the acquisition of two or more than two languages (e.g., Unsworth, 2013, p. 21). This is why we treat the labels *bilingual* and *multilingual* as interchangeable terms (see ▶ Sect. 1.2 for our reasoning).

Two aspects have been most prominent in the investigation and discussion of bilingual language acquisition. First, researchers have discussed the question of whether a bilingual child's languages develop as one system or as two separate ones (e.g., De Houwer, 1990, 1995, pp. 230–244; Meisel, 1990, 2001, 2011; Volterra & Taeschner, 1978; for a concise overview of such a discussion and some recent findings, see also Clark, 2016, pp. 384–393). For the last 20 or so years, researchers have mostly agreed that children acquire different languages as separate systems from early on but that interaction between these systems exists—the degree and manifestations of this cross-linguistic influence or transfer, again, are a much-debated issue (e.g., De Houwer, 1990; Genesee et al., 2008, pp. 73–75; Hulk & Müller, 2000; Meisel, 2001, p. 16, 2004, pp. 95–103; Paradis & Genesee, 1996; Serratrice, 2013a, pp. 87, 97; Unsworth, 2013, p. 31). Consequently, children growing up with more than one language have to learn two (or more) sound systems, two (or more) lexicons, two (or more) morphological systems, two (or more) syntactic systems, and two (or more) systems of use (e.g. Clark, 2016, p. 384). Second, scientific discussions have focussed on the differences between monolingual and multilingual language development. This has often led to identifying a deficit in the multilinguals' language proficiency. Although, as mentioned before, we reject such concepts, we find a comparison of monolingual and multilingual language acquisition processes which does not implement a monolingual bias to be helpful to highlight the specific characteristics and remarkable achievements of multilingual children. Furthermore, such unbiased comparisons increase multilingual children's visibility after the long-standing focus on monolingual children. Obviously, there are a number of differences between these two acquisitional processes. For example, a child acquiring one language will be exposed to this language and use it for longer periods of time than a child in a multilingual context will be exposed to and use each of the languages they acquire (e.g. Marchman et al., 2004; Nicoladis, 2006, p. 15; Nicoladis et al., 2012). For a child growing up multilingually, languages are likely to be domain-specific, which means they may be used primarily in school, at home, or with the grandparents. Furthermore, they may be more or less prestigious, spoken by more or fewer people in their social environment, or be the majority (often societal) language or the minority (often home) language. In contrast to monolingual children, multilingual children need to differentiate between or decide when to use which of their languages. In addition, while monolingual language acquisition is expected to always result in a somewhat similar level of proficiency, the outcome of bilingual language acquisition might be less homogeneous and vary in compositions of language skills and levels of proficiencies. Correspondingly, it has been claimed that "every bilingual child seems to have a unique constellation of language experiences and language abilities" (Place & Hoff, 2011, p. 1834), and we strongly endorse this view. The crucial question that arises in this context is: do children who acquire two (or more) languages still follow the same patterns, processes, and timing as monolingual children who acquire just one of these languages? Although "[c]hildren growing up in bilingual environments will have different experiences than those who encounter only one language, and these differences may have a profound impact on children's social, cognitive, and linguistic development" (Bialystok, 2007, p. 393), we find striking similarities between the monolingual and bilingual acquisition of a language: children seem to go through more or less the same processes on more or less the same schedule (e.g. Bialystok, 2001, p. 88; see also Delucchi Danhier & Mertins, 2018).

Before we delve into the details of the acquisition of one or more languages, a word of warning is in order: studies on bilingualism have long been inconclusive and contradictory in their findings. Two studies with the same focus and aim can result in very different findings. These contradictions, however, are partly due to the vastly different situations that different bilinguals find themselves in (for example in terms of time and order of acquisition or societal contexts) and partly due to methodological differences and even shortcomings of some studies, such as, varying and incomplete definitions of bilingualism, numerous ideas as to how to investigate this concept best, and limited use of objective tests to measure bilingual language abilities and use (Grosjean, 1998, p. 148; cf. Hulstijn, 2012; Treffers-Daller, 2018). The good news is, however, that empirical research on bilingualism has been gaining in systematicity and comparability in recent years and results are becoming less contradictory.

3.3.1 Acquiring Sound System(s)

The basis for all language learning, be it monolingual or multilingual, is the ability to discriminate sounds. While Serratrice (2013a, p. 90) proposes that "[t]he current evidence is increasingly pointing towards a model of speech perception development where simultaneous bilinguals do not lag behind monolinguals and perform just as accurately in their first year of life" and Unsworth, (2013, p. 24) concludes that, by and large, "the perceptual and phonological development of bilingual children is similar to that of monolinguals", slight differences have been found in the development of sound discrimination abilities between children growing up in monolingual and multilingual environments.

Language learning commences prenatally as fetuses are exposed to language sounds in utero. Shahidullah and Hepper (1994) found that fetuses can process prosodic patterns of language and music already in the last trimester of gestation. Byers-Heinlein et al. (2010) even found that newborns showed a significant preference for languages they had been exposed to in utero; monolinguals show a preference for one language and bilinguals prefer both languages (cf. Serratrice, 2018, p. 17). They further investigated that newborns that are born into a bilingual environment and are expected to acquire both languages were able to discriminate between English and Tagalog—the two languages they were exposed to in utero—presumably because these languages belong to different rhythmic classes: while English is a stress-timed language, Tagalog is a syllable-timed language. While it is not clear whether newborns can discriminate between languages of the same rhythmic class, 4- and 5-month-old bilingual children can differentiate Spanish and Catalan—two languages of the syllable-timed rhythmic class (cf. Bosch & Sebastián-Gallés 2001). At this stage, bilingualism is mostly influenced by exposure to language. However, within the first year of bilingual language acquisition, this exposure to more than one language results in physical differences in children. While all children are able to distinguish phonetic units in any language from birth—they are "universal learners" (Serratrice 2018, p. 18)—the brains of monolingual children lose parts of their flexibility and focus on only discriminating sounds of just one language (native contrasts) by the end of their first year of life. Since for monolingual children the range of their sound perception is subsequently limited to one language, they have the capacity to deepen and fine-tune their sound-discrimination ability and analyse the sounds on a phonemic level. Thus, monolingual children start developing their representation of meaningful sounds of their first language—its phonemic inventory—earlier than bilingual children do. As bilingual children have to keep what De Houwer (2021, p. 10) calls an "open ear" due to the higher level of variability in the linguistic input they are exposed to, their brains stay open and more flexible for a longer period of time (Garcia-Sierra et al., 2011). Behavioural studies of the bilingual acquisition of sounds have long been inconclusive as to whether or not bilingual children can discriminate phonemic contrast in both of their languages throughout their first year of life or whether they might lose this ability for one of the languages at some point only to rediscover it a little later (Bosch and Sebastián-Gallés 2003; Sundara & Scutellaro, 2011; cf. Serratrice, 2018, pp. 18–19). Studies using magnetoencephalography (MEG) and electroencephalography (EEG) have brought some light to this inconclusiveness.

Using MEG to measure the magnetic field produced by bilingual children's brains, Ferjan Ramírez et al. (2017) confirmed that 11-month-old bilinguals are able to acoustically discriminate sounds of any language and not just the sounds of the languages they are exposed to. At the same age, their monolingual peers were not able to discriminate sounds from other than 'their' languages but were already able to discriminate meaning-distinguishing phonemes from not meaning-distinguishing sounds in their L1. Similarly, EEG-based studies have shown that monolinguals turn from being able to discriminate sounds from different languages (non-native contrasts) at 7 months, towards only being able to discriminate sounds from their own language (native contrasts) at 11 months (Rivera-Gaxiola et al., 2005). For bilingual children, Garcia-Sierra et al. (2011) found that they turn towards discriminating language-specific sounds only at 10–12 months. At this very early stage of the language acquisition process, monolingual children appear to develop their sound system a little faster than bilingual children. However, as often is the case, this is only half of the truth.

For bilingual and monolingual children alike, the amount of input is of high influence when their discrimination abilities turn from lower-level acoustic to a more mature phonemic level. EEG studies have shown that a high amount of input supports the transition into more mature phonemic encoding by the age of 12–14 months (Garcia-Sierra et al., 2011; Garcia-Sierra et al., 2016; cf. Serratrice, 2018, p. 20). While the amount of absolute exposure is the underlying factor furthering the development of phonemic encoding abilities in monolingual and bilingual children, in bilingual children a higher relative exposure in Language A affects the development of phonemic encoding abilities only in Language A but not necessarily in Language B. Furthermore, Garcia-Sierra et al. (2011) have found that early development of more skilled phonemic discrimination abilities in English-Spanish bilinguals positively correlates with their word production at 15 months of age (see also Silvén et al., 2014; Serratrice, 2018, p. 21). Consequently, the development of sound discrimination abilities is not only a prerequisite of word learning but might even serve as a predictor for it.

While we see an overall similar pattern of sound perception, slight and only temporary differences between the acquisitional routes of monolingual and bilingual children can be assumed. In sound production, we do not see such differences: bilingual children start imitating the prosodic patterns of both of their languages already during the early babbling stage (Sundara et al., 2020) and bilingual and monolingual children start the different stages of production, namely babbling, holophrastic stage, etc. (cf. ▶ Sect. 3.3.2), at approximately the same age whilst continuing to develop their phonological language systems during their early childhood (cf. De Houwer, 2021, pp. 15, 27).

3.3.2 Acquiring Words: The Lexicon

The developmental steps towards the first word and, finally, an extensive language lexicon are overall the same for monolingual and bilingual children (cf. De Houwer, 2021, pp. 17–21). While learning how to speak requires mere exposure to language, building a lexicon is highly dependent on the quantity and quality of this exposure, that is the input provided to the child in its environment. In general, it has been suggested that bilingual and monolingual children employ the same word learning mechanisms to build their lexicons (e.g. Paradis, 2007, p. 19) and it has been found that their first words appear around the same time as do those of monolinguals (e.g. Genesee, 2003). Still, potential disadvantages of mulitlingual language acquisition are observed, mostly in studies targeting the development of bilingual children's vocabulary. A multitude of studies report a lag in expressive and receptive vocabulary development of bilingual children when compared to their monolingual peers (e.g. Nicoladis, 2006; Nicoladis et al., 2012, pp. 457–458; Pearson et al., 1997), even in the dominant language (e.g. Doyle et al., 1978). Other studies refute this finding and state that "no evidence of consistent differences between young bilinguals' and monolinguals' vocabulary sizes" (De Houwer et al., 2014, p. 1209, see also De Houwer, 2021) can be observed. Despite the often-reported delay, bilingual children tend to be within the same range of number of words acquired as their monolingual peers (Bialystok et al., 2010). But let us start at the beginning.

Somewhat simplified, two things are needed for a typically developing, monolingual or bilingual child to utter their first word: first, they have to be cognitively and physically able to produce the necessary sounds, meaning they have to identify them (see ▶ Sect. 3.3.1 on acquiring sound systems) and practice to produce them (via babbling and other uninterpretable utterances children produce prior to their first word); second, they have to imitate the combination of sounds to form a word. To not just utter but use a word within an appropriate communicative context, children also need to be able to understand the communicative function, so the general meaning, of the respective words. As perception precedes production, children tend to have a greater passive than active vocabulary, meaning they understand more words than they produce (De Houwer, 2009). While children as young as 6 months might understand words (Bergelson & Swingley, 2012; cf. De Houwer, 2021, p. 12), they tend to utter their first word only around their first birthday. This one-word stage in which the first word is uttered is followed by the holophrastic stage. In this phase, a single word fulfils a more complex communicative need and often represents a whole sentence. The first words children learn are content words, such as nouns, verbs, etc., whose meanings are usually over- or underextended. *Dog* might, for example, represent every animal that walks on four legs and has a tail, or it might only refer to the family dog. At the age of approximately 20 months, children enter the two-word stage, in which they combine two content words. The exact word-learning route is again highly individual: some children learn one word after the other and others 'save up their words' and suddenly use several new words at the same time (see De Houwer, 2021, pp. 17–19 for an overview of empirical studies on vocabulary size). While word-learning is expected to increase, words are also lost during this process, for example if children stop saying words they used to say (De Houwer, 2021, p. 17).

When comparing the lexical development of bilingual and monolingual children, studies have found differences (e.g. Nicoladis, 2006; Nicoladis et al., 2012, pp. 457–458; Pearson et al., 1997). They commonly find, for example, that bilinguals use fewer words than monolingual children in each of their languages individually. However, both languages combined, the vocabulary of bilingual children exceeds that of their monolingual peers. In her study, De Houwer (2021, p. 17) finds that, in general, "the total number of words that most 20-month-old monolinguals say is much lower than the average of 245" which, for example, Dutch-French bilinguals of the same age say (De Houwer et al., 2014). She also finds, however, that, in general, "[p]atterns of bilingual early lexical development reflect those found in monolinguals" (De Houwer, 2021, p. 17). This suggests that found differences might not be due to differences in the acquisitional processes as such but due to external factors. This claim is supported, for example, by De Houwer et al.'s (2014) study on

13- and 20-month-old Dutch-French bilingual and Dutch monolingual children in Belgium. In this study, De Houwer et al. (2014) controlled for the most common sociodemographic parameters, such as age, gender, age of onset of exposure, the families' socio-economic status, etc., and did not find any consistent differences in the vocabulary development between the two groups. Consequently, they argue "that if individual bilingual children appear to be slow in early vocabulary development, reasons other than their bilingualism [i.e. external factors] should be investigated" (2014, p. 1189–1190, quoted from original slightly modified). Studies like this, which control for external factors, such as different socio-economic statuses, the quality and quantity of the input, different ages of onset of acquisition, different domains of use (home vs. schooling), the prestige and status of the assessed language (societal vs. minority language), as well as the different study foci, such as the Total Vocabulary Score in one language or the Total Conceptual Vocabulary,[1] and do not find structural differences in the lexical development of bilingual and monolingual children, show that these external factors are likely to have affected the findings of earlier studies in which differences have been found. Consequently, these earlier findings (e.g. Nicoladis, 2006; Nicoladis et al., 2012, pp. 457–458; Pearson et al., 1997) should not be generalised unscrutinised.

However, scholars have moved to investigating the impact of some of these factors on studies on bilingual lexical development in more detail. It has been found that studies that do not find a significant difference between the vocabulary size of monolingual and bilingual children tend to investigate bilingualism in contexts in which both languages are of high status and prestige, for example, English and French in Canada (see Serratrice, 2018 for a short overview). Whenever minority languages of lower prestige than the societal language are involved, differences between the vocabulary size of bilinguals and monolinguals in an early stage of their development tend to be found. Silvén et al. (2014), for example, investigate the lexical development of Russian-Finnish bilinguals between the age of 13 and 36 months. They find that, overall, the bilingual group was slower concerning vocabulary growth. However, due to the higher prestige of Finish in comparison to their home language Russian, 18-month-old bilinguals produce more words and learn words in Finnish faster than their Finnish monolingual peers (Silvén et al., 2014). These findings are supported by, for example, Hoff et al.'s (2014) longitudinal study of Spanish-English bilinguals in Florida. They find that between 22 and 48 months of age, the total production vocabulary of bilinguals equals that of their monolingual peers if their languages are combined but that bilinguals with two Spanish-speaking parents gained more English words across the time of investigation than bilinguals with one English- and one Spanish-speaking parent and English-speaking monolinguals. Both studies suggest that the difference in status

---

1 For the Total Vocabulary Score (TVS), all words known by the child are counted while for the Total Conceptual Vocabulary (TCV), only one word per concept is counted. For the translation equivalents *Hund-dog* the TSV-score would be two while the TCV-score would be one as they describe the same concept. The TVS when limited to one language, is highly dependent on whether the more or less dominant language is tested, making the TCV a more accurate assessment (cf. Treffers-Daller, 2018 for an overview of vocabulary measurements).

between home and societal language influences vocabulary growth. However, in addition to the impact of language status on language acquisition (see also Gathercole & Thomas, 2009), these findings also show that quantity of input is a decisive factor for lexical development. In both studies, the groups that gained vocabulary most rapidly were the ones that had least exposure to it, when compared to the other groups (i.e. the Russian-Finish bilinguals, and the English-Spanish bilinguals with two Spanish-speaking parents). Hoff et al. (2014) also find that, in their study, native input often correlates positively with vocabulary size, suggesting that native input is more beneficial to the lexical development of a child than non-native input (see also Paradis, 2011; Serratrice, 2018, pp. 24–25 for an overview). However, we need to keep in mind that non-native input does not necessarily have to be of 'lower quality' than native input (cf. Armon-Lotem & Meir, 2018) and that nativeness is a problematic concept *per se*, in particular since newly emerging L1 varieties of, for example, English challenge old native speaker ideals (e.g. Buschfeld 2020a, 2020b; Hackert, 2012). To sum up, only small differences in lexical development between specific groups of bilinguals and monolinguals can be observed and these differences, if present at all, are of a quantitative rather than qualitative nature.

Findings on the lexical development of bilinguals have also been used to determine whether children can differentiate between their languages or use one undifferentiated lexicon for all their languages. In ▶ Sect. 3.3.1, we saw that children can differentiate between sounds of different languages from quite a young age. Genesee et al. (1996) have found that children can make appropriate language choices already at the one-word and two-word stages (ages 1–2). This means that children can consciously choose, for example, to use English words with an English speaker and German words with a German speaker, again supporting the dual system theory. This presumption is further supported by the fact that children learn *translation equivalents*, which are words for the same concept in each of the involved language (*Hund* and *dog*), already by the age of 13 months (De Houwer et al. 2006; cf. Serratrice, 2018). Studies of translation equivalents have shown that at early word production stages, translation equivalents make up up to 30% of the vocabulary and that bilingual children benefit from a potential phonological similarity of translations which, then, might cause their percentage to even rise (cf. Serratrice, 2018, pp. 18–19). Furthermore, one might even assume that being exposed to two languages might hinder or delay the processing of words, for example, in word comprehension. Children might be overwhelmed by the variability in their input. However, research findings suggest that a bilingual environment might even be beneficial to the development of word processing skills (cf. Serratrice, 2018).

Summing up, bilingual children may have lower vocabulary scores in each of the languages they acquire than their monolingual peers, but, as Bialystok (2001, p. 62) argues, are "surely more extensive in their communicative possibilities than any monolingual". Over the course of the years, the lexicons of monolingual and bilingual children grow. This growth, however, is increasingly influenced by child-external factors, such as language dominance and extent of exposure. Some bilingual children might increase their vocabulary evenly, some might develop more strongly in their language of schooling and some might even turn language dominance around after some years and become dominant in a language they have never been taught in (see ▶ Sect. 3.4 for a definition of language dominance).

3.3.3 Acquiring Morphosyntax

Acquiring language-specific morphosyntactic rules such as word order, inflectional morphology, and function words is, of course, based on the lexical development of a child. As described in Sect. 3.3.2, monolingual and bilingual children start to speak their first words around their first birthday. Once they start combining words, their morphosyntactic development sets in. Here again, monolingual and bilingual children appear to roughly follow the same paths (e.g. Bialystok, 2001, p. 67; Meisel, 1990, 2001, p. 12; Romaine, 1995, p. 217; Serratrice, 2013a, p. 99). In ▶ Sect. 3.3.2, we saw that the lexical development in a bilingual is influenced by their age and by child-external factors, such as quantity and quality of input in each language, domain of use for each language, status and attitudes towards each of their languages, etc. (cf. De Houwer, 2021, pp. 21–25). As morphosyntactic development follows lexical development, the production of grammatical structures is more variable across bilingual as well as monolingual children, especially when the development of certain abilities within specific age-ranges is concerned. The more words children know in (one of) their language(s), the longer their utterances in this language become.[2] Children learn to use language in relation to their reality. Consequently, children first acquire those (morphosyntactic) devices that are relevant in their life, meaning they ask *What?* prior to *When?* prior to *Why?*. This also holds true for morphological inflection, such as tense, and aspect. Similar to the acquisition of sounds and words, comprehension precedes production in the acquisition of morphosyntax. In most cases, by the end of their third year of life, bilingual and monolingual children can produce long and complex sentences and, by the age of 4, they can even tell short stories (De Houwer, 2009, 2021).

Despite these similarities in achievement and similar to the development of linguistic research on the lexical development of bilinguals, scholars are interested in looking into the details of morphosyntactic development to understand interdependencies, similarities, and differences within and across monolingual and bilingual children. We can investigate when and why the use of grammar occurs and whether the development of a grammatical system is universal or rather language-specific and usage-based, meaning whether rules and structures acquired in one language are automatically also available in the other. As mentioned above, scholars have initially believed that multilingual children acquire their many languages

---

2 Morphosyntactic (or grammatical) development is often measured based on the Mean Length of Utterance (MLU). While a difference in this measure might, e.g., reflect language dominance, it is highly dependent on the type of language under investigation. While MLU in languages such as Chinese is best assessed based on the used words, in languages such as English the MLU is best be assessed based on morphemes (cf. Treffers-Daller, 2018: 303–304; see Chap. 14 for some further details on measuring MLU).

as one system and separate their languages only towards the end of their acquisitional process (Unitary System Hypothesis, Volterra & Taeschner, 1978). However, currently scholars have shifted to believe that children acquire different systems for each of their languages from the earliest points of language acquisition (Dual System Hypothesis, cf. e.g. De Houwer, 2009; see also ▶ Sect. 2.3). This paradigm shift from believing in one holistic system for all languages towards assuming individual systems to exist has been caused by numerous studies that have found the languages of bilinguals to develop separately but in interconnected ways. Some have found strong within-language relations and weak across-language relations between grammar and vocabulary through measuring the language-specific grammar and vocabulary development of bilingual children (e.g. Conboy & Thal, 2006; Simon-Cereijido & Gutiérrez-Clellen, 2009; cf. Serratrice, 2018, pp. 31–34), others have found that bilingual children's "unilingual utterances (i.e., with words from just one language) use the morphosyntactic devices and rules of each of their languages separately" (De Houwer, 2021, p. 29). These findings suggest that within the same bilingual child, the grammatical development of one language can precede the grammatical development of the other language as both languages are separate but linked (cf. ▶ Sect. 3.4) systems. While morphosyntactic influences from one language to the other occur, in the very early stages of language development they have been found to be rare and not systematic (De Houwer, 2021, p. 29). At later stages of bilingual language acquisition, cross-linguistic influences become more frequent and systematic (cf. ▶ Sect. 3.4).

3.4 Language Choice and Cross-Linguistic Influence

So far, we have found that bilingual "children typically follow qualitatively similar developmental paths to those of monolingual peers (De Houwer, 1990; Meisel, 1989) and show evidence of early morphosyntactic separation" (Serratrice, 2018, p. 34). Despite all the similarities in acquisitional stages and rates of acquisition that have been reported for monolingual and bilingual children, individual variability has also been observed (De Houwer, 2021, p. 42, Meisel, 2004, pp. 95–96; see also Bialystok, 2001, p. 65 on the acquisition of the lexicon; Hervé & Serratrice, 2018 on the acquisition of determiners). This variability appears to be caused by a number of factors that—in combination and individually—influence the language acquisition process of bilingual children. These factors are typically divided into child-external factors that relate to the children's environment and child-internal factors that relate to the children themselves. Despite this quite straightforward differentiation, it is less straightforward to actually sort the many factors into the two groups and to separate their effect from one another (Chondrogianni & Marinis, 2011). In this textbook, we focus on the most commonly identified child-internal factor, age, and the most prominent child-external factor, language exposure.

Starting with the child-internal factor, age needs to be considered as "a proxy for increases in cumulative language exposure, cognitive maturity, memory skills, interactional skills, and much more" (De Houwer, 2021, p. 37). Older bilinguals tend to have higher language competencies, including more trained articulation skills, larger lexicons, a more complex morphosyntax, and more experience in social interactions. The age factor is, as we have seen in ▶ Sect. 3.2, one of the determinants of bilingualism. Based on the age of onset of acquisition, different acquisitional paths are entered, such as simultaneous or sequential bilingualism or second language acquisition (see ▶ Sect. 4.3 for an excursus into sequential multilingualism and second language acquisition). Age appears to correlate with but not necessarily causes variability, as more within-age-group variability in language use has been observed the older the assessed bilingual children. This variability is caused by developmental differences that develop or increase with age, namely articulatory training, processing skills, free will, and life experiences. By the age of two, children can adapt their language use to that of their interlocutors: they use different languages with different speakers depending on which language they are addressed in, which language they connect with their interlocutor, or which context they find themselves in (De Houwer, 2021, pp. 34–35; Serratrice, 2013a). A bilingual child who has been exposed to two languages at home and learns that one of these languages is used by all the visitors to their home might choose to speak this language more than the other language that is not shared by their visitors. Another child might experience the same thing but is used to speaking the not-shared language to family members and refused to use the shared language (Grosjean, 2021, p. 139). With increasing age, children start to realise the value and prestige of their languages, understand who shares these languages with them—and sometimes more importantly, who does not—and learn which language to (not) use in which contexts. One of the most important aspects which influences language competencies and, in turn, language choice is the cumulative amount of exposure the child receives to their languages. The more the child is exposed to a language, the more this language develops. Although cumulative language exposure increases with age, we consider it an independent child-external factor as it is provided by child-external sources.

While some children in dual or multiple language environments experience a fairly balanced amount and quality of exposure, most children receive (much) more exposure and experience in one language than in the other (De Houwer, 2009; Paradis, 2007, p. 17). Those rare bilinguals who have the same command of both of their languages are called *balanced bilinguals*. Most bilinguals, however, are *unbalanced*, as they are more proficient and more articulate in one of their two languages. Unequal exposure is likely to lead to unequally distributed language competencies between the two languages in a bilingual child (cf. Paradis et al., 2010; Zwanziger et al., 2005, p. 905) due to the fact that increased exposure or language input in one language causes this language to develop at a higher rate and with greater accuracy than the other language, in terms of active and passive vocabulary (e.g. Marchman et al., 2010; Scheele et al., 2010) as well as morphosyntactic development (Hoff et al., 2012). Once unbalanced exposure to a bilingual's languages, that is by hearing one language more often than the other or by favouring the context one language is used in over the context the other language is used in, affects the bilingual to be more proficient in one of their languages, we refer to this language as their dominant language. Language dominance is

> [t]he condition of bilingual people having one language in which they possess greater grammatical proficiency, more vocabulary, and greater fluency than the other language. This language may also be used more often than the other language. Most, if not all, bilingual children and adults have a *dominant language*. The dominant language can change throughout the life span, and a bilingual person can be slightly or highly dominant in one language. In bilingual children, dominance can affect language choice (choosing to use the dominant language more than the *nondominant language*) and rate of language development (the bilingual child's competence in the dominant language more closely resembles that of monolingual children who speak that language). (Paradis et al., 2010, p. 265, italics in original)

Once bilinguals participate actively and consciously in domains outside the home, for example, during childcare or playground interactions, the amount of exposure to a particular language might shift for the first time. A child who used to speak a non-societal language with one or both parents at home might refuse to use this language once entering societal language-based childcare as making new friends makes this new context more attractive than the home environment (see De Houwer, 2021, p. 50; Grosjean, 2010, p. 214 or similar observations on older children). New linguistic and non-linguistic experiences and qualitative or quantitative shifts in exposure or domains of language use often influence a bilingual's language choice and, consequently, their dominance not only during childhood but during the entire life span (e.g., Clark, 2016, pp. 394–395; Meisel, 2004, p. 94). Unsurprisingly, the relationship between language dominance and language exposure is tightly interlinked: with increased exposure, a language can become dominant, while, with language dominance, language exposure in the dominant language increases with an expansion of usage domains. In new communicative contexts, meaning in contexts that have not yet been assigned a language of use, the dominant language tends to be used first. Consequently, language dominance is a representation and result of variable experience and input and is often discussed in relation to other mechanisms of multilingual language acquisition such as language transfer. It may sometimes also be the reason for (temporary) loss of production in the non-dominant language (cf. De Houwer, 2021, p. 35).

In addition to the quantity of exposure to a language, the quality of exposure has shown to also be important for bilingual first language acquisition and outcome (e.g. Quiroz et al., 2010 on vocabulary development). The quality or richness of input is a complex notion in itself, and it encompasses factors and is guided by mechanisms (listed in Unsworth, 2013, p. 37–38; for a similar list, see Paradis, 2017, p. 28) such as:
(a) the input variety in terms of different sources of input (e.g. family, friends, reading, television; classroom input vs. community exposure; etc.; cf. Jia & Fuse, 2007; for the latter pair see Mougeon & Rehner, 2017)
(b) the number of speakers providing the input (e.g. Place & Hoff, 2011)
(c) the types of activities through which input is provided (e.g. Scheele et al., 2010)
(d) the question of whether the input-providers speak a standard or non-standard variety (e.g. Larrañaga & Guijarro-Fuentes, 2012)

(e) the question of whether the input-providers are native or non-native speakers (e.g. Cornips & Hulk, 2008; Place & Hoff, 2011)
(f) the number and type of literacy-related activities the child participates in (Scheele et al., 2010)
(g) the inferability of parental referential intention (Cartmill et al., 2013; discussed in Carroll, 2017, p. 8)
(h) socio-psychological factors such as belief systems, identity, language choice and attitudes, both on the part of the child learner and of the parents (cf. Carroll, 2017; De Houwer, 2017; Maneva, 2004, pp. 115, 119–120; see also Paradis, 2007, p. 23, and Bhatia & Ritchie, 1999 for a treatment of some such factors)

While we cannot discuss all of these factors in depth, this list gives us an impression of how complex bilingual first language acquisition is and how much it depends on individual life-trajectories. As a result, the outcome of this process is far more variable than that of monolingual language acquisition.

So far, we know that (1) most bilinguals are unbalanced, which means they have a dominant language in which they are more proficient, and that (2) bilinguals develop a language system for each of their languages. However, influences of one language on the other have repeatedly been found. These are called cross-linguistic influences (cf. Serratrice, 2013a, 2013b) and they have been observed for numerous language pairs, for variously complex and extensive language use, as well as on all levels of linguistic description (e.g., Hulk & Müller, 2000; Nicoladis, 2003, 2006; Paradis, 2001; Paradis & Navarro, 2003). The concept of cross-linguistic influences might be understood as strong support for the Dual System Hypothesis; if cross-linguistic influences exist, bilingual children must acquire their languages as separate systems. To further understanding of these systems and their interactions, much research has focused on the extent to which the two systems of a bilingual child interact, specifically on the nature and extent of cross-linguistic influence (Serratrice, 2013a, p. 98). Most frequently, cross-linguistic influence occurs from the dominant to the weaker language (e.g., Döpke, 1998; Gawlitzek-Maiwald & Tracy, 1996; see also Meisel, 2001, p. 35; Nicoladis, 2006, p. 16). However, it may also occur from the weaker to the stronger language (e.g., Kupisch, 2008) or independent of language dominance (e.g., Hulk & Müller, 2000). While cross-linguistic influences have been reported to occur on all levels of language, most studies have found cross-linguistic influence in morphosyntactic phenomena, such as the use of referential expressions (Serratrice & Hervé, 2015) or argument structure (Chan, 2010; cf. Serratrice, 2018, p. 34). Furthermore, cross-linguistic influence appears to be domain-specific, that is, for some reason, it occurs for some areas of grammar but not for others (Nicoladis et al., 2012; Paradis & Genesee, 1996). Hulk and Müller (2000) report cross-linguistic influence to occur in the domain of object drop but not for the acquisition of root infinitives in two bilingual children simultaneously acquiring Dutch and French and German and Italian. Several explanations as to why cross-linguistic influences seem to be not entirely systematic have been proposed. Some researchers suspect mechanisms and prerequisites that might facilitate cross-linguistic influence to occur, most prominently structural overlap/ambiguity (e.g., Döpke, 1998; Hulk & Müller, 2000; Müller & Hulk, 2001; Nicoladis, 2006). Other facilitating factors might be specific phases of the child's language acquisition process (e.g., Serratrice, 2005; Serratrice et al., 2004), language dominance, markedness of particular linguistic structures, and age of onset (e.g., Ball et al., 2001, p. 71; Kehoe 2002, p. 328; Lleó, 2002, p. 309; Paradis, 2001, p. 35; see also Paradis, 2007). Furthermore, cross-linguistic influences have been found to often occur for interface phenomena, such as discourse-dependent mood distinctions at the syntax/pragmatics interface (e.g., Hulk & Müller, 2000; Müller & Hulk, 2001; Serratrice, 2005), as these interfaces are assumed to be more vulnerable to cross-linguistic influence. A further factor that facilitates cross-linguistic influence is the specific language pairing, meaning the similarities and differences between the languages that a bilingual child acquires (Zwanziger et al., 2005, p. 908).

The conditions and mechanisms of cross-linguistic influences are still to be uncovered in their details. We know that not all children exhibit cross-linguistic influence even if facilitating linguistic conditions are met, but it is not clear what exactly predicts such differences between individual children (Gathercole & Hoff, 2007). It is assumed that linguistic criteria alone (e.g., interface phenomena and structural overlap/ambiguity) cannot account for cross-linguistic influence (see also Hauser-Grüdl et al., 2010). This leads the discussion towards other factors, namely language dominance and input (e.g., Unsworth, 2013, p. 32). In a larger-scale meta-analysis of research on cross-linguistic influence, Van Dijk et al. found that

> [l]anguage dominance, operationalized as societal language, was a significant predictor of cross-linguistic influence, whereas surface overlap, language domain and age were not. Perhaps an even more important finding was that definitions and operationalisations of cross-linguistic influence and its predictors varied considerably between studies. This could explain the absence of a comprehensive theory in the field. (2021, p. 1)

While cross-linguistic influence has widely been investigated in terms of the negative impact it may have on the acquisition of specific phenomena in the target language, often called negative transfer,[3] cross-linguistic influence has also been found to facilitate the acquisition of the other language (e.g., Meisel, 2004, p. 101; Nicoladis, 2006, p. 15; see the notion of positive transfer; for a discussion of the conceptual pair, see Odlin, 1989, pp. 36–38; for a more recent account, Bardovi-Harlig & Sprouse, 2017). The transfer of an aspect of language from one language to the other is mostly negative in case the two languages are different in this aspect and positive in case the languages are similar. However, it has also been shown how strong similarities between languages or linguistic characteristics and structural ambiguities can lead to negative transfer. Furthermore, it has been argued that cross-linguistic influences or transfer is more likely to occur the later a child starts

---

3 Although there are fine-grained differences between the notions of transfer and influence in terms of the hierarchical relations between the languages and their interactions with each other, we will use these terms synonymously.

to acquire their other language(s) (e.g., Pearson, 2009, p. 289). We return to the discussion of language transfer in ▶ Chap. 4, since it is a crucial factor of language change.

❓ Exercises

1. Find further definitions of the notions "bilingualism" or "multilingualism" and compare them. Discuss how they reflect the different manifestations and facets of the phenomenon so far introduced in the book.
   (a) Work in pairs. Each select one prominent multilingual (more than two languages) figure not introduced in this chapter and compile their sociolinguistic profiles. Present your profile to your partner and compare and discuss your two speakers with regard to how the factors introduced in this chapter have had an influence on their speaker profiles.
   (b) Compare their linguistic background with your own linguistic backgrounds and comment on the differences and similarities.
   (c) Think of a bi-/multilingual person in your environment. Develop an interview guideline relating to their multilingual experiences and ask them questions about those aspects of multilingualism already discussed in class (such as acquisition process, self-perception as a speaker of multiple languages, language myths). Also try to include further aspects that come to your mind that have not yet been discussed in class.
2. As famous linguist François Grosjean stated in the title of a 1989 paper: "The bilingual is not two monolinguals in one person". Discuss this claim from an acquisitional and social perspective.

Summary

In this chapter, we have focused on two main issues: firstly, we have tried to determine who can or should be considered multilingual and have realised that this issue is considerably more complex than expected. Multilingualism is not a binary category but a question of degree. Some (very few) speakers are purely monolingual and others are fully fluent and competent in two (or more) languages. Most people, as we have seen, must be located somewhere in-between these two extremes. Secondly, we have described and compared the processes of monolingual and bilingual first language acquisition without following the prevailing monolingual bias that is often reflected in such comparisons. Focusing on simultaneous bilingual language acquisition, we have concentrated on the factors most influential for bilingual language acquisition, such as the quality and quantity of input, language dominance, the child's linguistic experience, and potential cross-linguistic influences. These factors are all tightly interrelated, and their exact manifestations, interactions, and weights may vary not only according to the sociolinguistic context and the type of bi-/multilingualism, but also from child to child. While some studies have found delays in the linguistic development of bi-/multilingual children or (negative) cross-linguistic influences, recent research has shown that bilingual children ultimately catch up with their monolingual peers and even benefit from cognitive advantages (see Baker & Wright, 2021, pp. 142–164, for an up-to-date discussion).

References

Antoniou, K., Grohmann, K. K., Kambanaros, M., & Katsos, N. (2014). Is bilectalism similar to bilingualism? An investigation into children's vocabulary and executive control skills. In W. Orman & M. J. Valleau (Eds.), *BUCLD 38: Proceedings of the 38th Annual Boston University Conference on Language Development, 1* (pp. 12–24).

Antoniou, K., Grohmann, K. K., Kambanaros, M., & Katsos, N. (2016). The effect of childhood bilectalism and multilingualism on executive control. *Cognition, 149*, 18–30.

Armon-Lotem, S., & Meir, N. (2018). The nature of exposure and input in early bilingualism. In A. De Houwer & L. Ortega (Eds.), *The Cambridge handbook of bilingualism* (pp. 193–212). Cambridge University Press.

Baker, C. (2006). *Foundations of bilingual education and bilingualism*. Multilingual Matters.

Baker, C., & Wright, W. E. (2021). *Foundations of bilingual education and bilingualism* (7th ed.).

Ball, M., Müller, N., & Munro, S. (2001). The acquisition of the rhotic consonants by Welsh-English bilingual children. *International Journal of Bilingualism, 5*, 71–86.

Bardovi-Harlig, K., & Sprouse, R. A. (2017). Negative versus positive transfer. In J. I. Liontas (Ed.), *The TESOL encyclopedia of english language teaching*. Wiley-Blackwell.

Bergelson, E., & Swingley, D. (2012). At 6–9 months, human infants know the meanings of many common nouns. *PNAS, 109*(9), 3253–3258. https://doi.org/10.1073/pnas.1113380109

Bhatia, T. K., & Ritchie, W. C. (1999). The bilingual child: Some issues and perspectives. In W. C. Ritchie & T. K. Bhatia (Eds.), *Handbook of child language acquisition* (pp. 569–643). Academic Press.

Bialystok, E. (2001). *Bilingualism in development. language, literacy, & cognition*. Cambridge University Press.

Bialystok, E. (2007). Introduction: Language acquisition and bilingualism. Consequences for a multilingual society. *Applied Psycholinguistics, 28*(3), 393–397.

Bialystok, E., Luk, G., Peets, K., & Yang, S. (2010). Receptive vocabulary differences in monolingual and bilingual children. *Bilingualism: Language and Cognition, 13*, 525–531. https://doi.org/10.1017/S1366728909990423

Bloomfield, L. (1933). *Language*. Holt.

Bollnow, H. (1959). Engels, Friedrich. *Neue Deutsche Biographie, 4*, 521–527. [Online-Version]. Retrieved February 17, 2022, from https://www.deutsche-biographie.de/pnd118530380.html#ndbcontent

Bosch, L., & Sebastián-Gallés, N. (2001). Evidence of early language discrimination abilities in infants from bilingual environments. *Infancy, 2*(1), 29–49.

Bosch, L., & Sebastián-Gallés, N. (2003). Simultaneous bilingualism and the perception of a language-specific vowel contrast in the first year of life. *Language and Speech, 46*(2–3), 217–243.

Buschfeld, S. (2020a). *Children's English in Singapore: Acquisition, properties, and use*. Routledge.

Buschfeld, S. (2020b). Synopsis: Fine-tuning the EIF model. In S. Buschfeld & A. Kautzsch (Eds.), *Modelling world Englishes: A joint approach to postcolonial and non-postcolonial varieties* (pp. 397–415). Edinburgh University Press.

Byers-Heinlein, K., Burns, T. C., & Werker, J. F. (2010). The roots of bilingualism in newborns. *Psychological Science, 21*(3), 343–348. https://doi.org/10.1177/0956797609360758

Carroll, S. E. (2017). Exposure and input in bilingual development. *Bilingualism: Language and Cognition, 20*, 3–16.

Cartmill, E. A., Armstrong, B. F., Gleitman, L. R., Goldin-Meadow, S., Medina, T. N., & Trueswell, J.,C. (2013). Quality of early parent input predicts child vocabulary 3 years later. *Proceedings of the National Academy of Science (PNAS)*, 1–6. Retrieved June 7, 2018, from www.pnas.org/cgi/doi/10.1073/pnas.1309518110

Chan, A. (2010). The Cantonese double object construction with bei2 "give" in bilingual children: The role of input. *International Journal of Bilingualism, 14*(1), 65–85.

Chaojua, T., & van Heuven, V. J. (2009). Mutual intelligibility of Chinese dialects experimentally tested. *Lingua, 119*, 709–732.

References

Chevalier, S. (2015). Trilingual language acquisition. Contextual factors influencing active trilingualism in early childhood. .

Chondrogianni, V., & Marinis, T. (2011). Differential effects of internal and external factors on the development of vocabulary, morphology and complex syntax in successive bilingual children. *Linguistic Approaches to Bilingualism, 1*, 223–248. https://doi.org/10.1075/lab.1.3.05cho

Clark, E. V. (2016). *First language acquisition* (3rd ed.). Cambridge University Press.

Conboy, B. T., & Thal, D. J. (2006). Ties between the lexicon and grammar: Cross-sectional and longitudinal studies of bilingual toddlers. *Child Development, 77*(3), 712–735.

Cornips, L., & Hulk, A. (2008). Factors of success and failure in the acquisition of grammatical gender in Dutch. *Second Language Research, 28*, 267–296.

Coulmas, F. (2018). *An introduction to multilingualism: Language in a changing world*. Oxford University Press.

De Houwer, A. (1990). *The acquisition of two languages from birth: A case study*. Cambridge University Press. https://doi.org/10.1017/CBO9780511519789

De Houwer, A. (1995). Bilingual language acquisition. In P. Fletcher & B. MacWhinney (Eds.), *The handbook of child language* (pp. 219–250). Basil Blackwell.

De Houwer, A. (2009). *Bilingual first language acquisition*. Multilingual Matters.

De Houwer, A. (2021). *Bilingual development in childhood*. Cambridge University Press.

De Houwer, A., Bornstein, M. H., & De Coster, S. (2006). Early understanding of two words for the same thing: A CDI study of lexical comprehension in infant bilinguals. *International Journal of Bilingualism, 10*(3), 331–347.

De Houwer, A., Bornstein, M. H., & Putnick, D. L. (2014). A bilingual-monolingual comparison of young children's vocabulary size: Evidence from comprehension and production. *Applied Psycholinguistics, 35*, 1189–1211. https://doi.org/10.1017/S0142716412000744

De Houwer, A. 2017. "Bilingual language input environments, intake, maturity and practice." Bilingualism: Language and Cognition 20(1): 19-20.

De Houwer, A., & Ortega, L. (2018a). Introduction. In A. De Houwer & L. Ortega (Eds.), *The Cambridge handbook of bilingualism* (pp. 1–12). Cambridge University Press.

De Houwer, A., & Ortega, L. (Eds.). (2018b). *The Cambridge handbook of bilingualism*. Cambridge University Press.

Delucchi Danhier, R., & Mertins, B. (2018). Psycholinguistische Grundlagen der Inklusion—Schwerpunkt Bilingualismus. In S. Hußmann & B. Welzel (Eds.), *Do Profil—Das Dortmunder Profil für inklusionsorientierte Lehrerinnen- und Lehrerbildung* (pp. 161–178). Waxmann.

Döpke, S. (1998). Competing language structures: The acquisition of verb placement by bilingual German–English children. *Journal of Child Language, 25*, 555–584.

Doughan, D. (2021). *J.R.R Tolkien: A biographical sketch*. Retrieved May 6, 2022, from https://www.tolkiensociety.org/author/biography/

Doyle, A., Champagne, M., & Segalowitz, N. (1978). Some issues on the assessment of linguistic consequences of early bilingualism. In M. Paradis (Ed.), *Aspects of bilingualism* (pp. 13–20). Hornbeam Press.

Ferjan Ramírez, N., Ramírez, R. R., Clarke, M., Taulu, S., & Kuhl, P. K. (2017). Speech discrimination in 11-month-old bilingual and monolingual infants: A magnetoencephalography study. *Developmental Science, 20*(1), e12427.

Garcia-Sierra, A., Ramírez-Esparza, N., & Kuhl, P. K. (2016). Relationships between quantity of language input and brain responses in bilingual and monolingual infants. *International Journal of Psychophysiology, 110*, 1–17.

Garcia-Sierra, A., Rivera-Gaxiola, M., Percaccio, C. R., Conboy, B. T., Romo, H., Klarman, L., & Kuhl, P. K. (2011). Bilingual language learning: An ERP study relating early brain responses to speech, language input, and later word production. *Journal of Phonetics, 39*(4), 546–557. https://doi.org/10.1016/j.wocn.2011.07.002

Gathercole, V. C. M., & Hoff, E. (2007). Input and the acquisition of language: Three questions. In E. Hoff & M. Shatz (Eds.), *Blackwell handbook of language development* (pp. 107–127). Blackwell.

Gathercole, V. C. M., & Thomas, E. M. (2009). Bilingual first-language development: Dominant language takeover, threatened minority language take-up. *Bilingualism: Language and Cognition, 12*(2), 213–237.

Gawlitzek-Maiwald, I., & Tracy, R. (1996). Bilingual bootstrapping. *Linguistics, 34*(5), 901–926.

Genesee, F. (2003). *Educating second language children: The whole child, the whole curriculum, the whole community.* Cambridge University Press.

Genesee, F., Boivin, I., & Nicoladis, E. (1996). Talking with strangers: A study of bilingual children's communicative competence. *Applied Psycholinguistics, 17*, 427–442. https://doi.org/10.1017/S0142716400008183

Genesee, F., Paradis, J., & Crago, M. B. (2008). Dual language development & disorders. In *A handbook on bilingualism & second language learning* (3rd ed.).

Grosjean, F. (1989). Neurolinguists, beware! The bilingual is not two monolinguals in one person. *Brain and Language, 36*, 3–15.

Grosjean, F. (1998). Studying bilinguals: Methodological and conceptual issues. *Bilingualism: Language and Cognition, 1*(2), 131–149.

Grosjean, F. (2010). *Bilingual: Life and reality.* Harvard University Press.

Grosjean, F. (2020). How many are we? On the difficulty of counting people who are bilingual. Psychology Today. Retrieved November 4, 2022, from https://www.psychologytoday.com/intl/blog/life-bilingual/201209/how-many-are-we

Grosjean, F. (2021). Bilingualism in the family. In *Life as a bilingual: Knowing and using two or more languages* (pp. 115–140). Cambridge University Press. https://doi.org/10.1017/9781108975490.007

Grosjean, F., & Li, P. (2013). *The psycholinguistics of bilingualism.* Wiley-Blackwell.

Gumperz, J. J. (1982). *Discourse strategies.* Cambridge University Press.

Hackert, S. (2012). *The emergence of the English native speaker. A chapter in nineteenth-century linguistic thought.* Mouton de Gruyter.

Hamers, J. F., & Blanc, M. H. A. (2000). *Bilinguality and bilingualism* (2nd ed.). Cambridge University Press.

Han, H. (2013). Individual grassroots multilingualism in Africa town in Guangzhou: The role of states in globalization. *International Multilingual Research Journal, 7*(1), 83–97.

Hauser-Grüdl, N., Guerra, L. A., Witzmann, F., Leray, E., & Müller, N. (2010). Cross-linguistic influence in bilingual children: Can input frequency account for it? *Lingua, 120*, 2638–2650.

Hervé, C., & Serratrice, L. (2018). The development of determiners in the context of French-English bilingualism: a study of cross-linguistic influence. *Journal of Child Language, 45*(3), 767–787.

Hoff, E., Core, C., Place, S., Rumiche, R., Señor, M., & Parra, M. (2012). Dual language exposure and early bilingual development. *Journal of Child Language, 39*, 1–27. https://doi.org/10.1017/S0305000910000759

Hoff, E., Rumiche, R., Burridge, A., Ribot, K. M., & Welsh, S. N. (2014). Expressive vocabulary development in children from bilingual and monolingual homes: A longitudinal study from two to four years. *Early Childhood Research Quarterly, 29*(4), 433–444.

Hulk, A. C. J., & Müller, N. (2000). Bilingual first language acquisition at the interface between syntax and pragmatics. *Bilingualism: Language and Cognition, 3*, 227–244.

Hulstijn, J. (2012). The construct of language proficiency in the study of bilingualism from a cognitive perspective. *Bilingualism: Language and Cognition, 15*(2), 422–433.

Ilanguages. (2018). Retrieved February 2, 2022, from http://ilanguages.org/bilingual.php

Jia, G., & Fuse, A. (2007). Acquisition of English grammatical morphology by native Mandarin speaking children and adolescents: Age-related differences. *Journal of Speech, Language and Hearing Research, 50*, 1280–1299.

Kehoe, M. M. (2002). Developing vowel systems as a window to bilingual phonology. *International Journal of Bilingualism, 6*, 315–334.

Kupisch, T. (2008). Dominance, mixing and cross-linguistic influence: On their relation in bilingual development. In P. Guijarro-Fuentes, P. Larrañaga, & J. Clibbens (Eds.), *First language acquisition of morphology and syntax: Perspectives across languages and learners* (pp. 209–234).

Larrañaga, P., & Guijarro-Fuentes, P. (2012). Clitics in L1 bilingual acquisition. *First Language, 32*, 151–175.

References

Lleó, C. (2002). The role of markedness in the acquisition of complex prosodic structures by German-Spanish bilinguals. *International Journal of Bilingualism, 6,* 291–314.

Macnamara, J. (1967). The bilingual's linguistic performance—A psychological overview. *Journal of Social Issues, XXIII*(2), 58–77.

Maneva, B. (2004). 'Maman, je suis polyglotte!': A case study of multilingual language acquisition from 0 to 5 years. *International Journal of Multilingualism, 1*(2), 109–122.

Marchman, V. A., Fernald, A., & Hurtado, N. (2010). How vocabulary size in two languages relates to efficiency in spoken word recognition by young Spanish–English bilinguals. *Journal of Child Language, 37*(4), 817–840. https://doi.org/10.1017/S0305000909990055

Marchman, V. A., Martínez-Sussman, C., & Dale, P. S. (2004). The language-specific nature of grammatical development: Evidence from bilingual language learners. *Developmental Science, 7,* 212–224.

McLaughlin, B. (1978). *Second language acquisition in childhood.* Lawrence Erlbaum Associates.

Meisel, J. M. (1989). Early differentiation of languages in bilingual children. In K. Hyltenstam & L. K. Obler (Eds.), *Bilingualism across the lifespan: Aspects of acquisition, maturity and loss* (pp. 13–40). Cambridge University Press.

Meisel, J. M. (1990). Grammatical development in the simultaneous acquisition of two first languages. In J. M. Meisel (Ed.), *Two first languages* (pp. 5–22). De Gruyter Mouton.

Meisel, J. M. (2001). The simultaneous acquisition of two first languages: Early differentiation and subsequent development of grammars. In J. Cenoz & F. Genesee (Eds.), *Trends in bilingual acquisition* (pp. 11–41). John Benjamins.

Meisel, J. M. (2004). The bilingual child. In T. K. Bhatia & W. C. Ritchie (Eds.), *The handbook of bilingualism* (pp. 91–113). Blackwell.

Meisel, J. M. (2011). *First and second language acquisition: Parallels and differences.* Cambridge University Press.

Merriam-Webster. (1961). *Webster's third new international dictionary of the English language, unabridged.*

Mohanty, A. K. (2019). *The multilingual reality: Living with languages.* Multilingual Matters.

Mougeon, R., & Rehner, K. (2017). The influence of classroom input and community exposure on the learning of variable grammar. Bilingualism: Language and Cognition, 20, 21–22.

Morrill, John S. and Greenblatt, Stephen J. (Invalid Date). Elizabeth I. Encyclopedia Britannica. https://www.britannica.com/biography/Elizabeth-I.

Müller, N., & Hulk, A. C. J. (2001). Crosslinguistic influence in bilingual language acquisition: Italian and French as recipient languages. *Bilingualism: Language and Cognition, 4,* 1–21.

Nicoladis, E. (2003). Cross-linguistic transfer in deverbal compounds of preschool bilingual children. *Bilingualism: Language and Cognition, 6,* 17–31.

Nicoladis, E. (2006). Cross-linguistic transfer in adjective–noun strings by preschool bilingual children. *Bilingualism: Language and Cognition, 9,* 15–32.

Nicoladis, E., Song, J., & Marentette, P. (2012). Do young bilinguals acquire past tense morphology like monolinguals, only later? Evidence from French-English and Chinese-English bilinguals. *Applied Psycholinguistics, 33*(3), 457–479.

Odlin, T. (1989). *Language transfer: Cross-linguistic influence in language learning.* Cambridge University Press.

Ortega, L. (2014). Ways forward for a bi/multilingual turn in SLA. In S. May (Ed.), *The multilingual turn: Implications for SLA, TESOL, and bilingual education* (pp. 32–53). Routledge.

Oxford English Dictionary, (2023) "bilingualism, n."

Paradis, J. (2001). Do bilingual two-year-olds have separate phonological systems? *International Journal of Bilingualism, 5,* 19–38.

Paradis, J. (2007). Early bilingual and multilingual acquisition. In P. Auer & L. Wei (Eds.), *Handbook of multilingualism and multilingual communication* (pp. 15–44). Mouton de Gruyter.

Paradis, J. (2011). Individual differences in child English second language acquisition: Comparing child-internal and child-external factors. *Linguistic Approaches to Bilingualism, 1*(3), 213–237.

Paradis, J. (2017). Parent report data on input and experience reliably predict bilingual development and this is not trivial. *Bilingualism: Language and Cognition, 20,* 27–28.

Paradis, J., & Genesee, F. (1996). Syntactic acquisition in bilingual children: Autonomous or interdependent? *Studies in Second Language Acquisition, 18*, 1–25.

Paradis, J., Genesee, F., & Crago, M. (2010). *Dual language development & disorders: A handbook on bilingualism & second language learning* (2nd ed.). Paul Brookes.

Paradis, J., & Navarro, S. (2003). Subject realization and crosslinguistic interference in the bilingual acquisition of Spanish and English: What is the role of the input? *Journal of Child Language, 30*(2), 371–393.

Pearson, B. Z. (2009). Children with two languages. In E. L. Bavin (Ed.), *The Cambridge handbook of child language* (pp. 379–397). Cambridge University Press.

Pearson, B. Z., Fernández, S., Lewedeg, V., & Oller, D. K. (1997). The relation of input factors to lexical learning by bilingual infants. *Applied Psycholinguistics, 18*, 41–58. https://doi.org/10.1017/S0142716400009863

Place, S., & Hoff, E. (2011). Properties of dual language exposure that influence two-year-olds' bilingual proficiency. *Child Development, 82*, 1834–1849.

Quiroz, B. G., Snow, C. E., & Zhao, J. (2010). Vocabulary skills of Spanish–English bilinguals: Impact of mother–child language interactions and home language and literacy support. *International Journal of Bilingualism, 14*(4), 379–399.

Rivera-Gaxiola, M., Silva Pereyra, J., & Kuhl, P. K. (2005). Brain potentials to native and non-native speech contrasts in 7 and 11 month old American infants. *Developmental Science, 8*(2), 162–172.

Romaine, S. (1995). *Bilingualism* (2nd ed.).

Rowe, C., & Grohmann, K. K. (2013). Discrete bilectalism: Towards co-overt prestige and diglossic shift in Cyprus. *International Journal of the Sociology of Language, 224*, 119–142.

Scheele, A., Leseman, P., & Mayo, A. (2010). The home language environment of monolingual and bilingual children and their language proficiency. *Applied Psycholinguistics, 31*, 117–140. https://doi.org/10.1017/S014271640999019

Serratrice, L. 2005. "Anaphora resolution in monolingual and bilingual language acquisition." In A. Brugos, M.R. Clark-Cotton & S. Ha (eds.), Proceedings of the 29th Annual Boston University Conference on Language Development. Somerville, MA: CascadillaPress, 504-515.

Serratrice, Ludovica, Antonella Sorace and S. Paoli 2004 Crosslinguistic influence at the syntax-pragmatics interface: subjects and objects in English-Italian bilingual and monolingual acquisition. Bilingualism: Language and Cognition 7: 183–206.

Serratrice, L. (2013a). The bilingual child. In T. K. Bhatia & W. C. Ritchie (Eds.), *The handbook of bilingualism and multilingualism* (2nd ed., pp. 87–108). Wiley-Blackwell.

Serratrice, L. (2013b). Cross-linguistic influence in bilingual development: Determinants and mechanisms. *Linguistic Approaches to Bilingualism, 3*(1), 3–25.

Serratrice, L. (2018). Becoming bilingual in early childhood. In A. De Houwer & L. Ortega (Eds.), *The Cambridge handbook of bilingualism* (pp. 15–35). Cambridge University Press.

Serratrice, L., & Hervé, C. (2015). Referential expressions in bilingual acquisition. In L. Serratrice & S. Allen (Eds.), *The acquisition of reference* (pp. 311–333). John Benjamins.

Shahidullah, S., & Hepper, P. G. (1994). Frequency discrimination by the foetus. *Early Human Development, 36*(1), 13–26.

Silvén, M., Voeten, M., Kouvo, A., & Lundén, M. (2014). Speech perception and vocabulary growth: A longitudinal study of Finnish–Russian bilinguals and Finnish monolinguals from infancy to three years. *International Journal of Behavioral Development, 38*(4), 323–332.

Simon-Cereijido, G., & Gutiérrez-Clellen, V. F. (2009). A cross-linguistic and bilingual evaluation of the interdependence between lexical and grammatical domains. *Applied Psycholinguistics, 30*(2), 315–337.

Stavans, A., & Hoffmann, C. (2015). *Multilingualism*. Cambridge University Press.

Sundara, M., & Scutellaro, A. (2011). Rhythmic distance between languages affects the development of speech perception in bilingual infants. *Journal of Phonetics, 39*(4), 505–513.

Sundara, M., Ward, N., Conboy, B., & Kuhl, P. K. (2020). Exposure to a second language in infancy alters speech production. *Bilingualism: Language and Cognition, 23*(5), 978–991. https://doi.org/10.1017/S1366728919000853

Taxitari, L., Kambanaros, M., Floros, G., & Grohmann, K. (2017). Early language development in a bilectal context: The Cypriot adaptation of the Macarthur-Bates CDI. In E. Babatsouli,

References

D. Ingram, & N. Müller (Eds.), *Crosslinguistic encounters in language acquisition: Typical and atypical development* (pp. 145–171). Multilingual Matters.

Treffers-Daller, J. (2018). The measurement of bilingual abilities. In A. De Houwer & L. Ortega (Eds.), *The Cambridge handbook of bilingualism* (pp. 289–306). Cambridge University Press.

Unsworth, S. (2013). Current issues in multilingual first language acquisition. *Annual Review of Applied Linguistics, 33*, 21–50.

Volterra, V., & Taeschner, T. (1978). The acquisition and development of language by bilingual children. *Journal of Child Language, 5*(2), 311–326.

Wardhaugh, R. (2002). *An introduction to sociolinguistics* (4th ed.).

Zwanziger, E. E., Allen, S. E. M., & Genesee, F. (2005). Crosslinguistic influence in bilingual acquisition: Subject omission in learners of Inuktitut and English. *Journal of Child Language, 32*(4), 893–909.

Key Readings

Baker, C., & Wright, W. E. (2021). *Foundations of bilingual education and bilingualism* (7th ed.). Multilingual Matters.

De Houwer, A. (2021). *Bilingual development in childhood*. Cambridge University Press. https://doi.org/10.1017/9781108866002

Serratrice, L. (2018). Becoming bilingual in early childhood. In A. De Houwer & L. Ortega (Eds.), *The Cambridge handbook of bilingualism (Cambridge handbooks in language and linguistics)* (pp. 15–35). Cambridge University Press. https://doi.org/10.1017/9781316831922.002

Further Readings

Altarriba, J., & Heredia, R. R. (Eds.). (2018). *An introduction to bilingualism: Principles and processes* (2nd ed.). Routledge.

Chevalier, S. (2015). *Trilingual language acquisition. Contextual factors influencing active trilingualism in early childhood*. John Benjamins.

De Houwer, A., & Ortega, L. (Eds.). (2018). *The Cambridge handbook of bilingualism (Cambridge handbooks in language and linguistics)*. Cambridge University Press.

Linguistic Mechanisms, Processes, and Results

Contents

4.1 Introduction – 74

4.2 Language Contact – 74

4.3 Language Change and Its Mechanisms – 77
4.3.1 First vs. Second Language Acquisition and Language Change – 78
4.3.2 Factors of Language Change – 81
4.3.3 Mechanisms of Language Change – 87

4.4 Linguistic Effects of Language Change on the Recipient Language – 92

4.5 Language Change or Temporary Variation? – 95

References – 97

© The Author(s), under exclusive license to Springer Nature Switzerland AG 2023
S. Buschfeld et al., *Multilingualism*,
https://doi.org/10.1007/978-3-031-28405-2_4

4.1 Introduction

So far, we have read about historical reasons for the development of multilingualism in ►Chap. 2 and about the problematic issue of defining who can or should be considered multilingual in ►Chap. 3. In this chapter, we take the next step and discuss various situations that involve the use of more than one language in societies as well as in individual speakers. We start by looking into situations of language contact and their potential effects on the languages involved in such situations. Depending on the power relations between the involved languages, or rather between their respective speaker groups, language contact may result in language death, in new, mixed languages (cf. ►Chap. 5), or in contact-induced language change, which we assess in detail in the current chapter.

While keeping in mind that every situation of language contact and language change is unique and language change is not predictable, we learn about certain factors that influence the outcome of language contact and common mechanisms that are at work when speakers are confronted with the need (or wish) to use more than one language. To understand the mechanisms and processes that are at work in situations of multi-language use, we take a short excursus and learn about the differences between first and second language acquisition and the settings and outcomes that they often occur in. We focus especially on mechanisms of *code-switching*, *code-mixing*, *code alternation*, and *borrowings* and discuss how to differentiate between these practices. We end with an elaboration on one of the more recent concepts in multilingualism, that is *translanguaging*. Before we go into the details, we would like to remind readers that the list of factors and mechanisms we present is not comprehensive. We end the chapter by discussing what factors might cause permanent language change and which changes might only be temporary, for example as a part of youth language.

4.2 Language Contact

Multilingualism, that is, the use of more than one language by an individual or a social group, always involves language contact. While there are more or less complex and detailed definitions of language contact, in this book we refer to *language contact* as contact situations in which people use more than one language in the same place at the same time (see Thomason, 2001, pp. 1–3 for a discussion of possible definitions and contexts). Language contact is a phenomenon that is described mostly when referring to (larger) social groups, meaning (sub-)communities. It commonly occurs in communities that live in close proximity but speak different languages, such as speakers living at the German-Dutch border, or in communities into which another group of speakers has integrated. As the language of one of the most successful colonising nations in history, English has frequently come into contact with other languages and exhibits unparalleled numbers of current users around the globe. Language contact also occurs in individual speakers. Whenever speakers of different first languages use English in its function as a lingua franca to talk to each other, English and the respective first language (L1) may interfere within the respective speaker's language use. These contexts are discussed in more detail in ▶ Sect. 4.3.

In general, language contact is not uniform; it is context-dependent and varies in terms of intensity and stability. In some contexts, language contact is only temporary as one language is lost over time, for example through mobility or death of its speakers, and a multilingual community turns monolingual. An example of such a dying language might be Arvanitika, a variety of Albanian spoken in Greece (cf. Thomason, 2001, pp. 222, 226). In other contexts, such as Canada or Catalonia—a region in Spain—language contact is quite stable and the use of two languages or more is maintained. In multilingual societies, the language of the majority group is, most of the time, more dominant than the languages of minority groups. However, revitalisation processes can aim at turning a minority language into a dominant language, for example after years of being under colonial rule. The reasons for these different outcomes of language contact lie in the fact that the use of languages cannot be separated from power relations (cf. ▶ Sect. 2.2). As some languages are associated with more powerful speaker groups than other languages, in every multilingual context, there are language hierarchies at play that might shift and change over time. These shifts might occur (or not occur), for example, based on reproduced or resolved colonial power structures or economic dependencies of one speaker group or state from another. Depending on the nature and potential imbalances of these power relations in a specific contact situation, long(er)term language contact might lead to (1) contact-induced language change, (2) extreme language mixture, or (3) language death (cf. Thomason, 2001, p. 60).

Language death is the most tragic outcome of language contact and most often the result of voluntary or involuntary loss of language users. Speakers might shift voluntarily from their L1 towards another, often more dominant and powerful, language. Members of a minority group might shift towards an increased use of the language of the majority to facilitate, for example, their education or their job opportunities. This shift might be slow, starting with some families using the majority language instead of their L1/indigenous language in their homes. As more and more people integrate the majority language into domains in which the indigenous language used to be spoken, the use of this indigenous language is likely to be influenced and changed by the majority language. However, this is sometimes not the final outcome: as the usefulness of the indigenous L1 decreases in the eyes of its speakers over time, that is, in the course of decades or even centuries, they decide to no longer maintain their L1 but shift towards using the majority language as their 'new' L1. This decision is, of course, not necessarily one that is taken explicitly or implemented at a specific point in time; it is just something that happens over time when a speaker group experiences that it is easier for them to use the more powerful or majority language. The process of a speaker forgetting or unlearning a language is called *language attrition* and it often occurs in favour of another language (cf. Schmid, 2011; Stringer, 2013). In other contexts, often linked to globalisation, this shift towards a more powerful language is more quickly paced. While the grandparent generation might still have an interest in maintaining 'their' language and the cultural knowledge and traditions that are linked to it, the grandchildren generation is often more interested in wider communicative options and increased mobility and does not want to invest in learning or maintaining their grandparents' language. Such a quick shift can, consequently, result in multilingual families with grandparents who are L1 speakers of a language that their grandchildren do no longer speak or even understand comprehensively. Both of these scenarios are based on voluntary behaviour as language users decide to no longer maintain a language. However, language death might also result from more hostile circumstances, such as the violent or natural death of the language speakers or governmental or institutional discouragement of language use. In modern times, language policies (cf. ▶ Chap. 7) are often used to encourage the use or non-use of certain languages. As the influence of language policies might be quite drastic, the respective people's shift from one language to one that is more desired by powerful institutions, such as the government, might to be somewhere in-between voluntary and involuntary. The Singaporean government, for example, implemented the Speak Mandarin Campaign in 1979, which advised that Singaporeans of Chinese ethnicity should use Mandarin as the only Chinese language. This campaign has been very successful and has led Singaporeans to choose Mandarin over their L1 Chinese language, such as Hokkien, Teochew, or Cantonese, and to not maintain these other languages.

In language contact scenarios in which more than one language are maintained, either language change or language mixture can occur. While language change is quite common, and therefore discussed in more detail in the following section, language mixture, which in the extreme case leads to the emergence of a new language, is less frequent. Mixed languages are characterised by linguistic (sub)systems that have not been developed from one single source language—or at least it cannot be shown convincingly that these systems are rooted in just one of the source languages. Common examples of such mixed languages are pidgins and creoles but other forms of mixed languages exist, too (for further details and definitions, see ▶ Chap. 5; Thomason, 2001, pp. 157–221). Pidgins are languages that consist of a lexicon predominantly taken from one language and a grammar that is a combination of large chunks of grammatical structures from both (or all) languages involved. A pidgin is created *ad hoc* for intergroup communication and has no L1 users. Once the first generations of L1 users of the erstwhile pidgin are born, we typically speak of a creole language. Pidgins and subsequently creoles emerge in cases where no group can or wants to learn the other groups' language(s), even though the involved speaker groups need to communicate with each other. The emerging language tends to serve as the lingua franca between the speaker groups. Other mixed languages are created for intragroup communication and emerge in spite of already existing multilingualism. These mixed languages, therefore, do not serve as linguae francae but as a means to emphasise in-group similarities between members of the social group(s) involved (see ▶ Chap. 5 for further details on mixed languages). Let us now turn to a very frequent outcome of language contact: contact-induced language change.

4.3 Language Change and Its Mechanisms

Most often, language change is the result of language contact. As the ways in which languages might get in contact with each other differ (cf. ▶ Sect. 2.2 and Sect. 4.2), the resulting changes in the involved language(s) can vary considerably. *Contact-induced language change* is the outcome of language contact that is most interesting for us. It is commonly understood as one of the involved languages acquiring features from one or more other languages its speakers are in contact with. This transfer of features is possible on all levels of linguistic description, namely phonology, morphology, syntax, lexis, and pragmatics/semantics. However, language change can also be bidirectional. Which aspects of a language are transferred to which other language depends on various factors, such as the individual languages and speaker groups that are involved as well as their interrelations and the context of contact. While the presence of features of one language in another language indicates language contact, the absence of such transferred features does not negate a possible contact scenario. The fact that up to 75% of words in the English language are assumed to be loanwords from other languages shows that there has been contact between the English language and other languages, such as French and Latin (cf. Thomason, 2001, p. 10). However, language contact does not always result in loanwords entering one of the involved languages. This means that (1) the lack of loanwords from Language A in Language B does not mean that Language A and Language B have not been in contact. Furthermore, the number of loanwords in a language does not necessarily indicate the extent of language contact. The many French loanwords in the English language do not serve as proof that the contact between English and French speakers has been more intense than that between English speakers and speakers of a language from which less or no loanwords have entered the English language.

Contact-induced language change is highly complex and depends on the individual context. Although, in the course of this chapter, we present influential factors and mechanisms that often occur as part of processes of language change, the offered list is not comprehensive and can only partly explain how the complex linguistic realities occur and can be understood. Although we cannot predict language change, finding common patterns through probable generalisations and mechanisms can help us understand how and why languages change—or do not change—when in contact with other languages. To reduce the complexity of the discussion, we focus on cases in which language contact occurs between two languages. Unless indicated otherwise, the factors and mechanisms that are introduced in the following are also valid in language contact situations of more than two languages. Furthermore, we differentiate between contact-induced language change that involves speakers who are fluent speakers of the languages, meaning L1 speakers and very proficient second language (L2) speakers, and speakers who are less fluent, namely L2 speakers with incomplete learning in one of the languages. To understand the impact of language learning on language fluency and use, let us take a detour into the field of language acquisition.

4.3.1 First vs. Second Language Acquisition and Language Change

L1 and L2 acquisition vary due to multiple factors. The most often assessed factors in this respect are age of onset of acquisition, the (lack of) consciousness of the acquisition process, and ultimate attainment, that is the final outcome of the acquisition process. In very much simplified terms, L1 and L2 acquisition can be considered to be opposing poles on a spectrum of age, consciousness, and outcome. While monolingual L1 acquisition and multilingual, simultaneous acquisition of multiple L1s start at birth or even before (cf. ▶ Chap. 1 and ▶ Sect. 3.2), L2 acquisition is considered to start later in a person's life; some linguists suggest the age of 6 as a benchmark (De Houwer, 2021, p. 1). While L1 acquisition is an unconscious process that results in what is often called native-speaker competence—and there is much debate on what makes a native speaker and whether it is at all a useful concept (see our discussion of the concept of nativeness in ▶ Sect. 3.3.2)—L2 acquisition is mostly a conscious process of learning and its outcomes vary from basic to native-like proficiency. In general, the older the learner is when coming into contact with a new language, the more conscious the learning process might be. Learning in formal settings, such as school and other instructional settings, commonly involves the highest degree of consciousness, namely active learning of grammatical rules and vocabulary. Informal second language acquisition (SLA) often includes less conscious effort, for example if a language is learnt through exposure after migration. Sequential L1 acquisition ought to be placed somewhere in-between these two scenarios, leaning towards the pole of simultaneous L1 acquisition. As mentioned in ▶ Sect. 3.2, we follow the assumption that sequential multilingual acquisition starts at some point between the ages of 2 and 6, which means that sequential multilinguals make, what De Houwer calls, "monolingual experiences" (2021, p. 33). This describes a time in their lives in which they are in contact with only one language. Sequential multilinguals are often raised in contexts in which their home language differs from the societal language or the language of education. Consequently, they first acquire their home language quite similarly to a monolingually raised child and are introduced to the societal or educational language(s) only when entering institutions outside the home, such as childcare, kindergarten, or school.

Most important for our considerations is the ultimate attainment of L1 and L2 acquisition as well as potential occurrences of language contact in the course of these processes. Scholars agree that L2 learning can result in variable outcomes, especially when multilinguals are concerned (Baum & Titone, 2014; Bialystok & Kroll, 2018; Pierce et al., 2017). L1 acquisition is commonly expected to result in 'full competence'. A decrease of this 'full competence' in a speaker's L1 almost exclusively occurs due to a lack of use and is called *language attrition*. In comparison, L2 language learners' competencies may vary between understanding just a few words, having basic communicative skills, and having near-native fluency. Outcomes that differ from near-native fluency are often considered the result of incomplete or imperfect learning (cf. Thomason, 2001) and can occur in L2 acqui-

4.3 · Language Change and Its Mechanisms

sition as well as in sequential and even simultaneous multilingual acquisition. Often, the level of ultimately attained proficiency decreases with increasing age of onset of acquisition. As the differences in outcome and proficiency between sequential and simultaneous L1 learners tend to level off once they enter school or formal education (cf. De Houwer, 2021, p. 43), the so-called age effect is especially important for L2 learners. While the level of proficiency decreases with increasing age of onset, the likelihood of cross-linguistic influence or transfer increases (e.g. Pearson, 2009, p. 289; see ▶ Sect. 3.4 for more details on cross-linguistic influences in the context of bilingual L1 acquisition). Ultimately, L2 acquisition is always impacted by cross-linguistic influences or language transfer, as, by definition, an L2 learner "possesses complete knowledge of an L1" (Ortega, 2009, p. 31) which their learning of the L2 is based on and which has a more or less strong influence on their learning.

Cross-linguistic influence or transfer effects have been in the focus of L2 acquisition research since the first half of the twentieth century. Initially, similarities and differences between an L1 and an L2 were analysed to predict the learning process of an individual learner. This is known as the school of *contrastive analysis* (e.g. Lado, 1957; Stockwell et al., 1965) which postulates that similarities between the L1 and the L2 facilitate L2 acquisition while the learner will experience difficulties whenever their L1 differs from the target language, namely the L2 (e.g. Odlin, 2016, p. 1; Thomas, 2006, p. 302). While these assumptions have been shown to often hold, sometimes similarities between the two involved languages do not prevent learning difficulties and differences do not always cause problems. Consequently, there has to be more to L2 acquisition than formal correspondence between the L1 and the L2. While researchers still consider L1-L2 correspondence when trying to explain the emergence of learner language characteristics, such as language use that differs from the language use of L1 users, they also incorporate other leaner-internal mechanisms and learner-external factors that potentially influence an L2 learner's acquisition process.

One of the most important learner-external factors is the linguistic input learners receive. Especially but not only in the early phases of L2 acquisition, this input tends to be simplified to accommodate the lower level of proficiency of the individual learner. This phenomenon is often called linguistic accommodation. *Accommodation theory* is originally an socio-psychological model which aims at "predicting and explaining many of the adjustments individuals make to create, maintain, or decrease social distance in interaction" (Giles & Ogay, 2007, p. 293). These adjustments or accommodation might be realised by means of convergence or divergence (cf. Giles & Ogay, 2007 for an overview of Communication Accommodation Theory). This results in speakers altering their language use in various ways when communicating with an interlocutor who has a different proficiency level in their shared language. In the context of SLA, L1 speakers—or more proficient learners—of a language might, for example, simplify the morphosyntactic structure of their utterance, pay attention to careful pronunciation, choose informal vocabulary, or implement a combination of these choices when talking to a beginner learner of that language. This is referred to as convergence (sometimes it is also referred to as foreigner talk or teacher talk, e.g. Lightbown & Spada, 2007,

p. 34); the more proficient speaker converges to the needs and abilities of their interlocutor to facilitate or even enable communication. If a learner of English asks an L1 speaker of English, for example, "Where the toilets, please?", the asked person would facilitate successful communication if they said "The toilets are the second door to the right.", maybe even accompanied by holding up two fingers and pointing to the right. In contrast to *convergence*, however, speakers of a language might also choose to diverge, that is, to alter their language use in such a way that it impedes successful communication with their interlocutor. In our example, the L1 speaker could answer, for example, "Public conveniences can be found when exiting this room, turning right into the hallway. After having passed the internal staircase you will find them to your right." (see Lightbown & Spada, 2007, p. 34 for the inspiration of our example). In addition to showing the language learner that their language use is imperfect and that the more proficient speaker does not want to help, this answer would almost certainly cause the conversation to fail (see Niedzielski & Giles, 2008 on linguistic accommodation).

Turning towards learner-internal mechanisms, we focus on two very common processes: *simplification* and *overgeneralisation*. The process of simplification is characterised by the use of limited and structurally rather simple language (forms). While a proficient learner, for example, knows that *could* is the past tense form of *can* but can also be used as its polite form (Could you please pass the salt?), beginner learners often simplify and might use *could* only as the past tense for of *can*. Simplifications occur most often during the early phases of the L2 acquisition process, i.e., when the learner has only a limited target language repertoire, and decreases with increasing proficiency (cf. Ortega, 2009, pp. 116–117). Overgeneralisation is another important process of L2 acquisition and is defined as the transfer of rules or forms into contexts in which they do not apply. An example of overgeneralisation might be the use of *capelli* ('scalp hair' in Italian) to refer to body hair, in which case *pelo* would be the appropriate lexical choice. A common and important kind of overgeneralisation on the grammatical level is (over-)regularisation, which is the application of rules where they are not appropriate. A popular example of (over-)regularisation is the application of regular inflectional suffixes to irregular verbs, resulting in forms such as *go-ed or *eat-ed. While overgeneralisation and overregularisation might reflect that certain aspects of an L2 have not yet been acquired, their occurrence also shows that certain rules and regularities have been understood and internalised. Consequently, overgeneralisations only occur after a certain level of competence has been achieved by the learner and they occur in L2 and L1 acquisition (see, e.g., ▶ Sect. 3.3.2 on lexical overgeneralisation in L1 acquisition, for more details see VanPatten & Benati, 2015, pp. 154–155, 174). Transfer processes within a language, such as simplification or overgeneralisation, and across languages, such as cross-linguistic influences, are most often overcome in the course of the acquisition process. However, if the linguistic fetaures that result from these processes are consolidated, they can influence language change.

4.3.2 Factors of Language Change

As mentioned above, language change cannot be predicted. However, we can identify certain patterns of language change that are more or less likely to occur when languages come into contact with each other. As a first, quite general step, we can differentiate between direct and indirect effects of language contact. Direct effects of language contact are, e.g., linguistic features that are transferred from a source language into the recipient language. Indirect effects are effects of language attrition processes or changes that are based on earlier direct effects. By way of example, the word *fine* might first be transferred from the English into the German language and might be commonly used by (some) speakers of German. This would be a direct effect of language contact. The syntactic construction in which "fine" is often used in English, that is, "I'm fine with this", might then, in a second step, also be transferred into the recipient language German. Over time, German-speakers might use *Ich bin fine damit* (a literal translation of 'I'm fine with this' into German), instead of the more idiomatic *Ich bin damit einverstanden*. This would be an indirect follow-up effect of language contact as the structure is only transferred due to the previous transfer of *fine*. Language contact does not always cause features of a language to be transferred into another language or a direct effect to be succeeded by an indirect, follow-up effect. In turn, there is also no feature that, in principle, cannot be transferred into another language. Still, over the years, linguists have proposed rules that appear to guide contact-induced language change. While contact-induced language change tends to follow these rules, change is quite heterogeneous in its concrete realisations and counterexamples to these rules have been found. Although it is more likely that the transfer of lexical features from one language to another precedes that of grammatical features, language change can start with the transfer of grammatical features and, even though changes tend to simplify the recipient language, they can also make it more complex (e.g., Thomason, 2001). Consequently, rather than being used to exactly predict language change, the rules have been found to reflect the probability of a certain change to occur.

When investigating contact-induced language change, we follow Thomason (2001), who differentiates between *social* and *linguistic factors* as predictors of type and degree of language change. It is important to understand that these factors do not determine whether language change occurs or not. However, they influence the probability that language change occurs.

4.3.2.1 Linguistic Factors of Language Change

Linguistic factors that influence the realisation of contact-induced language change are typological differences or similarities between the involved languages, universal markedness (see definition below), and the degree of integration of features into the linguistic structure of the donor language (cf. Thomason, 2001, pp. 76–77). The typological distance between languages represents the degree of similarity between the languages in terms of, for example, their morphosyntactic structures. Generally, the likelihood of features being transferred from one language to another increases with the typological similarity of these languages. Whenever less fluent speakers are concerned, markedness seems to be the most influential of these factors (Greenberg, 1966; Jakobsen, 1941). Marked features are considered "structurally more complex, less frequent and therefore cognitively more salient" (Callies, 2013, p. 406) than their unmarked counterparts, such as dental fricatives which are rarely found in languages other than English. Consequently, they are also harder to learn and less likely to be known by language learners than unmarked features. This decreases the probability that marked features are transferred into the recipient language. Hence, it is unlikely that dental fricatives are transferred from English into another language while the regular and thus unmarked past tense morpheme {-ed} is more likely to be transferred into another language than any of its irregular (or subregular), marked equivalents, such as {-ept} as in *sleep–slept, weep–wept, keep–kept*. Whenever fluent speakers are concerned, markedness has less of an effect, as proficient speakers typically know both the marked and unmarked features of the language they acquire, and, consequently, can transfer both to another language. Finally, the degree of integration into the linguistic structure influences the probability of transfer. Features that are deeply embedded into the structure of a language, for example if they require the use of complex morphology or a complex subordinate clause, are less likely to be transferred into another language than features which are less embedded. In general, the more frequent, more easily accessible, and (structurally) more familiar features are more likely to be transferred into another language than rare, complex, and unfamiliar features. While the three linguistic factors presented in this paragraph are important to understand and determine which features of a language are more or less likely to be transferred into another language, social factors play a decisive role, too.

4.3.2.2 Social Factors of Language Change

The key function of a language is to serve as a communicative tool and means of expression for its users. Therefore, while certain properties of the involved languages can influence which features might be transferred from one to the other language, the social background of their users normally has an even bigger impact on language change (Thomason, 2001, p. 77). First and foremost, language change is influenced by attitudes speakers hold towards the languages involved. Speaker attitudes are a wild card in the context of language change: they are more influential than any other factor and can, therefore, motivate changes or prevent them from happening; speaker attitudes can overrule any linguistic likelihood (Thomason 2001, p. 77). To further systematise processes and mechanisms of language change, we discuss the influence of speaker attitudes on language change further below and first focus on other social factors, such as intensity of language contact and speaker fluency, and their effect on contact-induced language change (cf. Thomason, 2001, pp. 66–76).

Concerning the first social factor, it has been found that, in general, with increasing language contact intensity the likelihood of feature transfer from one language to another increases. Thomason (2001, p. 66) gives three main factors,

4.3 · Language Change and Its Mechanisms

which might influence language contact intensity: quantitative (in-)equality between speaker groups, socioeconomic (in-)equality between speaker groups, and length and intensity of language contact between speaker groups. The two types of inequality between speaker groups, namely an inequality in number and in socioeconomic status, tend to correlate with each other; the bigger group of speakers is often also of a higher socioeconomic status. In general, linguistic features are more likely to be transferred from the language of the bigger or socioeconomically stronger group to the language of the minority or socioeconomically weaker group than vice versa. Migration contexts might serve as examples: the bigger group, which often is the traditional, local population, tends to be of a higher socioeconomic status and (politically) more powerful than the smaller group of migrants. Therefore, when people migrate to another country and have lived in their new home for a while (i.e. for more than one generation), lingusitic features of the societal language are often transferred into the migrants' heritage language(s). This, however, does not mean that lingusitic features cannot be transferred from the smaller speaker group to the bigger one or from the speaker group of lower socioecomomic status to that of higher socioeconomic status; migrant speaker groups may also include linguistic features of their L1 in their use of the societal language. While these features often are initally results of language learning (i.e. incomplete learning), they can stabilise and be transferred into the language of the bigger speaker group of higher socioeconomic status. Furthermore, in some contexts, the bigger group is not the socioeconomically more powerful one. Most contexts of colonisation were characterised by the fact that the minority of settlers were socioeconomically and politically more powerful than the majority group of native inhabitants. In these cases, the majority (willingly or unwillingly) learnt the language of the minority. Consequently, while socioeconomic dominance tends to correlate with speaker number, its influence often overrides sheer numbers. Last but not least, the length of contact between speakers of two different languages factors into the intensity of language contact. The general tendency is that the longer two languages are in contact, the more likely interference occurs. While, as we have seen, the intensity of language contact has an influence on language change, the second social factor—speaker fluency—has been found to be even more influential.

For the longest time, speaker proficiency used to be assessed based on *native speaker competence* and functioned as measurement to differentiate native and non-native speakers (see ▶ Sect. 3.2 for a discussion why these terms are problematic). In the following, we do not differentiate between native and non-native speakers but rather refer to speaker fluency[1] and focus on the speakers' level of mastery of communication skills to differentiate between fluent (first and second language) speakers and less fluent/incomplete (second language) speakers (cf. Thomason,

---

1 Speaker proficiency focusses on the level of mastery of a language (competence in the Chomskian sense) while speaker fluency focusses mainly on language use (performance). As we do not want to assess a speaker's native-likeness—or support the ideology of the native speakers' hegemony, we will use the concept of speaker fluency.

2001, pp. 67–76). In sum, when combining the social factors of language change, namely language contact intensity and speaker fluency, three common scenarios of language contact between two languages (L_a and L_b) may occur:

1. fluent speakers of L_a and L_b, such as successful L2 learners as well as simultaneous or sequential bilinguals (cf. ▶Chap. 1), come in contact with fluent speakers of L_a in an L_a-speaking environment or with fluent speakers of L_b in an L_b-speaking environment.
2. speakers who are fluent in L_a and less fluent in L_b come in contact with fluent speakers of L_b in an L_b-speaking environment.
3. speakers who are fluent in L_a and less fluent in L_b come in contact with speakers of L_b in an L_c-speaking environment.

Considering the first of these scenarios, let us say Jo, an English language teacher from the Netherlands, migrates to the USA. In addition to being an L1 speaker of Dutch, she is a fluent speaker of English, which will be her primary means of communication in her new home. For her new flat, Jo has purchased an armchair which she refers to as *leunstoel* (Dutch for 'armchair') because it reminds her of the armchair that she used to sit in in her grandparents' house back in the Netherlands. Jo has decided to transfer a Dutch word into her use of English. From a linguistic perspective, her use of *leunstoel* might already turn it into a borrowing.[2] However, a borrowing is commonly recognised once it is also used by other people, for example by her friends who find the use of *leunstoel* charming and reproduce it (cf. Thomason, 2001, p. 67). This scenario is a typical case of borrowing, which starts with lexical features. Still, our example reflects only one version of scenario 1, as we assume that there are no Dutch speakers in Jo's social environment. In this case, Dutch borrowings will be mostly limited to content words as the borrowers (Jo's new friends) are not fluent in Dutch and would not be able to transfer structural elements into their L1, English. In case Jo's new social circle includes speakers of Dutch, the contact between the English and Dutch languages may increase and facilitate interference. This increased intensity of contact allows for less basic features, such as, function words and surface syntactical structures, to be transferred from Dutch into English—and vice versa. The bigger the group of bilingual speakers and the more favourable other social factors are towards transfer from Dutch to English, the more complex or more deeply embedded structures become subject to interference. Given the right circumstances, namely extensive bilingualism and social factors, such as language status and speaker attitudes, which favour language transfer, there are no constraints on which features of a language are transferred into another language. This is one more reason why language change is unpredictable.

The second scenario outlined above involves incomplete learning and a more or less predictable route of language change. Incomplete learning is characterised by the fact that some features of a language are not known by a language learner and

---

[2] In the following we adopt the term *borrowing* as referring to interference in cases that involve fluent speakers, that is, that do not involve incomplete learning.

can, therefore, not enter the interference process. Speakers who are not fluent in one of the two contact languages but communicate in a linguistic environment that is dominated by this language find themselves in a power imbalance. Imagine Jim, a fluent (or L1) speaker of English, decides to move to Spain. As he has taken Spanish classes in high school for 2 years, he is able to use Spanish for basic communication but is not a fluent speaker. In Spain, he is surrounded by Spanish speakers who do (choose to) not speak English, forcing him to alter—or shift—his primary language of use from English to Spanish. Jim, and potential fellow Spanish L2 speakers of English, represent a minority in this scenario as the local Spanish-speaking population is bigger as well as socio-politically more powerful. In case a (bigger) social group shifts from speaking the language of the less powerful social group—in our example English—towards speaking the language of the more powerful social group—in our example Spanish—this new language use could cause *substratum interference*. Substratum interference, in general, is characterised by the transfer of phonological or syntactic features before lexical features are transferred. However, it is not clear in advance which exact features of the substrate language will be transferred into the superstrate language (Thomason 2001, p. 75). This is different from the process of borrowing, which starts with lexical items and from there moves to other linguistic structures. In our example, substratum interference could proceed along the following steps: first, Jim would transfer some (phonological or syntactic) features of English into his use of Spanish. In addition, he will continue to learn Spanish and increase his mastery of Spanish. However, as we have learnt above, not all aspects of a language are picked up equally easily by language learners (see marked vs. unmarked features), which is why some features may never become part of his use of Spanish. Second, his social circle might eventually borrow (because they are fluent speakers of Spanish, see Footnote 5) some of the features of Jim's language and start using them themselves. Due to their close contact, a slight change in the superstrate language (Spanish, in our example) is a common result of language contact. In our example, the process of Jim and his local friends negotiating a common use of Spanish—which might, eventually, even spread to bigger social groups—causes the Spanish-speaking locals' use of their L1 to ultimately change. As the language use of both speaker groups can change, language change can be bidirectional, which means that substratum as well as superstrate interference can occur. Historically, superstrate interference, so linguistic shift of the more powerful speaker group towards the less powerful one, has commonly occured. One famous example is the acquisition of English by the French-speaking Normans who conquered England in the eleventh century after they had lost their French territories.

Last but not least, there is language contact between two languages in a linguistic environment in which another, third language is dominant (see scenario 3 introduced above). This scenario is most commonly found in communities that have been colonised by a power speaking a different language. Indian English, one of the varieties of English spoken in India, might serve as an example for language changes resulting from such a scenario. Although, as we have learnt in ▶Sect. 2.2, Hindi and English are the only official languages of India, it is a highly multilingual country, as its inhabitants speak many different languages and language varieties. Consequently, features of many different L1s have been transferred into the use of English in India. As English in India is not embedded in an English-dominant environment but in a linguistic environment characterised by multilingualism and linguistic diversity, linguistic changes in the English language used in India are more intense than they would be if English was the dominant language.

As we have seen previously, realities of contact-induced language change are always caused and influenced by a combination of linguistic and social factors and are considerably more complex than we can account for here. While the tendencies and interrelations presented above are simplifications of this complex reality, most of the time they are quite accurate and useful in assessing what will happen in case two speaker groups come in contact. However, as Thomason argues,

» [a]lthough a relationship of dominance and subordination between two groups of speakers is a powerful predictor of contact-induced change, with intensity increasing as cultural pressure on the subordinate group increases, and although the contrast between borrowing and shift-induced interference accounts for a great many differences in the linguistic results of contact, these are not the most powerful force in contact-induced change. (2001, p. 77)

The most powerful factor to trigger, prevent, and influence contact-induced language change are the speakers themselves, more precisely the speakers' attitudes which we turn to now.

4.3.2.3 The Influence of Speaker Attitudes on Language Change

While the social and linguistic factors that have been introduced so far certainly influence the probability that certain changes occur, it is the speakers who have to take the conscious or unconscious decision for or against the implementation of a certain known feature into their language use.[3] Some speech jurisdictions work hard to keep their languages pristine and unaltered by influences from other languages. An example of such a jurisdiction is France. In France, there is a long tradition of language policies promoting the use of French that resulted, among others, in the so-called *Toubon Law* which specifies that French must be used by official institutions, in official publications, and in communication (Zsombok, 2021, pp. 272–274). French speakers are continually reminded to use 'proper' French by social pressure as well as by law. When in 2013, the French minister for higher education and research, Geneviève Fioraso, introduced a draft law to allow the teaching of some university courses in English to attract international students, the *Académie Française*, the official authority of the French language, argued this idea would cause the depletion and marginalisation of the French language (e.g. Wiegel, 2013). Although the French language has changed, for example through the introduction of English borrowings, these policies have controlled the degree of change, at least to a certain degree and in official contexts. Unofficial language use has been found

---

3   One major exception to the 'speaker attitudes' wild card are some language contact situations that include incomplete learning, as features that are unknown to the speaker cannot be transferred into their language use (cf. Thomason, 2001, p. 79).

to be less influenced by purism than commonly expected (e.g. Martin, 2007; Walsh, 2014). While in France, the use of innovations appears to differ between contexts of use, other speech communities willingly borrow and transfer linguistic features from other languages to their own in all contexts of language use. Thomason (2001) uses the grammar of the Tanzanian Ma'a language that has been replaced almost completely by borrowed grammatical structures as an example. This practice allows the Ma'a speakers to not shift towards the more dominant languages they borrow from but to continue to speak their language as an identity marker, even if it has undergone changes over time. Sometimes, speaker groups even consciously decide to alter parts of their language to be more obviously different from other groups that speak a closely related language or variety. In these cases, again, the distinctive use of language serves as a marker of identity and can be used to underline differences from other speaker groups.

As has been shown so far, speaker attitudes are often based on identity constructions (see ▶Chap. 7 on language and identity) and can enhance or overrule any other (social or linguistic) influence on language change. Ultimately, speaker attitudes and the resulting conscious or unconscious language choices are further factors which make language change complex and unpredictable. The only thing we can be certain of is that contact-induced language change requires language contact. In the following, we move from general propositions about why languages change to individual speakers and how they might express this change, finding out about common mechanisms of language use that are commonly part of contexts of multilingualism or language contact.

4.3.3 Mechanisms of Language Change

Language change is typically initiated through the use of innovations by individual speakers. Simply put, one speaker has to start using their language differently for others to reproduce that use and for the new features to become implemented in the respective language. While language change is typically more likely on the phonological and syntactic levels when incomplete learning is involved, borrowing is the dominant mechanism for fluent speakers. Mechanisms that occur in or are a result of contact-induced language change include, for example, code-switching, code alternation, passive familiarity, negotiation, second-language acquisition strategies, bilingual first-language acquisition, and change by deliberate decision (see Thomason, 2001, pp. 131–153 for a more detailed overview of these mechanisms). These mechanisms can be combined or applied individually by multilingual speakers in language contact situations. While most of these mechanisms are available for fluent and less fluent speakers, they are more likely to be used consistently and implemented when used by fluent speakers than when used by less fluent ones. As discussing all the above-mentioned mechanisms in detail would go beyond the scope of this book, we focus on three of the most common ones, namely code-switching, code-mixing, and translanguaging, and show how they interrelate with the factors of language change that we have presented in ▶Sect. 4.3.2.

4.3.3.1 Code-Switching, Code-Mixing, and Code Alternation

Code-switching can be defined as "the use of material from two (or more) languages by a single speaker in the same conversation" (Thomason, 2001, p. 132) and it is the most extensively-studied mechanism of multilingual language use. We distinguish between intrasentential code-switching, which is the use of two (or more) languages within one sentence, and intersentential code-switching, that is, switching languages between sentences (cf. Myers-Scotton, 2002; Saville-Troike, 2003). While some scholars use code-switching and code-mixing interchangeably (MacSwan, 2019), in this book, we refer to intrasentential changes as *code-mixing* and to intersentential changes as *code-switching*. Code-switching and code-mixing potentially extent to all levels of language as they may concern pronunciation, word choice, and sentence or conversation structure. Furthermore, both processes can be used subconsciously or purposefully and fulfil various functions: they can be used to express social or cultural identity, humour, as well as (political) beliefs of various speaker groups and involve a combination of any languages (see Gardner-Chloros, 2009a for an overview). One of the most common functions of code-switching is that it can mark group belonging. As conversations that involve code-switching can only be followed by interlocutors that are at least able to understand the languages used, monolingual speakers are often excluded from such conversations. The use—or non-use—of specific languages within one conversation, consequently, can indicate group belonging or the lack thereof (see Gardner-Chloros, 2009b on the sociolinguistic factors of code-switching). Code-mixing, on the other hand, is often used to transfer a lexical item from one language to another to fill a lexical gap. This lexical gap might be a concept that cannot be translated from one language to the other or a concept which is missing in the speaker's lexicon or can, at least, not be retrieved fast enough from lexical memory. Consequently, most commonly, code-mixing involves words and short phrases (Thomason 2001: 136). Furthermore, code-mixing occurs more frequently in contexts that involve fluent speakers than in contexts that (also) involve less fluent speakers. This is due to the fact that language change involving less fluent speakers of one of the languages mostly occurs on the phonological and syntactic level of language. Code-mixing, by contrast, mainly occurs on the lexical level as explained above (Thomason, 2001, p. 137).

As code-mixing might, for example, be used to fill lexical gaps, it often results in a word from one language being adopted into a sentence structure that follows the grammatical rules of another language. This is quite similar to the process of borrowing, which Poplack and Meechan define as "the *adaptation* of lexical material to the morphological and syntactic (and usually, phonological) patterns of the recipient language" (Poplack & Meechan, 1995, p. 200, italics in original). Still, code-switching and borrowing are not identical processes, they can rather be understood as opposite poles of a continuum. This implies that a clear-cut differentiation between code-switching and borrowing is quite easy at the poles but becomes increasingly fuzzy in the centre. As argued by Thomason, code-mixing "is a mechanism whereby new forms and new structural features are introduced into a receiving language; once a code-switched [or in our case code-mixed] element is

4.3 · Language Change and Its Mechanisms

present, it progresses to permanence [...]" (Thomason, 2001, p. 36). In this latter case, we would speak of borrowing.

To distinguish the two concepts, borrowing and code-mixing, Thomason introduces four criteria: occurrence in the monolingual speaker's language use, nativisation, commonness of occurrence, and the free morpheme constraint (cf. Thomason, 2001, pp. 133–135). First, the use of an element from the source language by monolingual speakers of the recipient language can be understood as a strong indication that the element is fully borrowed into the language since the speaker would not have appropriate access to the source language. A monolingual, English-speaking student in a university classroom in North Carolina, USA, who told one of the authors that "it felt like a *déjà-vu* when I saw that car, man" was not aware that *déjà-vu* is a loanword from French and was quick at correcting the author's French pronunciation of the word. This hints towards *déjà-vu* being fully borrowed into the English language. Second, the incorporation of an element into the grammatical or phonological structure of the recipient language, commonly referred to as nativisation, is an indicator of borrowing. This might be the pronunciation of *déjà-vu* as /ˈdiʤə vu/ instead of the French /deʒavy/. A further example would be the attachment of a German inflection that marks dative case on plural nouns, as in on the English noun "computer" resulting in *Die Schüler sitzen an den Computern*. While nativisation is a marker of borrowing, the lack of nativisation does not necessarily mark a lack thereof, as some elements are borrowed into a recipient language together with their structural features. The third criterion, commonness of occurrence, is helpful only under certain presuppositions. While the more commonly an element is used in bilingual conversations, the more likely it is a borrowing, we cannot assume a causality here; just because a word is frequently used it is not automatically a borrowing. The lack of frequency, however, prevents a categorisation as borrowing. In case an element is used only once by a bilingual speaker (although this would be nearly impossible to prove), it is almost certainly an instance of code-mixing. The fourth and last criterion is a constraint to code-mixing. The Free Morpheme Constraint states that code-mixing does not occur on only one morpheme within a complex word (cf. Gardner-Chloros, 2009a, p. 96). Consequently, in case a word consists of morphemes from different languages, the morpheme from the recipient language must be borrowed rather than subject to code-mixing. By following these criteria, most manifestations of language contact in language use can be identified either as cases of code-mixing or as borrowings. However, and this is important to keep in mind, language use is highly complex and there are some cases of language contact within sentence boundaries that do not fit neatly into either of these categories. Similarly to the distinction between code-mixing and borrowing, in some cases of language contact code-switching has to be distinguished from code alternation.

In addition to code-switching (and code-mixing), code alternation is the most common mechanism used by fluent speakers of two or more languages. Code-switching and code alternation are both characterised by intact sentence boundaries, that is, languages are switched or alternated between sentences. One major difference between these concepts is that code alternation is not concerned with the co-occurrence of languages in one single conversation (cf. Thomason, 2001, p.

136). While code-switching is the use of both languages in the same conversation and, consequently, requires a certain level of fluency and language proficiency of all involved speakers, code alternation is defined by the use of just one language per conversation and might also include monolingual conversation partners. A multilingual's consecutive conversations with two monolingual language users represent code alternation if a different language is used in each of these (internally) monolingual conversations. A typical context of code alternation is a bilingual using one language at home and one language in school or at work, for example in contexts of migration or minority versus societal language use. Code alternation, however, can also occur in multilingual speaker groups that use only one of their shared languages. This occurs, for example, if the use of only one of the shared languages is considered appropriate in the respective social contexts, such as in official/government contexts. Especially in multilingual communities, the contexts of code-switching and code alternation can be hard to distinguish. As already described, the two mechanisms are differentiated by the (missing) occurrence of more than one language in the same conversation however sometimes it is hard to tell whether a conversation is new or continued. Consequently, it is difficult to determine the relevance of code alternation on language change. Commonly, the influences of code alternation on language change are expected to be weaker than those of code-switching and code-mixing. This expectation is based on a specific assumption about the activation levels of different languages in a multilingual's brain: although languages of a multilingual speaker are rarely completely deactivated, we know that a language that is not currently spoken is less activated than a spoken one. However, it is assumed that languages that are not used are less activated in code alternation than in code-switching or code-mixing situations, as in the latter situations both languages are potentially used in the same conversation and must be activated. Still, even in code alternation, elements of the other, less activated language(s) can influence the use of the activated and used language through, e.g., cross-linguistic transfer. Thomason (2001, p. 137) provides anecdotal evidence for this based on the following scenario: a Dutch-English bilingual is in a conversation with three friends; two are Dutch and one is American, who does not speak Dutch. With his two Dutch friends, he always speaks Dutch, and with the third friend, he always speaks English. As he alternates between English and Dutch, he notices what Thomason describes as "extensive though temporary interference in both his Dutch and his English [...], in the lexicon as well as in the grammar" (Thomason, 2001, p. 137). In case such instances of interference occur in multilingual communities, they can become fixed and may lead to language change.

Although code-switching and code-mixing have been found to be important mechanisms of language change and are prominent and well-researched phenomena in the field of multilingualism, current epistemological developments have questioned their very foundation, which is the existence of distinct languages in a multilingual speaker. As a result, translanguaging has been proposed as an alternative framework to discuss and understand multi-language use.

4.3.3.2 **Translanguaging**

The term *translanguaging* is used to represent a theoretical approach as well as a pedagogical practice in multilingualism and has raised some interest especially in the latter field (Vogel & García, 2017, p. 1; Wei, 2018, pp. 15–16, cf. ▶ Sect. 8.3.2.2). Translanguaging is a speaker-based approach that assumes multilingualism as the communicative norm and conceptualises language acquisition and use as based on cumulative linguistic repertoires, which can be defined as "the collective [linguistic] resources available to anyone at any point in time" (Blommaert, 2014, p. 85). In line with the central position of a cumulative linguistic repertoire, in translanguaging languages are understood as being flexible and fluid. The use of multiple languages is seen as a social practice rather than as the combination of the use of different individual languages that form multiple autonomous language systems in multilingual speakers. Consequently, translanguaging approaches understand commonly used notions, like *native speaker*, *mother tongue*, and individually named languages like *English* or *German* as socially constructed and artificial rather than linguistic facts (Duchêne & Heller, 2007; Heller, 2007; Vogel & García, 2017). Other terms that constitute a similar challenge to the traditional epistemology of language acquisition and use are "translingual practice" (Canagarajah, 2013), "translingualism" (Lee, 2018), and "metrolingualism" (Otsuji & Pennycook, 2010, see Canagarajah, 2013 or Pennycook, 2016 for an overview).

The translanguaging approach assumes that a speaker's linguistic resources are combined in one cumulative linguistic repertoire and does not differentiate between individual languages (see, e.g., Canagarajah, 2013; Vogel & García, 2017; Wei, 2018). Consequently, translanguaging is not concerned with concepts like level of proficiency or fluency. Instead, it is appreciative of emergent competencies in a language which in other approaches might be considered to be manifestations of incomplete learning. Speakers who use more than one language are assumed to access their respective linguistic repertoire and translanguage rather than switch between languages (see, e.g., Auer, 2005). Still, as Vogel and García argue, translanguaging embeds "the notion that while named languages and traditional language ideologies are socially constructed, they still have material effects" (Vogel & García, 2017, p. 6), so although individual languages are not understood as being clearly delimitable and fixed phenomena, translanguaging accepts that the separation of languages is meaningful in some social contexts and to certain speakers. While the framework of translanguaging emphasises the social and fluid nature of multilingualism and multilinguals in their language use, its strong focus on the individual speaker and their linguistic repertoires to some degree limits its applicability to assessing structural characteristics of language change in general.

4.4 Linguistic Effects of Language Change on the Recipient Language

After having found out about the prerequisites and mechanisms of language contact and change in ▶ Sects. 4.2 and 4.3, we now turn towards how language change is realised in the structure of the recipient, changing language. In sum, and of course quite simplified, there are three potential basic effects of language change on the structure of a language, which are the addition of features, feature loss without replacement, and feature loss with replacement (cf. Thomason, 2001, pp. 85–91). These effects are the same, whether language change is motivated by speaker-external, contact-induced factors or by speaker-internal, shift-based factors and they can occur on all levels of linguistic description.

New features, meaning realisations and characteristics on the various levels of linguistic description, are often added to a recipient language in order to satisfy the speakers' needs to communicate new meanings and concepts. Such needs, which cause the speakers of the recipient language to transfer features from the source language, might be conscious or unconscious. On a lexical level, additions are mostly conscious, for example when loanwords from a contact language enter a recipient language, such as "*entourage*" or "*pizza*" in English. Instead of developing a word for a new idea or concept, the word that describes this concept is transferred from a donor language into the recipient language. If similar concepts were already expressed by native words in the recipient language, the words that were previously used in the recipient language may take on a new meaning. An example of this is the English word "heaven". When the Vikings introduced their word "sky" into the Old English language, "heaven" came to be used to express the Christian heaven only, and not the blue or grey that we now call the sky. On a phonological level, the transfer of words and their pronunciation into a recipient language may have the effect that new sound features can be added to the receiving language. In some cases, the addition of phonological features into a language is also creative and might extend contexts of use, for example facilitate or even allow the use of taboo words. For example, Zulu speakers have added clicks, a phonological feature of Khoisan languages, to their use of taboo words. This alteration satisfies the cultural conventions and allows Zulu speakers to use these stigmatised words (e.g. Herbert 1990). Examples of the addition of morphological or syntactic features are the use of new cases in Lithuanian or the addition of *I* and *you* to the Thai pronoun scheme to reflect a higher degree of familiarity than the Thai pronouns (see Thomason 2001, p. 87 for these examples). The addition of features reflects the need for a more extensive linguistic repertoire or communicative reach of a language as it enables the representation of new concepts or new perspectives in the recipient language.

The remaining two effects of language change, namely feature loss with replacement and feature loss without replacement, do not necessarily reflect an extension of the linguistic repertoire of a language but might even occur for the opposite reason. Due to their conceptual proximity, we discuss these two effects of language change together on various levels of language. Lexical, phonological, morphological, and syntactic features are lost without replacement in cases of language contact, for example if the concept the respective feature stands for is no longer present in the respective speech community. Examples for this are the loss of voiced and voiceless dental fricatives in some varieties of Greek due to contact with the Turkish language in Asia Minor or the loss of a third numerical category, the dual, in Ethiopian Semitic (cf. Leslau, 1945, 1952). Another example might be the word *bushlips*, which has been created based on an utterance by former US president George H. W. Bush to read his lips (cf. American Dialect Society, 2021). The term referred to something primarily political that the speaker believed to be nonsense. Currently this word is rarely used, if at all, and is likely to be lost shortly as President Bush's utterance will no longer be relevant when referring to questionable political content. Feature loss with replacement, however, is much more common than feature loss without replacement. The replacement of the SOV word order in Finnish by the SVO word order (examples mostly taken from Thomason 2001, pp. 87–88) or the Old English third person plural pronoun *hē* that got lost in Modern English might serve as examples. As the need to express third person plural by a pronoun was not lost, this pronoun was replaced by a loanword from Old Norse, namely *they*. This change helped to reduce the ambiguity between the third person plural pronoun and the third person singular pronoun, which had existed before *they* came into use. On the phonological level, phoneme merger, that is the consolidation of one phoneme with another one into a new phoneme, is a frequent effect of language change. Unfortunately, phoneme mergers present us with the first limitation of our neat threefold categorisation of language change effects on the recipient language. Phoneme mergers may represent feature loss with replacement or feature loss without replacement. A phoneme merger thus is one of the more complex cases of language change in which a combination of effects or partial effects occurs. Let us go more into detail here: on the one hand and as mentioned before, phoneme mergers can be categorised as feature loss without replacement. This is due to the fact that the new, merged phoneme is (most often) not a one-to-one substitute of either of the original phonemes and the original phonemes are no longer used; they are lost. On the other hand, one could argue that the merged phoneme replaces the original one(s) as it combines (parts of) their use and is used instead of them. The most accurate description of phoneme mergers, however, appears to be that it is the result of partial loss and partial replacement and, hence, the combination of two effects of language change (see Thomason, 2001 for further details).

Again, we would like to remind the reader that language use and language change often do not include clear-cut concepts and processes. The reality of language use is complex and ever-changing as its primary function is to represent its speakers' complex and ever-changing linguistic and social needs. As a result, changes in the structure of the recipient language often have multiple causes and are rarely limited to just one of the above-mentioned effects. For example, a word might be transferred to a language and be used to refer to the original concept of the source language as well as to another concept that already exists in the recipient language. Alternatively, a word that is lost without replacement, for example "bushlips", might have only had a short period of use or an existing word might lose the broad concept it represents to a newly introduced, borrowed word but is still used for a more specific concept in the recipient language. The English word *deer*, for example, has been replaced by the Latin word *animal* but is still used for a more specific set of animals. Before we move on to the final part of this chapter and the question of how to distinguish language change from temporal variation, we would like to introduce two more types of language contact effects, convergence and relexification.

Simplified, *convergence* is "any process through which two or more languages in contact become more like each other" (Thomason, 2001, p. 89). While this definition might be easy to understand, it is not very helpful as it includes all language change processes. In case a word or a phoneme is transferred from a source language into a recipient language, per definition, these two languages become more similar to each other as they now share n+1 features. Usually, convergence is used to refer to two contexts of language change. Firstly, it is used in *Sprachbund* situations (cf. Thomason, 2001, p. 90), that is, in contexts in which languages are very similar to each other. Indicative of such a situation is the fact that the source of the shared features is unclear and the involved processes of language change or assimilation cannot be retraced. Secondly, convergence is used to stress the bidirectionality of language change. Throughout this chapter, we have used the terms source language and recipient language, which imply that interference is unidirectional: the source language provides the feature(s) that the recipient language incorporates. However, in many contexts of language contact, the involved languages either function as both source and recipient languages or, for example, bilingual speakers might converge both their L1s as source and recipient languages and use features of both languages (see migrant languages, ▶ Chap. 9).

Last but not least, there is *relexification*. In ▶ Sect. 4.3.2, we introduced the Ma'a language, whose grammar has been replaced almost completely by borrowed grammatical structures while its vocabulary has not been replaced. Relexification can be understood as a complementary process as it is "the replacement of most or all of a language's vocabulary by the vocabulary of some other language" (Thomason, 2001, p. 90), that is, an extreme form of borrowing. Theoretically, recurrent borrowing over a long period of time might cause the lexicon of a language to be replaced. However, to our knowledge, no example of complete relexification is known. This lack of complete relexification might be rooted in a social parameter as speakers tend to identify with the vocabulary of their language more than with the grammatical structures it uses: consequently, despite the replaced grammar, Ma'a speakers still identify with their language. However, once (almost) all words of a language have been replaced, meaning that relexification has occurred, the new version of the recipient language might not be perceived as the language the speakers are familiar with anymore. Thus, relexification might very well be influenced by social needs rather than purely linguistic ones and be based on conscious speaker choices. Speakers would normally not choose to give up their language completely.

4.5 Language Change or Temporary Variation?

It is a truism that all languages change constantly. There is no doubt about this. A group of people who spend a lot of time together is likely to assimilate their language use and develop a unique dynamic in their communication. After spending some time with a group of friends, you might have developed private jokes, a different pronunciation for some words, neologisms, etc. This, of course, is an aspect of language change, too, but a different kind from what we are concerned with here. These changes are called temporal variations and most of them are not likely to manifest and spread outside a specific small speaker group. Only in the rare cases in which they manage to spread throughout society as a whole will they cause overall language change. Very much simplified, the prerequisites of contact-induced language change are that contact occurs between at least two speaker groups and their respective languages. Whether this results in one or both of their languages assimilating to the other language is often influenced by the prestige of the involved languages and speaker attitudes. In case language change catches on, this assimilation must be reasonably extensive on a social and linguistic level. To convincingly show that this is what has happened to a language, that is to determine whether contact-induced language change or temporal and locally-bound variation has occurred, we again follow Thomason (2001, pp. 91–95) by introducing four requirements and a warning. To show that Language A has changed due to contact with Language B, first, Language B needs to be identified and we need to show that the contact between Language A and Language B has been long enough and close enough for language change to be triggered. This sounds quite straightforward but in cases of changes in smaller, less well-documented languages or due to contact situations that took place a long time ago, this might be difficult or even impossible to prove. Second, shared features between Language A and Language B have to be identified. This is the more convincing, the more similar features of Language B can be found in Language A on various levels. These features do not have to be completely identical but need to show a satisfactory degree of similarity. Of course, what degree of similarity satisfies this requirement depends on the language pair (or constellation) in question. This is also where Thomason's warning might be useful: shared features rarely occur by themselves and the more shared features can be identified on the different levels of linguistic description, the more convincingly one can argue for contact-induced language change to have occurred. Consequently, researchers should always consider the recipient language in its entirety to be able to identify various points of interference. Requirements three and four focus on how to prove that the language contact situation is the starting point of language change which must be done for all languages that are involved. Therefore, as a third requirement, one has to show that the features in question have not been present in Language A before its contact with Language B. As a fourth requirement, it has to be found that these features were present in Language B prior to its contact with Language A (see Thomason, 2001, pp. 91–95 for more details). In general, the argument for contact-induced language change is weakened but not automatically dismissed if one of these requirements is not met. Specifically, Thomason advocates that requirements one and two must be met and states that the final two requirements can often not be fulfilled. In these cases, the argument for a certain feature to be the result of contact-induced language change is weakened but still possible.

When concerned with a language contact situation and its complex dynamics, we might be tempted to conceptualise language contact as the sole cause for a particular language change. However, for a comprehensive understanding and to build a convincing argument for contact-induced language change to have occurred, we need to consider further potentially change-initiating factors, such as language-internal (i.e. structural) motivations or contact between more than two languages. Factors, processes, and mechanisms of language change are multiple and complex and so are its causes. Still, while language change is often initiated by adolescent or adult speakers, true language change, especially feature loss, has only occurred once children acquire these changes as part of their L1 repertoires (see Lightfoot, 2010 on I-language; McMahon, 1994). While adults have acquired the old structures, features, or words and can, in addition, choose to use the new ones, the old features are often gradually excluded from a language's repertoire once children no longer acquire them (see, for example, McMahon's (1994, pp. 134–135) assessment of the loss of nominal dative inflection in English) and the new features might stabilise over time (e.g. Buschfeld's 2020 study of children's English in Singapore).

❷ Exercises

1. Access the Oxford English Dictionary (OED, ▶ https://www.oed.com/) and find 10 loanwords that are now part of the English language. Compare your list with that of a fellow student. Were you aware that all of these words did not origin in the English language?
2. From your own experiences, what reasons other than migration may cause sequential multilingual acquisition to occur and what challenges do you think these learners have to face when starting to acquire their second (or third) L1?
3. Keeping this in mind, go to the map on the Ethnologue webpage (cf. ▶ Chap. 1, ▶ https://www.ethnologue.com/guides/how-many-languages) and pick three different languages in three countries from the map. Find out about their speakers, their local roles, and statuses. Are they minority languages, majority languages, spoken by many or a few people? For each language, find societies, social groups, or contexts in which the language might be acquired as part of simultaneous multilingual, sequential multilingual, and L2 acquisition.
4. Focus on codeswitching!
    (a) Explain why the example presented in the chapter represents code alternation and cannot be codeswitching: A typical context of code alternation is a bilingual using one language at home and one language in school or at work, e.g. in contexts of migration or minority versus environmental language use. Code alternation, however, can also occur, in multilingual speaker groups, e.g. if the use of one of the shared languages is considered inappropriate in certain social contexts, e.g. in official/government contexts.
    (b) Have you experienced instances of code-switching or code-mixing yourself? Have you ever included (one of) these practices in your speech? Can

you be sure these instances are not code alternations or borrowings? Take notes on why or why not.
    (c) Discuss your experiences and elaborations with a partner.
5. Most language change is temporal. In your environment, find three instances of language change and explain why they are or are not likely to remain temporal changes.

> **Summary**
>
> In this chapter, we have assessed linguistic processes and mechanisms that occur in multilingual speakers and/or settings. After outlining potential language contact scenarios, we have turned to linguistic transfer or interference. We have found that the likelihood of linguistic features to be transferred to another language depends on (1) linguistic factors, which are the typological differences or similarities between the involved languages, universal markedness, and the degree of integration of features, as well as (2) social factors, such as the intensity of language contact, speaker fluency, and speakers' attitudes towards the languages. We have seen that linguistic factors can be investigated and determined more easily than social ones. However social factors, and in particular speaker attitudes, have a great impact on language change and can certainly overrule any linguistic probability.
>
> In the course of the chapter, we have zoomed in on linguistic mechanisms that are widely used in multilingual contexts and by multilingual speakers. We have introduced and elaborated on code-switching, that is the intersentential use of more than one language, and code-mixing, that is the intrasentential use of more than one language. We have further discussed the notions of code alternation and the process of borrowing, as well as the relationships between these different concepts. Finally, we have introduced the concept of translanguaging as a mechanism of multi-language use. We return to translanguaging in ▶Chap. 8 and assess it from a pedagogical perspective. After introducing possible effects of language change on the recipient language, we have ended this chapter with a discussion of what factors might cause permanent language change and what changes might just be temporary.

References

American Dialect Society. (2021). *All the words of the year, 1990 to present*. Retrieved November 4, 2022, from https://www.americandialect.org/woty/all-of-the-words-of-the-year-1990-to-present#mill

Auer, P. (2005). Code-switching/mixing. In R. Wodak, B. Johnstone, & P. Kerswill (Eds.), *The SAGE handbook of sociolinguistics* (pp. 460–478). Sage.

Baum, S., & Titone, D. (2014). Moving toward a neuroplasticity view of bilingualism, executive control, and aging. *Applied Psycholinguistics, 35*, 857–894.

Bialystok, E., & Kroll, J. (2018). Can the critical period be saved? A bilingual perspective. *Bilingualism: Language and Cognition, 21*(5), 908–910.

Blommaert, J. (2014). Language: The great diversifier. In S. Vertovec (Ed.), *Routledge international handbook of diversity studies* (pp. 83–90). Routledge.

Buschfeld, S. (2020). *Children's English in Singapore: Acquisition, properties, and use*. Routledge.

Callies, M. (2013). Markedness. In P. Robinson (Ed.), *The Routledge encyclopedia of second language acquisition* (pp. 406–409). Routledge.

Canagarajah, S. (2013). *Translingual practice: Global Englishes and cosmopolitan relations*. Routledge.
De Houwer, A. (2021). *Bilingual development in childhood*. Cambridge University Press.
Duchêne, A., & Heller, M. (Eds.). (2007). *Discourses of endangerment: Ideology and interest in the defense of languages*. Continuum.
Gardner-Chloros, P. (2009a). *Code-switching*. Cambridge University Press.
Gardner-Chloros, P. (2009b). Sociolinguistic factors in code-switching. In B. Bullock & A. Toribio (Eds.), *The Cambridge handbook of linguistic code-switching* (pp. 97–113). Cambridge University Press. https://doi.org/10.1017/CBO9780511576331.007
Giles, H., & Ogay, T. (2007). Communication accommodation theory. In B. B. Whaley & W. Samter (Eds.), *Explaining communication: Contemporary theories and exemplars* (pp. 293–310). Lawrence Erlbaum.
Greenberg, J. (1966). *Language universals*. Mouton.
Heller, M. (2007). Bilingualism as ideology and practice. In M. Heller (Ed.), *Bilingualism: A social approach* (pp. 1–22). Palgrave Macmillan.
Herbert, R. K. (1990). The sociohistory of clicks in Southern Bantu. *Anthropological Linguistics, 32*(3/4), 295–315.
Jakobsen, R. (1941). *Child language, aphasia, and universals of language*. Mouton.
Lado, R. (1957). *Linguistics across cultures*. University of Michigan Press.
Lee, J. W. (2018). *The politics of translingualism—After Englishes*. Routledge.
Leslau, W. (1945). The influence of cushitic on the semitic languages of Ethiopia: A problem of substratum. *Word, 1*, 59–82.
Leslau, W. (1952). The influence of Sidamo on the Ethiopic languages of the Gurage. *Language, 28*, 63–81.
Lightbown, P., & Spada, N. (2007). *How languages are learned*. Oxford University Press.
Lightfoot, D. (2010). Language acquisition and language change. *WIREs Cognitive Science, 1*, 677–684. https://doi.org/10.1002/wcs.39
MacSwan, J. (2019). Sociolinguistic and linguistic foundations of codeswitiching research. In J. MacSwan & C. J. Faltis (Eds.), *Codeswitching in the classroom: Critical perspectives on teaching, learning, policy, and ideology* (1st ed., pp. 3–38). Routledge.
Martin, E. (2007). "Frenglish" for sale: Multilingual discourses for addressing today's global consumer. *World Englishes, 26*, 170–190. https://doi.org/10.1111/j.1467-971X.2007.00500
McMahon, A. M. S. (1994). *Understanding language change*. Cambridge University Press.
Myers-Scotton, C. (2002). *Contact linguistics*. Cambridge University Press.
Niedzielski, N., & Giles, H. (2008). Linguistic accommodation. In H. Goebl, P. H. Nelde, Z. Starý, & W. Wölck (Eds.), *1. Halbband: Ein internationales Handbuch zeitgenössischer Forschung* (pp. 332–342). De Gruyter Mouton.
Odlin, T. (2016). Was there really ever a contrastive analysis hypothesis? In R. Alonso Alonso (Ed.), *Crosslinguistic influence in second language acquisition* (pp. 1–23). Multilingual Matters.
Ortega, L. (2009). *Understanding second language acquisition*. Hodder Education.
Otsuji, E., & Pennycook, A. (2010). Metrolingualism: Fixity, fluidity and language in flux. *International Journal of Multilingualism, 7*, 240–254.
Pearson, B. Z. (2009). Children with two languages. In E. L. Bavin (Ed.), *The Cambridge handbook of child language* (pp. 379–397). Cambridge University Press.
Pennycook, A. (2016). Mobile times, mobile terms: The trans-super-poly-metro movement. In N. Coupland (Ed.), *Sociolinguistics: theoretical debates* (pp. 201–216). Oxford University Press.
Pierce, L. J., Genesee, F., Delcenserie, A., & Morgan, G. (2017). Variations in phonological working memory: Linking early language experiences and language learning outcomes. *Applied Psycholinguistics, 38*, 1265–1300.
Poplack, S., & Meechan, M. (1995). Patterns of language mixture: Nominal structure in Wolof-French and Fongbe-French bilingual discourse. In P. Muysken & L. Milroy (Eds.), *One speaker, two languages* (pp. 199–232). Cambridge University Press.
Saville-Troike, M. (2003). *The Ethnography of Communication-An introduction*. 3rd ed. Oxford: Blackwell Publishing.
Schmid, M. (2011). *Language attrition*. Cambridge University Press.

References

Stockwell, R., Bowen, J., & Martin, J. (1965). *The grammatical structures of English and Spanish*. University of Chicago Press.

Stringer, D. (2013). Attrition. In P. Robinson (Ed.), *The Routledge encyclopedia of second language acquisition* (pp. 48–51). Routledge.

Thomas, M. (2006). Robert Lado, 1915–1995. In K. Brown (Ed.), *Encyclopedia of language and linguistics* (Vol. 6, pp. 301–302). Elsevier.

Thomason, S. G. (2001). *Language contact. An introduction*. Edinburgh University Press.

VanPatten, B., & Benati, A. G. (2015). *Key terms in second language acquisition*. Bloomsbury Academic.

Vogel, S., & García, O. (2017). *Translanguaging. Oxford research encyclopedia of education*. https://doi.org/10.1093/acrefore/9780190264093.013.181

Walsh, O. (2014). 'Les anglicismes polluent la langue française'. Purist attitudes in France and Quebec. *Journal of French Language Studies, 24*(3), 423–449. https://doi.org/10.1017/S0959269513000227

Wei, L. (2018). Translanguaging as a practical theory of language. *Applied Linguistics, 39*(1), 9–30.

Wiegel, M. (2013, May 21). Regierung will Englisch an Universitäten erlauben. *FAZ*. Retrieved November 4, 2022, from https://www.faz.net/aktuell/politik/ausland/frankreich-regierung-will-englisch-an-universitaeten-erlauben-12189945.html

Zsombok, G. (2021). Prescribing French: A corpus-linguistic approach to official terminology in French newspapers. *Journal of French Language Studies, 31*(3), 270–293. https://doi.org/10.1017/S0959269520000204

Key Readings

De Houwer, A. (2021). *Bilingual development in childhood*. Cambridge University Press. https://doi.org/10.1017/9781108866002

Thomason, S. G. (2001). *Language contact. An introduction*. Edinburgh University Press.

Further Readings

Ellis, R. (2015). *Understanding second language acquisition* (2nd ed.). Oxford University Press.

Meisel, J. (2011). *First and second language acquisition: Parallels and differences*. Cambridge University Press.

Schmid, M. (2011). *Language attrition*. Cambridge University Press.

Linguistic Manifestations in a Multilingual World: Focus on English

Contents

5.1 Introduction – 102

5.2 Types of English Around the World – 102
5.2.1 The English as a Native, Second, and Foreign Language Distinction – 103
5.2.2 Pidgin and Creole Languages – 104
5.2.3 English as a Lingua Franca, English for Specific Purposes, and Grassroots Englishes – 106

5.3 Hybrid or Mixed Languages in Multilingual Settings – 109

5.4 But What's in a Name? – 113

References – 117

© The Author(s), under exclusive license to Springer Nature Switzerland AG 2023
S. Buschfeld et al., *Multilingualism*,
https://doi.org/10.1007/978-3-031-28405-2_5

5.1 Introduction

In ▶ Chap. 5, we zoom in on the results and linguistic manifestations of multilingual language acquisition, use, and language contact, with a particular focus on English-based or English-derived types of communication in multilingual contexts. As examples, we present both some of the most common and well-researched English-based contact varieties and modes of communication as well as recently emerging types. To that end, we introduce the *English as a Native Language, English as a Second Language*, and *English as a Foreign Language* classification, pidgins and creoles, and *English as a Lingua Franca* and related concepts such as *English for Specific Purposes* and *Grassroots Englishes*. In the second part of this chapter, we have a closer look at hybrid languages and mixed codes. We cannot discuss each type or usage context in all their details but approach their general conceptions from both their linguistic perspectives, that is, in terms of their characteristic features, as well as in relation to their genesis and emergence, that is, their sociolinguistic and acquisitional backgrounds.

We ultimately conclude and argue that all these notions are scientific, terminological constructs in the first place, and that the different types—be they varieties in the strict sense or usage types or modes of communication—are to be situated in a complex system of linguistic forms and their respective historico-political and sociolinguistic backgrounds. We argue that these categorisations are helpful means to describe and conceptualise these linguistic types but that their boundaries are rather fuzzy and that they can only be understood in relation to each other, this means as a Complex Dynamic System of languages and dialects/varieties (e.g. Ellis & Larsen-Freeman, 2009; Kretzschmar Jr., 2015; Schneider, 2020) in their multilingual ecologies (▶ Sect. 5.4).

5.2 Types of English Around the World

Ever since the early systematic spread of the English language worldwide (see ▶ Sect. 2.2 for a more detailed account), English has developed into one of the major players in multilingual scenarios since it came into contact with an unprecedented number of languages and cultures around the world. Its competitors were the languages spoken in the other empires at the heyday of European colonisation, that is, Spanish, Portuguese, French, Dutch, and German. They all left their traces around the world, too, but none of these languages was as successful as the English language in making their way into basically any corner of the world and staying 'for good'. Worldwide globalisation has even intensified the spread of English around the globe and has led to the emergence of yet other forms and usage types of English. Therefore, English around the world comes in many different forms and guises, for which linguists have created a number of terms and categories, and these manifestations are shaped by a variety of factors such as: (1) the historical and sociolinguistic background and entrenchment of English in a country or speech community; (2) the proficiency of its speakers; (3) its usage contexts and communicative intentions; and (4) ways of language acquisition, for example as mainly acquired as a first or second language in natural, untutored interactions, or by means of formal instruction via the school system.

5.2.1 The English as a Native, Second, and Foreign Language Distinction

In an attempt to account for the diversification of English worldwide, the World Englishes research paradigm emerged in the late 1970s/early 1980s and with it an impressive number of models, concepts, and terms aiming to capture the specific manifestations of English in these highly diverging historico-political and sociolinguistic scenarios. Amongst the first categories that have been created was the distinction into English used as a native, as a second, or as a foreign language. It goes back to one of the first formal attempts to classify and characterise different varieties of English, namely to Strang's (1970) classification of the global English-speaking community into A-, B-, and C-speakers. Classification into one of the three groups happens according to the context of English use and acquisition. Group A comprises the 'traditional' native speakers of English as found, for example, in the UK, the USA, and Australia. Groups B and C are made up of non-native speakers of English. However, while group B includes early childhood learners of English living in communities where "English has a special status" and is used "at the international, and possibly even the national level", for example in India and the postcolonial territories of Africa (Strang, 1970, p. 18), C speakers are foreign-language speakers of English in countries where English does not have a special status (Strang, 1970, pp. 17–18). Two years after Strang's (1970) contribution, Quirk et al. (1972, pp. 3–4) introduced "[a]n influential variant of her classification" (McArthur, 1998, p. 43). They assigned three potential categories of use to the English language, namely that of native language, second language, and foreign language, which largely corresponds to the earlier tripartite distinction introduced by Strang. This terminology has been widely adopted, used, and systematised in later publications on varieties of English under the labels *English as a Native Language* (ENL), *English as a Second Language* (ESL), and *English as a Foreign Language* (EFL). Following a common definition of the three categories, which again illustrates its relatedness to Strang's (1970) A-B-C speaker classification, the group of ENL countries consists of those territories where English is spoken as a native language by the vast majority of the population (e.g. the USA, Great Britain, and Australia). In ESL countries (e.g. India, Singapore, and Nigeria) English fulfils prominent intranational functions in a variety of possible contexts, for example in the education sector, the media, the political domain, and jurisdiction, and is used as the language of interethnic communication between groups of different language backgrounds. It typically coexists with other languages, most often one or more indigenous languages of the local population. In EFL countries (e.g. China, Spain, and Germany), English does not fulfil special intranational functions but is normally restricted to international communication and is mainly if not solely learnt through formal instruction (e.g. Quirk et al., 1985, pp. 4–5; Schneider, 2007, p. 12). Up to the present day, this distinction has been one of the most widely used classifications of World Englishes and its success has even been boosted through its implicit application as the conceptual basis of Kachru's (1985) "Three Concentric Circles of World Englishes", in which the "Inner Circle" accommodates ENL, while the "Outer Circle" includes ESL and the "Expanding Circle" EFL varieties.

5.2.2 Pidgin and Creole Languages

Another early approach to products of language contact are pidgin and creole studies. The first attempts to describe such speech forms actually date back as far as the second half of the eighteenth century. Such very early approaches, however, viewed these speech forms as merely corrupted versions of European languages. Non-prescriptive research on pidgins and creoles has its origin in the early 1970s (for details and an early account of the emergence of pidgin and creole studies, see Bickerton, 1976). Pidgins are speech forms that have evolved in high-intensity language contact between groups of speakers who do not share a language but need to communicate, often at short notice and in particular domains such as trade or labour. In these contexts, it was normally the less powerful group that tried to adapt to the linguistic needs of the more powerful group. The most widely-known context for the development of pidgin languages was the slave and labour trade found in the USA between the late 15th and the second half of the 19th centuries. The slave population had to acquire their masters' language in a very short time to be able to communicate with them, which is why they normally acquired the language only up to the proficiency level needed for this particular type of communication. Since no formal schooling was involved and language contact between the European languages spoken by the masters and the indigenous languages spoken by the slaves, who were mostly imported from Africa, was strong, pidgin languages emerged as reduced systems in that, for example, grammatical inflections were dropped and syntactic complexity was reduced in general. Often, pidgins have also been reported to be characterised by rather small vocabularies. When describing them as reduced, one, of course, takes on a prescriptive European perspective which compares these speech forms to the linguistic norms of the European lexifier languages, that is, the languages that provide the lexical and (to some extent) grammatical basis for pidgin and creole languages (e.g., the major coloniser languages English, French, Spanish, Portuguese, and Dutch). However, since communication was successful via these altered systems, such a stance is rather problematic since the term *reduced* may imply deficiency and inferiority.

Creole languages have normally emerged from their pidgin predecessors when the pidgins started to be acquired as first languages (L1s). A creole language is thus spoken as a first language by a speech community. In this process of nativisation, the variety normally undergoes expansion, for example in vocabulary, and builds up a more complex grammatical system again (for a more detailed account, see, e.g., Arends et al., 1994; Holm, 2000; Todd, 1990). Today, a wide number of pidgins and creoles exist around the globe, which cannot all be listed here, but ◘ Table 5.1 provides some examples of pidgins and creoles which are based on the four lexifier languages listed earlier.

Table 5.1 Some examples of pidgin and creole languages

Example	Lexifier language	Further comments
Krio	English	Sierra Leone Creole English
Nigerian Pidgin	English	Now a creole
Gullah	English	Also called Sea Island Creole English, spoken in the coastal regions of South Carolina and Georgia as well as in the northeast of Florida and the southeast of North Carolina
Haitian Creole	French	
Papiamento	Spanish/ Portuguese	Spoken in the Dutch Caribbean (Aruba, Bonaire, Curaçao, Sint-Eustatius, Saba, St. Maarten)
Berbice	Dutch	Extinct (as almost all Dutch-based pidgins and creoles) but formerly spoken in Guyana

► Example 5.1 provides insights into the structure and character of Tok Pisin, an English-based creole language spoken throughout Papua New Guinea.

► **Example 5.1**

An excerpt from Tok Pisin.

Am	*tete*	*avinun*	*mipela*	*mi*	*bin*	*go*	*waswas*
FILL	today	afternoon	1PL.EXCL	1SG	PST	go	wash

lo(ng)	*nambis*
PREP	beach.

Um, this afternoon we - I went to swim at the beach.

(Smith & Siegel, 2013, p. 221) ◄

In ► Example 5.1, we can still sense the English origin of Tok Pisin but also see that it is a highly restructured system, both in terms of lexis and grammar. It is clear that this and similar language forms deserve scholarly attention and should not be denigrated as corrupted versions of European languages. However, the question arises if pidgin and creole languages really require their individual research paradigm and could not, for example, be viewed as extreme forms of mixed and restructured varieties of, for example, English and thus be integrated into the World Englishes paradigm (cf. Mufwene, 2001, p. 18).

5.2.3 English as a Lingua Franca, English for Specific Purposes, and Grassroots Englishes

In the following, we introduce the three concepts *English as a Lingua Franca (ELF)*, *English for Specific Purposes (ESP)* and *Grassroots Englishes* in one subchapter for basically two reasons. First of all, they are more modes of communication/interactions than real variety types (cf. Buschfeld, 2021, p. 34). This is in line with Meierkord's (2012) "Interactions across Englishes" (IaEs) framework, which postulates that "the different Englishes potentially merge in these interactions", resulting "in the development of new emergent varieties" but not "*one* stable or even codified variety, but rather a heterogeneous array of new linguistic systems" (Meierkord, 2012, p. 2; italics in original). Secondly, they show substantial overlap in their conceptualisations and characteristics, in particular ELF and ESP (Schneider, 2013, p. 49). But let us start from the beginning.

ELF is the oldest and most widely-discussed of the three concepts. The notion refers to the use of English as the language of global inter-ethnic and inter-communal conversation in most contexts in which the interlocutors do not share a common language. As have most fields of research, the ELF paradigm has gone through a number of debates and changes in orientation over time that cannot all be discussed in this book. Still, we would like to provide two examples here. Whereas earlier research stated that "ELF interactions are defined as interactions between members of two or more different linguacultures in English, for none of whom English is the mother tongue" (House, 1999, p. 74), more recent, broader approaches include native speakers of English as possible participants in lingua franca encounters. Seidlhofer (2011, p. 7) therefore defines ELF as "any use of English among speakers of different first languages for whom English is the communicative medium of choice and often the only option". In addition to that, ELF has often been understood as a variety which can be categorised and described on the basis of specific linguistic characteristics, similar to EFL or ESL (for a discussion of the relationship between ELF and EFL and ESL, see Schneider, 2012). However, as, in particular, opposed to EFL, ELF is not oriented towards native speaker norms but focusses on successful intercultural communication (Hülmbauer et al., 2008) and is nowadays more understood as a linguistic practice than a variety or type of English. Still, Jenkins (2000) identifies a *Lingua Franca Core* (LFC), that is, pronunciation features that need to be retained according to the British or American English models and cannot be replaced by contact-induced alternatives to ensure successful communication between non-native speakers of English. In her blog "What is the Lingua Franca Core?", Laura Patsko (2013) sums up the LFC as follows: (1) most consonant sounds and the vowel /ɜː/ need to be kept and realised according to British English (BrE)/American English (AmE) standards; (2) most consonant clusters need to be preserved; (3) vowel length distinctions need to be kept, in particular before consonants; (4) appropriate grouping of words, that is, segmentation into meaningful tone units, and placement of nuclear stress should be ensured.

In our next mode of communication type, ESP contexts, which are prominently found in the tourism sector, English "serves as an auxiliary language, constituting ELF usage" (Schneider 2013, p. 48). Schneider takes an important step here by establishing a direct relationship between ELF and ESP that was not prominently highlighted before. He states that "[t]here is a substantial amount of overlap between ELF and ESP (in specific contexts); both are intrinsically related" (2013, p. 49). The study of ESP, however, is not all that new and has constituted a subfield of Applied Linguistics from the early 1980s (e.g. Kennedy & Bolitho, 1984; Robinson, 1991). Its focus has traditionally been on the use of English as used in specific domains, in particular in technology, but it also has a strong educational facet in that it has been suggested to be a subarea of TESOL (Teaching English to Speakers of Other Languages; Kim, 2008, p. 3). ESP has been further subdivided into subsections such as *English for Occupational Purposes* (EOP; Kim, 2008), *English for Academic Purposes* (EAP), and *English for Science and Technology* (EST), to name just the three main subtypes (cf. García Mayo, 2000, p. 15; Kim, 2008, pp. 5–6). The linguistic properties to be found for ESP are: (1) a specialised vocabulary geared towards a specific topic or activity (e.g. legal matters, technical domains), which is often incomprehensible to outsiders and whose stock is characterised by specific products of word-formation processes, for example, specific subject area-related affixes or acronyms; (2) a preference for certain grammatical structures in ESP texts, such as a strong use of passives and complex nominal groups; (3) specific textual properties and discourse conventions, which, for example, take into consideration the participants' role and status in the conversation as well as the linguistic needs arising from the activities the users are involved in (Kennedy and Bolitho, 1984, pp. 18–20; for a concise, more detailed overview, see Schneider, 2013, pp. 47–49).

In his 2013 article, Schneider focuses on scuba diving in Egypt as an example of leisure-activity ESP and its relationship to ELF. As in more general ELF encounters, divers, that is, instructors and tourists, from various countries meet and are forced to communicate in a link language, most often English, which is not the native language for many of them. In his linguistic analysis, Schneider points out a number of the characteristics that were identified in earlier research on other ESP contexts, for example, specific—in his case scuba diving-related—vocabulary items, semantic narrowing, specific word-formation types, transfers from various L1s feeding into the linguistic mix, for example *bottle* instead of *tank*—as used by German divers. In an analysis of dive site descriptions, he also identifies a number of general linguistic characteristics shared between geographical contexts, for example, the use of simple syntactic structures with mainly coordinated clauses and little subordination (except relative clauses) on the one hand, but the use of complex and specific vocabulary including many compounds on the other (Schneider, 2013, p. 53). Next to the general structural and discourse patterns that seem to be characteristic of scuba diving ESP, one needs to keep in mind the different varieties of English, native and non-native alike, that tourists and staff bring into the conversations. In such contexts, communicative success needs to be secured, in particular for a potentially dangerous activity such as scuba diving. Here, the importance of the LFC comes to the fore, which would help that instructions by the staff and instructors would be understood by everybody, no matter where they come from.

As a last type of English, also clearly related to the ELF paradigm, we turn towards a rather recent sub-area of English linguistics, that is, Grassroots Englishes. Amongst the first to mention this manifestation or, rather, mode of communication, Schneider (2016a) defines Grassroots Englishes as types of English which emerge from the grassroots, as opposed to elitist forms of English, which are associated with the traditional ELF paradigm. Grassroots Englishes are acquired in direct interactions rather than through formal education. Some Grassroots English speakers never had any formal instruction in English but teach themselves the language, for example, in search for better job opportunities in tourism or for higher turnover in trading. Therefore, Grassroots Englishes are the "products of strong personal instrumental motivation" (Schneider, 2016a, p. 9) and mostly emerge in less affluent societies, with limited opportunities for learning English (when approached from a scholastic perspective). The speakers' goal is to develop communicative ability rather than to achieve good grades or the ability to use the language correctly, that is, according to standard norms. Grassroots Englishes are spoken in diverse geographical settings, most prominently in marginalised, less-affluent countries or by individuals and speech groups that are structurally marginalised even though living in more affluent societies (see Han, 2013, p. 95 for a similar argument on Grassroots Multilingualism, which are discussed in more detail in ▶ Sect. 5.4). The following excerpt (▶ Example 5.2) provides an example of grassroots use of English in Bali, Indonesia.

▶ **Example 5.2**

Grassroots English use by a middle-aged male driver in Bali, Indonesia.[1] (Example from Schneider 2016a, p. 7; slightly adapted):

If [de] people going to [de] cem-, if now die, looking for good -, looking eh in Balinese calendar, when I can bring to cemetery, but if we do cemetery, around four o'clock, five o'clock, before [de], uh, sun down, maybe around uh five o'clock, and then, you get in, with many people. If here, if, uh, if I always come when the neighbor co-[?] dead, the neighbor have, uh, something, and then I hel(e)p him, evry[?], evry[?], uh, neighbor dead, yeah, neighbor, I have uh dead, I come. When I die, also come. When me lazy, only my family. There is this difficul' here in, uh, in Bali. Also, I am not from Lovina, when in Lovina I live with uh rented house, yeah, but I'm from the mountain here. If my neighbor in the mountain dead I come with motorbike, broooom. Sometime alone. If I have ceremony, one bike, four people: my daughter, my son, my wife, and suitcase behind. My daughter fourteen years, my son ten years, and small motorbike. But I have only one motorbike. Now I must try another motorbike. ◀

---

1 Explanatory notes on the transcription symbols used in the examples: [?] = best guess/unsure transcription; material in brackets = semi-phonological representation of speech material to highlight some of the phonological characteristics found in the speech sample.

▶ Example 5.2 illustrates a number of characteristics that have been identified as typical of Grassroots Englishes. First of all, the speaker has rather limited proficiency in English, most likely due to his mainly instrumental motivation to learn English, which is not guided by the desire to achieve native-like proficiency in English. This impression is fostered by, for example, incomplete sentences, false starts, repetitions, hesitation markers, and self-repairs. In addition to that, the excerpt shows a number of non-standard linguistic realisations, for example: the replacement of dental fricatives by alveolar stops (as indicated by the transcription of voiced dental fricative [ð] as [d] in ▶ Example 5.2); many zero elements in the syntactic structures the speaker produces, for example, zero pronouns ("if now die"), missing copulas ("When me lazy"), zero articles ("when I can bring to cemetery"), or a lack of person/number agreement ("the neighbor have") (see also Schneider, 2016a, p. 7). Again, we cannot go into real detail when it comes to the origin of such characteristics, but L1 transfer and general mechanisms of learning a second language such as simplification, overgeneralisation, or incomplete acquisition due to the reduced acquisitional context seem likely explanations.

Grassroots Englishes have been categorised as a special form of ELF or rather the non-elitist end of the ELF continuum (Buschfeld, 2021, p. 34), on which speakers range from high proficiency speakers, who often have learnt English in formal school contexts, oriented towards standard norms, to speakers with very low proficiencies who have acquired English in autodidactic ways outside the school context and limited towards a specific, oftentimes restricted purpose of using English (e.g. in trading or tourism contexts). Note, however, that proficiency in such conceptualisations is, again, determined by prescriptive ideas of standard language and norms of correctness/fluency.

5.3 Hybrid or Mixed Languages in Multilingual Settings

Hybrid or heavily mixed languages, for example, Englishes which include elements of other languages up to a point where they are no longer recognisable as Englishes to the untrained, non-linguist ear, have long been neglected in the history of English studies (Wright, 2000; see also Schneider, 2016b). Often, such hybrid languages were stigmatised as bad or broken languages. Fortunately, the ideal of language homogeneity and purity, which was behind much of such thinking, has been dismantled as a myth, a theoretical construct at best (e.g. Hickey, 2012). The ever-growing presence of English in many multilingual countries and contexts worldwide has produced new types of hybrid linguistic usage, in particular in contexts where English is not only the product of formal schooling, but where acquisition begins 'at the grassroots' (cf. ▶ Sect. 5.2) and English is used in people's everyday lives and is thus in strong contact and interaction with the other language(s) the speakers use (see the notion of transfer introduced in ▶ Sect. 4.3). Canagarajah (2013, p. 113) has called the everyday practice of such speakers "codemeshing", which results from "translingual practice". Such meshed codes have emerged in a number of countries and they creatively mix and blend English elements with elements from other languages. In the following, we introduce two examples of hybrid/ mixed codes, but many more of such linguistic manifestations exist around the world. Even though they have emerged and are nowadays spoken in totally unrelated geographical areas and contexts, such mixed languages show quite a number of interesting parallels when it comes to their sociolinguistic background and their linguistic properties. Even an overarching naming formula seems to have come into general usage, by linguists and laypeople alike. It typically consists of the first part of the respective local language to which an -(ng)lish is being added, for example, *Taglish*, a mix of English and Tagalog, or *Singlish*, the English-based colloquial and heavily Sinitic-influenced variety of Singaporean English (for further details and examples, see Schneider, 2016b).

Let us start our examples with one of the most well-known and most frequently discussed *mixed codes* Singlish, even though it is certainly closer to English and less mixed than some other potential examples. Singlish is the colloquial variety of Singaporean English, whose use has been strongly stigmatised by the government (see the Speak Good English Movement launched in 2000). The terms *Singlish* and *Good English* often have been used as contrasting notions and are conceptualised to be in binary distribution in public discourse (cf. Leimgruber, 2013, pp. 45–46). This official stigmatisation of Singlish as bad English, however, has experienced some alleviation in more recent years and Singlish clearly carries covert prestige, as many Singaporeans identify with it as their way of speaking English. It is characterised by a number of linguistic features that have found entrance into the variety via transfer from the other local languages spoken in Singapore, most importantly from Chinese, in particular Hokkien, but also from Malay and Tamil. One of the very prominent features of Singlish, for example, is the use of Chinese-derived discourse markers (Lim, 2004; see also Schneider, 2016b, p. 347). The following excerpt from a Facebook conversation between two young Singaporean women (▶ Example 5.3) illustrates some mixing of English and Chinese elements and the use of two of the Singlish-typical discourse markers.

▶ **Example 5.3**

A Singlish conversation (taken from Buschfeld et al., 2018, p. 35).

Female, 36: nice? no frog porridge this time? next time must *jio* me
Female, 38: Hahhaah u not in your hood mah. Yes. Ate up already 😊
Female, 36: Wah u 2 ate so much. U had the *kung bao* spicy one or spring onion?
Female, 38: Just 1 frog *kungpao* ◀

▶ Example 5.3 illustrates the Sinitic flavour of Singlish, that is, clear traces of the Chinese language and culture. *Jio*, from Hokkien, in this context means 'invite', 'ask someone out'[2]; the particle *mah* is used to indicate that a piece of information is obvious, *wah* is used as an expression of surprise. "Kung bao spicy" and "kung bao spring onion" are variants of a typical Sichuan dish. In the utterances "next

---

2   Personal conversation with one of the two speakers. We are grateful to the two speakers for granting their permission that the example can be used for linguistic purposes.

time Ø must jio me" and "Ø Ate up already", we find two typical grammatical features of Singlish, namely the use of zero subject pronouns and the use of "already", an aspectual marker transferred from Chinese, which reinforces past tense interpretation in Singaporean English (contrary to what we find in the traditional standard varieties of English, for which "already" is a marker of present perfect aspect). In addition to that, the example shows typical characteristics of online communication, namely the use of text message shorthands such as rebuses and grammograms (cf. ► Chap. 10), for example, "u 2 ate so much", "Just 1 frog kungpao".

How to exactly conceptualise Singlish, in particular also in relation to the standard variety of Singaporean English, and whether it should be considered a creole has been a question of some debate (for a summary of this debate see, e.g., Buschfeld, 2020a, pp. 11–15).

Another well-known mixed code, which is mainly based on French, is Camfranglais (CFA). The naming convention follows a similar pattern to that for the English-based mixed/hybrid codes. As is reflected in the blend of *Cameroon*, *Français*, and *Anglais* (French for 'English'), English is also an important donor element for this mixed language.

CFA is an extensively researched, strongly mixed sociolect and identity carrier, in particular for the urban youth in Cameroon. Linguistically, it integrates lexical items from several non-French languages "into a French morphosyntactic frame" (Kießling, 2005, p. 90), most prominently from English and Pidgin-English, but even some German as well as several local Cameroonian languages such as Duala, Ewondo, Basaa, and Bamileke-Ghomala'. Kießling (2005, p. 91, referring to examples from Chia & Gerbault, 1991) provides a number of examples illustrating this heavy language mixing (see ► Examples 5.4 through 5.7).

► **Example 5.4**

Le book-là c'est pour les mbindi, moi je suis mini.
('This is a children's game, I am too old for this.') (Chia & Gerbault, 1991, p. 275). ◄

► **Example 5.5**

Le test de linguistique étant sharp, j'ai préféré piak.
('The linguistics assignment was very difficult, I preferred to beat it.') (Chia and Gerbault 1991, p. 275). ◄

► **Example 5.6**

On a kick mon agogo.
('They stole my watch.') (Chia & Gerbault, 1991, p. 274). ◄

► **Example 5.7**

Il pense que je suis dumm.
('He thinks that I am stupid.') (Kießling, 2005, p. 91). ◄

In Examples 5.4 through 5.7 *mbindi* ('small', 'young') derives from Duala *mbìndì* ('small antelope'), *piak* ('take a turn, turn around a corner, escape') from Bamileke-Ghomala', *sharp* and *kick* from English, *agogo* ('watch') from Hausa, and *dumm* means 'stupid' in German (Kießling, 2005, pp. 90–91). Kießling (2005, pp. 97–100) also lists features of Camfranglais beyond the lexical level, such as hybridisation by affixation of the English gerund suffix-*ing* to non-English words, as in *lanc-ing [lãs–iŋ]* (from French *lancer* ('hurl')) or the over-application of non-productive French derivational suffixes such as in *ghettos-ard* ('someone who lives in the ghetto'). Camfranglais shares a number of linguistic characteristics with Cameroonian Pidgin English, which, in turn, derive from the Bantu languages of Cameroon (Kießling, 2021, pp. 115–116). Camfranglais, similar to Singlish, is mixed on a number of linguistic levels of description. Several studies (e.g. Schröder, 2007; Nchare, 2009) have described how "its emblematic lexicon is inserted into a French matrix" (Kießling, 2021, p. 121); still, its exact underlying grammatical framework has been an issue of some debate (cf. Kießling, 2021, pp. 121–122). Schröder (2007), for example, concludes that, depending on the speaker, Camfranglais is best referred to as relexified French (spoken by francophone Cameroonians) or relexified Pidgin English (spoken by anglophone Cameroonians) and has no homogenous, fixed grammatical system. In this respect, Kießling (2021, pp. 122–123) concludes that "it seems very likely that there is a continuum of CFA varieties spinning out between the poles of a francophone and an anglophone orientation", which is much in line with the fluid approach taken on languages, conceptions, and terminology we follow in this textbook. As was the case for the example from Singlish, our aim is not to provide an extensive feature overview of the mixed/hybrid codes presented here. They are meant as examples to illustrate the linguistic hybridity of some language varieties, be they based on English or any other language (for a more extensive feature overview of Camfranglais, see, e.g., Kießling, 2005, pp. 91–102, 2021, pp. 121–135; for a discussion and illustration of further examples of mixed/hybrid codes, see, e.g., Schneider, 2016b).

Similar to what has been observed for Singlish, code-mixing (in its neutral, simple meaning of mixing two or more languages; for a more detailed discussion, see ▶ Sect. 4.3.3.1) or even blending is one of the prime characteristics of hybrid/mixed languages. Besides the similar labelling strategies, hybrid/mixed languages are characterised by quite a number of similarities, both in terms of their linguistic properties and the sociolinguistic setting in which they evolve, no matter what geographical region or languages involved in the mix (Schneider, 2016b, p. 341). Oftentimes, the speakers of such mixed/hybrid codes are young, highly educated, multilingual speakers in urban settings. The codes themselves are strongly stigmatised and often rejected by official authorities, which is why they are "frequently perceived as informal icons of their [the speakers'] multilingual and multicultural experiences" and sometimes even hybrid identities (Schneider, 2016b, p. 350; addition our own), while, at the same time, as icons of a "resistance identity" (Castells, 1997; see Kießling, 2021, p. 115 for similar observations on the case of Camfranglais). The strong linguistic similarities between mixed/hybrid codes are, in fact, the result of highly similar linguistic mechanisms which underlie the emergence of such mixed/hybrid speech forms.

> **Think Tank**
>
> Think about what these mechanisms could be; you have already learnt about them in the earlier chapters of this textbook (in particular ▶ Chap. 4). Collect ideas and discuss them with a partner or in a small group. Explain where and how these mechanisms show in the examples introduced in this chapter (▶ Examples 5.1 through 5.7).

Still, we need to keep in mind that the intensity and type of language mixing and the exact manifestations can vary from context to context. Some varieties simply rely on heavy lexical borrowing from one language into the other, for example Denglish, Finglish, or Japlish (Schneider, 2016b, p. 341). Others are mixed even in the deeper strata of linguistic description and involve, for example, the morphosyntactic or pragmatic domains (e.g., Singlish). In such cases, "the amount and nature of mixing that is going on seems to be creating truly novel types of language varieties which are perceived as such by their speakers"; they are "comparatively stable and established" (Schneider, 2016b, p. 350). As examples for "intermediate options" Schneider (2016b, p. 350) names Spanglish, which is traditionally associated with more or less spontaneous code-switching practices, and Taglish, which relies on "continuously re-created mixed usage habits" (2016b, p. 350). However, as Schneider concludes, "in the absence of more solid evidence and descriptions of many varieties it seems impossible or at least premature to draw a line between such sub-types; they all blend into each other" (2016b, p. 350). While we are convinced that more evidence will clearly show that the boundaries between these types are rather fuzzy and anything but clear-cut, we show that this is not only true for this type of mixed languages but also for any kind of English-based speech form, and the same certainly also holds true for varieties of languages other than English (see ▶ Sect. 5.4 for a more detailed discussion).

While mixed/hybrid codes have attracted quite some scientific attention in the last couple of years, research on these linguistic systems is still in its infancy. As Schneider (2016b, p. 341) suspects, "[o]ne reason for this neglect may be their hybridity and the stigma that consequently is often associated with them", but we agree with him "that these young varieties are worth linguistic attention and analysis" (2016b, p. 341).

5.4 But What's in a Name?

> **Think Tank**
>
> Consider the language types introduced in ▶ Sects. 5.1 through 5.3 above. Where do you see differences and similarities between them? Collect at least three differences and similarities and discuss in a group/in class whether a strict separation of such types makes sense. The underlying question which should guide your discussion is: "How should these Englishes, hybrid/mixed languages, and performance types be accounted for from a conceptual, theoretical perspective?"

In the preceding sections of this chapter, the linguistic types and usage contexts have been discussed as more or less separate, still sometimes related concepts. In this respect, EFLs, ESLs, ENLs have been treated as part of the World Englishes paradigm, but EFLs have long been stigmatised as learner Englishes in non-postcolonial contexts and have often been denied true variety status. However, more recent research has shown that second language varieties of English can also emerge in contexts which were not formerly colonised by the British (e.g., Buschfeld & Kautzsch, 2014, 2017; Edwards 2016). It has been shown that ESL and EFL are not linguistically different in principle but are characterised by similar linguistic features and should therefore not be considered clear-cut categories but rather two ends of a continuum (e.g., Biewer, 2011; Buschfeld, 2013; Gilquin & Granger, 2011). More recent models in the World Englishes paradigm take these findings into consideration, most prominently the Extra- and Intra-territorial Forces (EIF) Model (Buschfeld & Kautzsch, 2017; Buschfeld, 2020b). Hybrid/mixed languages have been conceptualised as part of the World Englishes complex, too, but again as a somewhat special case and only, of course, if English forms a substantial part of the language mix (for a non-English example, see, e.g., Michif, a mix of French and Cree, e.g. Arends et al., 1994). Pidgins and creoles (see ▶ Sect. 5.2.2 for more details), on the other hand, have long been conceptualised as an independent language type and field of linguistic research, but that has been called into question in more recent times. Mufwene (2001, p. 18), for example, suggests to not make a strict distinction between English varieties and creoles. This seems convincing from a linguistic perspective since the linguistic characteristics found in these speech forms all go back to the same mechanisms of language acquisition and contact. What differs is the historical and sociolinguistic background, which, depending on the exact context, has simply led to different extents of language contact and thus of cross-linguistic influence, language mixing, and restructuring.

As discussed in ▶ Sect. 5.2.3, ESP and Grassroots Englishes can best be categorised as belonging to the ELF paradigm, since they constitute special cases of ELF usage, namely, highly specialised ELF and non-elite ELF uses, respectively. The ELF paradigm is clearly related to the World Englishes paradigm but it still constitutes an independent field of scholarly research.

We are not trying to advocate disposing of the different labels and concepts, they all contribute to our understanding and conceptualisation of the English Language Complex (for the term, see Mesthrie & Bhatt, 2008). Still, we need to ask ourselves how exactly all these variety types are linguistically discernible from each other. Buschfeld (2021, pp. 34–36) addresses this question in some detail, most prominently how Grassroots Englishes are really structurally and linguistically discernible from English-based pidgins and creoles (see Han, 2017, pp. 266–268 for a similar question and discussion). The answer, she argues, lies in their specific historical, political, and sociolinguistic developments and backgrounds as well as in a specific set of partly shared and partly specific extra- and intra-territorial forces (see Buschfeld & Kautzsch, 2017 for such a forces-based approach to World Englishes) working on the development of such speech forms. The linguistic characteristics of these types, however, are often of a similar nature. In a similar line of thinking, Han (2017) states that in traditional accounts of languages and varieties "the dividing lines between categories and stages seem more *social* than *linguistic*" (Han, 2017, p. 268; italics in original). However, such conceptualisations and the alleged differences between linguistic manifestations and types have to be approached not only from the World Englishes perspective but also with a language acquisition perspective in mind. There have been arguments in favour of conceptualising bilingualism as the exploitation of multilingual repertoires, challenging traditional views of languages as bound and clearly delimitable systems. Heller, for example, argues "for the notion that speakers draw on linguistic resources which are organised in ways that make sense under specific social conditions" (2007, p. 1).

So how can the linguistic manifestations discussed in the current chapter and others be conceptualised as part of the English Language Complex? As has been argued repeatedly, the boundaries between varieties and modes of communication are fuzzier than often suggested by their labels. Therefore, they should be pictured as part of a multidimensional matrix, as part of a Complex Dynamic System (for example Ellis & Larsen-Freeman, 2009; Kretzschmar Jr., 2015; Schneider, 2020), taking into consideration a variety of factors in their description (Buschfeld, 2021, p. 35):

- usage contexts (from individual to societal, from marginal/less affluent to affluent/elitist, from non-postcolonial, to postcolonial, to first language);
- communicative functions and intentions (from getting the message across according to situational needs and requirements to specialised language use in ESP and CMC (computer-mediated communication), to elitist conversation in academic circles);
- proficiency levels and types (from 'mute Englishes' (e.g., Wolff, 2010), to functional proficiencies, to balanced bilingualism);
- norm orientations (from non-existent norm orientations to exonormative and endonormative orientations).

Their exact manifestations are ultimately characterised by varying degrees of language mixing, cross-linguistic influence, and other mechanisms (as presented in ▶ Chap. 4), and are most importantly shaped by their very specific historical and sociolinguistic backgrounds.

Finally, we would like to encourage readers, researchers, and students of languages and multilingualism to leave behind the often employed but somewhat isolated Anglo-centric perspective and focus on the wider framework of multilingualism, without which we would not be able to understand the English-based linguistic outcomes introduced in this chapter, since these outcomes are always shaped by their wider linguistic ecologies. In this respect, Grassroots Englishes, for example, need to be pictured as a part of Grassroots Multilingualism. This notion was introduced by Han (2013, 2017) and "describe[s] the kind of multilingualism associated with globalisation from below, which is characterised by fluid forms, code-switching, and nonstandard linguistic features as a result of uninstructed expansion of multilingual repertoires for localized purposes" (Han, 2013, p. 84). It is indeed one of the newer dimensions of multilingualism and one of the many linguistic results of ever-growing globalisation and new forms of grassroots trading and communication. Han (2013), for example, investigates the multilingual practices of migrants of African and Chinese backgrounds and how they expand and negotiate their multilingual repertoires in Africa Town in Guangzhou, China. According to Han, grassroots exchanges do normally not take place in a stable communicative setting and at least one, if not both/all, conversational partners come from changing linguistic and/or cultural backgrounds (see also Han, 2017, p. 260). We immediately see the parallels between Grassroots Multilingualism and the notion of Grassroots Englishes as introduced in ▶ Sect. 5.2.3 and, even though originally not conceptualised as one, we argue that the two concepts are strongly related. In fact, the notion of Grassroots Multilingualism is a higher-level framework we need in order to fully understand and accommodate the concept of Grassroots Englishes (Buschfeld, 2021). English plays an important role, for example, in many migrant and refugee contexts (cf. ▶ Chap. 9), but not an exclusive one. Some communities of practice, such as Syrian refugees to North-Rhine Westphalia, primarily use other languages of practice (Wilson, 2021). Taking a more general multilingual perspective, thus, equips us with a much more powerful framework to capture today's multilingual realities.

❓ Exercises

1. Find one further example for two of the linguistic types or modes of communication introduced in ▶ Sect. 5.2. Compare them and discuss in what way they are similar and how they differ.
2. Explain the notion of language as a Complex Dynamic System and outline its advantages over earlier approaches towards languages, dialects, and varieties. You can either draw on your own examples or the examples presented in the chapter.
3. Try to find other linguistic types or modes of communication that have emerged as the result of multilingualism and language contact which are not covered in the chapter.
   (a) Outline their conditions of emergence and usage and provide some examples of their linguistic characteristics.
   (b) Compare them to the types/modes introduced in the presented chapter and discuss how they fit or do not fit into the general line of argumentation we have employed in the chapter.

Summary

In the present chapter, we have introduced and discussed a number of manifestations of language contact in multilingual settings with a focus on English-based language forms. As examples, we have showcased more or less traditional conceptions of the World Englishes paradigm such as ENL, ESL, and EFL, and hybrid/mixed languages but also types of English and modes of communication that are traditionally associated with neighbouring linguistic disciplines, such as pidgins and creoles and different manifestations of lingua franca uses of English, including ESP and Grassroots Englishes. We hope to have given a first idea that these forms are all related and that boundaries between them are often fuzzy. Furthermore, we have argued that these speech forms can only be fully conceptualised as parts of the multilingual ecologies they have emerged in. We therefore suggest approaching languages, dialects, and varieties from an overarching perspective, as part of a multilingual Complex Dynamic System, in which all these types interact and constantly influence each other, and in which the exact manifestations and interactions depend on a number of, for example, social, political, historical, demographic, individual, and societal factors (for the last aspect, see ▶ Chap. 6).

References

Arends, J., Muysken, P., & Smith, N. (1994). Pidgins and Creoles: An introduction. .
Bickerton, D. (1976). Pidgin and creole studies. *Annual Review of Anthropology, 5*, 169–193.
Biewer, C. (2011). Modal auxiliaries in second language varieties of English: A learner's perspective. In J. Mukherjee & M. Hundt (Eds.), *Exploring second-language varieties of English and learner Englishes: Bridging a paradigm gap* (pp. 7–33). John Benjamins.
Buschfeld, S. (2013). *English in Cyprus or Cyprus English? An empirical investigation of variety status.* John Benjamins.
Buschfeld, S. (2020a). *Children's English in Singapore: Acquisition, properties, and use.* Routledge.
Buschfeld, S. (2020b). Synopsis: Fine-tuning the EIF model. In S. Buschfeld & A. Kautzsch (Eds.), *Modelling world Englishes: A joint approach to postcolonial and non-postcolonial varieties* (pp. 397–415). Edinburgh University Press.
Buschfeld, S. (2021). Grassroots English, learner English, second-language English, English as a lingua franca…: What's in a name? In C. Meierkord & E. W. Schneider (Eds.), *The growth and spread of English at the grassroots* (pp. 23–46). Edinburgh University Press.
Buschfeld, S., & Kautzsch, A. (2014). English in Namibia: A first approach. *English World-Wide, 35*(2), 121–160.
Buschfeld, S., & Kautzsch, A. (2017). Towards an integrated approach to postcolonial and non-postcolonial Englishes. *World Englishes, 36*(1), 104–126.
Buschfeld, S., Kautzsch, A., & Schneider, E. W. (2018). From colonial dynamism to current transnationalism: A unified view on postcolonial and non-postcolonial Englishes. In S. C. Deshors (Ed.), *Modelling World Englishes in the 21st century: Assessing the interplay of emancipation and globalization of ESL varieties* (pp. 15–44). John Benjamins.
Canagarajah, S. (2013). *Translingual practice: Global Englishes and cosmopolitan relations.* Routledge.
Castells, M. (1997). *The power of identity.* Blackwell.
Chia, E., & Gerbault, J. (1991). Les nouveaux parlers urbains: le cas de Yaoundé. In E. Gouaini & N. Thiam (Eds.), *Des langues et des villes* (pp. 263–277). ACCT & Didier Erudition.
Edwards, A. (2016). *English in the Netherlands: Functions, forms and attitudes.* John Benjamins.
Ellis, N. C., & Larsen-Freeman, D. (Eds.). (2009). *Language as a complex adaptive system.* Wiley.
García Mayo, M. (2000). *English for specific purposes: Discourse analysis and course design.* Servicio Editorial de la Universidad del País Vasco.
Gilquin, G., & Granger, S. (2011). From EFL to ESL: Evidence from the International Corpus of Learner English. In J. Mukherjee & M. Hundt (Eds.), *Exploring second-language varieties of English and learner Englishes: Bridging a paradigm gap* (pp. 55–78). John Benjamins.
Han, H. (2013). Individual grassroots multilingualism in Africa town in Guangzhou: The role of states in globalization. *International Multilingual Research Journal, 7*(1), 83–97.
Han, H. (2017). Trade migration and language. In A. Suresh Canagarajah (Ed.), *The Routledge handbook of migration and language* (pp. 258–274). Routledge.
Heller, M. (2007). Bilingualism as ideology and practice. In M. Heller (Ed.), *Bilingualism: A social approach* (pp. 1–22). Palgrave Macmillan.
Hickey, R. (Ed.). (2012). *Standards of English: Codified varieties around the world.* Cambridge University Press.
Holm, J. (2000). *An introduction to Pidgins and Creoles.* Cambridge University Press.

House, J. (1999). Misunderstanding in intercultural communication: Interactions in English as a lingua franca and the myth of mutual intelligibility. In C. Gnutzmann (Ed.), *Teaching and learning English as a global language* (pp. 73–89). Stauffenburg.

Hülmbauer, C., Böhringer, H., & Seidlhofer, B. (2008). Introducing English as a lingua franca (ELF): Precursor and partner in intercultural communication. *Synergies Europe, 3*, 25–36.

Jenkins, J. (2000). *The phonology of English as an international language*. Oxford University Press.

Kachru, B. B. (1985). Standards, codification and sociolinguistic realism: The English language in the outer circle. In R. Quirk & H. G. Widdowson (Eds.), *English in the world. Teaching and learning the language and literatures* (pp. 11–30). Cambridge University Press for The British Council.

Kennedy, C., & Bolitho, R. (1984). *English for specific purposes*. Macmillan.

Kießling, R. (2005). "Bàk mwà mè dó"—Camfranglais in Cameroon. *Lingua Posnaniensis, 47*, 87–107.

Kießling, R. (2021). Grammatical hybridity in Camfranglais? In R. Mesthrie, E. Hurst-Harosh, & H. Brookes (Eds.), *Youth language practices and urban language contact in Africa* (pp. 115–140). Cambridge University Press.

Kim, D. (2008). *English for occupational purposes. One language?* Continuum.

Kretzschmar, W. A., Jr. (2015). *Language and complex systems*. Cambridge University Press.

Leimgruber, J. R. E. (2013). *Singapore English. Structure, variation, and usage*. Cambridge University Press.

Lim, L. (Ed.). (2004). *Singapore English: A grammatical description*. John Benjamins.

McArthur, T. (1998). *The English languages*. Cambridge University Press.

Meierkord, C. (2012). *Interactions across Englishes. Linguistic choices in local and international contact situations*. Cambridge University Press.

Mesthrie, R., & Bhatt, R. M. (2008). *World Englishes: The study of new varieties*. Cambridge University Press.

Mufwene, S. S. (2001). *The ecology of language evolution*. Cambridge University Press.

Nchare, A. L. (2009). *The morphosyntax of Camfranglais and the matrix language frame hypothesis*. New York University.

Patsko, L. (2013, November 21). *What is the Lingua Franca core?* ELF Pronunciation. Retrieved June 27, 2022, from https://elfpron.wordpress.com/2013/11/21/what-is-the-lfc/

Quirk, R., Greenbaum, S., Leech, G., & Svartvik, J. (1972). *A grammar of contemporary English*. Longman.

Quirk, R., Greenbaum, S., Leech, G., & Svartvik, J. (1985). *A comprehensive grammar of the English language*. Longman.

Robinson, P. C. (1991). *ESP today: A practitioner's guide*. Prentice Hall.

Schneider, E. W. (2007). *Postcolonial English. Varieties around the World*. Cambridge University Press.

Schneider, E. W. (2012). Exploring the interface between World Englishes and second language acquisition–and implications for English as a lingua franca. *Journal of English as a Lingua Franca, 1*(1), 57–91.

Schneider, E. W. (2013). Leisure-activity ESP as a special case of ELF: The example of scuba diving English. *English Today, 29*(3), 47–57.

Schneider, E. W. (2016a). Grassroots Englishes in tourism interactions. *English Today, 32*(3), 2–10.

Schneider, E. W. (2016b). Hybrid Englishes: An exploratory survey. *World Englishes, 35*(3), 339–354.

Schneider, E. W. (2020). Calling Englishes as complex dynamic systems: Diffusion and restructuring. In A. Mauranen & S. Vetchinnikova (Eds.), *Language change: The impact of English as a Lingua Franca* (pp. 15–43). Cambridge University Press.

Schröder, A. (2007). Camfranglais: a language with several (sur)faces and important sociolinguistic functions. In A. Bartels & E. Wiemann (Eds.), *Global fragments. (Dis)orientation in the new world order* (pp. 281–298).

Seidlhofer, B. (2011). *Understanding English as a Lingua Franca*. Oxford University Press.

Smith, G. P., & Siegel, J. (2013). Tok Pisin. In S. M. Michaelis, P. Maurer, M. Haspelmath, & M. Huber (Eds.), *The survey of Pidgin and Creole languages* (English-based and Dutch-based languages) (Vol. I, pp. 214–222). Oxford University Press.

Strang, B. M. H. (1970). *A history of English*. Methuen.

References

Todd, L. (1990). *Pidgins and Creoles* (2nd ed.). Routledge.
Wilson, G. (2021). Language use among Syrian refugees in Germany. In C. Meierkord & E. W. Schneider (Eds.), *World Englishes at the grassroots* (pp. 211–232). Edinburgh University Press.
Wolff, M. (2010). China's English mystery—the views of a China 'foreign expert'. *English Today, 104*(26), 53–56.
Wright, L. (Ed.). (2000). *The development of standard English 1300–1800: Theories, descriptions, conflicts*. Cambridge University Press.

Key Readings

Buschfeld, S. (2021). Grassroots English, learner English, second-language English, English as a lingua franca...: What's in a name? In C. Meierkord & E. W. Schneider (Eds.), *The growth and spread of English at the grassroots* (pp. 23–46). Edinburgh University Press.
Schneider, E. W. (2013). Leisure-activity ESP as a special case of ELF: The example of scuba diving English. *English Today, 29*(3), 47–57.
Schneider, E. W. (2016b). Hybrid Englishes: An exploratory survey. *World Englishes, 35*(3), 339–354.

Further Readings

Jenkins, J. (2007). *English as a lingua franca: Attitude and identity*. Oxford University Press.
Schneider, E. W. (2016d). World Englishes and English as a lingua franca: Relationships and interfaces. In M.-L. Pitzl & R. Osimk-Teasdale (Eds.), *English as a Lingua Franca: Perspectives and prospects* (pp. 105–114). Walter de Gruyter Inc.
Velupillai, V. (2015). *Pidgins, creoles and mixed languages. An introduction*. John Benjamins.

Societal Multilingualism

Contents

6.1 Introduction – 123

6.2 What Makes a Country or Society Multilingual? – 124
6.2.1 Measuring Linguistic Diversity – 124
6.2.2 Typologies and Frameworks of Societal Multilingualism – 128
6.2.3 Terms and Labels Expressing Language Status and Power Relations Amongst Speakers – 131
6.2.4 Contemporary Social Trends – 132
6.2.5 Language Policies and Attitudes – 134

6.3 Patterns of Multilingual Organisation – 135
6.3.1 Type I: Territorial Multilingualism Type A – 135
6.3.2 Type II: Territorial Multilingualism Type B – 137
6.3.3 Type III: Territorial Monolingualism – 138
6.3.4 Type IV: Predominantly Territorial Monolingualism with Urban Multilingualism – 139
6.3.5 Type V: Diglossia – 140

© The Author(s), under exclusive license to Springer Nature Switzerland AG 2023
S. Buschfeld et al., *Multilingualism*,
https://doi.org/10.1007/978-3-031-28405-2_6

6.4 Determinants of Multilingual Patterns – 141

References – 145

6.1 Introduction

The chapter on societal multilingualism focuses on the question "What makes a country or society multilingual?". As again this is a question of perspective and definition and depends on a variety of aspects, such as whether one takes into consideration the number of official languages a country has or the number of languages spoken on a daily basis independent of status, we provide a number of details and definitions for discussion. In general, we endorse the idea that societal multilingualism does not necessarily imply that all speakers are multilingual but that many languages are spoken side by side. For establishing linguistic profiles of multilingual countries, linguists often try to identify the number of languages spoken and used as well as their uses and functions. This, however, is not always easy for the reasons addressed in ▶ Sect. 3.2, most prominently the question of what constitutes a language and what does not.

We introduce different typologies and frameworks of societal multilingualism, for example the one suggested by Stewart (1968). He proposes ten major functions languages can fulfil, viz. official, provincial (in a specific region), wider communication, international, capital (a primary language in the capital), group, educational, school subject, literary, and religious. We present cases of multilingual nations and show how they can be very different when it comes to how languages distribute among these functions. In this respect, some linguistic systems occupy far more than one of these functions, and the distribution varies greatly from language to language and from multilingual nation to multilingual nation. Ultimately, we show that once more the picture is complex and defining multilingual nation-states and societies is a difficult encounter. In addition to that, we introduce different patterns of multilingual organisation (i.e. different types of societal multilingualism, see Stavans & Hoffmann, 2015, pp. 48–49) and discuss determinants of multilingual patterns (e.g. demographic factors, individual, sociopolitical, and sociocultural determinants). As part of the latter, we zoom in on contemporary social trends and show how developments such as ever-increasing migration have started turning even long-standing monolingual countries of the 'one language, one nation' type into culturally and linguistically diverse (and thus multilingual) contexts. Next to the examples used to briefly illustrate different types of multilingual organisation or to discuss the differences in functions languages can take in these contexts, this chapter introduces several case studies (i.e. Singapore, Namibia, German-speaking Switzerland, and St. Maarten in the eastern Caribbean) to showcase different types of multilingual organisation in different countries and speech communities. It is important to note that boundaries between the different types are not always clear-cut and multiple membership assignments to the different patterns introduced might be possible.

6.2 What Makes a Country or Society Multilingual?

In the following, we introduce different aspects which need to be considered for determining the multilingual status of a country or society. We start by introducing a way of measuring linguistic diversity, then present typologies and frameworks of societal multilingualism, and introduce terms and labels which express language status and power relations in a country or speech community. Finally, we consider the impact of contemporary social trends on societal multilingualism as well as language policies and attitudes and show how all these factors are important for determining what exactly it is that makes a country or society multilingual.

6.2.1 Measuring Linguistic Diversity

The 7151 living languages spoken today (SIL International, 2022) come with very unequal distributions and statuses. Just about 23 of these languages are spoken by half of the world's population (cf. ▶ Chap. 1), about 40% of these languages are endangered, many of them with less than 1000 speakers, and countries are characterised by very different linguistic diversity. ◘ Table 6.1 summarises the ten most multilingual, ◘ Table 6.2 the five least multilingual countries as reported by the Ethnologue (Eberhard et al., 2019).

◘ **Table 6.1** The ten most multilingual countries (simplified and adapted from Eberhard et al., 2019)

Country/territory	Established languages	Immigrant languages	Number of speakers
Papua New Guinea	840	0	4,213,381
Indonesia	707	3	222,191,197
Nigeria	517	7	163,317,444
India	447	6	1,257,421,714
China (mainland)	302	3	1,319,419,348
Mexico	287	5	125,535,200
Cameroon	274	1	10,228,065
Australia	226	93	22,693,732
United States	219	116	326,756,719
Brazil	217	11	204,653,402

6.2 · What Makes a Country or Society Multilingual?

Table 6.2 The five least multilingual countries (simplified and adapted from Eberhard et al., 2019)

Country/territory	Established languages	Immigrant languages	Number of speakers
Cayman Islands	1	3	74,840
Falkland Islands	1	1	2860
North Korea	1	0	23,300,000
Saint Helena	1	0	5900
Saint Pierre and Miquelon	1	0	6000

As can be seen from Tables 6.1 and 6.2, the differences in multilingual diversity between the ten most multilingual and the five least multilingual countries are immense. Saint Pierre and Miquelon is a self-governing French overseas archipelago near the Canadian province of Newfoundland and Labrador and the 242nd territory listed by the Ethnologue. We just present the extreme cases here and one might find slight differences in the rankings and number counts depending on the sources one draws on. Our aim here is to simply illustrate the high diversity and the huge differences between countries and not to report absolute numbers. These numbers are given to constant change and they cannot be taken at face value since they are strongly influenced by a number of factors, such as the size of the territory, overall speaker numbers, remoteness of the territory, and political system. These are the factors that may be considered responsible for the low number of both established and immigrant languages in the five least multilingual countries listed by the Ethnologue. Most of the islands and island groups (Saint Helena, Cayman Islands, Saint Pierre and Miquelon) come with comparatively small territorial sizes and speaker numbers. Saint Helena is additionally remotely located, 1859 km away from Angola (on the African continent) and 3286 km from Recife, Brazil, in South America. Until the commercial opening of the airport in 2017, the island could only be reached by boat on a 3-weeks cycle (apart from the occasional cruise liners landing on the island). The Falkland Islands, which consist of about 200 individual islands, cover more territory. Even though they lie only 395 km east of South Argentina, they are linguistically comparatively homogenous. What all these islands have in common is that they have English (or French in the case of Saint Pierre and Miquelon) as their official and basically only language, were more or less unoccupied upon European arrival during colonial times, are more or less difficult to access, and economically rather insignificant. In the case of North Korea, its linguistic homogeneity, despite a comparatively large population number, can be attributed to its ethnical homogeneity, which, in turn, can certainly be attributed to its history and current political orientation towards absolute centralisation.

This shows how the demographic, the geographical, but also the political background of a territory must be considered when assessing its linguistic setup. It is also important to put the number of languages spoken in a country or territory into perspective to measure its true linguistic diversity.

> **Think Tank**
>
> We saw that absolute speaker numbers must be contextualised and relativised in order to be realistically assessed. But how could linguistic diversity be relativised?
>
> Eberhard et al. (2019) suggest calculating an extension of Greenberg's (1956) linguistic diversity index, that is, the probability that any two, randomly selected people in a country or territory would speak different mother tongues (Lieberson 1964).[1] In the original article, Greenberg (1956) suggests calculating the index of communication H by dividing the population into groups of speakers according to their linguistic profiles, for example, monolingual speakers of language A, monolingual speakers of language B, bilingual speakers of A and B, and bilingual speakers of A and C (C not being spoken monolingually by any speaker in the country). If randomly selected people from these groups have at least one language in common, the product of the proportions of the respective groups are summed up. Here is an example calculation: In a population, 1/2 of the population is monolingual A, 1/3 is monolingual B, 1/12 is bilingual AB, and 1/12 is bilingual AC; no monolingual speakers of C and no bilingual speakers of BC exist. We calculate the product of those combinations that show an overlap:
>
> | Speakers' languages | Proportion |
> |---|---|
> | A and A | 1/2 × 1/2 = 1/4 = 36/144 |
> | A and AB | 1/2 × 1/12 = 1/24 = 6/144 |
> | A and AC | 1/2 x 1/12 = 1/24 = 6/144 |
> | B and B | 1/3 x 1/3 = 1/9 = 16/144 |
> | B and AB | 1/3 x 1/12 = 1/36 = 4/144 |
> | AB and AB | 1/12 x 1/12 = 1/144 = 1/144 |
> | AB and AC | 1/12 x 1/12 = 1/144 = 1/144 |
> | AC and AC | 1/12 x 1/12 = 1/144 = 1/144 |
> | **H-Index** (= sum) | = 71/144 = **0.493** |
>
> The sum of these products constitutes the index H, in our example 71/144 = 0.493. The linguistic diversity in our example would thus be rather low. Please note that in Eberhard et al.'s (2019) calculation, this value is subtracted from 1, so that 1 indicates the highest possible value and total diversity; 0 constitutes the lowest possible value and indicates that the country or territory is characterised by a complete lack of linguistic diversity often represented by monolingualism (cf. ◻ Table 6.3).

---

1 Note that the notion of *mother tongue* is a hotly debated issue as well and it is not always clear how exactly this notion is defined in any specific context. Since Eberhard et al. (2019) do not elaborate on this in their account, we assume that by *mother tongue* they refer to any language spoken from birth and/or from very early on in life with native-like proficiency measured against standard varieties of the particular language (e.g., British, American, or Australian English for the case of English).

6.2 · What Makes a Country or Society Multilingual?

◘ **Table 6.3** Linguistic diversity of countries in the world (highest to lowest; simplified from Eberhard et al. 2019)

Country	Index	Coverage	Established languages	Immigrant languages	Number of speakers
Papua New Guinea	0.988	100%	840	0	4,213,381
Cameroon	0.975	97%	274	1	10,228,065
Vanuatu	0.972	98%	110	6	196,298
Solomon Islands	0.968	99%	72	0	379,966
Central African Republic	0.953	93%	72	11	3,638,143
Democratic Republic of the Congo	0.951	94%	212	2	42,128,230
Chad	0.931	91%	130	1	8,865,556
South Sudan	0.931	81%	69	0	4,504,650
Uganda	0.930	98%	43	2	33,862,350
Kenya	0.927	94%	67	5	37,037,960

◘ Table 6.3 reports the indices for the ten most linguistically diverse countries in the world, according to the Ethnologue-based calculations by Eberhard et al. (2019). The *Coverage* column indicates the percentage of languages in the country for which population estimates can be reported.

Eight territories in their overall list (which we cannot fully present here) come with an index of 0.000, which is why we do not rank them here. These include Haiti (4 established, 0 immigrant languages, 6,960,600 speakers), Isle of Man (2 established, 0 immigrant languages, 88,000 speakers), San Marino (2 established, 0 immigrant languages, 25,000 speakers), Vatican State (2 established, 0 immigrant languages, 330 speakers), British Indian Ocean Territory (1 established, 0 immigrant languages, 4000 speakers), North Korea (1 established, 0 immigrant languages, 23,300,000 speakers), Saint Helena (1 established, 0 immigrant languages, 5900 speakers), and Saint Pierre and Miquelon (1 established, 0 immigrant languages, 6000 speakers).

As a comparison of ◘ Tables 6.1, 6.2, and 6.3 shows, Papua New Guinea is both the country with the highest number of languages spoken and with the highest linguistic diversity index. Most other countries listed in ◘ Table 6.1 are not part of the top-ten countries with the highest linguistic diversity; Cameroon is the only country that constitutes an exception here. The overlap between ◘ Table 6.2 and the list of eight countries that come with a linguistic diversity index of 0.000 is stronger, but still not completely congruent. The Cayman Islands and Falkland Islands, which rank as one of the least multilingual countries in ◘ Table 6.2, are not among the countries with a diversity index of 0.000. These observations clearly show that the degree of multilingualism cannot be determined on the sole basis of counting the languages spoken in a respective country. True linguistic diversity is of a more complex nature and this needs to be taken consideration in measuring it, as, for example, done in the linguistic diversity measurement introduced in this chapter.

Furthermore, establishing the multilingual framework of a country requires more than just measuring the languages spoken in it and its relative linguistic diversity. Linguists also take into consideration other factors, such as the uses and functions particular languages play in a country or region, to establish its linguistic profile. This is not always easy. Some reasons for this have been discussed in ▶ Sect. 3.2. In the following section (Sect. 6.2.2), we zoom in on typologies and frameworks of societal multilingualism to shed light on a variety of issues related to multilingual societies.

6.2.2 Typologies and Frameworks of Societal Multilingualism

As we all know, multilingual profiles of countries can vary, in particular with respect to the precise functions languages have in a particular society, their prestige, and, somewhat related to the latter point, their weight or share in the multilingual setup, that is, their usage and distribution frequencies. Stewart (1968) suggests a sociolinguistic typology and comparative framework for describing the functional distribution of languages in national multilingualism. In this framework, he takes into consideration "kinds of social, functional, and distributional relationships which different linguistic systems may have within (and to some extent across) national boundaries" (Stewart, 1968, p. 533). He points out the importance of the fact that linguistic systems differ in a variety of respects, for example, in their structures, histories, their relationship with other languages and dialects, the extent of codification (that is, their status as acknowledged, officially recognised grammatical systems), and in their manner of acquisition, that is, their transmission from generation to generation. He further argues that these factors have an important impact on the role a particular linguistic system may assume in a multilingual speech community. Along these lines, he suggests the following four attributes to classify linguistic systems into language types: (1) "*Standardization*, i.e., the codification and acceptance, within the community of users, of a formal set of norms defining 'correct' usage"; (2) "*Autonomy*, i.e., the function of the linguistic system as a unique and independent one"; (3) "*Historicity*, i.e., the linguistic system is known or believed to be the result of normal development over time"; (4) "*Vitality*, i.e., use of the linguistic system by an unisolated community of native speakers" (Stewart, 1968, pp. 533–539).

Another important factor for classifying national multilingualism is the specific sociolinguistic function a linguistic system fulfils in the speech community under observation. The relevant question to be asked here is: "For what purpose is a particular linguistic system used as a medium of communication in the nation?" (Stewart, 1968, p. 540). To this end, Stewart (1968, pp. 540–541) identifies ten general functions or roles languages may fulfil in a multilingual speech community (quoted from original; slightly adapted).

1. Official (symbol: o): the function of a linguistic system as a legally appropriate language for all politically and culturally representative purposes on a nationwide basis. In many cases, the o function of a language is specified constitutionally.
2. Provincial (symbol: p): the function of a linguistic system as a provincial or regional official language. In this case, the official function of the language is not nationwide but is limited to a smaller geographic area.
3. Wider communication (symbol: w): the function of a linguistic system (other than one which already has an o or p function) predominating as a medium of communication across language boundaries within the nation.
4. International (symbol: i): the function of a linguistic system (other than one which already has an o or p function) as a major medium of communication which is international in scope, for example, for diplomatic relations, foreign trade, tourism, etc.
5. Capital (symbol: c): the function of a linguistic system (other than one which already has an o or p function) as the primary medium of communication in the vicinity of the national capital. This function is especially important in countries where political power, social prestige, and economic activity are centered in the capital.
6. Group (symbol: g): the function of a linguistic system primarily as the normal medium of communication among the members of a single cultural or ethnic group, such as a tribe, settled group of foreign immigrants, etc. So strong can the association between linguistic behavior and group identity be that at times a linguistic system with a g function may serve as an informal criterion for ascertaining group membership.
7. Educational (symbol: e): the function of a language (other than one which already has an o or p function) as a medium of primary or secondary education, either regionally or nationally.
8. School subject (symbol: s): the language (other than one which already has an o or p function) is commonly taught as a subject in secondary and/or higher education.
9. Literary (symbol: l): the use of a language primarily for literary or scholarly purposes.
10. Religious (symbol: r): the use of a language primarily in connection with the ritual of a particular religion.

Of course, these usage contexts may overlap and some linguistic systems occupy far more than one of these functional slots. The distribution varies greatly across societies. In Quebec, for example, French can be used in all these functions, whereas in Vancouver, it is limited to only some of them (Stavans & Hoffmann, 2015, p. 41).

In some multilingual nations, more than one language may be used for the same function. For example, even though Dutch is the official language in St. Maarten, the former Dutch-colonised part of the eastern Caribbean Island St. Martin, the educational function is shared between Dutch and English; for a number of other functions, the two languages are clearly distributed (Buschfeld & Ahlers, 2022).

Table 6.4 Rating of degree of use (From Stewart, 1968, p. 542)

Class	Percentage of users
Class I	>75%
Class II	>50%
Class III	>25%
Class IV	>10%
Class V	>5%
Class VI	<5%

Furthermore, certain functions—and therefore the languages by which they are represented—play a much more dominant role in some societies than in others. In most contexts, for example, public communication and administration have a much greater impact on society as a whole than religious worship or literary and scholarly uses of language (Stavans & Hoffmann, 2015, p. 41).

For a precise description of national multilingualism, Stewart (1968, p. 542) further suggests a specification of the degree of use of a particular language in a multilingual speech community. To this end, he introduces six classes of different percentages of speakers measured against the overall population (◘ Table 6.4). It has to be noted, however, that this rating expresses the relative degree of use only and cannot be taken as an index of sociolinguistic importance. As we will see in ▶ Sect. 6.3, the size of the speaker group is not necessarily the ultimate guarantor of sociolinguistic success and superiority of a language. Furthermore, it needs to be kept in mind that measuring the exact degree of use of a particular language in a multilingual speech community according to the functions a language may fulfil is complex. As Stavans and Hoffmann (2015, p. 41) rightly point out, measuring the percentage of users a particular language has in a country as suggested by Stewart helps us approach the usage profile of a particular language but is, ultimately, meaningless if we do not know how often individual speakers use their language(s).

Once again, the picture is complex and defining multilingual nation-states and societies is as difficult as defining individual multilingualism, if not more. Multilingual societies are made up of individual speakers, but how is a multilingual individual to be defined (cf. ▶ Sect. 3.2)? How many active (or even passive?) speakers does a language need to have in order to be factored into the multilingual equation? How would this or the different functions languages fulfil and their interaction be measured and weighed against each other? All of these issues remain largely unclear.

6.2.3 Terms and Labels Expressing Language Status and Power Relations Amongst Speakers

Multilingual nations are normally characterised by ethnic diversity and often by unequal or at least unbalanced distributions of speaker numbers and/or power relations. This, too, has an influence on the status and the functions of languages within a multilingual setting. Linguists have a number of concepts and labels to categorise and express different kinds of relationship between languages. In the following, we introduce some of the most prominent ones. The *official* and *national languages* of countries are normally standardised linguistic systems, that is, languages which have undergone codification and are associated with the highest linguistic value and prestige. They are languages which have been assigned legal status by the government or administration. Note, however, that the notion of *standard* is a highly disputed and often challenged concept in modern linguistics since it comes with prescriptive associations of language correctness that often do not reflect realities of language use and are often imposed by a government. The term *official language* refers to the language(s) officially installed for public communication whereas *national languages* reflect the nationhood of a country. Often, official and national language(s) coincide, for example, German in Germany or French in France. However, for some countries, these functions do not overlap. Gabon, for example, has French as its official language and Fang and other Bantu languages as national languages. Australia, for example, does not have an official language, but English is the country's national language. India, on the other hand, has no national language, since the country accommodates more than 450 established and immigrant languages (cf. ◘ Table 6.1); English and Hindi have the status of official languages in India. Some countries have many official languages, for example, South Africa, which has 11 official languages; others have only one, despite strong ethnic heterogeneity, as is the case for Namibia.

Languages of wider communication or *lingua franca* status may be written or oral languages that fulfil communicative functions across speakers of elsewise different languages within and beyond a nation state (for a chapter-length discussion of these terms, see, e.g. Berns & Matsuda, 2020). Swahili would be an example used as a language of wider communication both within and across a variety of East-African nations; Bahasa Indonesia is the language of wider communication in the archipelago of Indonesia; and English is the prime example of a globally used lingua franca (cf. ▶ Sect. 5.2.3).

Other important labels which mainly signal and characterise power relations between speakers are *majority* and *minority language*. These are often used in direct contrast to each other, expressing demographic proportions of speakers of a particular language. However, the two notions also imply power structures in multilingual societies. In this respect, the minority group speaking the minority language is often considered as demographically, politically, religiously, ethnically, etc. inferior towards the larger, majority group in the society under consideration. As Hamers and Blanc aptly state: "A minority group is characterised by its powerlessness to define the nature of its relationship with the majority and therefore its own identity" (1989, p. 59; e.g., Edwards, 2010 for an informative overview of issues revolving around minority languages and a number of case studies; see also ▶ Sects. 2.2.1 and 4.2).

Linguistic minorities have further been subdivided into *autochthonous* or *indigenous linguistic minorities* and *non-indigenous linguistic minorities*. The former set of labels refers to those minorities that have long been part of a state or community, such as the Basques or the German-speaking South Tyroleans. Non-indigenous minorities, on the other hand, belong to groups that do not have long-established roots in a state or community, for example, first- or second-generation immigrants who normally live in larger groups of people in urban centres (e.g., in Europe or the US), such as Turkish people in the Netherlands. Along similar lines, the terms *old* or *historic minorities* have been contrasted with *new minorities* and relate to the historic entrenchment of a particular group in a country. Note, however, that such terms and labels have often come under criticism not long after their introduction due to the evaluative baggage as 'new' or 'old', 'indigenous' or 'non-indigenous', etc. they carry. Linguists and politicians strive for political correctness but the perception of what is politically correct and what is not may change just within a couple of years. In the US, for example, the term *minority language* has been replaced by *heritage language* (Stavans & Hoffmann, 2015, pp. 37–43 for a similar overview of terms and labels relating to multilingual speech communities).

6.2.4 Contemporary Social Trends

Even though multilingualism is not a recent phenomenon—we have refuted this myth in ▶ Sect. 2.3—a number of recent social trends have increased global multilingualism. Ever-growing migration, globalisation and internationalisation, language policies and education, as well as revitalisation programmes of linguistic minorities have turned even long-standing monolingual countries of the 'one language, one nation' type into culturally and linguistically heterogeneous contexts. The strongest factor in this context is migration/immigration, with ever-increasing migration waves having affected most of Europe's centres, in particular since the 1960s. These migrants and immigrants have come mostly from Africa, Asia, and Southern and Eastern Europe. In 2015, also known as the year of the "migrant crisis" (BBC, 2022), more than a million migrants and refugees, in particular from Syria, but also from Afghanistan and Iraq, Eritrea, and Kosovo, to name just a few, fled into Europe (for further information, see BBC, 2022). Still, the country with the highest number of immigrants is the US with 50.6 million foreign-born residents. Germany comes in second, with 15.8 million immigrants, followed by Saudi Arabia (13.5 million), Russia (11.6 million), the United Kingdom (9.4 million), and the United Arab Emirates (8.7 million), to provide just a few numbers and examples. Again, these numbers have to be seen in relation to the overall number of residents of a country. Taking this into consideration, the percentage of foreign-born residents amounts to 15% in the US, and as much as 88% in the United Arab Emirates (numbers as of 2020; World Population Review, 2022b). In particular, urban centres have attracted the major shares of these immigrants. London, Berlin, Paris, and Marseille are prototypical examples, often cited in the literature (e.g. Stavans & Hoffmann, 2015, p. 44). As of 2019, London accommodates approximately 3,331,000 foreign-born citizens, which are 37% of the total population (Office for National Statistics, 2020). Most of these people came to the UK from India, followed by Nigerians, Italians, Polish, and Bangladeshis (Trust for London, 2022). However, it is not only Europe being characterised by high numbers of immigrants. In Miami, Florida, 58.4% of its citizens are foreign-born, most of them from Europe and Asia but also from Africa, Oceania, as well as Latin and Northern America (numbers as of 2019; United States Census Bureau, 2019).[2]

All these people have brought their language(s) to these nowadays multi-ethnic hubs, which have, therefore, entered the multilingual equation of these speech communities (see the linguistic diversity index introduced in ▶ Sect. 6.2.1). If immigrants were not already multilingual upon arrival in the host country, many of them—and in particular second, third, etc. generations of immigrants—become multilingual very soon since they are normally exposed to their ethnic language(s) in the home and the language(s) of the host community, for example, in school.

Another, more recent trend that has promoted worldwide multilingualism is *globalisation*. Of the many aspects converging in the notion of globalisation, the following have essentially contributed to the unprecedented expansion in the use of the English language: internationalisation; new forms of tourism, and especially the development of mass tourism since the 1960s; the introduction of powerful and affordable personal computers in the 1980s, and the subsequent explosive growth of the internet and related forms of modern electronic communication; the development of English as the lingua franca of international trade. However, multilingualism has not exclusively been promoted by the increasingly worldwide spread of the English language. Languages such as Arabic or Mandarin Chinese, too, have emerged as trade languages for multilingual encounters in global cities between speakers who do not share a common language. This, in turn, has sparked the emergence of a new form of multilingualism, namely Grassroots Multilingualism, which has been introduced in ▶ Sect. 5.2.3.

---

2 Note that comparable numbers are difficult to find. Some sources count in all foreign-born citizens, that is, first-generation immigrants; some only count those with legal citizenship; some count both with legal and without legal citizenship; some sources also count in the following generations of immigrants; some others do not specify what the numbers are based on at all. The numbers for London and Miami are comparable since they both include foreign-born people with and without legal citizenship status.

6.2.5 Language Policies and Attitudes

As outlined in ▶ Chap. 1, political decisions in the former colonies of, for example, the British Empire have often introduced English and one or more local languages as the official languages of those nations and have thus promoted multilingualism on a political level. Still, English has repeatedly been deemed a "killer language", committing "linguistic genocide" by taking over the global linguistic market at the expense of local, and in particular, minority languages (e.g. Lucko, 2003; Skutnabb-Kangas, 2000). Indeed, for a long time, English was promoted at the expense of, for example, the aboriginal languages in the US and in the Antipodean area and at the expense of Scottish or Irish Gaelic in Scotland and Ireland. However, the trend to suppress minority languages at the expense of majority languages has not been observed for the English language only. It was a common strategy, in particular in eighteenth- and nineteenth-century Europe. The Spanish Bourbon dynasty, for example, systematically suppressed the use of Catalan, Basque, and Galician, a strategy again adopted by the Franco regime. This *une language, une nation*-ideal was already practised during the *Ancien Regime*, that is, in sixteenth to eighteenth century France (cf. ▶ Sect. 2.2.2). It is associated with a philosophy of language, nationhood, and identity that embraces unity and was adopted by statesmen on the basis of the assumption that socially and linguistically homogeneous states were easier to rule and control than societies with different languages and cultures. This attitude had prevailed far into the twentieth century. However, with the equal rights movements of the 1960s, voices were raised demanding civil rights for minorities, including linguistic rights. Political pressure as well as more liberal intellectual movements initiated a rethinking of these archaic language policies and the position of linguistic minorities and their languages in society. Official approaches to language revitalisation can be broadly divided into five categories: (1) school-based programmes; (2) children's programmes outside school (after-school programmes, summer programmes); (3) adult language programmes; (4) documentation and material development; and (5) home-based programmes. School-based programmes, either teaching the endangered language as a subject or pursuing bilingual education or even full-scale language immersion in the endangered language (cf. ▶ Chap. 8), have been employed in a number of countries. In Humboldt County, California, for example, the local Native American languages Tolowa, Hupa, Karuk, and Yurok are all taught through the public school system (Hinton, 2001, p. 7). We cannot discuss all types in detail here but interested readers are referred to, for example, *The Green Book of Language Revitalization in Practice* (Hinton & Hale, 2001) or *The Routledge Handbook of Language Revitalization* (Hinton et al., 2018). Education has always played a pivotal role in these developments, that is, in the spread of English but also for the promotion of minority languages in more recent times. However, there is, of course, no guarantee that multilingual language ideologies or even language revitalisation programmes will lead to a growth in speaker numbers of those minority languages. Power relations between linguistic communities and speaker attitudes cannot be overruled in the end and despite some clear progress in attitudes and language policies, old stereotypes often take a while to be fully dismantled.

In sum, we have seen that four central, strongly related trends have affected societies and individuals and increased their linguistic repertoires over the last centuries: colonisation, globalisation, the emergence of new linguistic minorities due to immigration, and, after a too long time of stigmatisation of linguistic minorities and their languages, the long-needed changes in language attitudes and language policies. However, no two multilingual states (and the same is true for individuals; see ▶ Chap. 3) are ever exactly identical. Still, linguists have identified some general patterns and types of multilingual organisation to be introduced in ▶ Sect. 6.3.

6.3 Patterns of Multilingual Organisation

When turning towards general patterns of multilingual organisation, it, too, holds that no two multilingual states are ever exactly identical. Still, some general patterns and types of multilingual organisation have been identified that help to describe and distinguish individual nations. Stavans and Hoffmann (2015, pp. 48–53) identify five such organisational types alongside two major criteria, namely "the relation between the number of languages used by a country's population and the incidence of individual multiple language use" (Stavans & Hoffmann, 2015, p. 48). In the following, we portray the major characteristics of the five types, that is, Type I: Territorial multilingualism type A; Type II: Territorial multilingualism type B; Type III: Territorial monolingualism; Type IV: Predominantly territorial monolingualism with urban multilingualism; and Type V: Diglossia (following the description in Stavans & Hoffmann, 2015, pp. 48–53). We provide examples for each type which are mostly based on our own research. ◘ Table 6.5 summarises the five patterns (adapted and slightly updated from Stavans & Hoffmann, 2015, p. 49).

6.3.1 Type I: Territorial Multilingualism Type A

Type I in Stavans and Hoffmann's typology, territorial multilingualism of type A, is characterised by a high incidence of individual multilingualism where several languages serve different functions in the territory. Namibia, a state in the southwest of the African continent, is a case in point. Due to its historico-political background of foreign domination and, in particular, the "scramble for Africa" (cf. ▶ Sect. 2.2.2.2), Namibia is an ethnically and linguistically diverse country; its diversity index amounts to 0.790 (diversity indices taken from Eberhard et al. 2019; see also ▶ Sect. 6.2.1). 50% of its overall 2.6 million inhabitants are Ovambos, 9% are Kavangos, 7% belong to the group of Hereros, 7% are Damaras, 5% Namas, and 4% Caprivian. 6% of the overall population are of European ancestry (mostly Afrikaners but also Germans), 6.5% are of mixed European and African ancestry, and 5.5% are listed as "other" (CIA, 2020).

As the result of this ethnic diversity, several African languages from different language families (e.g., Oshivambo, Kavango, or Otjiherero, Nama/Damara, or San) are regularly spoken alongside each other as are the three West Germanic languages, English, Afrikaans, and German (e.g. Böhm, 2003, p. 525).

◼ Table 6.5 Five types of multilingual organisations of nations

Type	Characteristics	Examples	References
I. Territorial multilingualism type A	Functional distribution between languages; High incidence of individual multilingualism	Luxembourg, Guinea-Bissau, Namibia, St. Martin/St. Maarten	Newton (1996), Benson (2003), Buschfeld and Schröder (2020), Buschfeld and Ahlers (2022)
II. Territorial multilingualism type B	All languages used for formal functions; Some separation for informal functions; High incidence of bilingualism or multilingualism among different ethnic groups	Singapore	Romaine (2004), Buschfeld (2020)
III. Territorial monolingualism	One official language for each region; Access to other languages seen as desirable but not essential	Canada, Belgium, Cyprus, Switzerland	Edwards (2001), Buschfeld and Vida-Mannl (fc), Vida-Mannl (2022), Ronan (fc)
IV. Predominantly territorial monolingualism with urban multilingualism	One official language in predominantly monolingual country; Concentration of linguistic minorities mainly in urban centres; Varying degrees of individual multilingualism among minority members	Barcelona, London, Berlin	Turell (2001), Edwards (2001), Wiese (2020)
V. Diglossia	(1) Two varieties of same language used for different functions; or (2) Two different languages used for different functions; Widespread individual multilingualism	German-speaking Switzerland, Paraguay, Greek-speaking part of Cyprus	McRae (1983), Barbour and Stevenson (1990), Dürmüller (1997), Rubin (1968), Arvaniti (2006), Buschfeld (2013)

Despite this linguistic diversity and even though Namibia was never a real British colony,[3] English has served as the only official language of the country ever since its independence in 1990. German, the former colonial language, has never had a far-reaching impact on the country, at least not when compared to

---

3   Note that Walvis Bay, a municipal borough in the Erongo region and the most important seaport of the country, was under British possession from 1878 to 1910—with an interlude of German possession at the beginning of World War I.

the influence the English language has had in many of the former colonies of the British Empire. However, German is still spoken particularly in the private domains by the population of German descent, and, to some extent, by mostly older parts of the indigenous population, whose ancestors had worked as servants in the households of the former colonisers. Since Namibia was long under a class C mandate exercised by South Africa, Afrikaans long fulfilled the role of the lingua franca of the country. However, it has been gradually replaced by English in this function (Buschfeld & Kautzsch, 2014; Buschfeld & Schröder, 2020). Nowadays, English and, to some extent still Afrikaans, function as official languages of the country and are used, for example, in administration and education. German and the local African languages are primarily ethnically distributed, this means that they are predominantly used within the respective speech groups. As the most widely spoken of the African languages, Oshivambo is partly used as the interethnic lingua franca in indigenous African circles. However, Afrikaans and, more recently, English are spoken by the majority of any ethnic group as the languages of wider communication. As a result, the degree of individual multilingualism is high, in particular in the indigenous African groups, who often speak Afrikaans and English alongside one or more ethnic language(s) (Buschfeld & Schröder, 2020).

The eastern Caribbean island of St. Martin is another interesting example of type A territorial multilingualism. However, it also shows traces of type IV since it is divided into a formerly French-colonised northern part, Saint-Martin, and a formerly Dutch-colonised southern part, St. Maarten. French is the official language of the northern, French part of the island, English and Dutch are both listed as the official languages of the southern part. The official languages of the two parts are thus different even though the island is no bigger than 34 sq mi. Furthermore, both parts are highly multilingual. They are characterised by strong ethnic and linguistic diversity due to slavery, migration, and tourism. The diversity indices of the two parts are both high, with an index of 0.689 in the French part and of 0.816 in the formerly Dutch-colonised part. In St. Maarten, English is the language most often spoken as a first language, even though it was also never truly colonised by the British. Dutch, Spanish, French, Papiamento (a Spanish-lexified creole), and a French-lexified creole (referred to as Creole) are spoken alongside the English language but much less frequently as an L1. According to a questionnaire-based study by Buschfeld and Ahlers (2022), English is the dominant language in most functional domains. A thematic analysis has revealed that it is particularly associated with the private and global domains, whereas Dutch is still perceived as the main language in the official domain. The two languages therefore occupy mainly different functional domains, even though some domains appear to be shared by the languages, such as the educational domain (Buschfeld & Ahlers, 2022).

6.3.2 Type II: Territorial Multilingualism Type B

With a linguistic diversity index of 0.758, Singapore is another highly multilingual nation and an example of type B territorial multilingualism (Type II). This type is very similar to type A territorial multilingualism. The only difference is that a number of languages have official language status and can be used anywhere in the country, even if people are not necessarily proficient in all of them. Singapore is composed of three major ethnic groups, namely people of Chinese, Indian, and Malay descents. Mandarin Chinese, Malay, and Tamil are recognised as official languages accordingly, as is English. Schooling officially takes place in the respective home languages of the children and in English. All four languages are used in administration, in court, and in the media. Traditionally, the respective ethnic languages of Singapore function as family and community languages. English, however, has been gaining ground as a home language, in particular in recent times. The 2020 Census of Population reports that in the group of 5–14-year-olds, 77.4% of the Chinese, 63% of the Malay, and 69.8% of the Indian segments of the population nowadays speak English as the most frequently used language at home (Department of Statistics Singapore, 2020, p. 29). It is certainly true that the situation in general has been characterised by "a noticeable shift towards wider use of English, and the increasing incidence of individual multilingualism" (Stavans & Hoffmann, 2015, p. 50). However, first trends towards monolingualism in English have been observed and discussed for Singapore (e.g., Mesthrie & Bhatt, 2008, pp. 221–222) and it has been speculated whether English in Singapore may follow suit with the example of Ireland, which developed into a mainly monolingual English country at the expense of Irish Gaelic (see Ronan and Buschfeld, 2023). Still, currently Singapore is far away from monolingualism, as our observations and the high linguistic diversity index suggest.

6.3.3 Type III: Territorial Monolingualism

Type III, territorial monolingualism, is found in states where different languages have official language status and are used as main languages in specific regions. Beyond the examples listed and discussed in Stavans and Hoffmann (2015), Cyprus might be seen as a case in point, though the situation in Cyprus is specific and the component parts, that is, the Greek-speaking and Turkish-speaking areas, come with different multilingual setups themselves (see our further elaborations on the Greek-speaking part of Cyprus as an example of Type V). Cyprus as a whole is yet another example of a divided nation-state which, of course, complicates the matter. From an official perspective, the northern part, the so-called Turkish Republic of Northern Cyprus (TRNC), is a self-declared state and officially only recognised by Turkey. Internationally, the whole island is considered to be the Republic of Cyprus (RoC) and the TRNC does officially not exist. De facto, however, the island is separated into a northern and a southern part. Therefore, it can be argued that it fulfils the general criteria of Type III since the two parts each have their own de facto official language, viz. Greek and Turkish, respectively. The separation of the northern part of the island in 1974 has caused the separation of the two major ethnic groups, that is, Greek and Turkish Cypriots and has caused Greek to vanish in the northern part and Turkish to vanish in the southern part. In the southern,

Greek-speaking part of the island, which is still controlled by the RoC, a number of adstrate languages, that is, languages spoken by larger, still minority population groups that have migrated to a country and mostly live alongside the indigenous population and "enrich[...] and expand[...] an existing contact scenario not from 'above' or 'below' but rather 'from the side'" (Schneider, 2007, p. 58), exist, most prominently Russian, which is spoken alongside the two dialects Cypriot and Standard Modern Greek. English was introduced to the island as a whole during the time of British rule (1878–1960) but has experienced a decline in functions ever since the island's division, most likely because it lost its function as inter-ethnic link language between Greek and Turkish Cypriots (e.g. Buschfeld, 2013; cf. Vida-Mannl 2022 on the current role and use of English in Cyprus).

In general, the linguistic situation in the TRNC differs significantly from the one in the Greek-speaking part of the island as it is strongly dominated by the Turkish language. Furthermore, English in the TRNC has not experienced a gradual decline but its recession was more abrupt. The reasons for this are, most likely, that the TRNC is internationally not recognised as a country and therefore not involved in international diplomacy or trade. Its economic and political structures are highly dependent on the support of Turkey, for example trade and travel have been possible only via Turkey since 1974. In addition, the majority of inhabitants in the TRNC are currently Turks who initially migrated to the northern part of Cyprus during the separation of the island to support the Turkish Cypriots and their descendants (Research Centre on Multilingualism, 2004). Due to this political, social, and economic power of Turkey over the TRNC, Turkish is undisputedly the most powerful and most important inter- and intranational language in North Cyprus. English is not central but holds two different roles: (1) in its function as a foreign language, it is primarily used as a medium of instruction to attract international students mainly from African countries to pursue their higher education in the TRNC; (2) it serves as a sign of Cypriotness for Turkish Cypriots, who are often still closely connected to the UK (Vida-Mannl 2022).

Both the southern and the northern part thus are by no means strictly monolingual speech communities—and which modern nation would be?—but the overall island fits the "[o]ne official language for each region; access to other languages seen as desirable but not essential" characteristics as stated by Stavans and Hoffmann (2015, p. 49). The situation in the Greek-speaking part, however, can also be characterised as diglossic, as discussed in ▶ Sect. 6.3.5.

6.3.4 Type IV: Predominantly Territorial Monolingualism with Urban Multilingualism

Type IV multilingualism often occurs in urban areas of otherwise mainly monolingual countries such as Spain, France, or Germany. Berlin, the capital of Germany, is a case in point even if it is maybe not comparable in size to some of our 20-million-inhabitants-plus cities, such as the three most populous cities Tokyo (37,274,000), Delhi (32,065,760), or Shanghai (28,516,904). Berlin, with its

3,570,750 inhabitants, ranks 131 in the list of World City Populations (2022 estimates, World Population Review, 2022a). Still, it is a growing, vibrant urban metropolis, which offers a broad range of ethnic and linguistic contact settings. It has been a language contact scene right from its origins in the thirteenth century, when speakers of Low German and Dutch met speakers of Sorbian, a Slavonic minority language still spoken in the Berlin vicinity. In more recent times, West Berlin (at the time when Berlin was still divided by the allies as the result of World War II) had been characterised by larger numbers of immigrants ever since the major labour immigration waves of the 1960s.[4] This turned in particular the working-class neighbourhoods of Berlin, such as Wedding, Neukölln, and Kreuzberg, into vibrant, multilingual communities. Today, 35% of Berlin's population has foreign roots, in particular Turkish, Arabic, and Polish (The Official Website of Berlin, 2022). Next to the coexistence of a variety of languages in these and similar neighbourhoods in other larger German cities, an urban contact dialect and new German vernacular, referred to as *Kiezdeutsch* ((neighbour-)hood German), is spoken in many of these multilingual areas. It has emerged as the result of language contact and is spoken in urban centres primarily amongst young people. *Kiezdeutsch* is a German-based mixed code (see ▶ Sect. 5.3 for further examples of mixed codes), which is characterised by, for example, language mixing and lexical and grammatical transfer from other languages such as Turkish or Arabic. It is, however, neither restricted to the influence of such languages nor to such speaker groups. *Kiezdeutsch* is a vibrant multi-ethnolect which is spoken in a number of German urban centres (e.g. Wiese, 2020, pp. 267–268; see also Wiese, 2012).

As we have seen, Berlin is no isolated case and ▶ Sect. 2.2 has shown that multilingual cities have been magnets for immigration, multiculturalism, and multilingualism from the earliest time of humankind. The fluid and heterogeneous character of urban speech communities makes multilingualism and contact in modern global cities particularly interesting and relevant for processes of linguistic innovation (see also ▶ Chaps. 5 and 12).

6.3.5 Type V: Diglossia

For our last case study, an example of Type V multilingualism, we return to the Greek-speaking, southern part of Cyprus. As outlined above, Greek and Turkish are the two official languages of the RoC. In everyday life, however, Turkish does not play a major role in the southern part of the RoC. The two most widely spoken languages (or dialects) are Standard Modern Greek (SMG) and Cypriot Greek (CG). Even though CG is supposed to be a dialect of SMG, it has been reported that they are not necessarily mutually intelligible (e.g. Arvaniti, 2006, pp. 18–19). CG is characterised by a number of specific linguistic characteristics on the differ-

---

4 East Berlin was not really affected by that due to the fact that contact between contract workers and East Berliners was not encouraged.

ent levels of linguistic description, that is, in terms of its phonetics/phonology, morphology, syntax, and its lexicon; it is even characterised by specific orthographic conventions (for an overview, see Arvaniti, 2006, pp. 23–30). The two dialects show clear functional differentiation in Cyprus. Therefore, the linguistic situation has often been described as diglossic. Following Ferguson's (1959) notion of *diglossia*, SMG corresponds to the H (high) variety, CG to the L (low) variety. As is typical for an H variety, SMG is learnt through formal schooling and is mostly used in formal types of writing and in formal oral communication such as news broadcasting. CG is mostly acquired at home and is used in personal, face-to-face communication among Greek Cypriots. It is also used in the media, but mainly for humoristic purposes, and in poetry (for details and further references, see Arvaniti, 2006, p. 20). It has to be noted, however, that the notion of *diglossia* is not uncontroversial. A number of researchers have argued that linguistic situations are actually too complex to be considered dichotomous and thus diglossic (e.g., Buschfeld, 2020, p. 260; Haeri, 2000, including further references). Still, it has been pointed out (Haeri, 2000; Caton, 1991) that, even if Ferguson's conception of *diglossia* is not linguistically deterministic and accurate, it bears some value for the speakers of such varieties in that it gives them a sense of understanding of what appears appropriate, historically and institutionally shaped language use in a given situation. As Arvaniti (2006, pp. 21–22) argues, this user-based principle clearly applies to Cyprus; "since the speakers see Cypriot and Standard Greek as distinct, and agree on which circumstances call for each variety, the situation is best seen as diglossic" (2006, p. 22).

6.4 Determinants of Multilingual Patterns

Finally, we would like to shed light on potential determinants of multilingual patterns, that is, factors that shape multilingual language use and determine the exact multilingual configuration of a society or nation. These include individual, sociopolitical, and sociocultural determinants which are associated with the languages, their speakers, and the wider political context of the community (mainly based on Stavans & Hoffmann, 2015, pp. 53–57).

When it comes to power structures and multilingual hierarchies between languages and speakers, various factors may influence a linguistic situation. First of all, the distinctiveness of a linguistic system in relation to the other languages or dialects 'competing' in the multilingual system may play a role, that is, its origin and typological setup, whether it is a dialect or standard form, whether it is a written or spoken system, etc. However, demographic factors of the group of speakers using the system also have an important influence on the overall linguistic situation. The size of the speaker group, its social composition and status, as well as its geographical location are crucial factors for the extent of multilingualism and language contact as well as the success of a language in a multilingual scenario. For example, it plays an important role whether speakers belong to an isolated group, located at the fringes of a country, cut-off from mainstream population and communication, or whether they live and operate right at the centre of the country and of everyday communication. If speakers of a minority language are isolated from each other or speakers of different minority languages are in extensive contact and use a third (majority) language as a lingua franca, the use of the minority language(s) may become more and more restricted and, in the worst case, the language(s) may eventually cease to exist.

Furthermore, the social status of the speakers of a language is an important determinant as it often becomes attached to the language itself. This, in turn, may influence speaker attitudes and whether other speakers voluntarily set out to learn and speak the language. This factor is so strong that it often overrides group size. As an example, bring to mind the linguistic success of the European coloniser languages in the era of colonisation between the fifteenth and twentieth centuries. Spanish, Portuguese, French, and in particular English are still spoken around the globe in destinations far from their countries of origin, even though the settler population was often in the clear minority upon arrival in the country. In such (and many other) contexts, language choice, that is, which language(s) speakers learn and use to what extent, is therefore rarely a question of free choice but depends on a number of factors. The socio-political power of speaker groups is a highly influential determinant as are language policies, ideologies, and beliefs (cf. ▶ Chap. 7). These factors determine the specific status of languages, for example, national and official language status (e.g., Japanese in Japan and German in Austria); joint official language status (e.g., Xhosa and Zulu alongside Afrikaans and English (and seven more languages) in South Africa); or regional official language status (e.g., Welsh in Wales or Gujarati in India). Linguistic marginalisation and extinction have long been the result of proscribed language status, that is, official restrictions and sanctions were imposed on speaking specific languages and against its users, for example, against the Inuits in Canada, native Indians in North and South America, Aborigines in Japan and New Zealand, etc. As discussed in ▶ Sect. 6.2.4, these times are fortunately over and changes in attitudes have taken place that have even led to attempts of revitalising these languages and their speaker communities.

As can be seen from this discussion, language policies have an important role in multilingual organisation. This is why it is important to understand what guides states in their language legislation. As Stavans and Hoffmann point out:

» Decisions of a general nature such as the degree of recognition of languages in multilingual states, their use and the rights granted to their speakers follow two basic principles: either a language is tied to a particular region or it is an attribute of the individual who has the right to use it anywhere. (2015, p. 55)

Two general principles can therefore be identified that guide states in language legislation. The first principle is the language-and-territory principle, which takes geographical criteria as markers of linguistic boundaries and considers language as belonging to a particular region. The second principle is the personality or language-and-identity-ideology (Myhill, 1999, p. 34), which underlines the inherent emotional and ideological connection between language and the individual who speaks the language.

The territoriality principle, for example, considers languages as being bound to particular regions and determines which language has official status in a region and is used in official contexts. In Canada, for example, Quebec is considered a monolingual French region. Belgium is characterised by two monolingual regions, Flanders, in which Flemish is spoken, and Wallonia, in which French is promoted. The German-speaking region in the East is bilingual as is the capital, Brussels, with Flemish and French as the main languages. India has a number of regional languages, which have official status in the regions they are associated with. Still, English and Hindi are the official national languages and can be used throughout the country; India is therefore characterised by territorial multilingualism (cf. Stavans & Hoffmann, 2015, p. 55).

The personality principle has found a number of advocates in modern linguistics, for example, Tove Skutnabb-Kangas and Joshua Fishman. Both of them emphasise the important role the mother tongue plays in a person's linguistic repertoire and for their well-being. Fishman equates the mother tongue with the speaker's soul (1989, p. 276), which, in turn, carries the inherent assumption that every person should have the right to use their language in whatever context. If a state or nation wanted to adopt this principle, it is clear that this cannot be done for the full state but only for groups of individuals. This can be a good solution for contexts in which various groups live and not one group claims historic or political ownership of a territory. Such a principle, which allows each major ethnic group to maintain their linguistic and cultural heritage, underlies the language policies of states such as the Fiji Islands or Singapore. In Singapore, for example, the three officially designated mother tongues are Malay, Mandarin, and Tamil. For quite a while (though not originally; cf. Gupta, 1994, p. 148), the mother tongue was assigned according to the child's ethnic group, but this regulation has been handled more liberally in recent times (cf. Leimgruber, 2013, p. 12). The aim of this mother tongue-oriented language policy in Singapore was to secure a strong cultural grounding for all Singaporeans, as the mother tongue was seen as "the vehicle of traditions and cultural values"; English, on the other hand, was long considered "the useful language of international trade and regional competitiveness" (Leimgruber, 2013, p. 12). By implication, this view would deny English the status of a legally accepted and suitable mother tongue in Singapore (Alsagoff, 2007, p. 36) and this idea has been clearly promoted by language policy makers. For example, Singapore's former Prime Minister Lee Kuan Yew stated in his Speak Mandarin Campaign Speech:

» One abiding reason why we have to persist in bilingualism is that English will not be emotionally acceptable as our mother tongue. To have no emotionally acceptable language as our mother tongue is to be emotionally crippled. We shall doubt ourselves. We shall be less self-confident. Mandarin is emotionally acceptable as our mother tongue. (1984)

However, the subsequent linguistic developments in Singapore have clearly shown that it is not always the policy makers who decide the fate of languages. English in Singapore, and in particular the colloquial variety Singlish, against which the political attacks of the 1980s and 1990s were primarily directed, has developed into a first language for an ever-increasing number of young Singaporeans (for further details, see ▶ Sect. 6.3.2). Still, and alarmingly, the negative governmental stance on English as a mother tongue is a much-debated issue in Singapore and strongly affects—if not unsettles—the linguistic identities of many Singaporeans.[5] In this respect, a study by Leimgruber et al. (2018) reports that often Singaporeans do not feel fully proficient even in the language they consider their most proficient/first language, since the government implies that the variety of English they speak is deficient since it is different from standard British English (e.g., the Speak Good English Movement propagated by the Singaporean government in 2000). Buschfeld (2020, p. 55) has argued this to be an alarming finding since it rests on the assumption that only traditional L1 speakers can be considered fully competent speakers of a particular language. If Singaporeans are not granted L1 speaker status and are being told that they speak a corrupted variety of English when using Singlish, how can they trust in their own linguistic proficiency and identity? If the mother tongue cannot be a self-chosen part of everybody's life, this clearly counteracts the essence of the personality principle introduced above. It is, therefore, high time that the recent emergence of new L1 speakers of English (also to be found in other Asian and a variety of African contexts) and their right to claim these varieties as part of their personal linguistic repertoires are taken into consideration by linguists and language policy makers alike (e.g., Buschfeld, 2020, pp. 55–64 for a more detailed discussion).

❓ Exercises

1. Do strictly monolingual nations or societies still exist? Work in pairs and collect information on this question. Prepare a discussion sheet. Include examples of societies that might still be considered monolingual and discuss why or why not this may still be the case.
2. Calculate the linguistic diversity index of the country you currently live in and another country you have been to or would like to go to (depending on the example you choose, it might be a bit tricky to find the relevant numbers). Read up on the languages that are used in these countries and their roles and discuss your findings in relation to the calculated numbers with a partner.
3. (Suggestions for project work): Work in pairs or small groups of three to four people. Select a multilingual country of your choice, maybe the country you currently live in, and gather as much information about its multilingual profile as possible. Concentrate on the three criteria "linguistic type", "function", and "degree of use" introduced by Stewart (1968). You may want to use the case study of Netherlands America presented in Stewart (1968, pp. 543–545) as a template, but make sure you bring in your own ideas. Present your results as a poster or padlet (or in similar format) in class.

---

5 We here use the term *mother tongue* instead of the more neutral L1, despite its ideological burden and controversial nature, since in Singapore, the terms "mother tongue" and "first language," often used interchangeably in the Language Acquisition literature, bear specific local connotations. The term "mother tongue" officially relates to the three official ethnic languages of Singapore, viz. Mandarin, Tamil, and Malay (Bokhorst-Heng et al., 2007, p. 424; Tan, 2014, pp. 319–320), and is assigned by the state; the term "first language", interestingly, captures the status of English (Gupta, 1998, p. 117).

Summary

In this chapter, we have introduced a wealth of issues related to multilingual societies, their emergence, definition, and general types. We have started discussing the question "What makes a country or society multilingual?", taking into consideration several relevant aspects. We have first looked into how to measure linguistic diversity and introduced some relevant terms and labels to address and express language status and power relations between speaker groups living in the same territory. We have further discussed typologies and frameworks of societal multilingualism as well as contemporary social trends that have boosted multilingualism in recent times (e.g. migration, globalisation and internationalisation, etc.), with a special focus on language policies and attitudes. We have subsequently looked into some general patterns of multilingual organisation, namely different general types of multilingualism to be found in societies around the globe, with a strong focus on actual case studies. Finally, we have introduced determinants of multilingual patterns, in particular the different factors that might influence the specific multilingual situation in terms of power structures and the multilingual hierarchies between languages and speakers, such as size of speaker groups and their social status. We again have zoomed in on language policies and how they determine multilingual patterns, and introduced two principles that have guided states in their language legislation, the language-and-territory principle and the personality principle.

References

Alsagoff, L. (2007). Singlish: Negotiating culture, capital and identity. In V. Vaish, S. Gopinathan, & Y. Liu (Eds.), *Language, capital, culture: Critical studies and education in Singapore* (pp. 25–46). Sense Publishers.

Arvaniti, A. (2006). Linguistic practices in Cyprus and the emergence of Cypriot standard Greek. *Mediterranean Language Review, 17*(2006–2010), 15–45.

Barbour, S., & Stevenson, P. (1990). *Variation in German: A critical approach to German sociolinguistics.* Cambridge University Press.

BBC. (2022). *Migrant crisis: Migration to Europe explained in seven charts.* Retrieved November 4, 2022, from https://www.bbc.com/news/world-europe-34131911

Benson, C. (2003). Trilingualism in Guinea-Bissau and the question of instructional language. In C. Hoffmann & J. Ytsma (Eds.), *Trilingualism in family, school and community* (pp. 166–184). Multilingual Matters.

Berns, M., & Matsuda, A. (2020). Lingua Franca and language of wider communication. In C. A. Chapelle (Ed.), *The encyclopedia of applied linguistics.* Wiley.

Böhm, M. (2003). *Deutsch in Afrika: Die Stellung der deutschen Sprache in Afrika vor dem Hintergrund der bildungs- und sprachpolitischen Gegebenheiten sowie der deutschen Auswärtigen Kulturpolitik.* Peter Lang Verlag.

Bokhorst-Heng, W. D., Alsagoff, L., McKay, S., & Rubdy, R. (2007). English language ownership among Singaporean Malays: going beyond the NS/NNS dichotomy. *World Englishes, 26*(4), 424–445.

Buschfeld, S. (2013). *English in Cyprus or Cyprus English? An empirical investigation of variety status.* John Benjamins.

Buschfeld, S. (2020). *Children's English in Singapore: Acquisition, properties, and use.* Routledge.

Buschfeld, S., & Ahlers, W. (2022). English around the World: New realities, new models, and the case of Sint Maarten. In A. Ngefac, H. -G. Wolf, & T. Hoffmann (Eds.), World Englishes and Creole languages today, vol. 1: The Schneiderian thinking and beyond. Lincom.

Buschfeld, S., & Kautzsch, A. (2014). English in Namibia: A first approach. *English World-Wide, 35*(2), 121–160.

Buschfeld, S., & Schröder, A. (2020). English and German in Namibia. In R. Hickey (Ed.), *English in the German-speaking world* (pp. 334–360). Cambridge University Press.

Buschfeld, S., & Vida-Mannl, M. (Fc.) English in Cyprus. In R. Hickey (Ed.), *The new Cambridge history of the English language* (pp. page numbers), vol. 4. Cambridge University Press.

Caton, S. (1991). Diglossia in North Yemen: A case of competing linguistic communities. *Southwest Journal of Linguistics, 10*, 143–159.

CIA. (2020). *The World factbook: Namibia*. Retrieved August 27, 2021, from https://www.cia.gov/the-world-factbook/static/b5ac4db93b3379cabced51723dda44c1/WA-summary.pdf

Department of Statistics Singapore. (2020). *Census of population 2020. Statistical release 1: Demographic characteristics, education, language and religion*. Retrieved January 22, 2021, from https://www.singstat.gov.sg/-/media/files/publications/cop2020/sr1/cop2020sr1.pdf

Dürmüller, U. (1997). *Changing patterns of multilingualism: From quadrilingual to multilingual Switzerland*. Pro Helvetia.

Eberhard, D. M., Simons, G. F. & Fennig, C. D., (Eds.) (2019). Summary by country. *Ethnologue: Languages of the world* (22nd ed.). SIL International. Archived from the original on April 28, 2019.

Edwards, J. (2001). Multilingualism and multiculturalism in Canada. In G. Extra & D. Gorter (Eds.), *The other languages of Europe* (pp. 315–332). Multilingual Matters.

Edwards, J. R. (2010). *Minority languages and group identity: Cases and categories*. John Benjamins.

Ferguson, C. A. (1959). Diglossia. *Word, 15*(2), 325–340.

Fishman, J. A. (1989). *Language and ethnicity in minority sociolinguistic perspective*. Multilingual Matters.

Greenberg, J. H. (1956). The measurement of linguistic diversity. *Language, 32*(1), 109–115.

Gupta, A. F. (1994). *The step-tongue. Children's English in Singapore*. Multilingual Matters.

Gupta, A. F. (1998). The situation of English in Singapore. In J. A. Foley, T. Kandiah, Z. Bao, A. F. Gupta, L. Alsagoff, C. L. Ho, L. Wee, I. S. Talib, & W. Bokhorst-Heng (Eds.), *English in new cultural contexts: Reflections from Singapore* (pp. 106–126). Oxford University Press.

Haeri, N. (2000). Form and ideology: Arabic sociolinguistics and beyond. *Annual Review of Anthropology, 29*(6), 1–87.

Hamers, J. F., & Blanc, M. H. A. (1989). *Bilinguality and bilingualism*. Cambridge University Press.

Hinton, L. (2001). Language revitalization: An overview. In L. Hinton & K. Hale (Eds.), *The Green book of language revitalization in practice* (pp. 1–18). Brill.

Hinton, L. & Hale, K. (Eds.) (2001). The Green book of language revitalization in practice.. Brill.

Hinton, L., Huss, L., & Roche, G. (2018). *The Routledge handbook of language revitalization*. Routledge.

Leimgruber, J. R. E. (2013). *Singapore English. Structure, variation, and usage*. Cambridge University Press.

Leimgruber, J. R. E., Siemund, P., & Terassa, L. (2018). Singaporean students' language repertoires and attitudes revisited. *World Englishes, 37*(2), 282–306.

Lieberson, S. (1964). An extension of Greenberg's linguistic diversity measures. *Language, 40*(4), 526–531.

Lucko, P. (2003). Is English a "killer language"? In P. Lucko, L. Peter, & H.-G. Wolf (Eds.), *Studies in African varieties of English* (pp. 151–165). Peter Lang.

McRae, K. D. (1983). *Conflict and compromise in multilingual societies*. Wilfried Laurier University Press.

Mesthrie, R., & Bhatt, R. M. (2008). *World Englishes: The study of new varieties*. Cambridge University Press.

Myhill, J. (1999). Identity, territoriality and minority language survival. *Journal of Multilingual and Multicultural Development, 20*(1), 34–50.

Newton, G. (1996). *Luxembourg and Lëtzebuergesch: Language and communication at the crossroads of Europe*. Clarendon Press.

References

Office for National Statistics. (2020). *Population of the UK by country of birth and nationality: 2020*. Retrieved March 10, 2022, from https://www.ons.gov.uk/peoplepopulationandcommunity/populationandmigration/internationalmigration/bulletins/ukpopulationbycountryofbirthandnationality/2020

Research Centre on Multilingualism. (2004). *Euromosaic III—Cyprus*. Retrieved December 10, 2022, from https://publications.europa.eu/en/publication-detail/-/publication/4dc487cf-3c39-40ac-9b97-c55110263a56

Romaine, S. (2004). The bilingual and multilingual community. In T. Bhatia & W. C. Ritchie (Eds.), *The handbook of bilingualism* (pp. 385–406). Blackwell.

Ronan, P. (Fc). English in Switzerland. In K. Bolton (Ed.), *The Wiley Blackwell encyclopedia of World Englishes*. Wiley Blackwell.

Ronan, P., & Buschfeld, S. (2023). From second to first language: Language shift in Singapore and Ireland. In M. Schmalz, M. Vida-Mannl, S. Buschfeld, & T. Brato (Eds.), *Acquisition and variation in world Englishes: Bridging paradigms and rethinking approaches*. De Gruyter Mouton.

Rubin, J. (1968). *National bilingualism in Paraguay*. Mouton.

Schneider, E. W. (2007). *Postcolonial English. Varieties around the World*. Cambridge University Press.

SIL International. (2022). *How many languages are there in the world?* Retrieved July 2, 2022, from https://www.ethnologue.com/guides/how-many-languages

Skutnabb-Kangas, T. (2000). *Linguistic genocide in education—or worldwide diversity and human rights?* Erlbaum.

Stavans, A., & Hoffmann, C. (2015). *Multilingualism*. Cambridge University Press.

Stewart, W. A. (1968). A sociolinguistic typology for describing national multilingualism. In J. A. Fishman (Ed.), *Readings in the sociology of language* (pp. 531–545). Mouton.

Tan, Y.-Y. (2014). English as a 'mother tongue' in Singapore. *World Englishes, 33*(3), 319–339.

The Official Website of Berlin. (2022). *35 percent of Berliners with foreign roots*. Retrieved March 25, 2022, from https://www.berlin.de/en/news/6092347-5559700-berlin-inhabitants-with-foreign-roots.en.html

Trust for London. (2022). *London's non-UK born population by country of birth (2010 and 2020)*. Retrieved March 10, 2022, from https://www.trustforlondon.org.uk/data/country-of-birth-population/

Turell, M. T. (Ed.). (2001). *Multilingualism in Spain: Sociolinguistic and psycholinguistic aspects of linguistic minority groups*. Multilingual Matters.

United States Census Bureau. (2019). *DP02—Selected social characteristics in the United States: Miami City, Florida. 2019: American Community Survey 1-year estimates*. Retrieved March 10, 2022, from https://data.census.gov/cedsci/table?g=1600000US1245000&tid=ACSDP1Y2019.DP02

Vida-Mannl, M. (2022). *The value of the English language in global mobility and higher education: An investigation of higher education in Cyprus*. Bloomsbury.

Wiese, H. (2012). *Kiezdeutsch. Ein neuer Dialekt entsteht*. C. H. Beck.

Wiese, H. (2020). Contact in the city. In R. Hickey (Ed.), *Wiley handbook of language contact* (pp. 261–279). Wiley-Blackwell.

World Population Review. (2022a). *World city populations 2022*. Retrieved March 25, 2022, from https://worldpopulationreview.com/world-cities

World Population Review. (2022b). *Immigration by country 2022*. Retrieved March 10, 2022, from https://worldpopulationreview.com/country-rankings/immigration-by-country

Key Reading

Stavans, A., & Hoffmann, C. (2015). *Multilingualism*. Cambridge University Press.

Further Readings

Aronin, L., & Singleton, D. (2008). Multilingualism as a new linguistic dispensation. *International Journal of Multilingualism, 5*(1), 1–16.

Edwards, J. (2008). Societal multilingualism: reality, recognition and response. In P. Auer & L. Wei (Eds.), *Handbook of multilingualism and multilingual communication* (pp. 447–467). De Gruyter Mouton.

Hinton, L., Huss, L., & Roche, G. (2018). *The Routledge handbook of language revitalization.* Routledge.

Multilingualism Between Identities, Ideologies, and Language Policies

Contents

7.1 **Introduction** – 150

7.2 **Identities** – 150
7.2.1 Defining Identities – 150
7.2.2 Language and Identity – 152

7.3 **Attitudes and Ideologies** – 157
7.3.1 Defining Language Attitudes – 157
7.3.2 Defining Language Ideologies – 158
7.3.3 Effects of Language Ideologies – 161

7.4 **Policies** – 164

References – 171

© The Author(s), under exclusive license to Springer Nature Switzerland AG 2023
S. Buschfeld et al., *Multilingualism*,
https://doi.org/10.1007/978-3-031-28405-2_7

7.1 Introduction

The question of who is multilingual is not only difficult to answer scientifically (cf. ▶ Sect. 3.2), but the answer to this question is also influenced to a very large extent by the societal and political contexts that speakers and speaker groups experience. This chapter addresses three factors that determine which languages speakers are likely to want to use within their habitats: identities, attitudes, and language policies; these factors constitute a gradient from personal choice to societal pressure. The chapter starts off by thematising the influence of speakers' identities on language choice and use. Further, it is shown that language use is not only determined by speakers' personal identities, but also by what the speakers are made to feel about their languages by other members of society, and that those members of society in turn are influenced by what their attitudes are about the other population groups. These feelings impact language ideologies. Having discussed identity and ideology, the chapter ends with insights into how language policies can contribute to the protection of multilingualism and of linguistic rights of minority and majority speaker groups.

7.2 Identities

In our globalised world, many people have left their country of birth, have parents who stem from somewhere else, or have experienced life in different countries. As a result, these people have been in contact with different cultures and different linguistic environments and may live with multiple identities. But what exactly is an identity? And what is its connection to language and culture? Let us explore these issues in more detail.

7.2.1 Defining Identities

Any individual can have multiple and multi-layered identities, and such identity construction is influenced by different aspects. Amongst these, we have ethnicity, race, nationality, migration, gender, sexuality, religion, social class, or language. However, beyond these relatively stable factors, identity is also formed by less stable, performative factors, such as power relations within the economic, cultural, or social fields (Block, 2006, 2007). In an influential study on identity in educational contexts, Gee (2001) argues that the following forces play a role in the construction of identities: (1) *nature-identity*: these are states of identity that we have received by forces of nature, such as being an identical twin; (2) *institution-identity*: these are identities that have been authorised by authorities within a society or institution, for example being a university professor or a citizen of a certain country; (3) *discourse-identity*: an identity that is ascribed to us in the course of a discourse with interactants, who value us in different ways; and finally, (4) *affinity-identity*: these are based on shared experiences within groups, such as fandom or other shared activities or experiences. Gee (2001, p. 101) is of the opinion that in western society all these identities coexist, but that the fourth one has gained in importance.

Gee's discourse-identity in particular shows that we are not totally powerless in creating identities because, to a certain extent, we can create identities for ourselves: we might want to present ourselves as a successful business person who has become powerful and wealthy through success, has a lot of money to spend, and can afford anything they want. If others view us as we would wish to be viewed, we have convinced them of this identity, and we have managed to create what can then be called an *achieved identity* (Gee, 2001). However, others may also disregard the identity that we have created for ourselves. People might refer to a person, in spite of their carefully created successful business person image, as a "jumped-up nobody" or even more traditionally as somebody "giving themselves airs and graces", and point to that person's humble past instead. They would hold on to an *ascribed identity* that does not match the one that the person might have wished to create for themselves. In reaction to such a view of others, the person in question may either accept the ascribed identity or continue trying to be recognised in terms of the desired achieved identity. However, unfortunately, identity construction is not an entirely free choice but is constrained by the social and societal contexts in which we construct our identity—not everyone can pass as super-rich or convince other people that they are successful, charismatic influencers. According to Gee (2001, p. 113), our identities are constructed in discourse and may reproduce social inequality, where the elites ascribe discourse-identities to the non-elites, who may internalise these ascribed identities and accept their own powerless identities as well as those of the more powerful elites.

As argued by Gee (2001), Block (2006, 2007), and others, identities nowadays are typically viewed as co-constructed by the speakers themselves in their interactions with others. The identities are also influenced by communities of practice, shared beliefs, and values. Block notes that identities develop through interaction with others in communities of practice, regardless of whether they have shared beliefs, motives, and values or not. Here *communities of practice* are defined as people who engage mutually in an endeavour (Block, 2015, p. 527). They develop across space and time and extend from local to global contexts and from immediate to long-term time scales. A community of practice may, for example, be people who are fans of a certain music style and its culture, hip-hop or rap for example, and participate in the culture attached to it. Or people who participate in a certain sport and its sports culture may be said to form a community of practice, be it soccer or other types of football, or horse-racing. Furthermore, communities of practice might also be formed by online-activities, such as gaming or online networks. Each individual may be seen as both being shaped by and shaping emergent social, cultural, and historical structures through negotiation processes during their lives. These processes of description and self-description and positioning and self-positioning lead to the construction of identities. The identities may be created in relation to other people that the individuals come in contact with, or they may be created in contrast to other people in case the individual wants to be different from their environment (Block, 2015, p. 527). This view of identity can be called a social constructivist approach (e.g. Evans, 2014): our interactions in society shape our identities. The identities of individuals are shaped by society as the individuals struggle against different population groups for power over economic, cultural, and social capital (Block, 2015, referring to Bourdieu, 1984). In addition, also socio-demographic categories are often said to be responsible for the formation of identities. Traditionally, these socio-demographic categories which are responsible for identity formation are said to be ethnicity, race, nationality, migration, gender, sexuality, religion, and social class. To these, we should also add language, which plays a further important role. On the one hand, it is spoken language which we use to express our identities. Block (2015, p. 529) adds that in addition to the way that we decide to speak, other semiotic and non-linguistic choices, too, can express our identity: body movements, gaze, or clothing for example. Interactional features also play a large role, and so do actions and mental processes like our way of thinking, our beliefs, and our values. All these features help to express who we are and who we want to be in our interactions with others.

7.2.2 Language and Identity

Important work on the role that language plays in identity construction has been carried out by Le Page and Tabouret-Keller (1985). Le Page and Tabouret-Keller studied language use amongst West Indian and Caribbean Creole speakers in London. Based on their work, Tabouret-Keller (1998) observes that language influences our identity construction along two important axioms: on the one hand, cultural transmission of identity is carried out through language, both inside and outside the family. On the other hand, the language choices that we make identify us as members of certain groups. In ▶ Sect. 2.2, we have seen that national identities have often been tied to specific languages. Being Portuguese, you would be expected to speak Portuguese, as a Russian you would speak Russian, as a Japanese, you would speak Japanese. The symbolic value of language as a marker of belonging to a certain group is often accepted and we argue that in addition to transporting linguistic content, our use and choice of language also function as a marker of identity. For this reason, a number of states that gained independence from a former coloniser have tried to (re-)establish a national language that is different from that of the coloniser. When India and Pakistan gained independence in 1967, Mahatma Ghandi tried to establish Hindustani as a common language; when Ireland strove for independence at the end of the nineteenth century, there was a huge surge in interest in the Irish language. Ousting the colonial language and returning to a local language symbolises a different national identity than that which had been imposed by the coloniser (Maher, 2017). Furthermore, regional divisions can also be epitomised by language. A Franco-Canadian is Canadian, but clearly belongs to one of the two linguistic majority groups of the country. Similarly, the Suisse-Romand(e) or the Suisse-Allemand(e) clearly identify as belonging to either the French-speaking or the German-speaking Swiss population.

7.2 · Identities

Linguistic choices are an important determinant in identity construction. According to Le Page and Tabouret-Keller (1985, p. 14), speakers use utterances as acts of identity, but in their utterances, they also display their search for their social roles. By either stressing their ethnic or their social solidarities or differences, speakers construct their identities in a discourse situation. These may change according to who speakers are speaking to in any given situation. Throughout speakers' lives, their identities evolve and change over time with changing circumstances of the speakers' lives. Identities can thus be argued to be socioculturally constructed narratives (Le Page & Tabouret-Keller, 1985; Eckert & McConnell-Ginet, 1992). We can make clear who we are or as who we want to be seen by varying sociolinguistic features such as accent or by making lexical, morphological, or syntactic choices. We may, for example, decide to use a slang term or a local dialectal lexical item to refer to something or someone, or we may use careful accent and diction, and indeed the choice of one or the other variety of language indexes who we are or who we want to be.

How important a role language plays in identity construction can be seen in two examples given in Tabouret-Keller (1998). On the one hand, Ancient Greeks classified everyone who they could not understand as barbarians, based on their speech, which sounded like *barbarbar* to the Greeks. These Ancient Greeks identified people who did not speak their language as belonging to a different group, as foreigners, on the basis of not understanding their language. In contrast to the Ancient Greeks identifying others, we can also use language to identify ourselves. Tabouret-Keller cites an interview with a Belizean school boy, who identifies as Belizean on the basis that he and other Belizeans speak Belizean Creole. Both self-identification and other-identification have in common that they create in-groups and out-groups: based on Gumperz (1982), we can distinguish a *we-group* that uses "our" language and a *they*-group that uses a different language. Linguistic features can be central in differentiating "us" and "them". For example, a minority language can be used as *we-code* to index solidarity and closeness within the in-group. This code may stand in contrast to a *they-code* that is used by the speakers of a majority language, which may index the power and authority that are held by the majority group.

Tabouret-Keller points to the possible drastic consequences of such linguistic out-group creation as described in the Old Testament, which describes an example of in-group versus out-group marking through the pronunciation of the Hebrew word *shibbólet*. After losing battle against the Gileads, the people of Ephraim tried to flee across the river Jordan, where Gilead soldiers were trying to intercept the Ephraimites. In order to find out who is an Ephraimite, the Gileads made every passer-by pronounce the word *shibbólet* (denoting the head of a stalk of wheat or rye). In contrast to the Gileads, the people of Ephraim pronounced the initial consonant not as [ʃ], but as an [s], and they were then identified as enemies and killed (The Bible, Book of Judges 12, pp. 5–6). As Tabouret-Keller (1998) argues, the use of specific linguistic features thus binds together individual identities and social identities.

We see that by using language in a certain way in interaction with the society around us, we are representing who we are or who we want to be. We can transport our identities through overall language choice: do you choose to speak a minority language when interacting with speakers who may (potentially) belong to a majority group—such as ordering a coffee in a bar in Dublin speaking Irish rather than English or addressing a police officer in San Sebastian in Basque rather than in Spanish? But linguistic identities can also be transported by lower-level choices such as using specific phonetic features, specific words and expressions, names, or syntactic structures. Specific phonetic features, such as using stops instead of dental fricatives, may, for example, index certain Irish identities when speaking English. The same may hold true for lexical choices, such as using the word *guard* instead of *police officer*, or employing the morphosyntactic feature of the *after*-perfect, such as "I'm not coming to the restaurant—I'm just after having my dinner", to indicate (recent) completion of an action. While these features have high currency in Irish English, speakers of the variety may use them or avoid them when speaking to speakers of other varieties.

As Tabouret-Keller (1998) observes, the use of languages creates or overcomes boundaries. She stresses that while a language may extend throughout a certain territory or nation, this does not necessarily need to mean that the same territorial identity has to prevail in all that area. Nevertheless, she argues that the longer a territorial identity is embedded in a language the stronger is the focus on language as a marker of internal coherence. In ▶ Chap. 2, we saw that after the French revolution, the use of the French language was pushed throughout France in order to increase national coherence. Tabouret-Keller argues that modern nation-states often justify their state-hood with the help of mother-tongue discourses, claiming that a union exists through a common language. Yet at the same time, such a state may incorporate territories in which the state ignores the languages and identities of the people inhabiting these territories and force the state's own languages on these people. As an example, she gives the French overseas territories of Martinique and Guadeloupe, which, as French territories, have French as an official language, rather than local languages.

Typically, the dominated population groups are expected to (learn to) master the dominant language. Tabouret-Keller points out that in such cases various distributions between citizenship identity, national identity, and language use identity can be found. The multilingual situations that arise in such cases can have different outcomes. For example, a multilingual speaker of a minority language may display language contact features when speaking the majority language. In cases where the speaker belongs to a less powerful population group speaking the majority language, this may lead to being discriminated against by the majority group or to the member of the minority group feeling inferior or excluded by the majority. An example of such linguistic discrimination are speakers of Irish or Irish English while Ireland was still under British administration and in the decades after independence. Of course, this example can be extended to other population groups worldwide who are dominated by powerful majorities.

By contrast, the observation of language contact features in multilingual speakers may also lead to bonding and feelings of similarity, recognition, and complicity among the speakers of this variety. The speakers may use the variety as their *we-code* to distinguish themselves from the dominant group of speakers of the majority language. Of this, we find ample evidence: expressing identity through the use of African-American Vernacular English, of Multicultural London English, or Multicultural Paris French, by using the French variety of Verlan-French, or by using German Kiezdeutsch, which is influenced by immigrant varieties of German (for details on the latter example, see ▶ Sect. 6.3.4). Thus, by deciding for a certain language from their repertoire or by using specific linguistic features in a given situation, a speaker creates an identity according to a given situation: a young central Londoner with Nigerian roots may decide to address a interlocutor in a conversation in Standard British English, in Igbo or Yoruba, or in Nigerian Pidgin English, depending on the circumstances in which the conversation takes place or on the level of rapport that the speaker wants to create with the interlocutor.

Depending on their attitudes to their own population group and other population groups, speakers may try and sound more like speakers of a different group than the one they originally belonged to. According to Giles' (1973) *accommodation theory,* speakers are likely to want to identify with a different population group than their own under specific circumstances. Typically, speakers feel most encouraged to identify with a different population group if they only weakly identify with their own group and if the language of their own group is not important to them. Speakers are also likely to want to identify with a different population group if they are dissatisfied with the status of their original social group. For example, this might be the case if they do not think that the ethnolinguistic vitality of their own group is strong or if they perceive the identity of their own group as vague. If they identify less with their own ethnic group than with other identity markers, such as profession, gender, or religious identity, they are also likely to identify with another population group. If a speaker wants to take on a new linguistic identity, a number of features need to be met. According to Tabouret-Keller (1998), the speaker, first, needs to be able to identify with a new group, they need to have access to the group to be able to observe them closely, they need to have a powerful motivation to join the new group, and, finally, they need to be able to modify their own linguistic behaviour sufficiently to be able to join the new group. In trying to become part of the new group, the speaker may either be encouraged or discouraged from doing so by their chosen group. Speakers or groups of speakers may ascribe a certain identity to other speakers or groups, they impose identities on the other group. We often find *imposed identities* in discourses about different population groups, who may be negatively ascribed as, for example, being lazy, dangerous, or criminal, and, on occasion, such discourses are also perpetrated by media. In the discourses between any speakers or groups of speakers, we may have *assumed linguistic identities*, often those of majority groups, which most typically are not contested. We may also have *negotiable identities* in the interaction if other participants of groups oppose the participant's identities (Pavlenko & Blackledge, 2004; see also ▶ Sect. 7.3 below). An interesting example of the construction of linguistic identity is given by Pavlenko and Blackledge (2004, p. 1):

> In 1948, Golda Meir, a Kyiv-born Jew, who later became the fourth Prime Minister of Israel, was the Israeli Ambassador in Moscow and attended a party, where a well-known Russian writer with Jewish background addressed her in Russian. Golda Meir answered – in English – that she did not speak Russian and asked him to speak English to her. The writer replied to her that he hated Russian-born Jews who spoke English. She replied to him that she was sorry for Jews who could not speak Hebrew, or at least Yiddish.

Here we see an example of the construction and negotiation of identities: even though two people with apparently similar background—Jews born in then-Soviet Union states—interact, a common language and a common identity are not established: the writer felt Russian and expected other people from the then-Soviet Union states to speak Russian, too. Meir, by contrast, felt Jewish and communicated that Jews should be able to speak Hebrew or Yiddish.

Overall, Pavlenko and Blackledge argue that in multilingual contexts identities are negotiated within the options which are available to the speakers within the sociohistoric contexts of the time and that different identity options are valued differently and may or may not even be available at different times. They further argue that some identity options are imposed on the speakers, others are assumed (uncontested) and yet others are negotiable (contested). Some people may also be in search of means to resist imposed identities and produce new identities (2004, p. 27).

As results of language and cultural contact situations, various outcomes can be found. Thus, as Maher (2017) indicates, different types of identity can arise and we can find multicultural multilinguals, monocultural multilinguals, or multicultural monolinguals. Particularly in the case of local minority languages coming in contact with majority languages, speakers may identify with the minority (language) culture, such as Welsh in Britain, Catalan in Spain, or Basque in France. Alternatively, especially in migration contexts, we may also find population groups who may want to shed their former identities, for example because they associate negative experiences with their former identities or because they do not experience their former identities as being valued. Alternatively, the migration experiences may also lead to double identities which are composed of the two cultures, such as Anglo-Irish, Irish-American, or Asian-American (Maher, 2017, pp. 93–94).

An interesting facet of multilingual, multi-ethnic, and multicultural contexts as we often find it in large cities or urban areas is that of *metroethnicity*. Maher (2017, pp. 92–93) argues that, particularly if you live in ethnically diverse environments, you may be able to choose certain ethnic affiliations for cultural reasons, such as the cultural capital that they carry. This might involve learning a heritage language because it makes you feel connected with a culture that you want to feel connected with because it carries this capital. Maher gives the example of the revival of the Irish language in urban Ireland. The cultural capital of the Irish language has been boosted by an international upsurge of interest in Irish music and culture, which, in turn, has made the language and its culture more attractive in its original territory again as well.

Even beyond marking identity, different languages have even been argued to influence how we see and understand the world around us. This approach is known as *linguistic relativism*, also known as Whorfianism or, with reference to Whorf's former teacher Edward Sapir, the Sapir-Whorf hypothesis. Whorf argued that we understand nature on the basis of the linguistic categories that we possess. In the earlier, strong version of the hypothesis, which was based on Ancient Greek and German humanist thinking, it was suggested that our language actually determines our worldview. However, it speaks against such a strong hypothesis that even speakers of those languages that do not distinguish, for example, different shades of green by using different words for them, or that do not have separate words for different types of snow, are conceptually able to see the differences within these categories without needing to verbalise them. As human cognition works similarly for all human beings, it seems questionable how different our understanding of natural categories could be.

Generally, we have seen that linguists typically view identities as co-constructed in the speakers' interactions with others. Identities can adapt and change over time depending not only on the speakers' environments but also on who we are interacting with at a given time and which image we want to portray to them. As such, our identities are influenced by the communities of practice we interact with, by our shared beliefs about what is desirable or not and what is valuable and what is not.

7.3 Attitudes and Ideologies

Cultural concepts of language and language users can manifest themselves in various guises: they can be observed in language attitudes, in the prestige of languages, in their standards, and in the results of language contact between the languages. Language ideologies may then be responsible for whether and how languages are acquired, and whether and how they are used in private and institutional discourse. Valorisation of linguistic communities and their languages has various effects on language contact situations and the multilingualism of speakers. If a language or language variety is not valued within a community, the speakers of that language may be less inclined to continue using their language, which leads to various outcomes for the affected language, such as higher or lower rates of borrowing in the languages involved in the contact situation, or even language shift and eventually language loss within minority groups (Woolard, 1998).

7.3.1 Defining Language Attitudes

Baker (1992, p. 10) points out that the status of a language in society can most readily be deducted on the basis of attitudes to this language. Attitudes are not a concrete but an abstract, hypothetical construct and must be inferred from people's external behaviour. Observing attitudes towards something or someone can help researchers to explain and predict behaviour towards this entity. Following Ajzen (1988), Baker defines an attitude as the "disposition to respond favourably or unfavourably to an object, person, institution or event" (Ajzen, 1988, p. 4, cf. Baker, 1992, p. 11). Attitudes are frequently seen as consisting of three components: the first is a cognitive component, which consists of the thoughts and beliefs a person will have towards an entity. The second component is affect, which refers to the feelings that somebody will have about an entity, such as hate or love. Finally, the third component is that of readiness for action, which relates to how willing a person is to act on their beliefs or their feelings; for example are they willing to actually join language classes (cf. Baker, 1992, pp. 12–13)? Generally, language attitude studies assume that while languages can be compared linguistically, speakers have subjective attitudes to languages which are based on the social status of the given speaker groups. It has been investigated (Giles & Smith, 1979; cf. Appel & Muysken, 1987, p. 19) whether language (varieties) themselves could be better or worse (inherent value hypothesis) or whether the evaluation of different varieties is influenced by attitudes towards speaker groups (imposed norm hypothesis). It could be shown that varieties were rated more or less positively by informants who know the sociolinguistic situation of the speakers, but that the ratings by informants who did not know the specific linguistic features and the population groups which the varieties were associated with were different.

On the one hand, attitudes to language are investigated by observing respondents' behaviour towards a language (*behaviourist approach*) or by assuming that there is an internal mental state that conditions people's behaviour towards a stimulus (*mentalist approach*). Typically, research on language attitudes takes the latter perspective and tries to determine mental states towards language by inferring attitudes from self-reported data or from behaviour. To do so, either questionnaire or interview studies are used, or the so-called *matched guise technique* (see ▶ Chap. 13 on how to collect linguistic data). In the latter, informants' attitudes towards a language are tested by recording a number of bilingual speakers in both of their languages and by asking the respondents about what their attitudes are towards the recorded speakers. Thus, informants may rate the recorded speakers as intelligent, successful, friendly, or trustworthy in one language and as unintelligent, unfriendly, unsuccessful, or unreliable when speaking in their other language. It has been shown that depending on which of the two languages are spoken by the speakers, the reported attitudes differ considerably. For example, early research on this was carried out on attitudes to English and French in Canada (Lambert et al., 1960). Lambert and his co-authors tested attitudes towards French-speaking and English-speaking Canadians. To do so, they played recordings of bilingual French and English speakers to French-speaking and English-speaking Canadians. They could show that the attitudes were considerably more negative towards a speaker when the speaker was speaking in French than when speaking in English. Notably, it was the French speakers who rated French-speaking Canadians more negatively than the English-speaking Canadians did (cf. Appel & Muysken, 1987, pp. 18–19).

7.3.2 Defining Language Ideologies

Ideologies have been investigated from various perspectives and different disciplines conceptualise ideologies differently. Thus, ideologies may be understood as mental phenomena with subjective representations, beliefs, or ideas. Following

7.3 · Attitudes and Ideologies

Blommaert and Verschueren (1998, p. 25), Horner and Weber (2018, 2020) define ideologies as fundamental and commonsensical ideas and attitudes related to aspects of social reality which are often normative. Ideologies may be seen as discursive rationalist reports of the world (Woolard, 1998, p. 6, referring to Gouldner 1976), but have more recently also come to be seen as not conscious and deliberate, but as behavioural, prereflective, and structural. By focusing on selective parts of reality only, ideologies can lead to simplification and stereotypes. Further, ideologies are often conceptualised based on the interests of certain, often powerful parts of society; in this approach, ideologies must be seen as dependent on the societies they exist in. Ideologies can also be used as tools to obtain or maintain social, political, or economic power of the social elites. For example, if one population group is systematically or repeatedly characterised in negative terms, this population group may be kept away from powerful positions in a society. In that respect, ideologies can also be understood as distortive. Woolard (1998, p. 7) points to Parsons (1959), who views distortions as well as selectivity as an essential part of all ideologies. Correspondingly, Woolard argues that truth is understood by some, especially Foucault (1970, 1980), as constituted only by discourses of power.

As argued above, languages, and our evaluations of them, are influenced by our attitudes to their speakers. These, in turn, are determined by our societies and cultures and are connected to identities, aesthetics, morality, and epistemology. Ideologies are based on societal divisions and all social institutions that perpetuate differences, such as religion, child socialisation, gender relations, nation-states, schooling, and the law (Woolard, 1998, p. 3).

Language ideologies can be found in linguistic practices and many researchers see cultural conceptions and social power as crucial features of (language) ideologies. The *one nation-one language ideology* has been mentioned as a key example of such an ideology (Coulmas, 2018; Horner & Weber, 2018; see ▶ Sect. 6.4 on the language-and-territory principle). A further frequently encountered ideology is the *standard language ideology*. By this ideology, in particular, linguistic capital is ascribed to certain varieties of a language, such as Standard British English or *Hochdeutsch* ('high German'). A good example of this standard language ideology is the promotion of Standard French by the *Académie Française*, whose use is proscribed for educational and political bodies and the media. Language uses that do not correspond to the standards that are set by the *Académie*, for example using loan words from English or other languages, are sanctioned as they contravene an ideology of *linguistic purism*, which aims to keep foreign elements out of a given language. However, there is opposition to such ideologies. Evans (2014, p. 31) points to the French sociolect of Verlan, which is based on modified French with the addition of North African and Eastern European lexical items, and is used to express a cultural identity that does not conform to these standard ideologies.

Further, ideologies are observed in talking about language at a meta-level, namely at metalinguistic or metapragmatic levels; even beyond what is said, meaning can be transported (Woolard, 1998, pp. 9–10). As a result of these factors, the point in analysing language ideologies is not only to analyse the social roots of these ideologies but also the question of how they transform the reality they comment on. For this, Woolard (1998, p. 11) refers to Eagleton (1991) and his concept of the performative aspect of ideology. In parallel to Austin's speech act theory (Austin, 1962), Eagleton sees ideology as in fact contributing to the creation of the social world which it describes. In earlier linguistic approaches, such as structuralism, ideologies were not considered to have much influence on language features. A number of newer approaches view this differently, however, and language ideologies are increasingly seen as shaping verbal practices and discourse genres. According to Silverstein (1985; cf. Woolard 1998), ideologies can affect linguistic structures, and in particular lead to analogical language change: aspects of experiences are generalised and then extended to broader categories, which, as a result, are restructured. Such restructuring of categories to make them more regular is due to the rationalisation of these categories. As an example of this, Silverstein (1985) presents the example of the use of 2nd person singular and plural pronouns by British Quakers. In English language history, the former 2nd person singular pronoun *thee/thou* had developed into a familiar (singular) pronoun *thou*, and the former plural pronoun *ye/you* became the more formal and polite *you*, which is still used today to denote both singular and plural. However, as the Bible used the familiar *thee/thou* form and as the Quakers believed that everyone was created equal and no-one was better than anyone else before God, they continued using the *thee/thou* forms. Silverstein argues that this linguistic behaviour reinforced a trend for non-Quakers, conditioned by social and societal changes, to increasingly abandon the *thee/thou* forms in order not to be taken for Quakers themselves (Silverstein, 1985, pp. 251–252). This example shows how groups of people (non-Quakers), who do not wish to be seen as belonging to a certain social group (Quakers), avoid using the linguistic behaviour that is associated with that particular group.

A similar case is presented by Kulick (1992), who shows how comparable language ideologies lead an entire community to increasingly shift from their own community language, Taiap, to a different language. In Gapun, an isolated village community in Papua New Guinea, the population traditionally used ritualised, gender-specific social practices. One of these language-specific practices carried out in the Taiap language was that women publicly expressed their anger in a discourse genre known by the Tok Pisin word *kros* ('anger'), largely using shouting and insults. These traditional expressions of anger are disparaged by men and perpetuated the role of women as irresponsible. Men, by contrast traditionally used language practices that focus more on all-male, seemingly more rational discourses in meeting-houses. In these male discourses, Tok Pisin, the widely used language of Papua New Guinea, is often used in addition to Taiap as it symbolises education and economic success. Kulick (1992) argues that in order to avoid being evaluated negatively for using traditional language practices, the practices themselves are increasingly avoided. For the Gapun community in Papua New Guinea this means that by using the national language Tok Pisin, community members can show their connection to the modern world. Using the local language, Taiap, by contrast, is connected with negatively valued aspects of life. Kulick (1992, pp. 294–295) argues that the use of such particular linguistic practices reinforces ideologies not only about language but also about gender and affect. In the case of Gapun and the use of the Taiap language, these ideologies are fuelling language shift and, eventually, most likely language loss. Kulick (1992, p. 282) points out that children were no longer learning the language, and by the time of his study, in 1992, nobody under 14 years of age was able to speak it. Thus, both Silverstein's and Kulick's examples show how social concepts about certain segments in a population group can change the linguistic behaviour of language communities.

7.3.3 Effects of Language Ideologies

The effects of language ideologies arguably become particularly apparent in multilingual communities. Questions of language maintenance or language shift can be viewed not only in sociolinguistic terms or in terms of historical language change, but also in terms of which ideologies cause such changes. Woolard (1998, pp. 16–17) points out that while the question of what causes language maintenance or alternatively language shift used to be seen as dependent on macro-social events. More recently, shifts or maintenance are thought to be due to people's belief about languages, social relations, or political and economic events. She outlines that public perception may only view the separate identity of a group, or this group's separate nationhood, as legitimate if this group speaks a separate language (cf. the concept of one nation—one language, introduced in ▶ Chap. 2 and revisited in ▶ Sect. 7.3.2). However, not all linguistic varieties will automatically be considered a language (see also ▶ Sect. 3.2). As Woolard shows, a language may not be accepted as a separate language by the larger population if a language only has a spoken but no written form. Also, public opinion may demand an official grammar of that variety in order to consider the variety a language—and not a 'mere' dialect. Languages may also be considered not to be 'proper' languages if strong language contact phenomena, like code-switching or creolisation, can be found in it. As a result, Woolard (1998, p. 18) argues that especially minority languages are often subjected to processes of standardisation in order to police the linguistic boundaries of such languages and to keep out unwanted influences from majority languages.

A different effect of language ideologies may be that ideologies can result in *indexicality*: once a linguistic feature or a specific variety is considered prestigious, users of this feature or speakers of this variety may be seen as having many other inherent positive values. This may, for example, be that they are seen as particularly intelligent or especially successful. Equally, language users who use stigmatised language features may be considered unintelligent or economically deprived. Such linguistic stereotyping can have even more negative effects: Woolard argues that where distinctive qualities are attributed to a speaker on the basis of this speaker's language variety, such as simple expressions, these speakers' language may automatically be perceived as simple, and anything that contradicts this stereotype will be ignored. This recursivity of stereotypes about the language users and the skewed perception of their language based on these stereotypes causes linguistic ideologies to be perpetuated.

As also pointed out by Coulmas (2018, pp. 63–64), while discrimination against population groups on various grounds, such as race, ethnicity, or social class, is usually considered illegal and unacceptable in democratic societies, discrimination on linguistic grounds typically is not: while somebody may not be discriminated against on the basis of their name or their skin-colour, their language variety may be deemed unacceptable or their pronunciation may be considered incomprehensible. Coulmas (2018) shows that, overall, ideologies are used to justify restrictions on language choices. This can be done by using language ideologies to connect individual languages with nations, heritages, and cultures. Ideologies can be used to make language policies, such as monolingualism, and their enforcement look rational and acceptable. Coulmas (2018, pp. 65–79) bases his argument on five questions. These are (1) whose language choices are restricted?, (2) who decides on restricting language choice?, (3) how restrictions on language choice are justified, (4) who enforces such restrictions and finally, (5) are such restrictions contested and who would contest them? First, he observes that, in contrast to religious choices which are free in many democratic countries, the language choices of different population groups are often restricted in modern states. Language choices are more frequently proscribed for individuals than for speaker groups. For example, there may be restrictions on which languages may be used for an oath of office or for a speech in parliament. Second, he observes that these restrictions are imposed at state level by statuary law, at (sub)-state level by institutional regulations, and at societal level by social attitudes. Third, he observes that such restrictions were historically justified by arguing that speaking minority languages leads to disadvantages for minority populations, but even now, it is seen as legitimate by some that language choices should be restricted by governments for the benefit of a state. If so, ideologies will be used to make this appear a reasonable choice. Fourth, Coulmas observes that the legitimate language is typically that of the socially dominant class(es), be it a minority in a country, such as colonisers, or a majority like larger population groups in a multilingual and multicultural state. This dominant variety is propagated in the school system. The use of other languages may either be proscribed against or the other languages may receive no recognition and no or insufficient funding and support. Finally, he observes that the restrictions of language choices are likely to be contested by the linguistically disadvantaged population groups—but examples can also be found where the majority language, especially if it is a world language or associated with economic success, may be preferred over local languages. In this assessment, Coulmas (2018, p. 78) argues that factors such as economic success and economic development play a large role.

Further, language ideologies may also determine the outcome of language contact at a lexical level. On the one hand, languages often borrow words for high-prestige concepts from high-prestige languages, such as Middle English borrowing *beef* from prestigious French *bœuf* ('cow'). Similarly, many contemporary languages copiously borrow cultural concepts from English. Yet not all borrowings necessarily indicate high regard for the contact language. Woolard (1998, p. 20) points to American English speakers' humorous misrepresentations of Spanish loan words which in fact show the disregard for not only the language but also its speakers. We also find negative regard for languages and speakers mirrored in negative connotations that a loan word may have in a language into which it is borrowed. Thus, the American English *shack* typically points to a house of a very low standard. This surely tells us something about the regard for the housing standards of speakers of the language from which this word was loaned into English, that is, the Irish Gaelic *teach* ('house'). The examples above have shown how ideologies can influence the use of language. In the following, two further examples of effects of language ideologies are described. The first example shows effects of conflicting standard language ideologies. The second example illustrates how languages can become symbols of political ideologies.

In Ireland, Irish was spoken well into the period after which British settlements had started. However, particularly during the nineteenth century, the number of Irish speakers dropped considerably and the use of English increased, largely due to socioeconomic reasons (e.g. Ronan, 2020). In present-day Ireland, there are some areas, largely in the more rural west of the country, where traditional varieties of Irish are still used as community languages. In contemporary Ireland, Irish is the first national language, even though it is not in fact spoken by every member of the population, and it is used daily by an even smaller percentage. English, by contrast, is the majority language and for the majority of the English-speaking population Irish is predominantly a subject that has to be taken in school. So on the one hand, we have a minority population of Irish speakers in rural communities who speak traditional varieties of the language and can be seen as the guardians of, and a resource of, the 'proper', traditional Irish language (O'Rourke & Brennan, 2019). On the other hand, during the last decades, an increasing number of all-Irish schools has also been founded, particularly in urban centres of Ireland. In those, after an initial acquisition phase, Irish is used as the sole language of instruction. This type of all-Irish school has facilitated a new movement of urban Irish speakers, for whom Irish is an L2 but may be either their main language in daily language use or play an important role in their lives. As it is a second language variety, however, this Irish typically exhibits strong influence by English language phonology as well as structural features which are due to language acquisition and language contact phenomena. If and where speakers of these two varieties, the traditional native speaker variety and the modern urban, 'new speaker' variety come into contact, two different ideologies clash. On the one hand, the traditional native speaker varieties are seen as the authentic legitimate variety of Irish and the Irish-speaking areas as the safeguards of the language (O'Rourke & Brennan, 2019). Every summer, Irish school students from all over the country are sent to these traditional Irish-speaking areas in order to improve their Irish in these natural settings. The traditional Irish is seen as the authentic standard language which is the ultimate goal of language acquisition. In contrast to the traditional native speaker varieties, the new varieties of Irish with their English-influenced phonology and structures are seen by many traditional speakers as deficient (e.g. Coughlan, 2021). On the other hand, language mixing in general, including code-switching, is frequent in Irish language use in the traditional Irish-speaking areas, particularly with younger speakers (cf. Coughlan, 2021), and both school students from outside the traditional Irish-speaking areas and new speakers of Irish from the all-Irish schools are typically taught to refrain from code-switching between Irish and English; violating this goal of linguistic purity of Irish is sanctioned. Coughlan (2021) shows how two competing ideologies are at work here: we find one standard language ideology, which aims for the traditional varieties of Irish and depreciates the new variety that shows influence from language contact features and is also the variety that is spoken by many non-proficient language learners. Yet, we find a second ideology, also a purist ideology, which sanctions against the—partly heavy—language mixing practices of (traditional) native speakers. In addition to purist language ideologies, language attitudes also play an important role here. Coughlan (2021, p. 58) points out that traditional Irish dialects are also often stereotypically viewed as backward, which can cause negative attitudes to these varieties in urban speakers and insecurities in the traditional speakers. The debate about the legitimacy of new varieties of Irish is ongoing and often fierce and leads to frequent dissatisfaction and disappointment amongst both speaker groups.

A strong example of this phenomenon can be found in language use in Northern Ireland, where in many cases political ideologies shape language use. Administratively, Northern Ireland belongs to the United Kingdom, while the Republic of Ireland separated from the UK after the Civil War in 1921. However, the Troubles, the violence that was particularly strong during the later 1960s, as well as the Peace Process during the late 1990s and afterwards make clear that societal divisions still existed in Northern Ireland after the independence of the Republic of Ireland and persist into the present day. The division has been caused by the Early Modern settlement of predominantly non-Catholic settlers from Great Britain in largely Catholic Ireland. Even though societal division largely focuses on religion, language enters the equation: Irish Gaelic, as the native language of pre-settlement Ireland, is associated with Irish identity, while many of the settlers of Ulster hailed from Scotland and spoke Scots. With the peace agreement in 1998, the language rights of the two population groups were recognised: both Irish and Ulster Scots obtained recognition and equal support. Already before this time, however, to speak Irish and to learn Irish was a strong identity marker of those Northern Irish who identified as Irish. In a similar vein, Wolf (2019) shows that those Northern Irish population groups, who are most often Loyalist and who identify with the United Kingdom most strongly, are likely to use Ulster Scots features in their spelling most extensively. Wolf finds that a high density of Ulster Scots features in the writing of loyalist writers correlates with strong unionist political views.

7.4 Policies

After focusing on how individual speakers position themselves towards their language use and how society as a whole views language uses, we now move on to the question of the roles that authorities play in the maintenance of multilingualism and in the protection of linguistic rights. Language policies may be defined as the policies of authorities, such as governments, supra-national bodies, or local authorities, towards linguistic varieties in their jurisdiction. Linguistic varieties could be either clearly defined languages or dialects or other varieties of a language. Language policies are typically enacted by language planning. In addition to (state) authorities, language planning activities may also be undertaken by interest groups or even individuals who work on behalf of a language. Original research on language planning focuses on the development of majority and minority languages. Particularly in the later part of the twentieth century, there was a strong focus on language planning in decolonising countries. Here, countries were often faced with decisions as to which language(s) should be used as national language(s) as the country decolonised (Appel & Muysken, 1987; Spolsky, 2004, pp. 5–6; Spolsky 2012a, 2012b, pp. 5–6).

Where a language planning process takes place, the first stage of such language planning includes a survey of all the language varieties used in a community (initial fact finding). Such a survey determines which languages are spoken in the community, by how many people, and what the status of these languages is. Then a decision is taken on which language varieties should be given official status (this is known as status planning), then on how to implement the use of the chosen varieties and to determine how to enable the chosen varieties to fulfil their tasks as official languages (corpus planning). The second phase of language planning activities determines the objectives of the language planning process. A key component is the selection of languages which are chosen and supported. There may also be minority languages for which support may be given and which may be used in public life, that is, in administration and education, while other languages may not receive support or even be actively suppressed, which may then even lead to the ultimate decay of these languages (minority language treatment). For those languages that are adopted for official use, codification may either already exist or it will be introduced, for example to create a basis for making teaching materials. This may be done by creating grammars or dictionaries, so that the language can be standardised for written use. In case no written form exists of a language at all, a writing system must be chosen to represent it (graphisation). As a final step in the language planning process, modernisation may be needed. If a language becomes a medium of official communication, it must be able to express modern and international concepts. For this, it may be necessary to create new discourse styles, for example to allow formal written discourses, and style manuals may be created for this. A central point is the use of this language for the expression of modern concepts. This can be achieved in different ways. On the one hand, loan words may be chosen from contact languages to express the new concepts. In the case of a decolonising country, this may be from the language of the former coloniser. Often, however, this is avoided in order to break up the power structures that were implemented during the country's colonisation and other methods are sought (Appel & Muysken, 1987, pp. 51–54). For example, in the modernisation of the Irish language after the independence of Ireland from Britain, concepts for which no word existed were created from existing materials to capture the sense of the English lexical items. Thus, "car" officially became a *gluaisteán* ('moving thing'), "bike" was a *rothar* ('wheel'), and "motorbike" became *gluaisrothar* ('moving wheel'). Somewhat later, a "hoover" was a *folúsghlantóir*, literally a "vacuum cleaner". However, these loan translations are not widely accepted amongst native speakers of the Irish language and the use of corresponding Anglicisations is common.

In the third stage of language planning, implementation of the planning activities takes place. Implementation works via publicising the results of the activities, for example, by providing word-lists for the languages, by publishing grammars and, importantly, by providing financial support for language maintenance activities and for the production of teaching materials, books, and communication in the given language. Finally, after the planning process, the success of the planning activities will be measured in an evaluation. Successful examples of language planning can be found, for example, in the introduction of Swahili in Kenya, Uganda, and Tanzania, in the introduction of Bookmål and Nynorsk in Norway, as well as in the revival of Hebrew as the language of Israel (Appel & Muysken, 1987).

Language planning activities are strongly influenced by sociodemographic factors, especially by the questions how many speakers a language has and how the speakers are distributed geographically, this means whether there are clear spatial divisions between speaker groups. Should a language already be distributed throughout a territory, that may make it a good candidate as an official language for that territory. Linguistic factors also play an important role: if a language is already modernised, it may also be a better candidate for the status of official language than a language which, for example, may be widely spoken but does not yet have a written form. A further linguistic factor is the degree of linguistic similarity amongst different languages. The easier a language is to learn for everyone who may be expected to use it, the more suited it will be as a official language. Further, socio-psychological factors are important in the choice of official languages. If attitudes towards a language and towards the speakers of that language are generally positive, this will make the language more likely to be accepted by wider population groups. Further, political factors are of key importance: each language policy will be determined by the overall policies towards any given population group. Governing authorities that do not want to promote stronger individual identities of specific population groups are less likely to allow these groups strong language rights. As examples of these, we may give the restriction of the language rights of minorities under the Franco dictatorship in Spain or the repression of Celtic languages in the Celtic countries under British administration. Finally, religious factors play a role. With the promotion of specific religions, the languages associated with these may also be promoted. A case in point here is the use of Arabic in a number of North-African countries.

In contemporary research on language policies, there is a strong focus on the inter-relatedness of different societal factors in language policies. These are the language practices in a community, the values assigned to the language varieties by the community members, and, finally, the management or planning efforts that are made by community members to modify the language practices of other members of the community (Spolsky, 2012a, 2012b, p. 5). Firstly, according to Spolsky (2004, 2005, 2012a, 2012b), language policies are strongly influenced by language practices, this means by the different languages and varieties that are used by the community as well as by language beliefs and ideologies. Language management and planning activities by stakeholders in society aim to introduce policies and plans which try to change the practices and ideologies within the communities. Secondly, language policies can apply to different levels of language varieties. While they can aim to influence the choice of a given language variety, they can also aim at different levels of linguistic description, such as the variety's pronunciation, spelling, grammar, or lexicon. In the lexical domain, it may be obscene language or profanity, or what is generally known as 'bad' language, which is targeted in particular. Thirdly, the domains of language policies can be found in speech communities of any size. Language policies start already on family level. Here certain languages or varieties may be encouraged or enforced over others, such as heritage languages over community languages, or use of 'bad' language or slang may be prohibited or sanctioned. Language policies can also be found in larger groups, such as sports teams, villages, or companies, which might define one language as an official team, community, or company language. Particularly important here are policies for educational institutions, especially for schools, as the decision which languages are used as medium of instruction plays an important role in language socialisation and language maintenance. Furthermore, language policies can be enforced by states or by organisations at supra-state level. Here, we may think of the European Union, whose member states' languages are official languages of the union but not all of these have working language status within the European Union institutions (Ammon, 2012). Finally, Spolsky emphasises that language policy is influenced by a complex set of both linguistic and non-linguistic factors, variables, and elements, which influence the outcome of any language management decisions that are taken by language managers.

As seen in ▶ Sect. 2.2, particularly during the nineteenth century, national identity was repeatedly tied up with monolingual policies. In the contemporary world, we still find countries which are officially monolingual (see the elaborations on linguistic diversity in ▶ Sect. 6.2.1). Spolsky (2004) gives Iceland as a salient example, whose population of just under 300,000 are supposed to be monolingual in Icelandic. He points out that other countries, which have had monolingual policies for partly long times, may still not have entirely monolingual populations. Thus, for example in France, regional minority languages persist and partly experience revivals. Examples here are Basque, on the southern border to Spain, or Breton in Brittany. This shows that restrictive policies do not necessarily need to meet with the success that language planners or language managers expect. For contemporary states, other than migration, a further feature has emerged that renders complete monolingualism of their population increasingly less likely, and this is the increasing spread of English as a global language. As a result of the international success of the English language, policies that aim for the purity of their local languages and that try to keep out English language vocabulary in particular, are challenged. In spite of official language policies which restrict the use of loan words by institutions, individual language users happily use English terms, such as many European French speakers using "weekend" rather than *fin de semaine*.

Even though many nation-states name one official language in their constitution, in many cases considerably more complex linguistic situations can be found (Spolsky, 2004, 2005). In addition to autochthonous, this means indigenous, minority languages, often immigrant languages are found. For example, in the United States, we find many different languages of the original population groups, namely the first-nation languages as well as immigrant groups from China, Vietnam, or Poland, maintaining their heritage languages. Where an official language exists, pupils who are not proficient in that language at the time they join the school system must be given the opportunity to learn the language. This may, for example, be the case where a former colonial language is chosen as official language and pupils with different home languages need to reach sufficient proficiency in the official language to participate in education. However, particularly after independence of a formerly colonised country or the formation of a new state, we could also imagine that a language or languages are selected as the new official languages which have not been used for official functions before independence. Under those circumstances, the new official languages may at first need to be codified or standardised. A case in point is the introduction of Hebrew as the official language of Israel after the formation of the state.

Where multilingualism is recognised in a state, the languages within the state will be given specific linguistic spaces. Language choices can in fact be highly political. Thus Maher (2017, pp. 75–90) points out that a government may choose a single language to govern a country and to use it to create a unified state. A good example of this is France after the French revolution (cf. ▶ Sect. 2.2). Original non-speakers of the language may have been forced into using French but may have felt less comfortable expressing themselves in that language than in their (minority) language. If one language is selected as the main language, other majority or minority languages may be supported, may not receive support, or may even be actively suppressed. In some cases, multilingualism can be a complication for states and, as a result, monolingualism is preferred. In this vein, Maher (2017, p. 77) quotes President Theodore Roosevelt stating in 1919 that "[w]e have room for but one language in this country, and that is the English language […]". As a result of such monolingual policies, large and multiple population groups may be separated from their languages. Spolsky (2004, 2005) observes that the distribution of linguistic spaces can be undertaken according to demography: specific linguistic or ethnic groups use a specific language. An example of this could be found in Ireland or Wales, where citizens may either identify as Irish speakers or Welsh speakers and expect to be able to use that language in official conversations, or they may self-identify as English speakers and expect to conduct official business through English. Further, the partition of linguistic space may be according to locality: speakers of one or the other language may be in the majority in particular locations rather than in others. This is the case in Canada, where the majority of French speakers live in the eastern province of Quebec and the other provinces are predominantly English-speaking. Language partition can also be on the basis of language function: depending on the context of language use—whether it is private amongst friends or family, or official in business or education—one or another language is used. An example of this can be found in German-speaking Switzerland, where the Swiss German dialect is used for private functions and in informal media and business settings and standard German is in education and formal media (for a more detailed discussion of types of multilingual societies and patterns of multilingual organisation, see ▶ Chap. 6).

While a country may be formally monolingual or have a small number of official languages, language rights of minority populations are increasingly taken into consideration. As Spolsky (2004, 2005, pp. 2158–2159) observes, already post World War I, the Treaty of Versailles and the League of Nations stipulated that language rights of minorities should be considered in the countries affected by the war and the resulting displacement of population groups. After World War II, first human rights and avoidance of discrimination were stipulated by the newly formed United Nations. Subsequently, the Universal Declaration of Human Rights in 1948 specified that, amongst other criteria, language should not lead to discrimination. In 1960, voluntary separate education systems were established, for example for parents who wanted their children to be educated in languages other than the majority language (see also ▶ Chap. 8), by the UNESCO Convention against Discrimination in Education. From the last decades of the twentieth century onwards, increasingly more international conventions were introduced which also permitted linguistic minorities within the general population to address public authorities through their minority languages—if, as Spolsky (2005, p. 2159) outlines, the groups are large enough in numbers and the languages are not too difficult to manage for the officials. As a result of increasing individual rights, language rights, too, have been receiving more political recognition and play an increasingly important role in determining the language policies of political bodies. As a result, linguistic pluralism is increasingly recognised and language rights of minorities are more and more accepted. However, it is the local, autochthonous languages which are more likely to receive recognition than languages of immigrant populations and different language policies may hold for these. A minimal approach to recognising other languages is to provide access to state services through other languages; one of the most inclusive approaches is the possibility to allow minority groups to offer education through their own languages—as long as the majority language continues to be taught as well (cf. ▶ Chap. 8). For example, in France there has been a long-standing drive for regional minority languages like Breton and Basque to be allowed as languages in which the final state-exams can be taken.

When determining contemporary language policies, Spolsky (2004, 2005) identifies four key factors as important determinants. First, this is the sociolinguistic situation of a country or community: it is important which varieties are spoken in the community, what their speaker numbers are, and their societal status. Where population groups and their languages are marginalised, they are also at risk of being ignored in language management. Second, identities within the community play a large role. A country or community may wish to either have a unified identity or promote such a unified identity by focusing on one language as providing one identity to all community members. However, this unity may not be accepted by everyone and alternative identities may be embodied by using different linguistic varieties (see, e.g., the use of French in France versus the development of Verlan as an identity marker). Third, the influence of international languages, and here English in particular, is strongly felt in language policies. With increasing globalisation, English is perceived as a key to economic success by many language users worldwide. Thus, a demand for access to English language competencies can be found both at grassroots level and at language planning level. The results may be on the one hand, as we have seen in the case of French language policies, to try and restrict the influence of English by the introduction of corresponding language policies. On the other hand, the results may be official attempts to try and facilitate language acquisition of English, or, correspondingly, of other global languages, as has, for example, been the basis for Singapore's language policy of "English-based bilingualism" (Tickoo, 1996, p. 438). Fourth, the linguistic rights of different population groups are increasingly being recognised not only due to civil rights movements but also due to international conventions.

In summary, contemporary language policies of a nation are influenced by the country's sociolinguistic situation, its national ideology, the influence of world languages like English, and the acceptance of language rights of different population groups (Spolsky, 2005, p. 2157). Ultimately, Spolsky (2005, p. 2162) endorses Fishman's (1971) observation that a nation with a tradition of national unity and a language that is associated with it is likely to have a monolingual language policy. For this, France would be a prime example. A nation with not one tradition but differing traditions which have their own associated languages, by contrast, is likely to try and enact territorial or demographic compromises. For this, Canada or Belgium are good examples. Nations without their own great traditions or cultivated own languages are likely to either use a colonial language or support the use of an international language, particularly English. Good examples of this are the Philippines or Singapore, but here, English is used alongside a number of local languages that have entered the countries for various reasons over the course of time. As to the effectiveness of language policies, attitudes are divided. Spolsky (2005, p. 2163) points out that as a rule, the success of language management policies cannot be taken for granted. He argues that attempts by states to suppress non-official languages do not always meet with success: in France, regional languages still have speakers and supporters; in the former Soviet republics, local languages are revitalised increasingly after the collapse of the former Soviet Union; and especially attempts of using language management policies to try and reverse language shift often fail. Spolsky names Irish here and he further points out that for Hebrew revitalisation of the language was achieved, but stresses that the resulting revitalised variety of Hebrew is different from the original variety that was to be revived. The same in fact holds true for the Irish language: the traditional variety of Irish is receding, but new speakers of the language lead to an increasing revitalisation. Here, too, however, the resulting new variety of Irish differs in various characteristics from the traditional one and opinions on the new variety are divided to say the least (Coughlan, 2021, cf. ▶ Sect. 7.3.3 above).

❓ Exercises

1. Research on language and identity (starting with Le Page & Tabouret-Keller, 1985) argues that identities are constructed discoursively. Consider your own language use during the day.
    (a) When talking to different people (family, friends, teachers, when shopping), can you observe that you talk to them differently? Do you construct your identity differently as a family member, friend, student, or customer—if so, what linguistic means do you use to do so (word choice, pragmatics, pronunciation)?
    (b) Do you use different languages or language varieties in these contexts? Which ones do you use and why?

2. Coulmas (2018, p. 67) points out that the language choices of members of parliament may be restricted. Imagine parliament in your own country. Assuming that a member of parliament has a first language that is not the majority language,

   (a) Should members of parliament be allowed to address parliament in their own first language? Why or why not?
   (b) Does it make a difference whether this language is a local minority language (for example Frisian or Sorbian in Germany, Welsh in Britain, Basque in Spain or France, Quechua in Argentina) or an immigrant language (for example Polish in the United States, Vietnamese in Canada)?

Summary

In this chapter, we have seen how identities, language ideologies, and language policies interact with multilingual language use in society. It has been shown that identity is built by various components, including language and language use. Identities may be assumed, imposed, or negotiated. Language is tightly interrelated with identity formation as it can be both a symbol of and a focus point for identity formation. Furthermore, languages can be used as in-group or out-group markers, this means to exclude or include other people from a group. Whether speakers want to be associated with a social or linguistic group to a large extent depends on attitudes towards that group. Further, it has been shown that language ideologies play a role in the treatment of language varieties and they determine whether a language is perceived as a desirable marker of one's identity or not. Prevalent ideologies which have an impact on language use are the one nation-one language ideology or the standard-language ideology. Ideologies may be transferred from speakers to their languages and they may have the effect that some languages or varieties are preferred over others and may even lead to neglect or even loss of language varieties. Finally, in the discussion of policies, it has been shown that language planning is an important aspect of language policies. Planning processes are crucial in multilingual situations, especially where minority languages are involved. Such processes have various stages, from fact-finding to implementation and evaluation, and can be influenced by various factors, such as sociodemographic, linguistic, socio-psychological, religious, or political factors.

References

Ajzen, I. (1988). *Attitudes, personality, and behavior*. Dorsey Press.
Ammon, U. (2012). Language policy in the European Union (EU). In B. Spolsky (Ed.), *The Cambridge handbook of language policy* (pp. 570–591). Cambridge University Press.
Appel, R., & Muysken, P. (1987). Language contact and bilingualism. .
Austin, J. L. (1962). *How to do things with words*. Harvard University Press.
Baker, C. (1992). *Attitudes and language*. Multilingual Matters.
Block, D. (2006). *Multilingual identities in a global city: London stories*. Palgrave.
Block, D. (2007). *Second language identities*. Bloomsbury.

Block, D. (2015). Researching language and identity. In B. Paltrage & A. Phakiti (Eds.), *Methods in applied linguistics* (pp. 527–540). Bloomsbury.

Blommaert, J., & Verschueren, J. (1998). *Debating diversity: Analysing the discourse of tolerance.* Routledge.

Bourdieu, P. (1984). *Distinction: A social critique of the judgement of taste.* Routledge.

Coughlan, E. (2021). Accommodation or rejection? Teenagers' experiences of tensions between traditional and new speakers of Irish. *Journal of Sociolinguistics, 25*, 44–61.

Coulmas, F. (2018). *An introduction to multilingualism: Language in a changing world.* Oxford University Press.

Eagleton, T. (1991). *Ideology: An introduction.* Verso.

Eckert, P., & McConnell-Ginet, S. (1992). Think practically and act locally: Language and gender as community-based practice. *Annual Review of Anthropology, 21*, 461–490.

Evans, D. (2014). The identities of language. In D. Evans (Ed.), *Language and identity: Discourse in the world* (pp. 15–35). Bloomsbury.

Fishman, J. A. (1971). National languages and languages of wider communication in the developing nations. In W. H. Whiteley (Ed.), *Language use and social change: Problems of multilingualism with special reference to Eastern Africa* (pp. 27–56). Oxford University Press for the International African Institute.

Foucault, M. (1970). The archeology of knowledge. *Social Science Information, 9*(1), 175–185.

Foucault, M. (1980). *Power/Knowledge.* Penguin.

Gee, J. P. (2001). Identity as an analytic lens for research in education. *Review of Research in Education, 25*, 99–125.

Giles, H. (1973). Accent mobility: A model and some data. *Anthropological Linguistics, 15*, 87–105.

Giles, H., & Smith, P. (1979). Accommodation theory: Optimal levels of convergence. In H. Giles & R. St Clair (Eds.), *Language and social psychology.* Blackwell.

Gouldner, A. (1976). *The dialectic of ideology and technology.* The Seabury Press.

Gumperz, J. J. (1982). *Discourse strategies.* Cambridge University Press.

Horner, K., & Weber, J.-J. (2018). Introduction. In K. Horner & J.-J. Weber (Eds.), *Introducing multilingualism. A social approach* (2nd ed., pp. 3–13). Routledge.

Horner, K., & Weber, J.-J. (Eds.). (2020). *Introducing multilingualism. A social approach.* Routledge.

Kulick, D. (1992). Anger, gender, language shift and the politics of revelation in a Papua New Guinean village. *Pragmatics, 2*(3), 281–296.

Lambert, W. E., Hodgson, R. C., Gardner, R. C., & Fillenbaum, S. (1960). Evaluational reactions to spoken languages. *The Journal of Abnormal and Social Psychology, 60*(1), 44–51. https://doi.org/10.1037/h0044430

Le Page, R. B., & Tabouret-Keller, A. (1985). *Acts of identity.* Cambridge University Press.

Maher, J. C. (2017). *Multilingualism. A very short introduction.* Oxford University Press.

O'Rourke, B., & Brennan, S. C. (2019). Regimenting the Gaeltacht: Authenticity, anonymity, and expectation in contemporary Ireland. *Language & Communication, 66*, 20–28.

Parsons, T. (1959). The social structure of the family. In R. N. Anshen (Ed.), *The family: Its functions and destiny* (pp. 173–201). Harper and Row.

Pavlenko, A., & Blackledge, A. (2004). Introduction. New theoretical approaches to the study of negotiation of identities in multilingual contexts. In A. Pavlenko & A. Blackledge (Eds.), *Negotiation of identities in multilingual contexts* (pp. 1–33). Multilingual Matters.

Ronan, P. (2020). English in Ireland: Intra-territorial perspectives on language contact. In S. Buschfeld & A. Kautzsch (Eds.), *Modelling current linguistic realities of English world-wide: The extra and intra-territorial forces model put to the test* (pp. 322–346). Edinburgh University Press.

Silverstein, M. (1985). Language and the culture of gender: At the intersection of structure, usage, antideology. In E. Mertz & R. J. Parmentier (Eds.), *Semiotic meditation: Sociocultural and psychological perspectives* (pp. 219–259). Academic Press.

Spolsky, B. (2004). *Language policy.* Cambridge University Press.

Spolsky, B. (2005). Language policy. In J. Cohen, K. T. McAlister, K. Rolstad, & J. MacSwan (Eds.), *ISB4: Proceedings of the 4th international symposium on bilingualism* (pp. 2152–2164). Cascadilla Press.

References

Spolsky, B. (Ed.). (2012a). *The Cambridge handbook of language policy*. Cambridge University Press.
Spolsky, B. (2012b). What is language policy? In B. Spolsky (Ed.), *The Cambridge handbook of language policy* (pp. 3–15). Cambridge University Press.
Tabouret-Keller, A. (1998). Language and identity. In F. Coulmas (Ed.), *The handbook of sociolinguistics* (pp. 315–326). Blackwell.
Tickoo, M. L. (1996). Fifty years of English in Singapore: All gains, (a) few losses? In J. A. Fishman, A. W. Conrad, & A. Rubal-Lopez (Eds.), *Post-Imperial English: Status change in former British and American colonies, 1940-1990* (pp. 431–455). Mouton de Gruyter.
Wolf, G. (2019). Studying dialect spelling in its own right. Suggestions from a case study. In B. Birte & C. Claridge (Eds.), *Norms and conventions in the history of English* (pp. 191–212).
Woolard, K. A. (1998). Introduction. In B. B. Schieffelin, K. A. Woolard, & P. V. Kroskrity (Eds.), *Language ideologies: Practice and theory* (pp. 3–20). Oxford University Press.

Key Readings

Block, D. (2007). *Second language identities*. Bloomsbury.
Le Page, R., & Tabouret-Keller, A. (1985). *Acts of identity. Creole-based approaches to language and identity*. Cambridge University Press.

Further Readings

Schieffelin, B. B., Woolard, K., & Kroskrity, A. (Eds.). (1998). *Language ideolgies: Practice and theory*. Oxford University Press.
Spolsky, B. (Ed.). (2012). *The Cambridge handbook of language policy*. Cambridge University Press.

Multilingual Education and Teaching

Contents

8.1 Introduction – 176

8.2 Why and When are Schools Monolingual or Multilingual? – 176

8.3 Multilingual Approaches in Schools – 180
8.3.1 Weak Multilingual Approaches – 180
8.3.2 Strong Multilingual Approaches – 182

8.4 Multilingual Third-Level Education – 188

References – 190

© The Author(s), under exclusive license to Springer Nature Switzerland AG 2023
S. Buschfeld et al., *Multilingualism*,
https://doi.org/10.1007/978-3-031-28405-2_8

8.1 Introduction

After we have introduced how multilingual countries have come into existence (▶ Chap. 2) and how diversely languages can function and be used within multilingual societies (▶ Chap. 6), we go into further detail about language policies (as introduced in ▶ Chap. 7) and see why certain languages are chosen as language(s) of education in various socio-political contexts—and why others might not be chosen. As discussed in ▶ Chap. 7, socio-political contexts play a large role in official language choice as governments can exercise extensive influence on the linguistic situation in multilingual countries. Which languages are selected as official languages in a country depends on various factors. These typically are factors of social demographics of the country, speaker numbers and the relative social positions of the speakers, but also political interests, such as the support of minority groups within a country, or religious considerations. We then turn to the key concern of this chapter and present a survey of different possible approaches to educational policies and language selection in teaching. Keeping in mind that monolingual ideologies still prevail, we assess educational approaches that include more than one language, i.e. multilingual approaches to education, and discuss in how far they really follow multilingual concepts. Multilingual education can refer to two types of education, (1) education that supports and promotes multilingualism and (2) a classroom in which multilingual students are educated but the practices do not promote multilingualism (see Baker & Wright, 2021, p. 209 on bilingual education). In the following, we learn to differentiate between these two types and see that the role and the use of language in education have been reconsidered and redefined, as has our understanding of language and multilingualism. In monolingual and *weak multilingual approaches*, the involved languages are considered to be separate entities within the speakers' minds and to be represented as distinct systems. In more recent approaches, however, the nature of language is considered to be dynamic and flexible and languages are considered to coexist within multilingual linguistic repertoires.

8.2 Why and When are Schools Monolingual or Multilingual?

As seen in ▶ Chaps. 2 and 6, many reasons for and realisations of multilingualism in societies exist. Some societies are officially multilingual, others promote just one official language but recognise the *de facto* multilingualism of the society and aim to maintain (some of) the involved languages, while yet others understand their unofficial multilingualism as a problem or even pretend to be monolingual (which is, if at all, very rarely the case, see ▶ Sect. 6.2.1). While some states offer monolingual administration and education services only, others follow multilingual approaches (see ▶ Sect. 6.2.5 for more details). The reasons for states to either promote or not promote multilingualism vary and often depend on the specific languages involved and the individual participants of—and their agenda in—the political decision-making processes. Power relations are often strongly reflected in a state's respective language policies (cf. ▶ Sect. 7.3.2) and have immediately obvious implications for the education system of the country and for linguistic choices: the language(s) of those social groups with the most political and/or economic power are often also the dominant language(s) in multilingual settings and those language(s) are chosen for educational contexts. Although, as we have seen throughout this book, most countries and societies are multilingual, many, particularly Western, countries have only one official language. Public education in another than the official language tends to be rare in such countries. An exception here is the English language, which has been introduced as a medium of instruction from primary to tertiary education level in a number of societies without being promoted as an official language.

In general, however, mainstream education is still mostly monolingual and offered in the official language(s) of a state. As education is a context in which certain language practices are legitimised (Stroud, 2003), mainstream majority language education may result in the understanding that the use of the dominant group's language and, subsequently, culture are the norm (Yiakoumetti, 2014, p. 22). While other languages can be part of this mainstream education, they are typically study subjects or L1s of minority language-speaking students and thus play a minor role in education. These language practices further solidify the already existing language hierarchies between majority and minority languages and often keep minority language-speaking students from maintaining and strengthening their L1. The strong focus on one language in this type of education is also visible in the fact that language assistance is commonly only offered if students are not proficient enough in the language of instruction to follow mainstream education, for example due to recent migration. In this case, additional language lessons might be offered. These language classes can either be implemented through another teacher entering the class and offering assistance to the minority language-speaking students or—more commonly—by taking these students out of their classes to work with them on their proficiency in the majority language/language of education. The latter option, however, also means that minority language-speaking students miss the content that is taught to their fellow students while they are absent. In both cases, the language-focused instructions are often provided by special language teachers and, as Baker and Wright (2021, p. 215) point out, are rarely coordinated with the respective curriculum. Consequently, while they might assist students in learning the language of education, they prevent them from receiving the same amounts of content-based instructions as their peers and their absence might also add a stigma of 'being different' to these multilingual students. Another possible way to cater for the needs of students who are less proficient in the language of education is to offer so-called *sheltered immersion* (Baker & Wright, 2021, pp. 215–218). Sheltered immersion is a practice in which the language of instruction is simplified so that students who are less proficient speakers of the language of education can also follow the instructions. A clear advantage of this practice is that instructions for proficient and simplified instructions for less proficient students are given by the same teacher, which allows classes to be heterogeneous and, very importantly, enables less proficient students to stay with their fellow students while they are still assisted in their language learning process. A disadvantage of all these approaches, however, is that they do not support the use of any other language(s) than the respective language of instruction and that they consider education from a strictly monolingual perspective. While a country that has two official languages might offer education in both languages, these languages are not mixed, instead the offered education is either in Language A or in Language B.

Monolingual approaches to education and practices of assisting students in assimilating to a monolingual class environment, that is by helping them improve their proficiency in the language of instruction, have another, considerably more severe disadvantage: they discourage students from using their L1s in case it differs from the language (or even variety) of instruction (Cummins, 2001; Yiakoumetti, 2014). Minority language speakers are typically educated within majority language frameworks. While the presence of other languages may be acknowledged, typically a diglossic situation is envisaged. In this case, there is one language, variety, or practice that is considered to be appropriate for the classroom, while the other is relegated to contexts like the home or the family. As we have shown in ▶ Chap. 1, the majority of children worldwide are growing up in multilingual environments. This fact has made the dominance of monolingual approaches to education, and the following propagation and reproduction of one mainstream culture, inappropriate—if it has ever been an appropriate one at all. There is another aspect, which makes language use in education more complex. In our current globalised world, we rarely find that only two languages are involved— one official language and one regionally determined minority language or variety. Instead, contemporary society, and thus the contemporary classroom, often unites multiple languages or linguistic varieties. Thus, old teaching approaches which treat linguistic and cultural diversity as problematic and presuppose linguistic homogeneity are increasingly obsolete and should be reconsidered. However, the implementation of multilingual approaches to education does not only reflect current social groups and societies more adequately. The introduction of such different multilingual teaching approaches is often also motivated either by a utilitarian and/or a human rights argument. While the utilitarian argument is based on the fact that minority language students perform better if they are taught bilingually—particularly if they are emergent bilinguals (Escamilla, 2006; Kosonen, 2005; Yiakoumetti, 2014)—the latter is based on the understanding that being taught in one's own language is a human right (May, 2005; Skutnabb-Kangas, 2000; see also ▶ Sect. 7.4).

While, in this chapter, we focus on the utilitarian argument for L1-medium education and it is beyond the scope of this book to elaborate on the discussion about linguistic human rights within educational contexts in great detail, we would still like to stress the importance of linguistic human rights. While linguistic rights in general enhance equality across speaker groups, they specifically empower minority or less-privileged speaker groups and especially so in the educational context, that is, when students' L1s become a medium of education. As Ball argues,

8.2 · Why and When Are Schools Monolingual or Multilingual?

> Language is not only a tool for communication and knowledge but also a fundamental attribute of cultural identity and empowerment, both for the individual and the group. Respect for the languages of persons belonging to different linguistic communities therefore is essential to peaceful cohabitation. This applies both to majority groups, to minorities (whether traditionally resident in a country or more recent migrants) and to indigenous peoples. (2021, p. 13)

Without L1-medium education, minority speakers might be (temporarily) excluded from participating in the social and cultural practices of the communities they live in. While minority speakers commonly assimilate into monolingual, majority language education as their proficiency in the majority language increases, for example after additional language instruction, initial separation is a marker of otherness and lacking appreciation and can hardly be overcome, even after the students have completed their educational journey.

Concerning the second line of argumentation, meaning the utilitarian argument, empirical evidence in favour of L1-medium education abounds. As numerous studies have shown, students are more likely to enrol in programmes and to be more successful on their educational journey in case they have the chance to be (even partially) educated in their L1 (e.g., Ding & Yu, 2013; Kosonen, 2005). Ding and Yu (2013), for example, investigated the success of students' college applications in China. They found that students who were educated based on a strong bilingual approach, in which the use of the minority and the majority language were required, were more successful in their college applications than peers who were educated based on a weak bilingual approach, in which the minority language was not prioritised (see Baker, 2011 and ▶ Sect. 8.3 for further details on strong and weak multilingual approaches). While this difference is partly due to specifics in the higher-education policies in China, it also suggests that multilingual education is not only more beneficial than monolingual education, but that the local importance of the involved languages and attitudes towards them are also influential. Furthermore, L1-medium education has been found to support literacy development (e.g. Cummins, 2000; Dutcher, 2004). Specifically, minority language education improves literacy in both the majority and minority language. This might be most relevant when considering the fact that the global majority of illiterate people live in areas in which formal education is not provided in their local, minority language (UIS, 2017). Other studies have found that L1-medium instruction is beneficial for students' learning outcomes merely in specific subjects, such as mathematics (Mohanty & Saikia, 2008). In sum, multilingual approaches to education are beneficial to multilingual and monolingual speakers, as the former are empowered within the local structures and the latter receive the opportunity to learn and appreciate other languages. However, especially in *de facto* highly multilingual countries, in which education is often offered in a majority or official language, parents might believe that they protect their children if they do not engage in multilingual and/or minority language-based instruction. This is often based on the belief that learning a local, less-valued language wastes their children's time

(Yiakoumetti, 2014, p. 19). Consequently, for a successful multilingual education, parents must be convinced of the benefits of their children's multilingual education and, at the very best, get involved. Further factors that help to implement and support multilingual approaches to education are (1) appropriately assessing (emerging) bilinguals' content and language skills to adapt to their educational needs, (2) integrating and using language awareness to create (socio-linguistically) meaningful education, and (3) involving translanguaging to enhance creative language use (Yiakoumetti, 2014, pp. 22–25; also see ▶ Sect. 8.3.2.2 on translanguaging).

As we can already see, various multilingual approaches that claim to support, enhance, or maintain more than one language within educational contexts exist. Let us now turn to some examples of education systems and approaches and find out about advantages, disadvantages, and problems they might come with.

8.3 Multilingual Approaches in Schools

Implementing a multilingual versus implementing a monolingual approach to education has a strong impact on different population groups. Some countries offer monolingual education, irrespective of the linguistic background of their students. England is a general case in point here.[1] If students or parents seek education through heritage or any other language, non-state, evening, or weekend classes must be attended. Other countries follow multilingual approaches to education which allow students of diverse linguistic backgrounds to make use of their home languages in the school system in order to validate their holistic linguistic competencies. These approaches allow monolingual students to learn additional languages from their peers as well as in class and support multilingual students in their "right to use, maintain, and develop their multiple languages." (Yiakoumetti, 2014, p. 14). Immersion programmes in Canada might serve as examples of these approaches. In the following, we discuss how different approaches can be classified and what key aspects are important to differentiate between weak and *strong multilingual approaches*.

8.3.1 Weak Multilingual Approaches

Weak multilingual approaches are approaches that include other languages than the majority/main language of education but do not aim to maintain or implement multilingualism in students or society. Foreign language classes are an examples of a weak multilingual approach, as they often do not result in students becoming fluent speakers of this foreign language due to very limited exposure to the language in only a few teaching hours. It has, for example, been found that after 12 years of French-as-a-Foreign-Language classes, many Anglophone Canadians are not fluent enough to communicate with Francophone Canadians in French (Baker & Wright,

---

1 Remember that the general monolingual approach to education includes foreign-language classes, such as for example French or Spanish classes, as part of the curriculum.

2021, p. 221). In some cases, however, foreign language classes as part of monolingual mainstream education are successful, such as English-as-a-Foreign-Language teaching in Slovenia or African countries. This, however, might be due more to the enormous motivation of people to become proficient speakers of English than to the educational approach in use. Another, quite successful approach that can be considered to be a weak multilingual one is *transitional bilingual education* (cf. Baker & Wright, 2021, pp. 218–219). This approach, too, does not aim to implement full multilingualism in the long run but to provide minority speakers with enough competencies in the language of education to follow mainstream education. It is a bilingual approach, in contrast to the language classes mentioned in ▶ Sect. 8.2, as minority speakers might be taught in their L1 for the first years of their educational journey while being also taught the language of mainstream education. After having gained a sufficient level of proficiency, irrespective of what the standards for this level might be, they will join the monolingual mainstream educational system. Although we still consider this approach to have shortcomings, it is a successful approach to assimilating minority speakers into the majority language education. Therefore, it is in some way an enabling approach: it enables minority speakers to use their L1, learn the language of education, and follow the content as prescribed in the curriculum. Other approaches that offer L1-medium instructions are less enabling, for example, the approach Baker and Wright (2021, p. 221) call "separatist education". This is an educational approach in which only the minority language is used and the majority language is not included. Separatist education is often disjunct from mainstream education and consequently not always possible. In countries in which schools have to be state-approved, such as in Germany, separatist education is possible only under specific circumstances and consequently less frequent than, for example, in the US, where individualised home-schooling is possible and frequently executed. Although Baker and Wright (2021) consider it to be a weak multilingual approach to education, we would argue for it to be a monolingual approach. Certainly, we consider it to be not enabling, as separating children from the majority language and the respective speaker group might result in them not being able to participate in the social and political structures of the society they live in.

Last but not least, international schools can be considered a form of weak multilingual education. International schools offer education in a prestigious world language. They offer education mostly in English but also in French, Chinese, or German, while being located in countries in which these languages are not widely spoken. In 2017, more than 8000 international schools that use English as the medium of instruction existed worldwide (Wechsler, 2017) and numbers are constantly rising. International schools are a prestigious, well-recognised, and often costly alternative to public mainstream education for local and international students. These international schools might follow an international curriculum (International Baccalaureate) or a UK- or US-based curriculum. These schools are particularly attractive for expatriates or temporary residents who would like their children to either be able to continue their education in another country and/or to gain an internationally valid school qualification. However, international schools have also become more popular with local parents who want their children to become global citizens, educated in an international setting. In some international schools, a limited amount of instruction is provided in the local language and, at least for these local students, this combination of world and local language would count as multilingual education that results in—rather than aim at—multilingualism. We call approaches that aim for multilingualism, multiliteracy, and often types of multiculturalism strong multilingual approaches.

8.3.2 Strong Multilingual Approaches

The strongest multilingual and multicultural effects on students and societies are created through strong multilingual approaches to education that aim, initiate, promote, and maintain multilingual language use in students and in societies. Strong multilingual approaches to education are sometimes also called *language immersion* approaches. While, in the course of its global rise to success, various formats and practices of language immersion have been developed, these educational approaches are characterised by aiming at enrichment. Specifically, immersion approaches do not aim for the assimilation of one speaker group to another (more dominant and powerful) one but aim to create an inclusive, pluralistic, and multilingual ideology towards diverse language use and speaker identities. We must distinguish between three main groups of programmes: (1) immersion programmes that combine a local majority and one or more local minority languages, so languages that are spoken in the society the programme is implemented in; (2) programmes that combine only majority languages of the society or state they are implemented in; and (3) programmes that combine a local—often majority—language and another world language of high prestige (Baker & Wright, 2021, pp. 227–249). Let us look at some examples and go into further detail on how these multilingual immersion programmes are and can be implemented.

All of the above-mentioned programmes aim for (1) a high language proficiency in all languages involved (multilingualism), (2) the acquisition of reading and writing skills in all languages (*multiliteracy*), (3) academic achievements of students at least similar to the achievements of students in mainstream education programmes, (4) positive attitudes to different cultures and multiculturalism, and (5) critical consciousness towards social and linguistic inequalities (cf. Baker & Wright, 2021, p. 230; Arias & Markos, 2018; Cervantes-Soon et al., 2017; Howard et al., 2018). In immersion schools, all involved languages are of equal status and of equal importance. Teachers are ideally competent speakers of these languages and communication in and outside of the classroom, such as during lunch breaks, on the playground, or letters to the parents, include all languages. Unsurprisingly, not all immersion programmes—or better not all actual realisations of immersion programmes—have been able to achieve these goals. Most important for the successful implementation of immersion approaches is the socio-political context in which they are implemented. Specifically important are the socio-economic and linguistic background and the specific combination of students within the individual classes, the prestige and status of each of the involved languages within the local social and national context, and the political agenda that is followed. What is also important are factors like the age at which children start education in more than one language and the amount of time students can participate in immersion programmes. Whether immersion programmes are implemented in primary education only or also in secondary and tertiary education has a strong influence on the outcome and success of multilingual education.

For the idealised outcome of raising and educating balanced multilinguals, all aspects of the programme should be balanced and/or multilingual. Students should be provided with an equal amount of lessons in each language and each subject should be taught in each language to prevent that one specific language could be correlated with, for example, sciences or humanities. In order to create equality of the languages in the speakers' minds, there has to be a strict policy determining who is taught in which language when, and at what point languages alternate. One way to do that is to teach all students in one language in the mornings and in the other language in the afternoons and alternating this pattern every year. A realisation of this might be that all students, let us say in grade five, are taught in English in the mornings and Spanish in the afternoons and students in grade six are taught *vice versa*. In other programmes subjects might be taught in certain languages for one week and in the other the next week. One half of the subjects might, for example, be taught in English one week and in German the next and the other half of the subjects is taught in the respective other language. For this to work, all teachers have to be fluent speakers of the languages involved. While the language exposure through instruction might be balanced in these cases, the overall amount of exposure to each language might still differ due to the language dominance of the students. To ensure a fully balanced exposure to both languages in cases in which students are dominant in one of the languages, their language dominance would need to be counterbalanced by an increased use of the non-dominant language as language of instruction or by grouping these students with fellow students who are dominant speakers of the other language. Consequently, while all types of immersion education share many similarities, it might be useful to differentiate them further in order to identify different motivations, beneficiaries, outcomes, and goals.

While, in theory, dominance could be levelled out as described above, in practice this is rarely successful. School settings can neither counterbalance a majority language's dominance in extracurricular settings nor can students be grouped in such a way as to perfectly counterbalance each other's language dominance. While this might not be too big a disadvantage from a linguistic perspective, the impact of extra-linguistic factors often increases with the dominance of one of the involved languages. Once one language becomes dominant, the motivation to use the other languages often decreases, and so does these languages and their speakers' status and prestige. Immersion programmes that combine majority and world languages and those that combine minority and majority languages potentially suffer considerably from such effects of language dominance. As mentioned above, immersion programmes of the former type often combine (one of the) majority languages of the respective location and one the most wide-spread world language. As most often English is the world language of choice, let us take such a programme as an example. In these programmes, English and (most often) one majority language are used as mediums of instruction. Since the student bodies tend to consist of local students—that is unlike at international schools—the world language is used more often to balance out the dominance of the local majority language. This type of immersion education is often chosen by parents who want their children to be educated in major languages like English, Chinese, or French—in addition to the most prestigious local language spoken in such contexts. The goal for these parents is not necessarily to raise multilingual speakers who identify with their local multilingual reality, but who are fluent speakers of a language that has a wider international communicative reach. Immersion programmes that combine majority and world languages tend to focus on the future perspective of the students rather than their present linguistic needs or heritage.

The other type of immersion approaches to multilingual education that is often strongly affected by language dominance are the programmes combining majority and minority languages. Immersion education that combines minority and majority languages focuses on the students' linguistic heritage, their present realities, and certainly tries to support the minority language as part of the students' future. These programmes aim to teach students who speak a local minority language as their L1 and students who speak a local majority language as their L1 in both (or all) these languages. Consequently, this type of immersion education does not aim to assimilate minority speakers to their majority language-speaking peers but to raise multilingual speakers of both (or all) languages. Depending, for example, on the combination of students in a class, one language might, however, become the dominant one. Still, the majority speakers are also taught to become fluent speakers of minority languages, which makes the various speaker groups within a society more equal and facilitates the development of a shared identity. This fact is one of the most valuable aspects of immersion education in general.

One subcategory of this type of immersion programme that should be mentioned explicitly here is heritage language education. Heritage language education is essentially based on the argument that being educated in one's L1 is a human right. It is often limited to kindergarten and elementary school education and aims to offer minority language students, from local minority groups or with a history of migration, the possibility to develop higher levels of proficiency in their home language. While these programmes sometimes aim to enhance multilingualism and to support the role and the status of the heritage language within the respective society or speaker group, most of these programmes support the minority language speakers only for some time and do not target the majority language speakers at all. Consequently, heritage language programmes range somewhere between weak and strong approaches to multilingual education.

Finally, immersion education might combine majority languages only. Canada, the country of origin of this approach, might serve as an example here. French and English are the official languages in Canada, while the majority of inhabitants are predominantly English-speaking. In the 1960s, parents in a suburb of Montréal decided that they wanted their Anglophone children to also become fluent and literate in French to be able to communicate with French Canadians and to participate in French-speaking Canadian culture as well as English-speaking Canadian culture, while still achieving the same academic goals as their monolingual peers (cf. Lambert & Tucker, 1972). This new type of bilingual education initially started in kindergarten but in the course of time various additional options for entering or pursuing immersion education have developed in Canada. As both languages are considered to be prestigious and are treated equally with respect to importance and exposure within these educational settings, no speaker group is favoured and students are educated with the explicit goal to become bilingual, bicultural, and biliterate Canadians. As, typically, students are more fluent in one of the involved languages, the other has to be acquired during the first years of education. Building (also) on the success of language immersion programmes in Canada, the method of Content and Language Integrated Learning (CLIL) has spread in Europe (Mehisto, 2012). CLIL is an efficient way of teaching a language while still teaching content and is presented in the following.

8.3.2.1 Content and Language Integrated Learning (CLIL)

The principle of Content and Language Integrated Learning (CLIL, e.g. Coyle et al., 2010) is a commonly used method of integrating multiple languages into an educational approach while also focusing on successful content instruction. In CLIL approaches, subjects such as, for example, geography or sports are taught through the medium of a target language other than the state or majority language. Consequently, CLIL can be described as "a dual-focused educational approach in which an additional language is used for the teaching and learning of both content and language." (Coyle et al., 2010, p. 1). This additional language of instruction may be a world language, especially English (e.g. in Germany or Switzerland), or it may be a territorial minority language, such as Irish in Ireland or Romansh in Switzerland. CLIL approaches have gained popularity especially in Europe, where they are considered to be partly built on the success of the Canadian immersion programmes (Baker & Wright, 2021, p. 249). Quite similarly to the early years of immersion approaches, in CLIL approaches the target language is not 'just' used as a vehicle for content transmission but also taught as a subject itself. CLIL is a didactical method rather than an approach to education and its success in implementing multilingualism in students correlates strongly with the extent of its use, thus using CLIL as a teaching method can be part of monolingual as well as weak and strong multilingual approaches to education. An example of CLIL as part of a monolingual approach to education is students in Germany being taught geography in English for 90 minutes a week in grades 7–9. An example of immersion or heritage language education via CLIL can be found in Wales if Welsh students are being taught history in Welsh throughout their secondary education. CLIL is an umbrella term and possible realisations can vary widely. Unaffected by that, many researchers and teachers support this teaching method, and they do so for several reasons:

» First, learning a language may be quicker when it is via an integration of language and content, and much slower if just learnt as a language. Second, CLIL ensures a student gains language competence in academic domains and not just in social communication. Third, such an integration of language and content is efficient. Two outcomes can be achieved at the same time: learning a language and subject-matter learning. Fourth, CLIL provides a communicative approach to second language teaching that emphasizes meaningful and authentic communication. (Baker & Wright, 2021, p. 250; see also Ball et al., 2016; Ozóg & Marsh, 2009)

Despite all this support, implementing CLIL teaching requires a lot of preparation, which includes changing teacher education, adapting testing practices, and revising curricula. It consequently requires a strong motivation by policymakers to invest in multilingualism. In Europe, the vision of Europeanisation, referring to

European citizens being multilingual and speaking at least two European languages, is enhanced by the use of CLIL teaching. CLIL teaching has the potential to influence the ideology and identity of learners, (future) parents, and policymakers towards multilingualism. There is another approach to teaching multiple languages that has the potential to change our language policies and the very basics of our understanding of what language is and how it is used and accessed, and this approach is translanguaging.

8.3.2.2 Translanguaging

We have seen in the preceding chapters that many multilingual language users deploy their languages depending on the respective situations, often blending different languages or varieties (e.g. ► Chap. 7). In recent years, the use of flexible, situationally dependent language practices that engage the speakers' full linguistic repertoire has become known as *translanguaging* (García & Wei, 2014) and the use of this approach as a teaching philosophy has been termed *translanguaging pedagogy* (García et al., 2016).

The aim of translanguaging pedagogies is to allow students to use their full linguistic repertoires in order to reach the overall learning goals of the school curricula and to gradually increase competencies in the local majority language. In order to increase the competencies in the target languages, resources in all the students' languages can be drawn upon and students—as well as teachers—with different competence levels in the different languages support each other in the language and knowledge acquisition processes.

Translanguaging pedagogy approaches have the purpose to provide support to multilingual students who show emerging competences in the majority language, which typically is the main language of instruction. The goal of translanguaging approaches is to enable students to master academic content in the language of instruction. Such academic content may in fact be challenging not only for emergent bilinguals but also for monolingual students whose academic language competencies are not yet fully developed. For example, like emerging bilinguals, also monolingual students may not have come in contact with academic style levels or with the specific vocabulary of certain school topics in their home environment and may need to acquire this in the classroom context. In order to be able to deal with academically challenging content, multilingual students may benefit from their knowledge in a language or languages other than the language of instruction. To master challenging content, the students' home language may be harnessed: teachers may allow students to research the target content in the students' home languages. In addition to using home languages, also different ways of knowing may be used to master the respective content. For example, in subjects like geography or social studies, the students may draw on personal experiences, such as firsthand knowledge gained during personal visits of certain places, or they may be able to draw on the knowledge of family members in addition to what is learnt from the teaching materials. The validation not only of the learners' linguistic competencies, but also of their previously acquired knowledge, will support the students' multilingual identities by signalling that their competencies are valuable and valued. This validation will therefore also support the learners' socio-emotional development; particularly minoritised communities can be given the opportunity to contribute to the majority culture and to enrich it.

Support of the learners' multilingual development can take various forms. Critically, learners will be allowed to use multilingual resources such as dictionaries or sources in other languages and to work with other learners with similar linguistic backgrounds. Group work will allow students to learn from other, more advanced learners and to develop solutions together, which would then typically be presented in the main language of instruction. In this way, the weaker students can contribute their own experiences and knowledge to solving the task while learning the academic vocabulary in the target language. All the linguistic resources of the learners can be drawn upon and are thus validated as a legitimate resource instead of being branded as low-value or illegitimate. This experience then contributes to the socio-emotional well-being of the learners. Teachers using a translanguaging approach evaluate not only the language-specific progress in the target language, but also take into consideration the learners' general linguistic performance by considering for which tasks the learners can use all their linguistic resources. To do so, the teachers have to subscribe to a translanguaging stance that values the learners' multilingualism and allows them students to use different languages in the classroom. To enable students to do so, collaboration is fostered between learners so that they can learn from each other. A multilingual ecology is created in the classrooms which provides and encourages the use of multilingual resources and multilingual work practices with language shifts between the language resources.

> **Think Tank**
>
> Translanguaging instructional design cycles start with the exploration of a topic, in which learners work on their own. In a next step the new knowledge is evaluated through critical thinking and discussion. This is followed by an imagination stage, in which the learners consider how to apply this knowledge or how to make it more accessible. In all these steps, the full linguistic resources can be drawn upon. Then, the results are presented in the language of instruction at a presentation stage and at this point the relevant linguistic competencies in the language of instruction will be employed by the learners, before the final step of implementing the knowledge can be taken, for example by passing it on to audiences outside the classroom. In order to follow such an instructional design, the teachers will have to cede a certain amount of classroom control: they will have to come to terms with work being carried out in their classrooms in languages they are likely not to understand. The trade-off for ceding this amount of control is that the learners' multilingual resources can be employed and are valued, which improves the students' learning outcomes as well as their socio-emotional wellbeing.
>
> If you are a teacher or are planning to become a teacher, think of a topic of instruction that you could teach to learners whose linguistic competences in the majority language are emerging at the moment and plan how you could implement a translanguaging approach to teach this topic.

Let us illustrate the use of multilingual approaches by a study of linguistic practices in German classrooms. In the industrial region of the Ruhr Valley, some residential areas may have very heterogeneous population groups. As an example, in the German city of Dortmund, the north inner city is linguistically and culturally very diverse and has seen sizeable immigration into the school system by students without any German language skills at the end of the 2010s. In some regular classrooms, less than 10% of the students' home language might be German. As a result, teachers, who may be monolingual German speakers, may have some knowledge of educational languages like English or French, or may be heritage speakers of other languages themselves, have to teach students with varying proficiency levels in German who are, in addition, speakers of home languages that are as diverse as Polish, Romanian, Turkish, Kurdish, Arabic, Dari, or Farsi (Ronan, 2022; Ronan & Melles, 2022). In such a context, monolingual approaches will not represent best practice, neither in terms of harnessing students' linguistic competencies, nor in terms of validating home cultures and student identities. Allowing learners to employ their home languages where needed in order to help them understand academic content in the German target language can improve their academic achievement, speed up the acquisition of target structures, and have positive effects on their socio-emotional well-being.

8.4 Multilingual Third-Level Education

Quite similar to primary and secondary education, tertiary education is often offered in the local majority language and has shifted towards implementing multilingual approaches to teaching. However—and unlike in primary and secondary education—the involved languages tend to not vary as widely. While multilingual approaches to teaching can also be found at the level of tertiary education, they most often include a combination of English and a majority language. The implementation of English as a language of instruction is often understood as a sign of internationalisation. English, in tertiary education, fulfils various functions: it grants access to knowledge; it attracts international students and academics; it boosts these students' future employability; and it potentially improves the university's position in international rankings (Lasagabaster, 2015, pp. 265–266; Wilkinson, 2013).

As mentioned before, the language of knowledge transfer—at least at state universities—is most often a language that is locally-bound to the location of the university. In France, non-language contexts such as economic or statistics classes are commonly taught in French, in Germany, they are commonly taught in German, and in the UK, they are commonly taught in English. Respective other languages are used in language classes; English literature is commonly taught in English and introductory classes to Italian grammar in Italian, independent of the location of the university. However, this division of language functions has started to change—especially when the English language is concerned. English has lost its restricted function as a subject of study and functions primarily as a vehicle of knowledge transfer, due to globalisation and the increasing global connectedness and mobility across national borders. Furthermore, introducing English-medium study programmes reflects the high prestige of English as an international language of business and universities aim to provide their students with the necessary linguistic tools to participate in international commercial and scientific discourse through these programmes (e.g. Ammon & McConnell, 2002). Due to the use of English being extended from functioning only as a subject of study to also being (a) language of instruction, any content can be taught context- and location-independently: it might be taught in English anywhere by anyone to anyone, provided students and teachers have the necessary language competence (cf. Vida-Mannl 2022). This flexibility potentially attracts foreign students: to study in Denmark, prospective students do not necessarily have to speak the local language Danish, they can navigate their academic and private lives using English.

In addition to the increased accessibility when using English as the medium of instruction, English-medium education is often equalled with high-quality education (Lasagabaster, 2015, p. 266). Consequently, for universities, it is essential to include English-medium study programmes into their offers in order to achieve high positions in university rankings and remain or become attractive and prestigious for prospective students. In addition, its implementation is a fruitful way "to seize part of the major English-speaking countries' market share of international students" (Lasagabaster 2015, p. 265) and increase the institution's economic profit, as, for example, in the EU, non-EU the students often pay higher fees than local, EU students (Holborow, 2013, p. 233). While the flexibility and mobility that is enabled by the global spread of English present a great opportunity for people to travel and get in touch with different people, cultures, and customs, the extensive spread of English in the field of higher education comes with a huge disadvantage: English-medium education is predominantly monolingual and, hence, dominates local languages. Ultimately, English has become so dominant in higher education that it suppresses multilingualism. While there are immersion approaches to higher education, monolingual, mostly English-medium or majority language-medium education, is the norm. English has grown into a gatekeeper of access to education—in higher education more than at any other level of education.

❓ Exercises

1. Education in one's L1 is a linguistic human right. Assemble arguments in favour and against monolingual approaches to education. Get together with a partner and discuss your arguments.
2. The European Union and UNESCO have long been promoting linguistic human rights and the maintenance of minority languages and local varieties. Get together in groups and find out about at least two projects that enhance local multilingualism. Present your results in class.
3. Which languages or varieties are part of your local society? Try to find educational and cultural projects that support this language diversity, e.g. local variation or minority or indigenous languages in your home town or home country.

Summary

In this chapter, we have defined and distinguished between monolingual and multilingual approaches to education and assessed the socio-cultural and political circumstances under which either of these may be used or is more or less likely to be used. We have presented that, although the majority of people around the globe are multilingual (cf. ▶ Chap. 1) and most countries are linguistically diverse (cf. ▶ Sect. 6.2.1), mainstream education is predominantly monolingual in (one of) the majority language(s). This might have a devalorising effect on the other languages that are present in the respective society. While monolingual approaches to education do not completely exclude other languages, for example as the content of learning, they aim for the assimilation of minority language-speaking learners to their majority language-speaking peers. Multilingual approaches to education, by contrast, aim to implement and support multilingualism, multiculturalism, and multiliteracy. We have distinguished between weak multilingual approaches, for example implemented in international schools, and strong multilingual approaches, such as heritage language classes or immersion programmes. To illustrate how multilingual approaches to education might be realised, we have introduced two popular multilingual teaching methods, that is, Content and Language Integrated Learning and translanguaging. Finally, language choice in higher education has been assessed. While primary and secondary education potentially become increasingly multilingual, higher education seems to be increasingly English-based. English is understood as a global language by universities and (prospective) students and is implemented for both parties' social and economic enhancement. In so doing, local languages increasingly disappear in higher education settings, making global higher education more and more monolingual.

References

Ammon, U., & McConnell, G. (2002). *English as an Academic Language in Europe: A survey of its use in teaching*. Peter Lang.

Arias, M. B., & Markos, A. (2018). Recent research on the three goals of dual language education. In M. B. Arias & M. Fee (Eds.), *Profiles of dual language education in the 21st century* (pp. 3–19). Multilingual Matters.

BAAL. (2021). *Recommendations on good practice in applied linguistics* (4th ed.). Retrieved from November 4, 2022, from https://www.baal.org.uk/wp-content/uploads/2021/03/BAAL-Good-Practice-Guidelines-2021.pdf

Baker, C. (2011). Foundations of bilingual education and bilingualism. In N. Hornberger (Ed.), *Types of bilingual education* (pp. 206–220). Multilingual Matters.

Baker, C., & Wright, W. E. (2021). *Foundations of bilingual education and bilingualism* (7th ed.).

Ball, P., Kelly, K., & Clegg, J. (2016). *Putting CLIL into practice*. Oxford University Press.

Cervantes-Soon, C., Dorner, L., Palmer, D., Heiman, D., Schwerdtfeger, R., & Choi, J. (2017). Combating inequalities in two-way language immersion programs: Toward critical consciousness in bilingual education spaces. *Review of Research in Education, 41*, 403–427.

Coyle, D., Hood, P., & Marsh, D. (2010). *Content and language integrated learning*. Cambridge University Press.

Cummins, J. (2000). *Language, power, and pedagogy: Bilingual children in the crossfire*. Multilingual Matters.

References

Cummins, J. (2001). Bilingual children's mother tongue: Why is it important for education? *Sprogforum, 19*, 15–20.

Ding, H., & Yu, L. (2013). The dilemma: A study of bilingual education policy in Yi minority schools in Liangshan. *International Journal of Bilingual Education and Bilingualism, 16*(4), 451–470.

Dutcher, N. (2004). *Expanding educational opportunity in linguistically diverse societies* (2nd ed.). Center for Applied Linguistics.

Escamilla, K. (2006). Monolingual assessment and emerging bilinguals: A case study in the US. In O. García, T. Skutnabb-Kangas, & M. Torres-Guzmán (Eds.), *Imagining multilingual schools: Languages in education and globalisation* (pp. 184–199). Multilingual Matters.

García, O., Ibarra Johnson, S., & Seltzer, K. (2016). *The translanguaging classroom*. Caslon Publishing.

García, O., & Wei, L. (2014). *Translanguaging: Language, bilingualism and education*. Palgrave Pivot.

Holborow, M. (2013). Applied linguistics in the neoliberal university: Ideological keywords and social agency. *Applied Linguistics Review, 4*(2), 229–257.

Howard, E. R., Lindholm-Leary, K., Rogers, D., Olague, N., Medina, J., Kennedy, B., Sugarman, J., & Christiane, D. (2018). *Guiding principles for dual language education* (3rd ed.). Center for Applied Linguistics.

Kosonen, K. (2005). Education in local languages: policy and practice in Southeast Asia. In *First languages first: Community-based literacy programmes for minority language contexts in Asia* (pp. 96–134). UNESCO.

Lambert, W. E., & Tucker, G. R. (1972). *Bilingual education of children: The St. Lambert experiment*. Newbury House.

Lasagabaster, D. (2015). Language policy and language choice at European Universities: Is there really a 'choice'? *International Journal of Applied Linguistics, 3*(2), 255–276.

May, S. (2005). Language rights: Moving the debate forward. *Journal of Sociolinguistics, 9*(3), 319–347.

Mehisto, P. (2012). *Excellence in bilingual education: a guide for school principals*. Cambridge University Press.

Mohanty, A., & Saikia, J. (2008). Bilingualism and intergroup relationship in tribal and non-tribal contact situations. In G. Zheng, K. Leung, & J. G. Adair (Eds.), *Perspectives and progress in contemporary cross-cultural psychology* (pp. 163–172). International Association for Cross Cultural Psychology.

Ozóg, C., & Marsh, D. (2009). CLIL: An interview with Professor David Marsh. *International House Journal of Education and Development, 26*.

Ronan, P. (2022). Linguistic inclusion of school-age immigrants in Ruhr valley schools from a teacher's perspective. In A. Auer & J. Thorburn (Eds.), *Approaches to migration, language and identity* (pp. 199–222). Peter Lang.

Ronan, P., & Melles, W. (2022). Linguistic inclusion of school age immigrants in Ruhr valley schools: A translanguaging perspective. In P. Ronan & E. Ziegler (Eds.), *Language and identity in migration contexts* (pp. 277–296). Peter Lang.

Skutnabb-Kangas, T. (2000). *Linguistic genocide in education—or worldwide diversity and human rights?* Erlbaum.

Stroud, C. (2003). Postmodernist perspectives on local languages: African mother tongue education in times of globalisation. *International Journal of Bilingual Education and Bilingualism, 6*(1), 17–36.

UIS (UNESCO Institute for Statistics). (2017). *Fact sheet no. 45*. Retrieved November 4, 2022, from http://uis.unesco.org/sites/default/files/documents/fs45-literacy-rates-continue-rise-generation-to-next-en-2017_0.pdf

Vida-Mannl, M. (2022). *The value of the English language in global mobility and higher education: An investigation of higher education in Cyprus*. Bloomsbury.

Wechsler, A. (2017, June 5). *The international-school surge*. The Atlantic. Retrieved November 4, 2022, from https://www.theatlantic.com/education/archive/2017/06/the-international-school-surge/528792/

Wilkinson, R. (2013). English-medium instruction at a Dutch university: Challenges and pitfalls. In A. Doiz, D. Lasagabaster, & J. M. Sierra (Eds.), *English-medium instruction at universities: Global challenges* (pp. 3–24). Multilingual Matters.

Yiakoumetti, A. (2014). Language education in our globalised classrooms: Recommendations on providing for equal language rights. In M. Solly & E. Esch (Eds.), *Language education and the challenges of globalisation: Sociolinguistic issues* (pp. 13–31). Cambridge University Press.

Key Readings

Baker, C., & Wright, W. E. (2021). *Foundations of bilingual education and bilingualism* (7th ed.). Multilingual Matters.

García, O., & Wei, L. (2017). Bilingual education. In O. García, A. M. Y. Lin, & S. May (Eds.), *Encyclopedia of language and education* (Vol. 5, 3rd ed.). Springer.

Lasagabaster, D. (2015). Language policy and language choice at European Universities: Is there really a 'choice'? *International Journal of Applied Linguistics, 3*(2), 255–276.

Further Readings

Lee, J. W. (2018). *The politics of translingualism—After Englishes*. Routledge.

Wei, L. (2018). Translanguaging as a practical theory of language. *Applied Linguistics, 39*(1), 9–30.

Multilingualism in the Modern Age: Emergent Contexts and Current Perspectives

Part III of the textbook introduces current perspectives on multilingualism; in particular, multilingualism in emergent contexts. Many of these contexts are the result of our modern age, especially globalisation and resulting large-scale migration, tourism, and technological advancements. Many of the topics addressed in this part of the book have only recently entered the research agenda of linguistics; some have, to our knowledge, not yet been addressed in textbooks on multilingualism at all.

Contents

Chapter 9   Multilingualism in Migrant and Refugee Contexts – 195

Chapter 10   Multilingualism in New Media – 217

Chapter 11   Multilingual Pop Music – 235

Chapter 12   Linguistic Landscapes – 253

Multilingualism in Migrant and Refugee Contexts

Contents

9.1 **Introduction** – 196

9.2 **Migration Contexts** – 196

9.3 **Modes of Communication in Migration Contexts** – 198
9.3.1 Super-Diverse Settings – 198
9.3.2 Communication in Super-Diverse Settings – 203

9.4 **Multiethnolects** – 204
9.4.1 Introduction to Multiethnolects – 205
9.4.2 Linguistic Features of Multiethnolects – 206
9.4.3 Why Are Multiethnolects Used? – 209

9.5 **International Diasporas** – 210

References – 214

© The Author(s), under exclusive license to Springer Nature Switzerland AG 2023
S. Buschfeld et al., *Multilingualism*,
https://doi.org/10.1007/978-3-031-28405-2_9

9.1 Introduction

While neither voluntary nor forced migration are new developments, modern globalisation with increased personal global networks and with improved transport options has made not only international migration but also intercontinental migration a more common phenomenon. Arguably, the decision to migrate internationally is also facilitated by global information options provided by the internet, as well as the already very well-documented international diasporic networks, which would help to provide initial support for somebody deciding to migrate to a new country. In the current chapter, we focus on language contact scenarios arising from migration. We start by outlining different migration contexts and introduce terminology that is used to describe different migration situations. Then we engage with characteristics of the communication found in specific migration contexts and put a special focus on super-diverse settings. Super-diverse settings may result in the rise of multiethnolects. We outline characteristic features of such multiethnolects and discuss well-known examples. To close this chapter, we move beyond localised language varieties and consider the impact international diasporas can have on linguistic developments.

9.2 Migration Contexts

The term *migration* is used in many contexts and can, generally speaking, be explained as indicating displacement from one location to another. A well-known instance of migration is the displacement of many different peoples around the Mediterranean region during the first millennium of the Christian Era. Throughout the millennia, especially with increasing contemporary globalisation, migration has become an international phenomenon and the reasons for migration are diverse. As a result, the terminology used in migration discourse reflects the varied reasons that lead people to migrate. In trying to categorise different types of migration, the Council of Europe,[1] for example, refers to temporary labour migrants, often also called guest workers. It is usually expected that these will return to their home country at some point in their lives, for example when retiring from working life. Further, there are highly skilled business migrants. These are professional people who typically work for international or multinational employers and join their employer's staff in a different country. A further group of migrants are called irregular migrants, undocumented, or unauthorised migrants. These do not have the necessary documents and permits for legal entry into a country. Additionally, there are different types of forced migrants. According to the terminology of the United Nations High Commissioner for Refugees (UNHCR), these may be refugees. Refugees are defined as people who cannot return to their home country due to fears of prosecution, for example because of race, religion, or political opinions. While refugees have an internationally recognised status, asylum seekers are seek-

---

[1] ▶ https://www.coe.int/en/web/compass/migration (last accessed 22.03.2021)

ing international protection but their refugee status has not yet been determined. In addition, migrants may also be internally displaced persons. These are people fleeing from conflict, violence, or any type of disaster, but they do not cross country borders while doing so and remain in their country of residence. All these groups may also be joined by members of their families at later stages, leading to the migration of family members. Finally, migrants who return to their home countries after periods in a foreign country are known as return migrants. As the Council of Europe points out, in highly developed countries, public discourse is typically concerned with immigration from developing countries. Yet in fact, the largest migration by far is constituted by country-internal migration, with numbers of internal migration being four times as high as those of external, that is international, migration. Further, the majority of migrants (60%) move between similarly developed countries and only 37% of international migrants leave a developing country for a developed country.

Migrant groups who cross country borders or those who move between different linguistic regions within their own countries typically have to accommodate linguistically to their new environment in order to integrate into their new societies and in the process typically have to learn new languages. Coulmas (2018, p. 238) argues that both foreign people and foreign linguistic elements experience assimilation pressures when entering a new society. However, just as some loan words and concepts from one language may be very acceptable and desirable in a society, others may not be welcome and may not receive recognition by the majority population of that society. Similarly, migrants may also be more or less welcome and be more or less expected to assimilate into their new environment. Highly skilled and business migrants may often not see any need to learn the language(s) of their host communities. For example, American or British business migrants may be able to lead their lives through English and send their children to international schools, where they are educated through English (cf. ▶ Sect. 8.3.1). International experts from non-English-speaking countries may decide to do the same and lead their lives in their host countries neither through their native languages nor through the local languages but through the international lingua franca, English.

When migrants enter the societies of their host country, the host country may have various responses to them. The host country may not take any integration measures, linguistic or otherwise, or they may put an emphasis on teaching the local language(s) to the immigrants. Such linguistic and cultural integration measures may either try to support the migrants' multilingualism or they may try to promote linguistic and cultural assimilation of the migrants into the host community. For the immigrants, a good command of the host country's majority/official/dominant language will typically lead to better employment opportunities in the new environment, as shown for, amongst other countries, Israel (Chiswick & Repetto, 2000) and Germany (Dustman & van Soest, 2002). Chiswick and Repetto (2000) point out that also for the host countries the investment into the linguistic resources of the migrants pays off: on the basis of data from Israel, they determine that for their study the costs of a 6-month full-time language course and the resulting proficiency are off-set by 20% increased earnings during the working life as a result of this higher fluency in the language. The investment into language courses, for immigrants, results in a high rate of return of investment into the human capital of the new members of society. However, yet again if migrants do not speak the local languages (yet), those migrants who are English speakers have a lower loss in wages than speakers of other languages. This is due to the value that English as the language with the globally highest communicative potential adds to its speakers (cf. Vida-Mannl, 2022).

9.3 Modes of Communication in Migration Contexts

We have seen that different migration patterns can be distinguished. We have further argued that once they have arrived in their host countries, migrants most typically are under pressure to accommodate linguistically to their environment, though this pressure may be less severe in some contexts than in others. We now turn towards contexts where migrants from various different backgrounds interact and cause specific linguistic and cultural practices to emerge.

9.3.1 Super-Diverse Settings

The population movements that societies experience can lead to new social realities. This has been and is true for major displacements of peoples, for example after wars and natural catastrophes, and also for individual migration due to the search for personal safety or for better living conditions. This is also true for population movements that are conditioned by the search for better economic opportunities (Capstick, 2020). While we have seen in ▶ Sect. 9.2 that the majority of migrants move regionally or between similarly developed countries, industrialised nations, mainly in the global north, attract immigration from diverse backgrounds. In his much-cited work, Vertovic (2007) discusses factors that shape immigrant experiences in their destination countries. The basis of his discussion is formed by the development in Britain from the early 1990s onwards. The interaction of different factors leads to social conditions which Vertovic describes as *super-diverse*, that is, they are influenced by multiple parameters.

The concept of *super-diversity* emphasises those societal complexities which are "distinguished by a dynamic interplay of variables among and increased number of new, small and scattered, multiple-origin, transnationally connected, socio-economically different and legally stratified immigrants […]" (Vertovic, 2007, p. 1024). Not least due to its colonial past, Britain in general, and London in particular, have a long history of population diversity. Between the 1950s and 1970s, London became the home of people from many former colonies because post-war Britain was in urgent need of a large labour force to rebuild the country. More recently, migration to Britain stems from smaller and more diverse groups, who do not have the post-colonial citizenship rights that the earlier migrants were given (Vertovic, 2007, pp. 1027–1028).

Vertovic identifies different key factors that have a strong influence on the experiences, opportunities, and trajectories of the recent immigrants. First, he discusses country of origin. This involves different ethnicities, languages, and various religious identities—even amongst the same faiths. A further large role is played by the migration channels. These determine the legal status of the migrants and the conditions of their stay. Official status is often dependent on the forms of *human capital*, namely education and skill-sets, that the migrants bring along: official status is dependent on different types of work-related migration, study visas for foreign students, or family status—which may give spouses and family of legal permit holders the right to residence. The legal status of asylum seekers and refugees is less secure and often more transitory because rejections are frequent. Rejected claims for asylum or refugee status will sometimes not lead to the claimants leaving the country but may lead them to stay in the country in a form of irregular residence. Equally precarious conditions are experienced by illegal and undocumented immigrants, who are excluded from legal rights and entitlements and from official employment. A further important determinant of a migrant's status is played by gender: asylum seekers are mostly male; work-related migrants in the health- and domestic service systems are overwhelmingly female. Also, females from some geographic regions (South Asia, Middle East, North Africa) tend to have lower employment rates than their male counterparts. This, we would expect, is likely to lead to more precarious social conditions for these females than for their male counterparts although their legal status might be the same.

It is a notable feature of immigration that new immigrants often settle in areas with high employment opportunities, especially if immigrants from the same country of birth have already settled there and can provide a support network (Vertovic, 2007, pp. 1041–1042). Such networks can lead to sizable cultural and linguistic communities in specific places, such as Cypriots living in the London Borough of Haringey. Vertovic notes, however, that the policies by local authorities and communities also play an important role in the formation of such communities, for example as immigrants were increasingly dispersed throughout different regions of the country. While the dispersal of immigrants may challenge networking with their own linguistic communities, it can lead to increased social integration with non-migrant population groups. This is shown for example by recent studies in the German context. Migrants who settle in areas which are geographically remote from their own support networks are likely to feel better integrated and are more likely to engage with the German population than migrants who settle in areas where they find a strong support network amongst their own community (Hallenberg et al., 2018). However, contemporary urban spaces like London may still not only show high concentrations of immigrants, but they may also have a high diversity of immigration from different regions, which then leads to a high diversity index.

Typically, when immigrating into a new country, the immigrants stay in contact with families and friends outside the new country of residence. This retention of transnational contacts is facilitated by changed communication technologies and social media (cf. ▶ Sects. 9.5 and 10). As a result of these technologies, diasporic communities can maintain stronger ties with their areas of origin and their resulting transnationalism has an impact on the practices of migrant communities. Vertovic (2007) reports that international financial networks make money transfer to home communities easier, that the number of transnational marriages has increased and so has international telephone communication—a fact that is even truer with the arrival of enhanced internet and social media technology. As a result, international migrants can keep in touch with their families at home and with their home cultures (cf. ▶ Chap. 10).

Thus, the growing socio-cultural diversity and more varied immigration patterns in the 1990s and 2000s, as well as the immigrants' continued strong links with their countries of origin form the basis of a new super-diversity in societies (Vertovic, 2007). In response to these developments, new approaches need to be found at an organisational level to provide services to super-diverse population groups with different needs. At a personal level, evidence shows that super-diversity leads to new forms of cosmopolitanism and to the emergence of new multilingual identities, such as multi-ethnic language identities discussed in ▶ Sect. 9.4. A linguistic result of super-diversity is that in such environments, language use is likely to go beyond the local majority language, with the possible addition of other local minority language materials. Additionally, language use may be influenced by various immigrant populations and new and complex linguistic resources are shared by globalised citizens through their contacts with translocal, deterritorialised linguistic varieties (cf. Blommaert, 2010). Where many people with diverse repertoires come together and interact, multilingual language use patterns become even more complex.

In a pre-globalised world, the distribution of languages was characterised by a language-in-place (Blommaert, 2010, pp. 5–7), where languages move through space horizontally and show variation along variables of class, gender, or age. This is now being replaced by sociolinguistics of mobility, created by language-in-motion, which is characterised by the interaction of the different, layered spatial and temporal frames in which language users move: in addition to horizontal spaces like regions or neighbourhoods, we also find vertical stratification according to the migrants' social, cultural, or political distinctions. More recent migrants settle in areas where other migrants already live and often the new migrants join networks of earlier migrants, where they receive advice and support. These networks are then very diverse and complex linguistic repertoires result from the interaction of speakers with very different linguistic backgrounds. Local languages are mixed with the migrants' languages and linguae francae. Typically, the more settled linguistic communities influence the linguistic landscape to a larger degree and do so more visibly: shopfronts and posters are more likely to display their languages than those of the more recent migrants (see also ▶ Chap. 12 on linguistic landscapes). The resulting language practices mean that the immigrants have very specific linguistic repertoires, which combine skills from specific contexts in combination with fragments of diverse languages. Blommaert (2010) refers to these language competencies as *truncated repertoires*: repertoires which consist of unevenly distributed, specialised resources drawn from different sources which are mastered to different extents.

Blommaert illustrates the concept of truncated repertoires with an example of a Nigerian woman in a Flemish-speaking area of Belgium, shopping in a Turkish-owned bakery. The resulting conversation would mix local Dutch with English and possibly some German, always depending on the extent of the speakers' language competencies. Visiting a Pakistani-owned telecommunications shop, more English is likely to be used, and in communication with the children's school teachers, Nigerian English would meet the English of the Flemish-speaking teachers. With the children, Dutch and English would be used (most likely together with the mother's own native language(s)), and for contacts with home and the diasporic community, native languages or other languages from home are used. For formal conversations in Dutch in official contexts, the children often have to mediate linguistically. Such linguistic repertoires are both very locally and very internationally oriented. Only parts of the repertoires are transferrable from one to other situations, especially to situations where standard language varieties are required. In other contexts, where languages and language varieties which do not conform to the local linguistic standard are used, the individuals who use those varieties do so to signal their belonging to their communities. The language varieties that are used serve as indexes of the individuals' belonging to their communities (Blommaert, 2010, pp. 9–13).

In Blommaert's approach, mobility affects the conception of language: linguistic resources can change their value, function, or ownership. Language has become a phenomenon which can be described on the basis of different scale-levels: on sociolinguistic scales, orders of indexicality, and polycentricity. Globalisation (and international migration) can cause shifts across these scales. Discussing sociolinguistic scales, Blommaert (2010) argues that scales are a useful metaphor for conceptualising sociolinguistic phenomena. They express space as a stratified and power-invested commodity. While social events unfold in space, they also unfold in time. Blommaert (2010, p. 35) shows how a social event can be conceptualised at a local (or personal), situated level. The example is that of a Ph.D. student telling their tutors: "I'll start my dissertation with a chapter reporting on my fieldwork", and the personal level becomes clear, for example, in the use of the personal pronoun *I*. The same situation could also be conceptualised at a translocal, general level. This is the case if a tutor tells their students: "We start our dissertations with a literature review chapter here", with the pronoun *we* indicating a larger context into which the PhD student is expected to fit. This example illustrates how a personal, local situation can be transported, that is, 'upscaled' from the student's personal statement to a general, impersonal situation, which has general validity and lays down a normative rule: the Ph.D. student says they want to do something, the tutors, who represent the norm-approach, replace the *I* by the *we* and the intentional *will* by the generic present *start*. The student discusses their own plan, the tutors lay down the rules on what the general approach is *here*. Blommaert generalises this observation and conceptualises "time and space" at a "lower scale" level: the student refers to their own momentary and local, situated experience. At a "higher scale" level, the more general and normative levels, the "time and space" levels are Timeless and translocal, widespread respectively. Blommaert gives further examples of such vertical moves, in which higher (social) scale levels prevail over lower scale, individual concerns: these are impersonal/collective concerns prevailing over the personal/individual ones, the decontextualised concerns over the contextualised ones, and so on (Blommaert, 2010, pp. 35–36). In this analysis,

Blommaert shows that high levels of power invoke the right to determine the scale levels when presenting or interpreting an event. Vertical scale levels define who can lay down the social order in their statements. Scalar processes introduce shifts between spaces and they introduce new concepts of time and space and new action patterns. Language is organised by different scales, and a certain order organises it. Power plays an important role in the organisation of these principles.

Another ordering principle is *indexical order*, a metapragmatic principle which organises the pragmatics of language. Indexical order produces patterns of similarity and stability, such as for example register differences, which are expressed by various small patterns, and identify the speaker as a member of a particular community, such as academic, lawyer, medical doctor, or others. Such indexical orders may come to represent prevalent, prestigious, or standard versions of a language, or they may index a non-standard, non-prestigious variety. How any given society at any given time interprets the relative ordering of the different varieties or languages depends on the society's *orders of indexicality*. As some varieties are perceived as more or less prestigious, orders of indexicality illustrate the value that a society gives to a linguistic variety and to the speakers who use this variety. Depending on the context, different groups can be seen as an authority or as the power-holders. Also depending on the context of the interaction, different types of discourses may be appropriate. For this reality, Blommaert (2010, pp. 39–41) uses the concept of *polycentricity*. He points out that in each interaction, many different roles and many different agents may be involved (teachers and fellow students in a class; bride(s), groom(s), guests, and a person officiating at a wedding) and the situational focus may be on one of these participants, but not on the others. Yet, some of these participants will always prevail over others due to their inherently higher status or authority: for example, in the asylum process, the voice of bureaucracy in the host country will systematically prevail over that of the asylum seekers. As people move across different orders of indexicality, Blommaert argues, they can predict—or even steer—communication patterns less successfully than in their own linguistic environment. This has considerable impact on language use in a globalised environment, and thus on language use in migration contexts: when language users cross the scale levels to a new communication context, which lies outside a language users' normal communicative context, these language users may not meet the linguistic expectations of the power-holders in the discourses. This is the situation that the Nigerian immigrant in Blommaert's example finds herself in when talking to the Dutch school teachers. In order to move from the periphery towards the centre of society, the prevalent discourse must be acquired.

Overall, Blommaert (2010) construes language in such super-diverse settings as a mobile resource, which can form local systems defined by their own local functions and norms. Language users try to use their language resources in situationally appropriate ways, even though they may not have full command of all the registers of the individual languages feeding into their linguistic repertoires. While new local discourses may arise, dominant discourses are still shaped by power holders. Blommaerts' approach is described here in some detail as it provides a good explanation for the sociolinguistic factors that influence the language uses that we observe in globalised migration contexts. Local repertoires arise which are influenced by personal and by local multicultural experiences. These both coexist and compete with supra-local, national or even supra-national discourses. We can see this in Blommaert's example of a migrant who negotiates local repertoires and is—to some point—challenged when faced with the local dominant bureaucratic discourses. Blommaert (2010) argues that in our globalised times, we need to renew sociolinguistics that takes the dynamics of population movement into account. We see similar phenomena at work where local or national varieties of a language coexist, and where the local varieties are influenced by multilingual and multicultural contacts. This coexistence and competition of varieties is found, for example, in vernacular Irish English or in a basilectal Caribbean or Singaporean English strongly influenced by local languages and cultures, which coexist with the acrolectal versions of the same variety that make the mainstream discourses. Speakers who want to enter dominant educational or administrative contexts in those communities are expected to start using the more standardised version of the variety, which shows fewer traces of the multilingual origins of the variety.

9.3.2 Communication in Super-Diverse Settings

In migration contexts where speakers with diverse linguistic backgrounds need to communicate, even very reduced communicative repertoires can be used efficiently for "survival communication" (Harrington, 2018). In his study, Harrington (2018) investigates linguistic practices in a community of asylum seekers in Ireland who are of varied linguistic backgrounds and live in a reception centre in rural Ireland. While in general native-speaker English communication, the basic high-frequency vocabulary of spoken language is at about 2000 words, Harrington (2018) finds that the immigrants who contributed to his corpus communicate with a basic vocabulary of about 100 words, which is exploited to the maximum extent possible to enable communication.

These words used by these migrants mainly consist of personal pronouns (*I, you, they*), function words, basic nouns related to contexts relevant to the environment in the accommodation centre, for example *people, language, country,* or *time,* but also nouns like *problem, school,* and *house. Good* is the most frequent adjective and in the top-100-word list, the only other adjective is *different*. Adverbs are not among the top-used category. Verbs that have a high share in the interactions are the communication verbs *talk, speak, say* and *tell,* and also verbs of mental state and cognition like *know, think, want, like,* and *understand,* as well as the general action verb *do* and the modal *can. Eat, help,* and *listen* are not among the top attested ones anymore and are only used by smaller numbers of speakers. Very frequent are deictic markers, such as *this, that, now,* or *here,* which allow the speakers to situate themselves in discourse and in relation to other discourse topics. Discourse markers are rare, except for a general use of *so* in various contexts. Expressions denoting attitudes, stance words, like *really* or *anyway,* are hardly used, the only exception being *just*. These expressions are particularly used to negotiate inter-speaker relationships, for example as down-toners to avoid face threats. These, however, are not exploited in the basic communicative situation (Harrington, 2018).

Harrington reports that in spite of its very restricted register and in spite of uncanonical language use, the language used by the immigrants often does not seem deficient. This is due to the extensive use of interactional markers in the investigated community, especially the response token *yeah*, which is used with various functions in the conversations with the other participants to maintain a share in and exercise subliminal control over the conversation. Another frequent item with a similar function is *okay*. Harrington notes that conversations in general are very cooperative, with turn-taking respected and speakers generally providing a lot of mutual support. Importantly, structures which are used by more proficient speakers are adopted and incorporated into the less proficient speakers' own repertoire. Thus, Harrington (2018), for example, describes how certain L2 speakers of English within the community cut conversational routines down and only use the second half of adjacency pairs, that is, of paired utterances that usually appear together, such as question and answer. For example, more proficient speakers of English, such as Nigerian L2 speakers of English, might anticipate an as yet unasked question and use the second half of the question-answer adjacency pair only. Thus, instead of requesting something, the speakers might use what normally is a typical answer to the question that remains unasked, for example saying *fine* without the question that normally precedes the answer being asked at all. Such language practices were then replicated by the less proficient speakers in Harrington's data set. Like this, specific linguistic forms can arise and spread in such communication-centred varieties, in which the speakers are concerned with communicative efficiency and not with grammatical correctness (Harrington, 2018; see ▶ Sect. 5.2.3 on the grassroots acquisition and use of language). In general, Harrington (2018) characterises the communication that takes place in this highly diverse context with very restricted language competencies as maximising the possible use of known vocabulary and extending its meaning, and as exploiting minimal responses to control the continuation of interaction.

If they are used frequently enough, multilingual- and multicultural varieties (see also Capstick, 2020, pp. 145–180) may eventually reach the status of a specific linguistic variety of a language. The spread and emergence of specific varieties and the linguistic outcome of such diverse and super-diverse contacts within a confined geographic area are illustrated with the help of case studies on two super-diverse varieties, Multicultural London English and Multicultural Paris French.

9.4 Multiethnolects

Nowadays more people live in urban areas than in rural areas and the trend towards urbanisation is increasing. According to the UN, by 2050 two thirds of the population will live in urban areas (cf. Coulmas, 2018, p. 132). As urban areas have a long history of attracting immigration, they have long been melting pots of different cultures and varieties of language, which has turned them into centres of language

9.4 · Multiethnolects

contact and change. Particularly cities that are rich in language resources offer opportunities for speakers of many different language varieties to interact. This may lead to the development of multiethnolects, which are discussed in the following sections.

9.4.1 Introduction to Multiethnolects

We have seen in ▶ Sect. 9.3 above that the interaction of speakers of different languages can lead to the development of specific multilingual language practices. The interaction of different languages and linguistic varieties is particularly likely to happen when the speakers of these different varieties form common social networks. Wherever social networks of speakers of different languages form, we can see the emergence of new language varieties, which have new language features that were not previously used by speakers of a certain social or ethnic group. Often, members of multilingual and multi-ethnic social networks are fairly young, and the language varieties that emerge in their diverse social networks contain phonetic, grammatical, or discourse-pragmatic features which have been assembled from various languages. The new varieties have thus been referred to as *multiethnolects* and have been defined as language varieties that are "born in the informal spontaneous talk of multi-ethnic peer groups; a defining characteristic is that they are used by (usually monolingual) young people from non-immigrant backgrounds as well as by their bilingual peers" (Cheshire et al., 2015, p. 2). These multiethnolects draw on a large repertoire of features associated with different language varieties but also with innovative language use in the community. Much-discussed examples of such varieties are *Multicultural London English* (MLE, e.g. Cheshire et al., 2015) or *Multicultural Paris French* (MPF; Cheshire & Gardner-Chloros, 2018), *Kiezdeutsch* in Germany (Wiese, 2009; see also ▶ Sect. 6.3.4), or Rynkebysvenska in Sweden (Kotsinas, 2001).

Cheshire and Gardner-Chloros (2018, p. 161) describe the typical genesis of such a multi-ethnic variety of a language. In the development of a multi-ethnic urban variety, its speakers usually grow up in a strongly multi-ethnic setting. Children who do not speak English at home receive their majority language input, in this case English-language input, mainly from peers or from siblings who also speak the MLE variety and may also have had limited exposure to the local majority language. In the multilingual communities, already young children use variety-specific features, and this is due to the fact that the multilingual children receive restricted English language input in their homes (Cheshire et al., 2013, p. 11). As a result, very diverse input models exist for the young speakers and a high tolerance of variation and considerable potential for innovation develops in their language practices because the speakers draw on a very diverse feature pool. When these speakers reach adolescence, variety features can stabilise and new varieties can form amongst these speakers. The community-specific features then spread within multi-ethnic friendship groups, and from there on they may be passed on beyond the multi-ethnic communities. As a result, such a multiethnolect can become a vernacular variety that is the unmarked language variety of some speakers; in the case of MLE, the variety of many, particularly young, working class London speakers (Cheshire et al., 2015, p. 3). This variety contains features of both one or more immigrant varieties of English, in this case Jamaican English, and of a vernacular dialect, such as Cockney English.

9.4.2 Linguistic Features of Multiethnolects

Multiethnolects have been observed in a number of different languages. So far, we have mentioned Multicultural London English, Multicultural Paris French, *Kiezdeutsch* in Germany, and Swedish *Rynkebysvenska*. Other multiethnolects discussed in the literature include Dutch *Straattaal* (Cornips & De Rooij, 2013), Norwegian *Jallanorsk* (Opsahl & Nistov, 2010), or the Danish *Københavnsk multietnolekt* (Quist, 2008). In spite of being based on different languages, the linguistic features of such different multi-ethnic varieties show a number of common characteristics. Putting a focus on MLE and MPF, Cheshire et al. (2015, p. 6) observe that in multiethnolects, we are particularly likely to find evaluative adjectives, intensifiers, and phrases with interpersonal and ritual functions, including swear words and taboo words. Thus, in MLE, which has strong Caribbean and Jamaican Creole features, we find *blood* and *bredren* for 'friend', or *cuss* for 'defame', and *tief* for 'steal', which all are of Jamaican origin. MPF uses the Arabic expressions *wallah* ('swear by Allah'), which is also found in many other urban varieties, or *starfoullah* ('I swear'), as well as the quantifier *brat* ('many'). The Romani terms *bicraver* ('to sell or steal'), *maraver* ('to hit'), or the evaluative adjective *narvalo* ('crazy') are also used. In addition to loanwords, we can also observe the use of innovative lexical items. For example in the French multi-ethnic variety *Verlan*, we can find the creations *meuf* ('woman, girl'), which has been innovatively created from French *femme* 'woman' or *keuf* ('police officer'), innovatively created from *flic*, which is colloquial for 'police officer' (cf. McAuley & Carruthers, 2020, p. 168).

In terms of phonetics and prosody, in some cases the phonetic system of the multiethnolect is simplified compared to that of the majority language. For example in MLE, the distinction between the definite articles [ðə] and [ðiː], as in *the pear* and *the apple*, is not made and, similarly, the variation between indefinite articles *a* and *an* is dropped (Cheshire et al., 2015, p. 8). Phonetic influences that can be found in the multiethnolects are less easy to pinpoint to particular input varieties than loanwords are (cf. Cheshire et al., 2015, p. 7). A widespread use of [ʃ] instead of [s] has been explained as the influence of Moroccan Arabic or Berber on Dutch. Even though it also shows similar features, Turkish is considered a less likely source due to sociolinguistic reasons. In MLE, the FACE and GOAT vowels are near-monophthongs, which makes them similar to Jamaican patois, but Cheshire et al. (2015, p. 8) point out that West African or Indian Englishes may also have contributed, and that monophthongal realisations are often the result of second language acquisition processes. Similarly, other phonetic simplifications that have been identified in other multiethnolects, such as the loss of a glottal constriction in Danish or changes to the tone system of Norwegian, can also be understood as features of general second language acquisition. In multi-ethnic French varieties, a glottal onset of vowels has been observed particularly with speakers of North-African origins, as in *Il n'est jamais /ʔ/arrive /ʔ/à l'école* ('He has never arrived at school'; McAuley & Carruthers, 2020, p. 169). In the prosodic system, a number of multiethnolects show a levelling of vowel length: while long vowels become shorter, short vowels become longer, which may lead to the creation of new rhythmic patterns of multiethnolects compared to standard varieties of the languages. This change, too, has been attributed to the influence of language contact (Cheshire et al., 2015, p. 9).

In multiethnolects we can also find simplifications in the inflectional system. Various authors observe that inflections are levelled in different contact varieties (Cheshire et al., 2015). Simplification of gender-marking has been observed for different Scandinavian languages, general levelling of inflections—comprising case, number, and gender marking—has been observed for German multiethnolects (Wiese, 2009), and the regularisation of irregular inflections to usage of regular inflectional endings has been observed for MPF as well as for MLE. Here forms like *childs* (instead of *children*), or *mans*—but also *man, men* or *mens*—(instead of *men*) have been observed (Cheshire et al., 2015, p. 10). Further, *man* has been extended to describe a group of (male) people and from there on further towards the use as a first person singular pronoun where the speaker positions himself as a member of a group of males in general. An example of this is "didn't I tell you man wanna come see you I don't date your friends I date you […]" (Cheshire et al., 2015, p. 10). Here the pronoun *man* refers to the male speaker himself and constructs him as a member of the group of any male person.

A further frequent change in the use of the nominal paradigm is the use of bare nouns after verbs, especially verbs which semantically imply the directionality of an action, without the use of an expected preposition (Cheshire et al., 2015). This has been observed in various contact varieties.

► **Example 9.1**

"*Wir gehen McDonalds*" [German].
  ('We go McDonalds')
  ('We are going to McDonalds.') (Example from German Ruhr Valley, Ronan, P.c.) ◄

Similar examples of leaving out prepositions have been observed in English-based multiethnolects, such as *I'm going school*, or in Swedish multiethnolects (Cheshire et al., 2015, p. 11).

Beyond morphosyntactic changes, syntactic changes are also frequently reported. Freywald et al. (2015) report that the usual word-order pattern of verb-second in main clauses in Dutch-, German-, Swedish-, and Norwegian-based multiethnolects is changing. In the standard varieties of these languages, the subject is placed after the verb if another element is present before the verb. In the multiethnolects of these languages, additional elements, especially simple or complex adverbials, can be found before the verb. Instead of the standard language verb-second order, the syntactic pattern XSVO arises.

> ▶ **Example 9.2**
>
> *"I dag hun lagde somalisk mat"* [Norwegian].
> ('Today she made Somali food')
> ('Today she made Somali food.') (Freywald et al., 2015, p. 83) ◀

> ▶ **Example 9.3**
>
> *"GEStern isch war KUdamm"* [German].
> ('Yesterday I was Ku'damm')
> ('Yesterday I was at Ku'damm.') (Kurfürstendamm = street in Berlin; Freywald et al., 2015, p. 83) ◀

Research on some multiethnolects also reports that question structures are reordered. For example, in MPF, we find embedded questions where the question word does not introduce the embedded question clause but remains in the position where the referent of the question word would have been found in a simple positive clause.

> ▶ **Example 9.4**
>
> *"Je sais pas il est où"*.
> ('I know not he is where')
> ('I don't know where he is.') (Cheshire et al., 2015, p. 13) ◀

This structure of embedded questions is also found in other varieties of French, but it is more frequent in MPF than in other informal varieties (Cheshire et al., 2015, p. 13, Gardner-Chloros & Secova, 2018). In the use of this feature, too, we can observe how a complex structure, the embedded question, is simplified and restructured along the lines of a more frequent structure of the language, a simple main clause.

However, we do not only find specific features in the lexicon and structure of multi-ethnic varieties. We also find innovative patterns of language use such as innovative pragmatic patterns. An interesting pragmatic feature of MLE is the use of relative markers to differentiate topic (what the sentence is about) from comment (what is said about the topic). In standard varieties of English, *that* or *which* are usually used to refer to inanimate antecedents—the noun which is modified by the relative clause—while *who* is used to refer to human antecedents. In MLE, *who* is used as a relative marker if the antecedent of the relative marker is the topic of the conversation, that is, what the conversation is about. *That*, by contrast, is used as a relative marker to refer to an antecedent which will not become the topic of further communication. The functional split between the two relative pronouns can be explained in terms of animacy and salience: as argued above, *who* is used to refer to animate referents in Standard British English, while *that* is used for inanimate referents. As a human/animate referent is more likely to become a topic of discussion than an inanimate thing, *who* can be reinterpreted as a pragmatic marker for the topic of a conversation (Cheshire et al., 2013, 2015, pp. 13–14).

A second pragmatic marker which has been reinterpreted in MLE is the question tag *innit*. The invariant form *innit* is used in different southern varieties of English both as a question tag and as a follow-up, a reaction to something that has been said (Pichler, 2016, p. 64). In MLE, the function of *innit* has been extended to

9.4 · Multiethnolects

marking new information and to marking the topic of conversation (Cheshire et al., 2013, p. 14, Pichler, 2016).

> ▶ **Example 9.5**
> I mean, the sister innit she's about five times bigger than you innit Mark? (Cheshire et al., 2015, p. 14). ◀

As we have seen, the innovations that can be observed in multiethnolects can be attributed to a number of different factors. In some cases, they are directly derived from language contact with the contact languages, especially lexical features like the use of the loan of *starfoullah* ('swear' in MPF) or of *wallah* ('swear by Allah') in various languages and their multi-ethnic varieties (Cheshire et al., 2015, p. 16), or such as the presence of phonetic features like the glottal onset in the multi-ethnic French of North African speakers as in /ʔ/*école* ('school') (McAuley & Carruthers, 2020). Further, innovations may be due to the impact of second language acquisition. This may be the case for example for simplifications of grammatical systems, such as gender systems in the multi-ethnic variety. Further, features that are present in the contact languages and also have a marginal presence in the local majority language may be overused or overextended in the multiethnolect. We find this, for example, in the pragmatic extension of *innit* in MLE. An additional example of this is the lack of the embedded question structure without inversion of the question word as in multicultural varieties of French *je sais pas il va où* (lit.: 'I don't know he goes where?'; Gardner-Chloros & Secova, 2018). These and other examples show multiethnolects often follow similar cross-linguistic principles of language change and innovation (see also Cheshire et al., 2015).

9.4.3 Why Are Multiethnolects Used?

The multiethnolects introduced and discussed in this chapter show considerable evidence of being based on large and varied feature pools, they show strong evidence of language contact, and they display features of language innovation. Not all multiethnolects seem to show the same amount of grammatical innovation, however. Cheshire and Gardner-Chloros (2018, p. 162) point out that even though some innovations are used in MPF, most forms are not used more frequently by bilingual speakers or speakers with multi-ethnic friendship groups than by monolingual speakers. In order to account for this higher degree of standardisation in MPF than in multiethnolects of other languages, Cheshire and Gardner-Chloros suggest that various features can play a role. These may be language policies in former colonies, national ideologies, as well as educational and integration policies. In France, intensive French classes are provided for non-francophone school children with the aim of making them proficient in the French standard language (cf. ▶ Sect. 8.1). Further, the prestige variety of French, that of the *Île de France* in the Paris region, has traditionally been the only prestige variety. The linguistic purity of French in the public domain is further ensured by language laws, which regulate against the use of foreign language influences. When speakers use a non-standard variety of French this is often interpreted as lacking the competence to use the standard language. Otherwise, using a non-standard variety can imply that the speakers want to dissociate from French society at large (McAuley & Carruthers, 2020, pp. 163–165).

As we have seen above, some of the features of the multi-ethnic varieties could be explained as results of second language acquisition processes, for example, the imperfect acquisition of gender marking or other inflectional marking. But using only this explanation to account for multiethnolects in general would fall short on various grounds. Though these features may often originate in language acquisition or contact scenarios, speakers who are fully competent in the standard varieties choose to use them, too. This explanation would also fail to explain why monolingual speakers of the majority languages may use features of the multiethnolect even though they are not influenced by language acquisition phenomena themselves. To explain these factors, we need to consider the sociolinguistic, political and demographic contexts in which the features are used and ask why the speakers decide to use the features. If we do so, we are likely to find that the usage of multiethnolects constitutes acts of identity and that they are used to emphasise the speakers' multicultural identities. So far such multi-ethnic urban varieties are mostly associated with young speakers (Cheshire et al., 2015, p. 20) and are often criticised as corrupt and non-standard (Coulmas, 2018, p. 226) and they and their speakers may be despised by majority-language speakers who adhere to strong standard language ideologies (Kirchner & Fox, 2021). For these reasons, the features of the multiethnolects may not become absorbed by mainstream varieties. Yet for the speakers of such urban vernaculars, the multiethnolects may serve to create a speaker identity that incorporates their super-diverse environments, including local features, language acquisition features, and features of contact languages (McAuley & Carruthers, 2020). Having such a unique identity can then serve as a badge of honour. However, recent research has also found that some features of multicultural varieties are taken up in urban varieties. This is found for TH-stopping in particular, a feature that can be found both in learner varieties and in various L1 and L2 varieties of English. This feature is argued to have been taken from Multicultural Urban English and adopted by certain subcultures, in particular grime and dancehall, and employed by speakers identifying with these cultures to enact tough identities (Drummond, 2018; cf. Capstick, 2020, p. 196).

9.5 International Diasporas

In the preceding sections of this chapter, we have seen how migrants may be influenced by contacts with the new host societies. We have further seen how the host societies may become more diverse due to multinational and multi-ethnic contacts, and how, as a result, language use can also become more diverse. The interaction between host society and migrants is only one aspect of migration. The other aspect of migration is the connection that migrants are likely to continue to have with their countries of origin. The migrants may form *diasporas*, networks of transnational migrant communities, which may consist of individuals, groups, or organisations. Diasporas have been defined as a "postnational space", which redefines "the relationship between nation, soil and identity" (Ponzanesi, 2020, p. 3) which migrant communities experience outside the geographically bounded spaces of their places of origin. Thus, we may speak of the Irish diaspora in Britain, or the Basque diaspora in the United States or elsewhere. In the diaspora, migrants may connect with new communities, but they can also hone their existing social networks with their home communities (Ponzanesi, 2020). Before the arrival of the internet, maintaining contact with home communities was often costly or cumbersome. Diasporic associations may have existed where many immigrants from the same background were found, such as Irish associations in London, Boston, or New York. In earlier times, diasporic contacts with the homelands were sustained through writing letters, telephone calls, or travelling to the country of origin where affordable or possible, for example for holidays or family occasions. In the late decades of the twentieth century, satellite television then made it possible for diasporic communities to take a passive share in events in their home communities. With the arrival of digital communication, keeping up active and passive contacts with the home communities has become both easier and cheaper, and as a result, networks with the home communities can be maintained with considerably more ease.

In illustration of digital diasporas, let us consider the case of the international Basque diaspora. Oiarzabal (2012) shows how members of the Basque diaspora use Facebook. In contrast to many offline associations, membership in online groups is free of charge, does not involve having to travel to specific places, and is open to all interested persons—regardless of whether they can prove Basqueness. The investigated members of the Basque diaspora state that they join Basque associations to keep in contact with other Basques, with Basque culture, or other Basque associations and also to get to know new Basque people. Basque associations further help the diasporic members to be informed about Basque projects and activities, events in the Basque Country, to affirm and reinforce their Basque identities and Basque culture, and to learn more about the culture. On Facebook, the members of the diaspora continue their offline friendships into the online sphere, but they also become friends with people who they did not know before because they are members of their own Basque association or because they are Basques. Facebook is a valued tool for diasporic interaction because it facilitates interaction, provides fast and easy information, and allows contacts with other Basques worldwide. Social networking sites are thus seen as having a positive impact on diasporic communities. They allow community members more comprehensive contacts and thus facilitate the maintenance of their home identities. Being better informed also increases the community members' social capital in the online and offline world. Online community building allows members of diasporic communities to maintain or strengthen their ties with their homelands—be they their place of origin or the place they identify with. This community building often takes place on various online platforms, as well as in the offline world and thus leads to diverse and overlapping networks independent of time and space.

By maintaining closer contacts with the home community, the diasporic communities, as Ponzanesi (2020) points out, can experience an extension of the social control of the home community over the diasporic communities. As a result, the diasporic communities may perpetuate nostalgic, conservative, or reactionary attitudes. By contrast, they are of course also very likely to provide the homeland communities with information about the host countries and their culture and they are likely to act as linguistic mediators and bridge builders between home and host country. Continuing close contacts with the homelands on the one hand may lead members of the diaspora to perpetuate linguistic influences of their home communities which are reinforced by those continuing contacts. On the other hand, the diasporic communities are of course also likely to introduce features of other international linguistic varieties into their communities at home, and from their home communities into their networks in their countries of residence.

In addition, the digital diasporas themselves may also constitute communities or communities of practice of their own, which unite community members both from homelands and digital diasporas (also see ▶ Chap. 10). One such case is the Nigeria and Nigerian-interest centred online community ▶ www.nairaland.com, described by Heyd and Mair (2014), which unites Nigerian locals, diasporic communities, and other participants with an interest in Nigeria. On this platform, the language is English, and Nigerian Pidgin is also used, providing a "Cyber-Nigerian" ethnolinguistic repertoire (Heyd & Mair, 2014, p. 249), which can be used to mark an ethnic identity online. In this online space, Nigerian Pidgin English is used as a digital vernacular which provides participants in the forum with social capital. The authors show that metalinguistic discussions take place and these tie language use to identities. The elements of Nigerian Pidgin are used to act out these identities. The use of the pidgin on the site and the metalinguistic discussions about it further provide some users with a basis to learn Nigerian Pidgin on and from the site.

But given the specific online setting of the language varieties used on the digital platform, different elements and influences mix: in addition to Nigerian variety-specific features, features of netspeak and items from other varieties of Englishes, which Nigerian speakers are either in contact with or whose speakers also interact on the Nairaland platform, contribute to this digital repertoire. Typical examples of such a blended repertoire are the expressions ITK, "I too know" used for a smart Alec, and JJC, "Johnny just come", used for a naïve new immigrant and transferred to the digital variety (Heyd & Mair, 2014, pp. 259–260).

Interested members of this online community need not be in the Nigerian homeland or even hail from the homeland, instead, they can participate in the deterritorialised, mediatised, and commodified discourses. The use of Nigerian Pidgin as well as the use of other specific features of Nigerian English and of the online register used on the website provide users with social capital for interacting on the site.

❓ Exercises
1. Compare immigration and emigration in your country.
    (a) Where do immigrants mainly come from?
    (b) Where do emigrants mainly emigrate to?
    (c) What are the reasons for immigration to and emigration from your country?
2. Consider Multicultural Urban Varieties.
    (a) Grime star Stormzy uses his variety of Multicultural London English in his lyrics. Work through the opening lines of his "Shut up" and try and

9.5 · International Diasporas

identify features that are not typical of British Standard English. Can you find any that are typical of MLE?

"State your name, cuz." "Stormzy innit?" "And what're were we doing today" "Rappin' innit?" "Yeah?" "Fuckin' rappin.'" "Yeah? Fire in the park—let's go" "Man try sayin' he's better than me. Tell my man shut up." "Shut up!" "Mention my name in your tweets. Oi, rudeboy, shut up." "Shut up." "How can you be better than me? Shut up." "Shut up." "Best in the scene? Tell my man shut up! Couple man called me a backup dancer. Onstage at the BRITs, I'm a backup dancer. If that makes me a backup dancer, the man in your vids, backup dancer. The man in your pics, backup dancer. Man wanna chat about backup dancer. Big man like me with a beard. I'm a big man, how the fuck can I backup?" (▶ https://www.youtube.com/watch?v=RqQGUJK7Na4. Accessed: 15.09.2021.)

(b) Do similar urban varieties of your own language exist in your country of residence? Find information on them, if you can. Who speaks them?
(c) Can you observe any of the features that have been observed in the multi-ethnic varieties in this chapter also in the multi-ethnic varieties in your own countries?

Summary

In this chapter, we have introduced different types of migration. We have argued that both the type of migration and the integration measures taken by the host countries influence the extent of linguistic assimilation by the migrants in their host country. How the language of the host country is used by the immigrants is meaningful from a sociolinguistic point of view as the migrants' linguistic behaviour is typically perceived as showing their degree of overall assimilation to the host society. Yet we have argued that often immigrants have truncated repertoires of linguistic competencies based on the contexts in which they use their repertoires. We have shown that, initially, those repertoires can be very restricted but still serve to communicate efficiently. When the speakers are well established in their host societies, and in particular when they interact in multilingual contexts, features that index multilingual—and multicultural—identities may be kept and deliberately emphasised in order to enact an identity that is different from that of mainstream society. Particularly in highly diverse contexts, this may lead to the formation of multiethnolects. We have observed that many features of such multiethnolects can be traced back to language contacts with specific languages, but we have also seen that other features could be caused by general language contact phenomena and processes of second language acquisition. Further, we have argued that international diasporas of speaker groups of particular linguistic backgrounds can cause bidirectional language contacts: the speakers in the diasporic communities may introduce features of their own home languages into the language of the host country and features of their host countries' languages may spread to the home countries and influence non-diasporic varieties.

References

Blommaert, J. (2010). *The sociolinguistics of globalisation*. Cambridge University Press.
Capstick, T. (2020). *Language and migration*. Routledge.
Cheshire, J., & Gardner-Chloros, P. (2018). Introduction: Multicultural youth vernaculars in Paris and urban France. *Journal of French Language Studies, 28*(Special Issue 2), 161–164.
Cheshire, J., Kerswill, P., Fox, S., & Torgersen, E. (2013). Language contact and language change in the multicultural metropolis. *Revue Francaise de Linguistique Appliquée, 18*, 63–76.
Cheshire, J., Nortier, J., & Adger, D. (2015). Emerging multiethnolects in Europe. *Queen Mary's Occasional Papers Advancing Linguistics, 33*, 1–27.
Chiswick, B. A., & Repetto, G. (2000). IZA discussion paper 177: Immigrant adjustment in Israel: Literacy and fluency in Hebrew and earnings. In S. Djajic (Ed.), *International migration: Trends, policy and economic impact* (pp. 204–228). IZA Institute of Labour and Economics. Retrieved November 4, 2022, from https://www.iza.org/de/publications/dp/177/immigrant-adjustment-in-israel-literacy-and-fluency-in-hebrew-and-earnings
Cornips, L., & De Rooij, V. A. (2013). Selfing and othering through categories of race, place, and language among minority youths in Rotterdam, The Netherlands. In P. Siemund, I. Gogolin, J. Davydova, & M. Schulz (Eds.), *Multilingualism and language contact in urban areas: Acquisition–development–teaching–communication* (pp. 129–164). John Benjamins.
Coulmas, F. (2018). *An introduction to multilingualism: Language in a changing world*. Oxford University Press.
Drummond, R. (2018). Maybe it's a grime [t]ing: th-stopping among urban British youth. *Language in Society, 47*(2), 171–196.
Dustman, C., & van Soest, A. (2002). Language and the earnings of immigrants. *Industrial and Labor Relations Review, 55*, 473–479.
Freywald, U., Cornips, L., Ganuza, N., Nistov, I., & Opsahl, T. (2015). Beyond verb second—a matter of novel information-structural effects? Evidence from Norwegian, Swedish, German and Dutch. In J. Nortier & B. A. Svendsen (Eds.), *Language, youth and identity in the 21st century: Linguistic practices across urban spaces* (pp. 73–92). Cambridge University Press.
Gardner-Chloros, P., & Secova, M. (2018). Grammatical change in Paris French: in situ question words in embedded contexts. *Journal of French Language Studies, 28*(2), 181–207.
Hallenberg, B., Dettmar, R., & Aring, J. (2018). *Migranten, Meinungen, Milieus.* vhw-Migrantenmilieu-Survey. Retrieved April 18, 2021, from https://www.vhw.de/fileadmin/user_upload/07_presse/PDFs/ab_2015/vhw_Migrantenmilieu-Survey_2018.pdf
Harrington, K. (2018). *The role of corpus linguistics in the ethnography of a closed community: Survival communication*. Routledge.
Heyd, T., & Mair, C. (2014). From vernacular to digital ethnolinguistic repertoire: The case of Nigerian Pidgin. In V. Lacoste, J. Leimgruber, & T. Breyer (Eds.), *Indexing authenticity. Sociolinguistic perspectives* (pp. 242–266). de Gruyter.
Kirchner, R., & Fox, S. (2021). Multicultural London English and its speakers: a corpus-informed discourse study of standard language ideology and social stereotypes. *Journal of Multilingual and Multicultural Development, 42*(9), 792–810. https://doi.org/10.1080/01434632.2019.1666856
Kotsinas, U. B. (2001). Pidginization, creolization and creoloids in Stockholm, Sweden. In N. Smith & T. Veenstra (Eds.), *Creolization and contact* (pp. 127–155). John Benjamins.
McAuley, D., & Carruthers, J. (2020). Investigating perceptions of Banlieue French: Problematising theory and methods. In C. Mar-Molina (Ed.), *Researching language in superdiverse contexts* (pp. 159–182). Multilingual Matters.
Oiarzabal, P. J. (2012). Diaspora Basques and online social networks: An analysis of users of Basque institutional diaspora groups on Facebook. *Journal of Ethnic and Migration Studies, 38*(9), 1469–1485. https://doi.org/10.1080/1369183X.2012.698216
Opsahl, T., & Nistov, I. (2010). On some structural aspects of Norwegian spoken among adolescents in multilingual settings in Oslo. In P. Quist & B. A. Svendsen (Eds.), *Multilingual urban Scandinavia. New linguistic practices* (pp. 49–63). Multilingual Matters.

References

Pichler, H. (2016). Uncovering discourse-pragmatic innovations: Innit in Multicultural London English. In H. Pichler (Ed.), *Discourse-pragmatic variation and change in English. New methods and insights* (pp. 59–85). Cambridge University Press.

Ponzanesi, S. (2020). Digital diasporas: Postcoloniality, media and affect. *International Journal of Postcolonial Studies, 22*(8), 977–993. https://doi.org/10.1080/1369801X.2020.1718537

Quist, P. (2008). Sociolinguistic approaches to multiethnolect: Language variety and stylistic practice. *International Journal of Bilingualism, 12*, 43–61.

Vertovic, S. (2007). Super-diversity and its implications. *Ethnic and Racial Studies, 30*(6), 1024–1054.

Vida-Mannl, M. (2022). *The value of the English language in global mobility and higher education: An investigation of higher education in Cyprus*. Bloomsbury.

Wiese, H. (2009). Grammatical innovation in multiethnic urban Europe: New linguistic practices among adolescents. *Lingua, 119*, 782–780.

Key Readings

Blommaert, J., & Ramption, B. (2011). Language and super-diversity. *Diversities, 13*(2), 1–21.

Kerswill, P., & Williams, A. (2005). New towns and koineisation: linguistic and social correlates. *Linguistics, 43*, 1023–1048.

Further Reading

Harrington, K. (2018). *The role of corpus linguistics in the ethnography of a closed community: Survival communication*. Routledge.

Multilingualism in New Media

Contents

10.1 Introduction – 218

10.2 The History of Multilingual New Media – 218

10.3 Practices of Multilingualism in New Media – 220
10.3.1 Multilingual Sites – 220
10.3.2 Multilingual Language Use on the Internet – 220

10.4 Benefits and Pitfalls of Multilingual New Media – 224

10.5 Two Case Studies – 226
10.5.1 Multilingual Exchanges in YouTube Comments – 226
10.5.2 Appropriating your Idol: Instagram – 230
10.5.3 What the Sample Studies Show Us – 233

References – 234

© The Author(s), under exclusive license to Springer Nature Switzerland AG 2023
S. Buschfeld et al., *Multilingualism*,
https://doi.org/10.1007/978-3-031-28405-2_10

10.1 Introduction

The rise of the world wide web in general has changed global language practices as it allows language users to communicate across geographical and linguistic boundaries. In particular the arrival of *Web 2.0*, which offers internet users the possibility to create their own content and to interact with other users' content, allows both national and international interaction at an unprecedented level. Given this, the internet and social media sites have turned into major sites of linguistic practices in general and of multilingual practices in particular. The use of multilingualism on the internet is a fairly recent development still, and this chapter showcases the internet and social media as sites of multilingual practices. The chapter starts with a brief outline of the development of online media. Then, we discuss multilingual practices on the internet and in social media. After this, we add our point of view to the discussion whether online media are a threat to multilingualism, or whether they are beneficial for it. We conclude this chapter with two case studies on multilingual language use in social and online media, namely on multilingual language practices in YouTube comments and in Instagram comments.

10.2 The History of Multilingual New Media

Communication technologies and new media are omnipresent in the lives of most of us today. While we are working—be it online or offline—we are likely to have emails coming in, and friends and family are contacting us on social media sites and messaging apps. We, as users of these technologies, make the technologies work for us, but at the same time, the technologies themselves are also shaping our own worlds and, in what is referred to as domestication of technologies (see e.g. Barton & Lee, 2013), we have started to take this for granted. An outcome of the impact of communication technologies on our lives is that there are changes to the way in which we communicate, and thus the way how we use language. This is true on a micro-level: pragmatic principles that regulated turn-taking, that is, who has the right to speak when in a conversation, and face work, the use of politeness in interaction, have to differ when we chat electronically and when we do so face-to-face. It is also true on a macro-level: communities of practice, such as online gamers, have turned international. Also, speech communities are spread more widely and can communicate across wider spatial distances than they used to. For example, a speaker of Nigerian English may now talk to their home community from New York or from Dublin. While in the early days of digitisation speakers of minority languages might have kept in touch with the speech communities in their homelands through—increasingly cheaper—phone calls and via satellite TV, today's more sophisticated multimedia technologies allow digital participation in home cultures for everyone who lives in a global diaspora. Androutsopoulos and Juffermans (2014, p. 2) argue that digital media have moved from serving as containers of cultural products to facilitators of deterritorialised interaction, and this deterritorialised interaction not only connects members of a diasporic community

10.2 · The History of Multilingual New Media

with their home cultures, it additionally allows members of the host communities to participate in the cultural interaction with any digitalised community. As a result, language practices, as well as their analyses, are changing: in the past, multilingual language use was conceptualised as mixing static language systems, for example in the analysis of code-switching. Now, new approaches investigate multilingual practices by seeing them as fluid systems, as is done in translanguaging approaches (cf. ▶ Sect. 8.3.2.2).

Arguably, the birthday of the first of our new media was in 1991, when the world wide web saw the light of day. The first world wide web had fewer users than today and, even more importantly, before the arrival of *Web 2.0*, web pages were largely static and allowed only little interaction between consumers and the authors of web page content. This changed in the early years of the new millennium, with the arrival of *Web 2.0* and its new possibilities for participation, interaction, and, as a result, for digital social networking. Mayor networks like Facebook, Instagram, or YouTube and their interactive functions would not have been possible without *Web 2.0*.

In its early days, the internet was English-speaking and arguably, the prevalence of English in the early internet increased the global spread of English even more rapidly. In 1998, more than 80% of websites were in English. German, Japanese, French, and Spanish accounted for one-digit percentages. By 2012 websites in English only accounted for 55% of all websites. Today, the web uses many, potentially all, languages (Barton & Lee, 2013; Lee, 2016; Coulmas, 2018). By 2020, English is still in the lead, but other languages are catching up. While more than a billion speakers of English use the internet, 0.8 billion speakers of Chinese do so, followed by Spanish and Arabic speakers; the numbers of Arabic show the largest growth (Internet World Stats, ▶ https://www.internetworldstats.com/stats7.htm). The proportion of English language websites amongst the most popular global websites has also decreased from 80% in 1998 to 55.3% in 2015 as reported by Lee (2016). However, by 2021, the data source for Lee's study, ▶ w3techs.com,[1] reports a slight rise again of English language websites to 60.5% of the main global websites. Thus, there has been a strong increase of websites in languages other than English, but English has clearly been able to hold its position as a major player on the world wide web. It remains to be seen whether the trend for other languages to continue demanding a larger share of the internet continues. After all, in many respects, Romanised scripts are still easier to use on the internet than, for example, Arabic or Chinese writing systems, and English is still growing in importance as an international language and language of science (Lee, 2016).

Given the increased access to international communication tools worldwide, it is not surprising that users employ internet-based media for global communication, both in the still prevalent language(s) of the internet and in their own languages. For this reason, when we think about multilingualism and researching multilingualism, we have to keep a firm focus on analysing new media as a prime location for multilingual practices, not only of younger users.

---

1 W3techs (2021). ▶ http://w3techs.com/technologies/overview/content_language/all.

10.3 Practices of Multilingualism in New Media

With the arrival of the possibilities that new media offer to language users, the questions of which languages could, would, or should be used have become relevant in these media. The international reach of new media has not only created sites for multilingual language practices online, but the language practices have also sparked the interest of linguists working on multilingualism. In the following, we explore how multilingualism is used on new media, that is on the internet and, more specifically, on social media sites.

10.3.1 Multilingual Sites

The arrival of the interactive *Web 2.0* has offered numerous possibilities for multilingual contacts. We may find web pages which offer the same or similar content in different languages, such as Wikipedia, or we may find resources where different languages are used on one page, for example on bilingual news sites, such as the website of the bilingual Spanish-Basque newspaper *Gara*. In addition to websites on which the owners provide multilingual content, further options for multilingual interaction can be found in users' comments on news sites or blogs, on sharing sites like Youtube and in their users' comments, or in personal networking spaces like Instagram, Facebook, Twitter, Flickr, or TikTok, to name only some of the most popular ones. On personal networking spaces, multilingual practice can vary widely. Barton and Lee (2013, pp. 44–54) mention the following slots in which language practices can be observed: username, profile-information, postings, tags, or hashtags. To these, we should of course add the comments by the various users of the sites, which may be in their first languages or in other commonly understood languages. In order to help users decode content in other languages, some sites offer their users help with multilingual content. Often this is done through the use of translation sites such as Google Translate or Bing. Barton and Lee (2013, p. 63) point out that the option exists for Facebook users to have content which they do not understand translated into a language they understand. Tripadvisor, too, uses Google Translate to supply comments in the users' own or preferred languages. Where a translation option is not available on the chosen site itself, many users will choose to input data into a translation site in order to be able to engage with web content in other languages.

10.3.2 Multilingual Language Use on the Internet

In addition to multilingual sites, many users choose to employ multilingual practices themselves. As Barton and Lee (2013, pp. 56–60) note, multilingual users consider the following factors when interacting online. They take into account who the target audience is in terms of location, education, linguistic, social, and cultural background. While first languages may be used, language users often agree that an international language, English, should be used to communicate with those who do not share the local language (Barton & Lee, 2013, p. 56). The decision which language to use is based on who the intended viewer is. The intended viewers may be the whole online community, or listed online friends, or real-life friends. Discussing language choice on Flickr, Barton and Lee (2013) argue that here the language is usually selected on the basis of what the intended target audience speaks. If the social media user knows the audience in real life, a language that is shared by the group is chosen. However, if the intended audience is unknown or consists of both known and unknown members, then English is used. The choice of language also depends on how people want to appear to their viewers (Barton & Lee, 2013, pp. 56–57), whether they want to be seen as part of a local or clearly delimited community or as a global citizen. The choice of a language or languages for this task is, at least partly, based on the audience that the writers want to reach, and thus is a form of audience design (cf. ▶ Sect. 11.4). By using multiple languages, including English as a lingua franca, the users can underline their global identities, by using a specific language, such as Chinese or Spanish, the users partly interact with their local networks, and partly display their local identities to a global network. This use of both global and local identities is known as *glocalisation* (Lee, 2016, pp. 57–60).

In addition to whether the post is aimed at one's local contacts, or whether it wants to reach an international audience, language choice also depends on what kind of content is posted (Barton & Lee, 2013, p. 58) and on how the social medium is used, whether it is used informally and personally or in formal and business contexts. So, while we may ask whether a website is (predominantly) in one language or another, a media user may decide creatively and strategically which language to use depending on the individual context (Lee, 2016, pp. 34–36).

Generally, various opportunities exist for multilingual interaction and users are free to make their own micro- and macro-choices that go beyond the question of which main languages they choose. All these multilingual encounters of media users will form part of the users' translingual practices (Barton & Lee, 2013, p. 60). The notion of translingual practices refers to communicative practices across different communities, for example if users within a multilingual country communicate with each other, or if users communicate with speakers of different languages in different countries. In the latter case, the users are likely to use a lingua franca such as English. Further, diasporic communities may communicate in their common language and additionally they may use language varieties which are influenced by language practices from both their host communities and their countries of origin.

However, new media language is not identical across the different media, and different levels of formality can be found in new media language. The different media, and the different language choices made on them, additionally determine whether, and if so to what extent, multilingualism is used at all in these media. We find that there are strong differences between mass media and user-generated content, and there is a strong impact of style level and audience on these choices. Mass media and content of higher stylistic levels will typically show less multilingualism than user-generated content does. Where mass media display multilingualism, we will often find use of a local language plus a dominant or lingua franca variety, such as English (cf. Lee, 2016). In user-generated content, by contrast, we often find different multilingual practices, for example on such social media sites like Facebook, Instagram, or in comments on YouTube videos, and possibly in comment sections of international sites like Tripadvisor or Amazon, or on news sites or blogs. The user-generated, partly multilingual content on such large international media sites addresses a subset of target audiences amongst the general users of the sites, and this subset is directly addressed through the choice of language.

Such user-generated content, particularly on social networks, allows users to purposely create groups that maintain languages and identities internationally (Androutsopoulos, 2013; Androutsopoulos & Juffermans, 2014; Lee, 2016). In his work, Androutsopoulos (2013) draws parallels between digital social networks and non-digital urban social networks. He argues that in our globalised world, both cities and digital networks are sites of translocal contacts which also enable multilingual practices. He points out that nowadays social processes in general depend on mediation for communication flow, which may be digital. Digital networks can be used to enable both local and transnational communication flows, and these can maintain mutual relationships and language practices.

In a study of multilingual practices on Facebook, an example of networked multilingualism, Androutsopoulos (2013) frequently finds a special communicative situation in the interactional practices: in contrast to real life, Facebook friends from different contexts are addressed at the same time, be it close or extended family, friends, colleagues, or further national and international networks. Addressing all these different recipients together has been referred to as context collapse (Androutsopoulos, 2013). In cases of intercultural or international communication, Facebook users often select English to address both the local L1 speakers of a different language and international, English-speaking networks. Alternatively, the users may specifically address one subset of their network by choosing a language that does not include the entire network but restricts the audience to network members of that language group. He argues that by using such language practices, users employ a key function of code-switching, namely addressee specification. In this, the choice of language makes clear to whom a certain utterance is addressed.

Androutsopoulos (2013) investigates the language practices of a group of teenage secondary school pupils with Greek backgrounds in Germany. To this end, he researches language use on Facebook walls, in different multilingual *wall events*. Wall events are the sequences of posts shown on the Facebook wall, which consist of at least one post and all the potential comments on that post. His study shows how the pupils, who are multilingual in Greek, German, English and with further, more restricted competencies in other languages, use their multilingualism in a way that is determined by genres, thematic context, and their own and their interactants' preferences.[2] The main languages are Greek and German, and language choice depends both on language competence and context. Other outside influences, such as the use of youth slang or especially the discussion of media in other languages, can cause further, typically more local, language shifts. Androutsopoulos (2013) finds that these language uses can include monolingual moments as well as multilingual uses. The choice of languages is determined by the multilingual language users' communicative routines of their digital literacies which may be close to oral language practices. Overall, Androutsopoulos' example shows how the social medium Facebook is used by a network of multilingual users to create and maintain their identities.

A further example of a medium that is used to reach an international community is YouTube. From its beginnings in 2005, YouTube has turned into a highly successful international site which is not only used for sharing media but also for commenting on their content. According to YouTube figures,[3] at the end of the year 2020, YouTube had more than two billion users who logged in monthly, and it offers local sites in more than 80 languages. Every minute, more than 500 h of content are uploaded. In his study on YouTube as a site for multilingual practices, Schneider (2016) points out that YouTube is explicitly community oriented in allowing not only setting up but also subscribing to channels, providing comment space and email link distribution options. As such it is not only an entertainment website and a cultural archive, but can also generate mass movements and income as a site for advertisements and through revenue sharing programmes. Schneider argues that while the majority of its content is user-generated, its lack of professional standards means that it is the professionally created content that is the most viewed. The majority of the most frequently viewed videos on Youtube are professional music videos, and in late 2020, of the 20 most frequently viewed, 16 videos use the English language, 2 videos feature Spanish, one is in Korean, and one in Russian.[4] One formerly most frequently viewed video, the Korean Pop *Gangnam Style*, had been overtaken at that time by another Korean-produced feature, an English language children's song, *Baby Shark Dance*, with over 7.5 billion views in early 2021.

Schneider (2016) evaluates the usefulness of YouTube for linguistic analysis and emphasises the use of World Englishes and their representation in the language of the people speaking in the videos. In doing so, he distinguishes between metalinguistic clips, which deal with language issues either by describing them or by mocking them, and natural clips, which use a certain linguistic variety either naturally or consciously and functionally in order to reach a specific audience. Natural clips may have the advantage over sociolinguistic approaches that they avoid the observer's paradox: the observer's paradox is the problem that when tell-

---

2 Greek and German multilingualism is particularly interesting here as different but structurally compatible scripts are used in the two languages. As a result, Greek script may be used or Greek may be more or less narrowly transliterated into Romanised script.
3 At ► https://blog.youtube/press/ (last accessed 02.01.2021).
4 ► https://influencermarketinghub.com/most-viewed-youtube-videos/ (last accessed 02.01.2021).

ing the informants what the researchers want to find out, the informants may be caused to change their linguistic behaviour and avoid the forms the researchers are trying to investigate (see ▶ Sect. 13.4.2 for further explanation and discussion, and ▶ Sect. 14.2.1 on ethical aspects of the data collection process). However, even though YouTubers may not expect their language use to be investigated by researchers, many YouTubers will be using their language very consciously as a means of self-presentation because their performances are public and potentially widely viewed. In metalinguistic clips, the language attitudes of the producers play an important role in how a variety is displayed and evaluated, often in comparison with other varieties. In that, Schneider points out, the presenters/uploaders show themselves to be aware of self-representation, of cultural differences, and of their identities and perspectives. While Schneider (2016) has some reservations about using YouTube as a source of linguistic data, he cautiously recommends it for its easily accessible, wide availability. Overall, he considers it a good source for exposure to varieties, or, in spite of contextualisation and representativeness problems, a source of varied data. Thus, in a given video clip, qualitative features—the presence of particular items—can be examined, and features may also be quantified. In the context of a study on multilingualism, a researcher might be interested in questions like how many different languages are used in a given clip and who uses them for what. Or we may ask what lexical items or grammatical structures are used which have developed under the influence of language contact.

In a further linguistic study based on YouTube, Sharma (2014) investigates diasporic Nepali discourse in YouTube comments. Sharma shows how comments in the medium are used as spaces of diasporic involvement with the nation of origin. The study illustrates how the site is used for identity building of the diasporic community. In comments on a YouTube video featuring the Health Minister's speech at a United Nations meeting, the commentators evaluate the minister's language competencies. By doing so, they manifest their own language attitudes and ideologies as members of an international, diasporic community in relation to a representative of their country of origin. In this approach, then, it is not the producers of the videos, as discussed by Schneider (2016), but the commenters of the video who portray the awareness of the cultural features expressed in the minister's language, and who take an evaluative stance on the linguistic features and thus on the cultural attitudes expressed towards them. How the linguistic practices of the commenters themselves can be exploited is discussed in ▶ Sect. 10.5.

10.4 Benefits and Pitfalls of Multilingual New Media

We have seen in ▶ Sect. 10.2 that the largest part of internet content is dominated by global or majority languages. As shown above, the most frequently used languages on the internet are English, Chinese, Spanish, and Arabic. However, regardless of their first language, media users often use English to communicate with non-local, international readers or readers whose language is unknown. For users of minority languages, the international character of many media may mean that there will always be readers or viewers who are not able to interact in the minority language. This is likely to lead to the authors using the majority language instead to reach larger audiences. Thus, Androutsopoulos (2013) cautions that minority languages can come under pressure from majority languages when they are used online. He points out that if minority languages are predominantly used only in genres that are closely related to a specific culture or if they are mainly used to bracket majority language content, this can be a sign of the majority language exercising pressure on the minority language community.

These observations suggest that new media are likely to give the death blow to small languages. In how far this is the case is also discussed in Lee (2016, pp. 91–92). As we have seen in ▶ Sect. 4.2, minority languages have indeed often been threatened by coming into contact, and thus into competition, with majority languages. However, online media also offer the possibility to create content for and by linguistic minority communities. As such, the online media carry potential for the maintenance of minority languages since they allow global, fast, and comparatively cheap distribution of content. Language materials can be shared and online classes can be made accessible to interested users worldwide. As such, online media are an efficient way for communities to obtain content which could otherwise not be produced or distributed in an economically viable way.

Coulmas (2018, pp. 198–200) gives the example of Wikipedias that are created, often by very few individuals, in minority language varieties such as Extremaduran, Franco-Provençal, or Palatinate. Further, there are Wikipedias in earlier varieties of languages, such as in Latin or Old English. For such minority languages, Wikipedia provides the possibility to be used in a written format, and this, as Coulmas points out, offers status enhancement to the languages by bringing them into the digital age. The pages would then also be visible to and usable for members of widely dispersed speech communities. Thus, the internet can provide a lifeline for such small languages and their users and can help to preserve minority languages across space and time by providing, for example, free dictionaries and grammars. Yet, like Androutsopoulos (2013), Coulmas argues that the internet may also speed up the extinction of endangered languages, especially in the context of previously isolated communities, by bringing them into contact with majority cultures and languages. Due to these contacts with majority languages, the minority language may be reduced to usage in increasingly restricted domains outside the requirements of modern life, which may lead to the decline of the minority language. Thus, cyberspace can be seen as both a chance and a risk, especially for endangered languages. However, cyberspace is no doubt here to stay and is continuing to increase its hold on our life. If users can be provided with the option to obtain media content in a minority language, then this is certainly preferable to having to use only majority languages online. As Lee (2016, pp. 23, 103) points out, it is not only on the internet that the viability of a minority language is decided but in its broader societal context.

Research into the sociolinguistics of minority languages online also shows that minority languages can indeed be maintained by creating international networks. The issue is also very important in the context of global mobilities, which can lead to a potentially worldwide spread of communities and their languages. International migrants can use new technologies to keep in contact with their languages and their cultures in dedicated forums or groups. If you are a Welsh speaker anywhere in the world, you may join Facebook groups of Welsh expats anywhere around the globe, or you may follow any Welsh speaker on Twitter. You may also decide to turn into Welsh Flickr/Fflicr to share photographs from Wales or comment on them in Welsh and join virtual communities in addition to your real-life ones. Barton and Lee (2013, pp. 64–65) give the example of international members of the Assyrian community, who use Assyrian for identity construction in English language chatrooms. The majority language content is bracketed by greetings or signing off in the minority language or Assyrian is used for specific cultural Assyrian topics to underline Assyrian identity construction by language choices. Like this, a global community can be maintained in spite of geographic distances.

In such written practices of language use, minority languages or other formerly uncodified languages can profit. Social media sites provide only a low threshold for the production of a written form of any language. And by receiving a written context, otherwise non-written oral language practices can become validated. Languages can expand their repertoires from being a non-standardised language, such as Colloquial Egyptian Arabic, which used to be considered too informal to be written, to an increasingly written language which is accepted and acceptable in more and more contexts (Barton & Lee, 2013, p. 64).

New media have developed into means of communication that take central positions in the lives of particularly younger population groups, who spend large amounts of time interacting on these media. As time and particularly space constraints play only a small role here, new networks based on various interests emerge on a daily basis and may transcend group and national boundaries.

10.5 Two Case Studies

Major strands in online multilingualism research are surveys of linguistic diversity in online media, research on linguistic features, pragmatic, or sociolinguistic factors of multilingual writing or multilingual discourse analysis, and finally ethnographic research on why and when users use certain languages or language practices (Lee, 2016, p. 124). In the following, we introduce two small-scale studies situated in a feature analysis paradigm as examples of research that can be carried out within the context of multilingualism in new media. Both studies offer insights into translingual practices in user-generated content in online media. The case studies are further intended to offer ideas for research topics and research methods that can be used in the examination of online media (for further details, see ▶ Sect. 14.2.1).

10.5.1 Multilingual Exchanges in YouTube Comments

YouTube has been identified as a valuable resource for linguistic research, and for research on varieties in particular (Schneider, 2016; cf. ▶ Sect. 10.3). In addition to the language practices that can be observed in the videos themselves, the viewers'

10.5 · Two Case Studies

comments can also be analysed in terms of the attitudes that are displayed towards the posted content and the language use in it (Sharma, 2014; ▶ Sect. 10.3). Further, the viewers' comments can be a research topic in their own right as, first, posts from a multilingual country are likely to trigger multilingual comments and second, clips with an international appeal may generate responses in the viewers' languages. The small case study (Ronan, In prep. a[5]) presented here investigates (1) which languages are triggered in responses to a video clip that uses English in a lingua franca context, and (2) how interaction takes place between the poster and the commenters. To this end, content from a channel based in India has been selected, which is a strongly multilingual country that uses English as one of its official languages. As the intention of the study is to observe maximally natural language behaviour, the focus was on instructional videos that deal with a topic that is potentially interesting to a very varied audience without having a focus on any linguistic or otherwise educational issues.

For this, a video has been selected from an Indian gardening channel, which, in order to protect the channel owner's privacy, we shall refer to here as *M's Gardening Techniques*, which has more than half a million subscribers. The exact location of the channel owner is not given except for stating that it is in India. All the channel's videos show the suggested techniques in great visual detail and provide either no comments at all or only give sparse key information in the form of English subtitles, which will encourage viewing by a multilingual audience. From a large number of posts, a video clip was selected that has an appropriate number of comments for a small sample study, namely "Double Grafting On One Mango Tree!!!". At the time of its analysis in early 2021, the video had more than a million views and 239 comments. These comments consist of 154 comments and 85 responses to comments. In order to determine the language choices in the comments, comments in unknown languages were entered into Google Translate and the auto-detection of the language was used to determine the language.

The channel's name is in English, *M's Gardening Techniques*, and the hashtags posted for the video address an English-using audience, namely #mangografting #double, #juckfruitgrafting. The description of the video likewise is in English. Comments on the video clip mostly either thank the channel owner for uploading the video or engage, mainly negatively but also positively, with the music. A large number of comments ask further questions on details of the content of the video. Given the language choice in the clip and the contextualisation of the clip as well as the English language name of the channel, it is not surprising that the English language predominates in the comments. Of the 239 comments, we find that 128 are in English. A further 23 consist of English and Hindi in almost equal parts. ◘ Table 10.1 gives an overview of the language choices in the comment section.

◘ Table 10.1 shows that about 80% of the comments are in English, in a combination of English and Hindi, or in Hindi alone. Other commenters use other Indian languages from the region, that is, Bengali, Urdu, and Nepali. Languages from further afield are Indonesian, Filipino, or Vietnamese, and we also find lan-

---

5   Ronan, In prep. a. *Multilingual practices in YouTube comments.*

◻ Table 10.1 Language choices in the comment section

Language	Examples	Percentage of the total 239
English	128	53.55%
Hindi	43	18%
Hindi/English	22	9.3%
Spanish	9	3.8%
Indonesian	6	2.5%
Indonesian/English	1	0.4%
Chinese	4	1.7%
Bengali	3	1.25%
Portuguese	2	0.8%
Nepali	1	0.4%
Urdu	1	0.4%
Filipino	2	0.8%
Vietnamese	1	0.4%
French	1	0.4%
Emoticon/no text	7	2.9%
Unclear	8	3.3%
Total	**239**	**100%**

guages from other parts of the world, such as Spanish, Chinese, Portuguese, and French. Their presence reflects the large number of global internet users who commented on the video.

In the multilingual practices, we can observe some linguistic preferences. Looking at the use of Hindi versus English, we find that bilingual practices manifest particularly frequently in the use of these languages, which is very likely to be due to the extensive bilingualism in these languages. In Hindi posts, we find code-mixing, that is, the insertion of individual words from another language into a matrix language (cf. ▶ Sect. 4.3.3.1). In these cases, the technical terms that are related to the content of the video repeatedly are in English, for example *grafting* or *mother plant*, e.g., in *Grafting kaliya atcha hai* ('grafting kalia is stuck') or *Mother plant kya hota hai bhai* ('what is a mother plant, brother?'). Interestingly, we also repeatedly find that the names of the months are in English, for example in the mixed Hindi-English post *July August best hota hai* ('July and August are best').

Another interesting feature of multilingualism to look at are address terms as they also show strong multilingual practices. On the one hand, we have a very for-

10.5 · Two Case Studies

mal term of address, *sir*, which is used repeatedly in English, and its Hindi counterpart *sar*. On the other hand, Hindi and other (Indian) languages in the corpus repeatedly use address terms translating into English as "brother", such as in Hindi *bhai*, as in for example *Bhai kyun ebkuuf banatr ho* ('Brother why are you so good?'), or *thanks Bhaiya ji* ('thank you brother'). In Bengali we likewise find *Vai apnar Sathe Kotha Bolte chai* ('Brother I want to talk to you'). These practices are then also found in the English language conversations, as in [...] *I am try to this one. Thanks brother*. Interestingly, there are also instances of *broo*, both in English and in other languages, for example Indonesian *Waaauu keren banget mas brooo* 👍 (...) ('Waaauu really cool brooo 👍'). The vernacular English *bro* here seems to have been perceived as functionally equivalent to the 'brother' element observed in a number of languages from the region. It is appropriated not only into the common language English, but from there on it is also transferred as a loan word into other regional languages.

A further exciting topic of study here is the use of multilingual practices of the commenters and the channel owner, as well as between the various commenters. The interactional patterns between the users of the different languages are instructive: in principle, comments may be in any language, even though the commenter may not expect the channel owner to master that language. If we look at the channel owner, we find that his replies, which are given to about a third of the comments, are in English and Hindi. He uses these languages also to reply to another Indian language, Bengali. There are two replies to comments in Bengali, one in English and one bilingual Hindi-English. The comment is on the Bengali question কলম করার পারফেক্ট সময় কখন ('When is the preferred time to pen?'). The answer is "July August.. Best time". Similarly, a French comment is replied to in English. The comment is *Vous avez fait du très bon travail* ('You have done very good work'); it receives the answer "Thanks". Whether this exchange was enabled by using translingual practices (Barton & Lee, 2013) such as online translation tools or not is not known, of course. There are no answers by the channel owner to the other Romance languages used, that is, Spanish and (Brazilian) Portuguese. Further, three Chinese comments are found in the corpus, two of these show some English language elements. Of the three Chinese comments, the monolingual one receives a reply by another YouTuber in Chinese. Of the seven Spanish comments, two receive answers in Spanish by other YouTubers. There are no replies on any of the Portuguese comments. This illustrates nicely how not only local networks are created through the channel owners and their posts, but also global networks of language users who rely on finding other YouTubers with competencies in their language(s). However, some linguistic problems also emerge. Thus when one commenter asks in Hindi: *Sar gil lagaka kitna din rakna ha* ('Sir, how many days have you spent applying *gil*?'), this question remains unclear as the channel owner asks for confirmation of the term in Hindi *Gil matlab kia hai..?* ('*Gil* means *kia*?').

Another feature that is interesting in this context is the scripting of the various languages. As Androutsopoulos (2013, cf. ▶ Sect. 10.3) points out, languages may either be scripted in their own scripts or in Romanised transliterations. Thus, for the contributions in Hindi, we partly find Devanagari scripts, but various contributions are also spelled in Romanised letters. This is particularly the case where the comments are bilingual in Hindi and English, such as *Yaar first wali scion ulta lagae ho* ('your first scion is upside down'). Non-Romanised spelling is rare overall, though we find four examples of Hindi and one example of Nepali in Devanagari script, two examples of Bengali in Bengali script, one example of Tamil in Tamil script, and one example of Urdu script. All four examples of the Chinese comments contain Chinese characters.

In addition to the topics sketched in this section, other research could be interested in features of the individual languages used here, such as, for example, language contact features in the English language. In general, this example shows that comments on YouTube videos can be very rich sources of research on many aspects of multilingualism.

10.5.2 Appropriating your Idol: Instagram

Instagram is a social networking site that has gained strong popularity since its launch in late 2010. Huang and Su (2018), for example, call it the most popular networking site amongst young people, with 60% of the American users being between 18 and 29 years old. Its users are mainly female and 80% of the users live outside the USA, with user figures growing especially in Asia and South America (Huang & Su, 2018). Instagram is owned by Facebook, and, in contrast to Facebook, its user-numbers among the younger population are still increasing considerably. In their Taiwan-based study, Huang and Su (2018) show that most users have an above-average education, a college education or higher, at least if they belong to an age group which makes this possible. We find similar demographic information on Wikipedia (s.v. "Instagram"[6]), stating that users in Taiwan are more urban than rural, mainly under 35, more female than male, and that a large proportion of users have participated in or are participating in third-level education. Even though the main motivation of Instagram users in Huang and Su's (2018) study was to look at posts, interacting with others in comments and Likes also played a very large role. Thus, Instagram does also contain significant amounts of written content, which makes it an interesting source for the evaluation of a predominantly urban and younger user base with an apparently above-average education. Often, it is exactly this user base which we would expect to display features of metrolingualism. To find clarify this, we have conducted a small-scale sample study on how far features of multilingual language use can really be found. Thus, in this study of Instagram posts (Ronan, In prep. b[7]) we aim to find out (1) whether we can indeed find multilingual practices in Instagram comments, and (2) if so, how these multilingual practices manifest. To do so, we have selected data from an Instagram account that is potentially of interest particularly to a young, international audience, and which is likely to trigger multilingual practices. The account chosen for

---

6 ▶ https://en.wikipedia.org/wiki/#Users (last accessed 07.01.2021).
7 Ronan, P. (In prep. b.) *Constructing multilingual identities on Instagram. The case of multilingual comments on Instagram.*

10.5 · Two Case Studies

this is a fan account for the Irish actor Saoirse Ronan, who, as a teenager and now a young woman, has gained an international reputation with a wide variety of films of different genres. As the films are available in English, it is to be expected that they might trigger either English language or multilingual interaction.

At the time of the study, the Instagram account chosen, *@saorseronan*, had nearly 4000 posts and more than 100,000 followers. In order to allow for a detailed study of the language practices on the account, a post was chosen that had around 100 comments, namely a post from February 2020 with 116 comments. The post shows the actor in the context of one of her early films, when she was 13 years old. The comments have been analysed manually. Posts in languages that we could not translate ourselves were entered into Google Translate to determine the language and to obtain a rough translation of the content. In a second step, attestations of different languages were counted, then instances of multilingual practices were determined quantitatively and qualitatively.

In analysing the data, we found that one possible site of multilingualism in social media, hashtags (Barton & Lee, 2013), were hardly used in this particular post. The only hashtags used were two in the monolingual English post, pointing to the actor and the film to which the post is connected. The comments, however, showed notable multilingual practices. In total, seven different languages were found in the comment section, as well as a number of comments which used only emojis and no language. In the comments on this post, English had a clear lead, followed by the use of emojis only, and then Korean, Spanish, and further languages. A quantitative overview is given in ◘ Table 10.2.

That English is the most frequently used language is not surprising given that both the Saoirse Ronan's fan-page as well as the film to which the post is related are in English. A high percentage of comments in Spanish may represent the large

◘ Table 10.2 Overview of languages used in comments on @saorseronan post

Language	Total	Of which bilingual
English	68 (58.6%)	0
Spanish	10 (8.6%)	1 (10%)
Korean	14 (12.1%)	1 (7.1%)
Chinese	1 (0.9%)	0
Japanese	1 (0.9%)	0
Filipino	1 (0.9%)	1 (100%)
Portuguese	1 (0.9%)	1 (100%)
Emoticons only	20 (17.2%)	0
Total	116 (100%)	4 (3.4%)

internet presence of Spanish speakers. What seems more unexpected is the large number of comments in Korean. Given Huang and Su's (2018) study which points to a very high prevalence of Instagram in Taiwan, it seems well possible that comparative social demographics and comparable user figures might also be found in Korean Instagram users, who might then be very interested in a young female international actor. Examples are 천사같아[8] ('she looks like an angel') or 엄청 청순해 ('very innocent'). Interestingly, we find that the Korean comments, with one exception, are strings of comments addressed to specific other users, which are then followed by one or two replies. Thus, specific small communities of Korean language users are created in these comments. In the other groups of languages, there were no further examples of such community building via direct addresses in the sample data, but we would expect this to be used by other speaker communities as well. Inside the larger fan community, this language practice then serves to create a language-specific in-group whose language choices exclude the majority group from the smaller group's conversation.

Further, the data also gives us insights into interesting multilingual practices. One Korean user sums up the gist of her more extensive Korean post in English, 눈동장에 별이 박힌 듯 하다. *Her eyes are star…*. While the English is a very short note of the gist of her statement, the Korean translates as "there seems to be a star stuck in the pupil". The other three multilingual examples, too, include English language content. We find two examples of code-mixing, introducing English expressions into the matrix language, for example Spanish *Tu en primaria heavy* ('You will be the first *heavy*'). Finally, we find some code-switching where English language content complements the Portuguese matrix language content by adding an English phrase: *você é um anjo, I love you* ('you are an angel, I love you').

While interactions on an English-language site about an English-speaking media personality has been chosen for study here, particularly the study of sites of non-English language personalities is also interesting. If we compare the Instagram comments on posts by a Turkish-German male actor, *@mehmetkurtulusofficial*, this not unexpectedly predominantly yields Turkish, German, and English posts, as well as further posts in other languages. The interaction between apparently bilingual Turkish-German speakers in the comments displays similar phenomena to those observed in the comments discussed above: insertion of frequently used Turkish language phrases into German, for example *Baba* ('dad'), or of the phrase *vallaha* ('I swear'), or insertion of English language phrases into French, such as *Good luck pour tous vos films. Mehmetkurtulus* ('Good luck for all your films. Mehmetkurtulus.').[9]

In general, this sample study illustrates a research methodology that can be used to determine multilingual practices on Instagram, or indeed on other (social) media sites from both qualitative and quantitative viewpoints. Similar studies can of course also be carried out on comment sections in other social media. Data is plentiful and out there for the take, and in particular, studies on language practices on TikTok, which has been launched more recently, are still scarce. Further detail and information on studying online data is also provided in ▶ Sect. 14.2.1.

---

8 ▶ https://www.instagram.com/p/B8yu6CVlH4J/ (last accessed 08.01.2021).
9 ▶ https://www.instagram.com/p/CF1mqmQntdh/ (last accessed 08.01.2021).

10.5 · Two Case Studies

10.5.3 What the Sample Studies Show Us

The two shortly sketched studies show clearly that multilingualism in digital space can provide us with telling examples of how contemporary multilingual practices are transferred to online genres. The linguistic practices are fluid and shaped by situational preferences. Language users blend their language repertoires fluidly, making use not only of languages, expressions, or idioms but also of different scripts to suit their individual purposes and preferences. Online language practices show their users' language competencies as well as their translingual practices, informed by their identity construction and their audience design. In this, they are supported by the diverse multilingual resources that can be drawn upon.

? Exercises
1. Consider the YouTube clip, "Manglish VS Proper English ~ ??!!", at ▶ https://www.youtube.com/watch?v=W0Nk4dFCHZA, introduced in Schneider (2016). The main language used in this clip is English.
   (a) Determine how many non-English lexical items are used in this clip and what they are used for.
   (b) Can you determine any grammatical structures in the English sentences that are used that stem from language contact, that is, that have their origin in a language other than English?
2. Select the profile of an international figure on Instagram.
   (a) Which language(s) does the person post in?
   (b) Which language(s) are used for the comments?
   (c) For what purposes are the different languages used?
3. Consider any social network channel in multilingual contexts. The interaction might be between local minority and majority languages, or the interaction might include local languages and other (international) languages.
   (a) Investigate which languages are found in the data set.
   (b) Can you identify specific contexts in which one or the other language(s) are used?
4. Research the multilingual social media use of somebody you know and ask them to work with you. Investigate their data to find out which languages they are using and in which situation they seem to be using that particular language. In a second step, conduct a guided interview or questionnaire study with them to find out why they think they have chosen a specific language in a specific post (cf. ▶ Chap. 13).

Summary
In this chapter, we have discussed the role of the internet in the use of multilingual practices. We have shown that user-generated content enables users to select the language or the languages that they use on the basis of their own linguistic preferences, the needs of their audience, and on the basis of the linguistic identity the language users want to create for themselves. We have shown that multilingual language practices often either involve local majority languages or global languages or both of

these. We have argued that, on the one hand, this use of global or majority languages can pose a threat to small and particularly isolated minority languages by exposing them to more powerful languages, but on the other hand, minority languages can also be invested with prestige by their use in written form in an international medium. Further, the possibilities of the internet also allow global diasporas to form and offer further support to linguistic minorities. We have additionally provided two small-scale sample studies, which use multilingual comments from YouTube and Instagram sites to study multilingual practices, and these have further illustrated the formation of international online communities.

References

Androutsopoulos, J. (2013). Networked multilingualism: Some language practices on Facebook and their implications. *International Journal of Bilingualism, 19*(2), 185–205.

Androutsopoulos, J., & Juffermans, K. (2014). Digital language practices in superdiversity: Introduction. *Discourse, Context and Media, 4*(5), 1–6.

Barton, D., & Lee, C. (2013). *Language online: Investigating digital texts and practices*. Taylor and Francis.

Coulmas, F. (2018). *An introduction to multilingualism: Language in a changing world*. Oxford University Press.

Huang, Y.-T., & Su, S.-F. (2018). Motives for Instagram use and topics of interest among young adults. *Future Internet, 10*(8), 77. https://doi.org/10.3390/fi10080077

Lee, C. (2016). *Multilingualism online*. Routledge.

Schneider, E. W. (2016). World Englishes on YouTube: Treasure trove or nightmare? In E. Seoane & C. Suárez-Gómez (Eds.), *World Englishes: New theoretical and methodological considerations* (pp. 253–282). John Benjamins.

Sharma, B. K. (2014). On high horses: Transnational Nepalis and language ideologies on YouTube. *Discourse, Context and Media, 4*(5), 19–28.

Key Reading

Lee, C. (2016). *Multilingualism online*. Routledge.

Further Reading

Androutsopoulos, J., & Staer, A. (2018). Moving methods online: Researching digital language practices. In A. Creese & A. Blackledge (Eds.), *The Routledge handbook of language and superdiversity* (pp. 118–132). Routledge.

Barton, D., & Lee, C. (2013). *Language online: Investigating digital texts and practices*. Taylor and Francis.

Multilingual Pop Music

Contents

11.1 Introduction – 236

11.2 The History of Multilingualism in Music – 236

11.3 Multilingualism and Language Use and Choice in (Pop) Music – 237

11.4 Reasons for Employing a Particular Singing Style or Multiple Languages or Dialects – 241

11.5 A Short Resumé – 243

11.6 Manifestations of Multilingual Pop Music in the Twenty-First Century – 243

References – 249

© The Author(s), under exclusive license to Springer Nature Switzerland AG 2023
S. Buschfeld et al., *Multilingualism*,
https://doi.org/10.1007/978-3-031-28405-2_11

11.1 Introduction

Nearly 40 years ago, Peter Trudgill's (1983) ground-breaking study investigated accents of British rock and pop vocalists, more specifically how they used an accent different from the one they spoke. In the present chapter, we assess the development of research in the field of multilingualism in modern pop music. We show that, in general, linguistic research on multilingual pop music is still in its infancy but is increasingly gaining interest and importance. First, we provide a brief overview of multilingualism and language use and choice in pop music, with a focus on earlier studies and the development of multilingual pop music. We then zoom in on the different reasons and motives for singers to employ a particular singing style or to perform in more than one language or variety/dialect (for a discussion of the relationship between languages, varieties, and dialects, see ▶ Sect. 3.2). We further present some example songs against the background of the different phenomena and motives for multilingual language use in music as introduced in the present chapter. In addition to that, we apply some of the concepts introduced and discussed in ▶ Chap. 4 to the songs. To this end, we discuss notions such as, for example, code-mixing, code-switching, borrowing, and translanguaging from a more practical perspective and show how transfer phenomena also occur in singing accents, as a means of expressing personal and cultural identities.[1]

11.2 The History of Multilingualism in Music

> » Multilingual singers know that music is one of the few truly universal languages. It communicates to people regardless of their ability to comprehend the lyrics, and it has the ability to evoke a response in babies and animals alike. (Koyfman, 2020)

Music has always been an important property of human life, with a long history in human existence. Investigating the history of music, Altenmüller (2018) dates the origin of human music back to Neanderthal times. Ever since then, music has been a means of sending messages, expressing emotions and culture, and affecting humans and their lives in a number of positive ways. In the present chapter, we look into multilingual music, with a special focus on modern pop music, that is, such music genres that are consumed by broad audiences all around the world (see Werner, 2018, pp. 4–7 for a discussion of related aspects and terms).

Multilingualism is widespread in modern musical genres. Some artists use it to perform their own multilingual identities, but it is also simply used to express modern, hip, and urbane lifestyles. However, multilingual pop music has not always been equally popular. For quite a while, English has been the lingua franca of modern pop music ever since blues and jazz music took root in the United States at

---

1 We are grateful to Lisa Westermayer for her invaluable input on the chapter and for sharing her musical expertise with us.

the turn of the twentieth century and later on spread around the world.[2] When the Beatles and the Rolling Stones entered the global scene in the 1960s, they caused a worldwide hysteria and set the standards for modern, English-based pop. As Ed Vulliamy (2019) points out in *The Observer*: "Pop stars once had to sing in English to win global fame". According to him, however, the tide seems to be turning and "[n]ow Spanish and other languages are taking over". He continues to describe the journey of modern pop music going multilingual. According to the 2021 report of the International Federation of the Phonographic Industry (IFPI, 2021), which represents the worldwide music recording industry, recorded music revenues have strongly increased worldwide, with Latin America clearly leading the way, closely followed by Asia, Africa, and the Middle East. Many of these productions are still in English, predominantly in American English[3] (AmE) (Westphal & Jansen, 2021, p. 190), but pop music also displays a wide range of different varieties of English and interactions of English with other languages. The European and also the US and UK markets have experienced a change from 'English only' towards multilingualism in the music industry in recent times. Shakira producer Sebastian Krys told the Rolling Stone magazine in 2018 that "[y]ou simply can't have a global No 1 any more without a hit in Mexico and Spain" (Vulliamy, 2019).

Next to these recent changes towards linguistic heterogeneity and multilingualism in pop music, it should be kept in mind that English has not always been the number one language of music. Latin was the lingua franca of music for a long time and was later replaced by its closest descendant, Italian, as the international language of music (Vulliamy, 2019). While currently English is the primary language of music, this seems to be changing once again, towards the use of languages such as Spanish, but also towards multilingualism in music—which is often still based on English but not exclusively so.

11.3 Multilingualism and Language Use and Choice in (Pop) Music

Linguistic research on the use and choice of language in pop songs has only recently gained true momentum, despite Trudgill's (1983) early and influential study of how AmE accents dominated pop music, even with singers who speak another variety of English as their first language. Trudgill (1983) investigates how and why singers change their accents when they switch from speaking to singing and exposes six underlying tendencies in the sung productions of British pop singers from the late 1950s and early 1960s, namely: (1) the voicing of intervocalic /t/, as in *better* (t-flap-

---

2 Note however, that this trend has not been equally strong around the world. France, for example, has tried to counteract the influence of English as a lingua franca in pop music ever since by always making sure that a particular quota of French music is being aired in the first place and, in general, French bands seem to be less oriented towards English than bands from other countries.
3 We would like to stress that no one American (or British) English exists. We use American English/AmE to refer to what is considered the standard variety.

ping); (2) the raising and shortening of /ɑː/ to [æ], as in *dance* or *half*; (3) rhoticity; (4) the monophthongisation of /aɪ/ to [aː], as in *life* or *my*; (5) the weakening of /ʌ/ to [ə], as in *love* or *done*; and (6) the unrounding of /ɒ/ to [ɑː], as in *body* or *top*. The crucial point here is that all six features are strongly associated with AmE and while these features do occur in British varieties of English, according to Trudgill, "no single British variety has all these features, and the vast majority of singers who use these forms when singing do not do so when speaking" (Trudgill, 1983, p. 252). Trudgill draws on three central sociolinguistic approaches to explain such behaviour: (1) Accommodation theory (Giles, 1973; Giles & Smith, 1979), that is, the observation that speakers—and in our case singers—adjust their language to create social proximity to their interlocutors; (2) the notion of appropriateness of style, that is, the idea that specific situations require a specific use of language; and (3) Le Page's theory of linguistic behaviour (1968, 1975, 1978; Le Page et al., 1974). The latter approach is quite similar to Giles and Smith's theory but focusses less on the relationship between the parties involved in a conversation than on the speaker's desire to identify with a particular group, whose immediate presence is not necessarily required. In this line of thinking, British pop singers tried to sound American because "Americans have dominated the field, and cultural domination leads to imitation: it is appropriate to sound like an American when performing in what is predominantly an American activity; and one attempts to model one's singing style on that of those who do it best and who one admires most" (Trudgill, 1983, p. 254). However, in his comparison of the late 1950s and early 1960s Beatles and Rolling Stones songs with songs by randomly selected artists from the 1970s, Trudgill observes a decline of AmE pronunciation features in the British artists. He explains these observations by a change of genre towards "British themes and locals" (Trudgill, 1983, p. 260) and a change in cultural domination, that is, a decline in the exclusive gravity of the United States in worldwide cultural affairs. Recent publications confirm this observation, such as Jansen and Gerfer's (2022) investigation of the Sheffield Indie rock band *Arctic Monkeys*. They find that "[w]hile convergence toward a mid-Atlantic mainstream accent is detectable, salient Northern English variants remain a clear trademark and Turner [the *Arctic Monkeys'* lead singer] further includes idiosyncrasies that create an individual singing style" (Jansen & Gerfer, 2022, p. 156; our addition). Beal (2009) even interprets the Arctic Monkeys' Northern English singing accent as a deliberate choice and means to express their aversion against the profit-oriented, US-based music industry.

Following Trudgill's seminal contribution on the topic, similar publications on the accents of pop artists appeared, which, however, diverge from Trudgill's approach—and each other—in how they explain the variation between speaking and singing accents (e.g. Morrissey, 2008; Simpson, 1999). Simpson's (1999) USA-5 model has proven particularly influential amongst these. It picks up on Trudgill's identification of particular AmE singing variants but, for unknown reasons, leaves out tendency five, that is, the weakening of /ʌ/ to [ə]. Even though the remaining five tendencies identified by Simpson correspond to Trudgill's observations, the audience is not assigned an important role in the accent selection of the singer, as the selection of a particular accent is solely related to the singer's own identity and role models. We cannot go into further detail here, since this would lead us too far away from the actual aim of the chapter, that is, to look into multilingual pop songs. However, we can conclude that the few older existing publications mainly focus on the representation of accents in pop music. They present various, mostly sociolinguistically motivated explanations for differences between speaking and singing accents. However, later studies have also taken up physiological reasons for explaining such differences, that is, the actual production of sung materials and the physiology of the articulatory organs (e.g. Morrissey, 2008). Still, most of these studies are not based on representative empirical data sets. They investigate particularly conspicuous features in individual songs of individual artists and try to explain them as part of a broader picture, but without much systematicity in their investigations. In addition to that, most studies investigate the language of music super stars who try to accommodate to the global market and adapt their choice of accents to it. These may, therefore, not be natural but influenced by the expectations of a global and commercialised music scene. Therefore, such analyses cannot unveil the natural and subconscious reasons for the observed changes between singing and speaking accents. Westermayer (2019)[4] aims to answer exactly this question and finds that three Australian indie artists all share the same phonological properties in singing but not in speaking. She shows that their singing accents consist of variants that are either easier to sing in general, for example because they are more sonorous, or that are easier to sing in specific musical contexts, like an unvoiced /t/ in staccato phrasings.

Furthermore, much of the research so far has focussed almost exclusively on British pop superstars. However, in an age where pop music is moving away from a "standard" English-based monolingual ideal, this constitutes a shortcoming in the research paradigm, not the least since it is far from clear whether the conclusions drawn in such analyses apply to non-British singers as well (Westermayer, 2019, p. 4). Even though research on non-British singers and multilingual pop songs still has not taken centre stage in linguistics, a number of studies have emerged, in particular in the last 15 years. In an early article, Androutsopoulos & Scholz (2003) look into the appropriation of rap music in different European countries, based exactly on the above observation that music is no longer necessarily dominated by the US or UK cultures but that, for example, local rap, characterised by the use of the local languages, can be found in many parts of the world today. Several studies, in particular on hip hop culture and rap language, have followed since. Akande (2012, p. 237), for example, points out that "[i]n principle, multilingual practices, including use of dialects and languages which are not natively spoken in a community, fits [sic!] in well with the hip hop aesthetic". However, he also shows how some of the features borrowed from other languages or dialects (in his study African-American Vernacular English and Jamaican Creole or Patois in Nigeria) are not fully understood when it comes to their linguistic and cultural context, which, in turn, may come at the expense of authenticity.

---

4   See also Westermayer, L. In prep. *My home is calling me: regionality versus physiology in the songs of Husky.*

Looking into multilingual songs, English is often involved in the multilingual music mix, no matter what genre. Bremner (2015), for example, investigates the use of Réunionese Kreol together with English in popular dancehall songs in the French overseas department of La Réunion. Jansen and Westphal (2017, 2022) consider varieties of English and investigate the use of Caribbean English creole features in songs performed by Barbadian singer Rihanna and Trinidad and Tobagian artist Nicki Minaj and how they act out and express their Caribbeanness. Still, multilingual songs which do not include English exist, too, such as the 2018 remix of the Namika song *Je ne parle pas français* (Beatgees Remix; feat. Black M), which features German and French to more or less equal parts. However, the phenomenon of multilingualism in pop songs is not as new as it might seem from the examples provided so far—which makes it even more surprising that it has only recently attracted the interest of linguists. For example, the Beatles hit "Michelle", which employs a mix of French and English, dates back to 1965. Other, even earlier multilingual songs exist as well, mostly combining majority languages such as English and French and English and Spanish but also smaller languages like Gaelic and Welsh (for a more detailed overview and some further examples, see John, 2015, pp. 160–164). Thus, as is true for individual and societal multilingualism in general, multilingual music is not an exclusively recent phenomenon (c.f. ▶ Sect. 2.2 for a detailed discussion of the historical dimensions of multilingualism). The strong increase in multilingual songs and their gain in worldwide popularity and successful commercialisation, however, is a phenomenon of the last 20 to 30 years. John (2015, p. 158) attributes this to the general development of the music market towards a 'world music' as well as to general processes of globalisation, migration, new regionalities, and the interactions of such factors. Furthermore, multilingual songs from the 1950s, 1960s, and 1970s are normally dominated by one language, while the other language is sprinkled in here or there. The second language serves as a symbol or signal for foreign cultures and countries, making the song more interesting and exotic in an era when global travelling was not as common and widespread as it is today and distant countries were often out of reach. Multilingualism in such songs was normally reduced to only few but culturally significant words and often restricted to the chorus or other exposed parts of the song, as, for example, in "Buona sera, signorina kiss me goodnight" (Louis Prima: *Buona Sera*, 1956), "Voulez-vous coucher avec moi?" (Labelle: *Lady Marmelade*, 1974), "Qué Será, Será" (Doris Day, 1957), and many more. The same can be found for older non-English-based songs such as the German hits *Merci Chérie* (Udo Jürgens, 1966) or *Fiesta Mexicana* (Rex Gildo, 1972), to mention just a few (examples taken from John, 2015, pp. 164–165). This emblematic use of additional languages in pop songs has remained an important function up until now, but its precise manifestations have changed since the 1980s. For one, the emergence of music videos has added an additional means of expressing and integrating foreign cultures. In addition to that, the second language has gained in importance over time (John, 2015, p. 165), up to a point where nowadays, we find extremely mixed lyrics in which a matrix language cannot always be clearly recognised, as, for example, in Moe Phoenix' *Aicha* (2018), which features Arabic, German, and French.

John (2015, p. 169) attempts a classification of the formal compositions of more recent multilingual songs but finds that, even though particular patterns which find recurring application exist in multilingual songs, the variety of manifestations of multilingualism in pop songs is elusive. Still, a common pattern of multilingual songs seems to be the distribution of languages between chorus and refrain, and variations thereof. Other, though less frequent, patterns that have been identified are a switch of languages from stanza to stanza (e.g. Altan: *Tá Mo Chleamhnas Á Dhéanamh*, 1987) or the successive occurrence of the two languages, as in Xavier Naidoo's *Ich kenne nichts* ('I don't know anything'; 2002). Very rare is the language change from line to line (but see, e.g., Gilles Vigneault: *I Went To The Market*, 1976; examples from John, 2015, p. 169). Oftentimes such language change between clearly definable entities such as stanza or line serves as a vehicle to illustrate cultural diversity, and the intended political message is to portray influences from foreign cultures not as a threat but as an enrichment (John, 2015, p. 170). More recent songs, such as the ones discussed in ▶ Sect. 11.6, take this aim to another level by a strong, yet not necessarily random, mixture of languages (e.g. Cro: *Meine Gang (Bang Bang)*, 2014; see ▶ Sect. 11.6, ▶ Example 11.2 for a discussion). In contrast to older multilingual songs, in which balanced proportions of two different languages were rather rare (John, 2015, p. 170), modern pop songs often employ two (or even more) languages at more or less equal levels, as, for example, the remix of the Namika song *Je ne parle pas français* (Beatgees Remix; feat. Black M, 2018) mentioned above.

11.4 Reasons for Employing a Particular Singing Style or Multiple Languages or Dialects

In ▶ Sect. 11.3, we have already touched on some of the potential reasons or motivations for employing a particular singing style, language, or dialect that may not be the artist's own. Let us go into some more detail in the following. Above, we have already outlined the earlier and long-standing orientation towards AmE as a linguistic role model in popular songs and the shift (back) towards local voices. The motivations for these two trends can, for example, be approached by Bell's audience design framework and the notion of referee design (Bell, 1984, 1992). According to the audience design framework, speakers accommodate their language use to their addressees. Referee design extends this general approach to a third party, that is, away from the actual addressee and towards an absent reference group. The Americanisation of pop culture and music discussed above constitutes such a case (Jansen & Westphal, 2022, p. 315). The artists are often not Americans themselves and do not necessarily address an American audience but, for example, a British one (see, e.g., the study by Trudgill, 1983), even though one has to keep in mind that normally mainstream artists try to address a global audience not restricted to a particular society in the first place. In this line of thinking, Gibson & Bell (2012) argue that AmE can be considered the unmarked, default singing accent, not necessarily associated with the USA but simply with mainstream music. They further suggest that accents other than AmE express a particular regional belonging or simply a rejection of mainstream music. Still, even though long neglected in linguistic research, the audience plays an important role as the counterpart of artists and thus in their performances (e.g. Bell & Gibson, 2011, p. 563; Jansen, 2018). As Jansen and Westphal (2022, p. 314) point out: "The audience carefully scrutinizes and evaluates how performers act on and off stage. It expects to be entertained by skilful performances. Ultimately, the audience plays a decisive role in assessing whether a performance and, in turn, the performer is successful".

This makes all artists national and/or international pop personas, that is, it gives them "a publicly projected role which can consist of interacting real as well as artificial identities or alter egos. These can have different voices which display co-existing identities" (Jansen & Westphal, 2022, p. 314; see also Jansen & Westphal, 2017, p. 5; Trudgill, 1983, pp. 158–160). However, as Jansen and Westphal (2022, p. 314) also point out, "[m]ost performances where an artist displays their persona are not authentic in a traditional sociolinguistic sense but stylized linguistically, since language use, from writing lyrics to singing, is planned and rehearsed, and visually, by staging performers and songs in music videos".

In this respect, the general aim of specific language choices in music and in particular of marked choices, that is, those diverging from one's own or cultural expectations or the generally assumed linguistic standards, is the negotiation of identities (see also, e.g., Jansen & Westphal, 2022) through taking on specific personas. As briefly pointed out above, such negotiation seems to fall within two general categories: on the one hand, multicultural and multilingual singers aim to express their truly multilingual or multidialectal identities, as in the case of Rihanna (and others such as Shakira and the Namibian-German Kwaito artist EES, as discussed in ▶ Sect. 11.6). On the other hand, artists seem to act out particular roles or identities, for example, to signal specific group membership or at least the wish thereof (Beal, 2009; see also the sociolinguistic explanations discussed for the choice of accents in ▶ Sect. 11.3). Studies on this latter case often also investigate issues such as authenticity (e.g., Gerfer, 2022), as singers of dialects and languages that are not their own have been criticised for using fake, that is, not authentic, language (e.g., Sarpeah, 2017). Finally, it seems that some artists simply want to be considered hip and trendy and, therefore, employ a specific language mix in their songs, which often reflects the language of the youth spoken in a particular country (see the example of German hip-hopper Cro, as discussed in ▶ Sect. 11.6). This is similar to the earlier trend to sound American since both are forms of referee design (see also Jansen & Westphal, 2022; Morrissey, 2008 for similar lines of argument).

11.5 A Short Resumé

Summing up our more theoretical approach to the topic of multilingual (pop) music, multilingual songs have been present in the music industry from very early on. Their presence on the music market, their functions, and their manifestations, however, have changed over time. Multilingualism in music has developed from the occasional song, sprinkling in a second language for symbolically indexing the exotics of foreign cultures and peoples in prominent parts of the song, to highly linguistically mixed songs of two or more languages, which express and signal the strong cultural heterogeneity of our modern, globalised world. As pointed out above, artists express their own cultural and linguistic identities or the heterogeneous cultural setup of their bands, with band members coming from different linguistic cultures. Furthermore, multilingual songs are a means of expressing a transculturally construed aesthetic concept, by often also crossing musical genres (for details, see John, 2015, p. 172). An example of genre-crossing can be found in "Temple of Love" by The Sisters of Mercy feat. Ofra Haza (1992), in which traditional Dark Wave is mixed with stylised-sounding oriental female vocals. In this respect, songs have also been created or modified for commercial reasons, expressing such transcultural aesthetics, for example Herbert Grönemeyer's (feat. Amadou & Mariam) 2006 Football World Cup song *"Zeit, dass sich was dreht / Celebrate The Day / Fetez cette journée"* (John, 2015, pp. 173–174).

We cannot address the full picture and complexity of the developments and manifestations of multilingual pop music in this chapter. Some aspects have only been addressed superficially, others have been left out altogether, such as the ironic, parodic, and thus derogatory implementation of two or more languages in the same song. In the same sense, the chapter cannot include all languages, cultures, and geographical regions which may find expression in multilingual songs but is admittedly biased by the linguistic and cultural backgrounds of the authors. Still, in ▶ Sect. 11.6, we present and discuss different songs which exemplify the main criteria introduced in the earlier sections of the present chapter. We further consider what our examples illustrate in terms of the linguistic mechanisms of being multilingual introduced in ▶ Chap. 4. We also discuss the artists' potential motivations behind the use of different languages, dialects, or accents in one song, though, naturally, this part is in many ways rather speculative. The analysis of both the lyrics and the pronunciation of these examples can, of course, be expanded to any multilingual song.

11.6 Manifestations of Multilingual Pop Music in the Twenty-First Century

In the following, we provide excerpts of the lyrics of three songs. For the example from the South-African hip hop group *Die Antwoord*, we further discuss phonological results of language contact by reference to particular pronunciation features found in the oral representation of the song. We discuss all examples with reference to the notions and observations introduced in ▶ Sects. 11.2 through 11.5. The discussions of these songs cannot take up every theoretical aspect discussed above and are therefore never comprehensive, since this would go far beyond the framework of this chapter. We simply point out aspects that can be discussed on the basis of these songs and text excerpts as examples for potential approaches to multilingual (pop) songs. We start our hands-on discussion by looking into the lyrics of EES, an Namibian-German Kwaito artist, who performs his German-based but clearly mixed identities and multilingual repertoires in his songs. In his song "Alles Beste" (cf. Example 11.1), he creatively mixes (low) German, English, Jamaican Patois, and Afrikaans elements.

▶ Example 11.1

Excerpt from "Alles Beste" (EES feat. The Hunta); English translation by Buschfeld & Schröder (2020, p. 342).

Bin final back in NAM, war lekka bei den Jerries,
('I'm finally back in Namibia, it was nice with the Germans,')
Man Ihr kennt moss,—ich bin der Hunta,
('Well you do know me—I'm the hunter,')
Wo imma Partie is, da bin ich moss da,
('Wherever there's a party, I'm definitely there')
[…]
Heute is mein Tach, Heute kriech ich lekka,
('Today is my day. Today I get nice,')
Ich zieh mein T-shirt aus, und fahr lekka aufn Trekka!
('I take off my t-shirt, and nicely drive on the tractor') ◀

The song is mainly based on German, featuring the variety of low-German mainly spoken in the North of Germany (e.g., *Tach* and *Trekka* as indicators of the low-German variety). Occasional insertions from English (e.g. *final back*) and Afrikaans (e.g. *lekka, moss*) make up the multilingual character of this song. Afrikaans *lekka* in this context translates to 'nice', *moss* is a popular Afrikaans filler word, which is used in all Namibian languages for emphasis. It is similar in meaning to *actually* (cf. Mandus, 2016, glossary). By doing so, EES does not create an artificial mixing of languages but acts out an authentic, German-based but multilingual, multicultural persona and possibly reflects how German-descendant Namibians make use of their linguistic repertoires in their everyday lives. Next to the German core, in particular the first line of the song (see the full version of the song online, e.g., https://www.youtube.com/watch?v=UrhwdU7Knsk) is sung in Jamaican Patois, interspersed with Afrikaans elements, before turning back to German. As the Jamaican Patois parts are sung by EES himself, they constitute another example of an artist not singing in their native language for reasons of transcultural aesthetics. The authenticity of such crossing (Rampton, 1995) has been discussed in the literature (e.g. Akande, 2012, p. 237; Gerfer, 2022; ▶ Sect. 11.2) and it is, of course, questionable whether this part of his persona is really authentic. Very likely, this is not the case and is just used to emphasise the Reggae-like character of the song, in an attempt of referee design.

In other songs, EES even integrates local African languages, for example in the song "Never Over", which features the Herero-descending group *Ongoro Nomundu*. In this song, African-Herero musical styles and linguistic elements are mixed with EES' Hip Hop-Reggae-fusion music. The musical and linguistic elements are presented in a clear pattern with the refrains being performed in English and the rest of the song in Otjiherero. What adds to the local African colour of the song is that EES sings the English elements in a local African variety of English, which features prototypical characteristics of African Englishes, such as consonant cluster reduction and the monophthongisation of diphthongs (cf. EES feat. Ongoro Nomundu: *Never Over*, 2014). Since it can be assumed that this is not his native variety of English, we are again confronted with a presumably inauthentic persona of his, even though, in an interview, EES claims a clearly German-African hybrid identity: "*Wir sind so basically die vergessenen Deutschen ... Und den Rest machen wir alles African style*" ('We are basically the forgotten Germans ... And the rest we do African style'; EES TV—teaser); so maybe the African-based parts of his persona are not all that inauthentic after all (for a discussion of this example in the context of language use in present-day Namibia, see Buschfeld & Schröder, 2020, pp. 341–342).

The 1990-born German hip hop and pop artist Cro, on the other hand, exhibits a different type of multilingualism in his songs. He makes use of extensive code-mixing between German and English, as illustrated in Example 11.2.

▶ **Example 11.2**

Excerpt from "Meine Gang (Bang Bang)" (Cro, 2014), English translation by Buschfeld (2021, pp. 37–38).[5]

Ich bi-bi-bin nicht Drake, doch hab' Love für die Crew, meine Dawgs
('I'm not Drake but I have love for the crew, my dawgs')
Alle Boos sind im Club, but I don't give a fuck
('All the uncool guys are in the club, ...')
Und alle Babes sagen, 'Boah, du bist straight hier der Boss.'
('And all babes say, "Wow, you're clearly the boss here."')
Egal wie viele Tapes ich record'
('No matter how many tapes I record')
Und ich sag', 'Bitch, get off, keine Zeit für dich, Hoe.'
('And I say, "Bitch get off, no time for you, hoe"')
Bin unterwegs mit meinen Doggys, also scheiß mal auf Cro
('I'm on tour with my doggies (a German youth language variant of dawgs, indicating submissiveness), so don't give a shit about Cro')
G-G-Gangsterattitüde, Motherfucker (ah!), life is a hoe
('Gangster attitude, motherfucker ...')
Und meine Gang ist eigentlich broke, aber immer wieder high von dem Dope, oh, oh
('And my gang is actually broke, but again and again high on dope')

---

5 We are grateful to Simon Kautzsch for providing explanations on the youth language related slang terms.

Digga, Digga, meine Gang ist voller Chicks oder Atzen
('Dude, dude, my gang is full of chicks and fellas')
Die bis Mitternacht ratzen, aufsteh'n, obwohl sie noch nicht wach sind
('Who sleep until midnight and get up even though they are not awake yet')
Lieber ficken statt quatschen (ah!), Jimmys lieber spliffen statt klatschen
('Who rather fuck than chat (ah!), Jimmies who rather smoke spliffs than drink (alcohol)')
Kein bisschen erwachsen, but ain't nobody fuckin' with my motherfucking gang
('Not a bit grown-up, but …'). ◄

Example 11.2 illustrates the fluid transitions between languages. Many, in particular young people in Germany indeed integrate the English language into their daily language repertoires in similar ways, depending on the context, speakers, and general intentions, even though their proficiency in English might be limited to the absolute basics, which often depends on their age and level of formal education. Still, it can be assumed that the motivation behind multilingual language use is different for Cro than for multi-ethnic and multilingual singers such as EES, who have grown up in strongly multi-ethnic and multilingual societies. As has been observed in ► Sect. 11.3, hip hop has long been an essentially American and thus English-speaking genre. Even though many other languages have claimed the genre for themselves in more recent times, its (African-) American-based associations still often persist in the consumers' minds. In an attempt of partial crossing, Cro embraces this American hip hop identity by incorporating English elements into his songs while still foregrounding his German identity, as the matrix language of his songs is clearly German. By doing so, he addresses Germans as his main audience and Germany as his main commercial market and at the same time picks up elements of English-derived German youth language (e.g. "[…] *du bist straight hier der Boss*", "[…] *lieber spliffen statt klatschen*") and English as the main language of the global hip hop culture ("[…] *but ain't nobody fuckin' with my motherfucking gang*"). This adaptation of (American) English is also an example of referee design (cf. ► Sect. 11.3), since a non-American singer addresses his audience, which is mainly German, by incorporating features in his singing that are clearly not part of his - or his main audience's - mother tongue. This can also be interpreted in terms of Beal's (2009) approach of indexicality, that is, the observation that artists and bands adapt their language according to prevailing genre-specific stereotypes such as the real-hip-hop-requires-gangster-rapper-US-English cliché.

Another interesting observation that can be made on the basis of the excerpt from Cro's lyrics (and also his other songs and songs by other German artists) is more linguistic in nature and refers back to what has been discussed in relation to multilingual practices in ► Chap. 4. In lines such as "*Alle Boos sind im Club, but I don't give a fuck*", we find intrasentential code-switching, which we refer to as code-mixing; and, indeed, when looking at the song excerpt as a whole, we would also argue that it constitutes an example of code-mixing, rather than switching, since the going back and forth between languages is rather intense and seems unsystematic at first sight. However, this is not entirely true. A more systematic look at the lyrics reveals that often English words or phrases are employed to create a consistent rhyme scheme, as, for example, between the lines "*Und ich sag', 'Bitch, get off, keine Zeit für dich, Hoe.' / Bin unterwegs mit meinen Doggys, also scheiß mal auf Cro*". This observation corroborates our line of argumentation that the example from Cro is far more artificial and put-on than the use of multilingual lyrics in Example 11.1. While Cro appears to be acting out a persona that is not genuinely his own, EES performs his multilingual and multicultural identity in his songs.

In addition to that, our former observation that we find a mixture of German, German-based youth language, and English further illustrates how the boundaries between code-switching, code-mixing, and linguistic borrowing are not clear cut. It can be argued that words such as "straight", "*spliffen*", "nice" (as found in others of his songs), etc. do not constitute instances of code-mixing but permanent borrowings since they seem to have been taken over into German by the younger generations of speakers (see ▶ Sect. 4.3.3.1 on code-mixing).

Our next example comes from the South African hip hop group *Die Antwoord*. This song is not presented here for its multilingual lyrics even though it features two languages, namely English as the matrix language and Afrikaans as interspersions to mark the multi-ethnic and multilingual identity of the group. On the basis of this example, we would like to show how multilingualism and multiethnicity can also be expressed by means of other linguistic features than multilingual lyrics. In the spoken introduction to their song "Enter the Ninja" (see, e.g., https://www.youtube.com/watch?v=cegdR0GiJl4), Ninja explains: "Check this! Proudly present South African culture. In this place, you have a lot of different things; blacks, whites, coloureds; English, Afrikaans, Xhosa, Zulu, Watookal. I'm like all these different things, all these different people, packed into one person" (Die Antwoord, 2010). He explicitly states his multi-ethnic identity in this introduction. This shows that his distinctly White South African English pronunciation patterns, such as the use of dental stops instead of dental fricatives (e.g. /tɪŋs/ instead of /θɪŋs/) or the extensive use of trilled r, and his use of linguistic elements from Afrikaans, such as "*Met fokol kos, skraal*" ('kick back rough language'), are genuine parts of his own linguistic identity. Therefore, he seems to be presenting an authentic persona.

Last but not least, we would like to highlight yet another function of code-switching and thus multilingual language use in pop songs. In his song "Beauty & Stupid" (1996), Hide mixes Japanese and English at more or less equal shares but again not randomly.

▶ **Example 11.3**

Excerpt from "Beauty & Stupid" (Hide, 1996), lyrics from Musixmatch, with modifications by Lisa Westermayer.

気絶する様な 行為の中気持ち売る様じゃ
恋も泡腰を振る数 数えてもとても本気にゃなれない *Ai ai*
あなた好みの *Sixty-nine*いやよやめては *OK sign*
もしも愛なら 紛い物で栗の花咲きゃ *Bye bye bye bye*
You make me love, love
I give you my gun, gun
名前知らない2人のままなら分かり合えちゃったのにね

> I, I, I, I, I just wanna make love
> だけど I, I, I, I, I don't wanna fall in love
> あれやこれやと こんがらがっちゃうの
> いつのまにやら そんななっちゃうの
> 白い谷間で 微睡んでいれば
> 胸の何処かが ズキズキ Shakin, shakin
> かなり Cool に 気取ってても
> やっぱりシュールな 心模様
> 避けて通れぬ 甘い wanna にみごとはまって Ah, ah, ah
> Is this love potion?
> Youve got love machine gun
> 殺し文句は dynamite な涙つぶした 君の Smile
> Beauty and stupid, A-ha-ha (Baby love you, love you like an animal)
> Beauty and stupid, a-ha-ha
> A-ha-ha A-ha-ha A-ha-ha A-ha-ha ◄

Going into the details and exact translation of the Japanese material would go far beyond the aim of this chapter. We would rather like to illustrate how Hide uses the English language to address or rather circumvent expressions and words which are considered taboos in Japanese society, in this case metaphors and explicit mentions of sex and sexual love (e.g. "*Sixty-nine …OK; I give you my gun, gun; I, I, I, I, I just wanna make love*"). This is reminiscent of a function of code-switching which has already been suggested by Thomason (2001, p. 133; ► Sect. 4.4), that is, the use of another language as euphemism, for example, to soften the effect of an unpleasant, or in this case tabooed, statement.

❓ Exercises

1. Go to the song *Enter the Ninja* on Spotify, YouTube (► https://www.youtube.com/watch?v=cegdR0GiJl4) or any other music streaming platform and listen to it. Try to identify further typical South African English pronunciation patterns in the song. Simply describe what you hear if you do not know the proper linguistic terminology. Also identify the Afrikaans elements in the lyrics of the song and discuss the band's potential motivation for including them in the song.
2. Select a multilingual song you like, present it to the class, and analyse it according to the criteria introduced above, that is, linguistic mechanisms at work and potential motivation for the artist. Explain your considerations.

Summary

In this chapter, we have outlined the development of multilingual music and linguistic research relating to the use of languages, varieties, and dialects in (pop) songs. We have further presented and discussed a variety of reasons for artists to either sing and perform in a language or dialect which is not their own or to make use of more than one language or variety in one song. In this respect, we were able to identify two general sets of reasons, which means those related to the performer's actual multi-ethnic and multilingual identity and those related to the audience's expectations and stereotypes of a specific music genre. In addition to that, we have discussed some of the mechanisms of multilingual language use presented in ▶ Chap. 4 in relation to how they find application in multilingual songs. We finally want to state again that the label *multilingual* in our understanding does not only pertain to songs which feature two or more languages but also to songs in which a variety of a language is being used next to the 'standard' language. We have further included songs in which singing accents or grammatical structures reflect the multilingual identity and repertoire of the singer, even though the song is superficially only presented in one linguistic system.

References

Akande, A. (2012). The appropriation of African American vernacular English and Jamaican Patois by Nigerian hip hop artists. *ZAA, 60*(3), 237–254.
Altenmüller, E. (2018). *Vom Neandertal in die Philharmonie: Warum der Mensch ohne Musik nicht leben kann*. Springer.
Androutsopoulos, J., & Scholz, A. (2003). Spaghetti Funk: Appropriations of hip-hop culture and rap music in Europe. *Popular Music and Society, 26*(4), 463–479.
Beal, J. C. (2009). 'You're not from New York City, you're from Rotherham': Dialect and identity in British Indie music. *Journal of English Linguistics, 37*(3), 223–240.
Bell, A. (1984). Language style as audience design. *Language in Society, 13*, 145–204.
Bell, A. (1992). Hit and miss: Referee design in the dialects of New Zealand television advertisements. *Language and Communication, 12*(3/4), 327–340.
Bell, A., & Gibson, A. (2011). Staging language: An introduction to the sociolinguistics of performance. *Journal of Sociolinguistics, 15*(5), 555–572.
Bremner, N. (2015). Keepin' it real? Engaging in language politics in Réunion through the juxtaposition of English and Réunionese Kreol in dancehall music. *Journal of Romance Studies, 15*(1), 111–130.
Buschfeld, S. (2021). 'Grassroots English, learner English, second-language English, English as a lingua franca …: What's in a name?', in C. Meierkord & E. W. Schneider (Eds), World Englishes at the Grassroots (pp.23–46). Edinburgh University Press.
Buschfeld, S., & Schröder, A. (2020). English and German in Namibia. In R. Hickey (Ed.), *English in the German-speaking world* (pp. 334–360). Cambridge University Press.
Cro (feat. Danju). (2014). Meine Gang (Bang Bang) [Song]. Retrieved June 6, 2021, from https://genius.com/Cro-meine-gang-bang-bang-lyrics
Gerfer, A. (2022). Authentic crossing? Jamaican Creole in African dancehall. In J. T. Farquharson, A. Hollington, & B. Jones (Eds.), *Contact languages and music*. The University of the West Indies Press.
Gibson, A., & Bell, A. (2012). Popular music singing as referee design. In J. M. Hernández-Campoy & J. A. Cutillas-Espinosa (Eds.), *Style shifting in public: New perspectives on stylistic variation* (pp. 139–164). John Benjamins.
Giles, H. (1973). Accent mobility: A model and some data. *Anthropological Linguistics, 15*, 87–105.
Giles, H., & Smith, P. (1979). Accommodation theory: Optimal levels of convergence. In H. Giles & R. St Clair (Eds.), *Language and social psychology*. Blackwell.
Hide. (1996). *Beauty & Stupid* [music video]. YouTube. Retrieved July 6, 2022, from https://www.youtube.com/watch?v=a5sqDJGkY6Y
IFPI. (2021). Global music report 2021. Retrieved from https://www.ifpi.org/ifpi-issues-annual-global-music-report-2021/.

Jansen, L. (2018). Britpop is a thing, damn it: On British attitudes toward American English and an Americanized singing style. In V. Werner (Ed.), *The language of pop culture* (pp. 116–135). Routledge.

Jansen, L., & Gerfer, A. (2022). The Arctic monkeys live at the Royal Albert Hall: Investigating Turner's "lounge singer shimmer". In V. Werner & C. Schubert (Eds.), *Stylistic approaches to pop culture*. Routledge.

Jansen, L., & Westphal, M. (2017). Rihanna works her multivocal pop persona: A morpho–syntactic and accent analysis of Rihanna's singing style. *English Today, 33*(2), 46–55.

Jansen, L., & Westphal, M. (2022). Caribbean identity in pop music: Rihanna's and Nicki Minaj's multivocal pop personas. In A. Hollington, J. T. Farquharson, & B. Jones (Eds.), *Contact languages and music*. UWI Press.

John, E. (2015). Zweisprachige Songs: Sprachmuster transkultureller Inszenierungen. In D. Helms & T. Phleps (Eds.), *Speaking in tongues* (pp. 157–176). transcript-Verlag.

Koyfman, S. (2020). *When music is multilingual: 10 artists who perform in other languages*. Babbel Magazine. Retrieved May 12, 2022, from https://www.babbel.com/en/magazine/10-artists-who-perform-in-other-languages

Le Page, R. B. (1968). Problems of description in multilingual communities. *TPS*, 189–212.

Le Page, R. B. (1975). Polarizing factors: Political, social, economic, operating on the individual's choice of identity through language use in British Honduras. In J. G. Savard & R. Vigneault (Eds.), *Les États Multilingues* (pp. 537–551). Laval University Press.

Le Page, R. B. (1978). Projection, focussing, diffusion. Society for Caribbean Linguistics Occasional Paper, 9.

Le Page, R. B., Christie, P., Jurdant, B., Weekes, A., & Tabouret-Keller, A. (1974). Further report on the sociolinguistic survey of multilingual communities. *Language in Society, 3*, 1–32.

Mandus, A. (2016). *Light and shadow in Namibia. Everyday life in a dream country*. Palmato Publishing.

Morrissey, F. A. (2008). Liverpool to Louisiana in one lyrical line: Style choice in British rock, pop and folk singing. In M. A. Locher & J. Strässler (Eds.), *Standards and norms in the English language* (pp. 193–216). Mouton de Gruyter.

Rampton, B. (1995). *Crossing: Language and ethnicity among adolescents*. Longman.

Sarpeah, A. (2017, August 21). *The fake patois used by Shatta Wale, Stonebwoy, others can't be labeled as Dancehall*. Ghbase.com. Retrieved March 10, 2019, from https://www.ghbase.com/fake-patois-used-shatta-wale-stonebwoy-others-cant-labeled-dancehall-root-eye/

Simpson, P. (1999). Language, culture and identity: With (another) look at accents in pop and rock singing. *Multilingua—Journal of Cross-Cultural and Interlanguage Communication, 18*(4), 343–368.

Thomason, S. G. (2001). *Language contact. An introduction*. Edinburgh University Press.

Trudgill, P. (1983). Acts of conflicting identity: The sociolinguistics of British pop-song performance. In P. Trudgill (Ed.), *On dialect—social and geographical perspectives* (pp. 141–160). New York University Press.

Vulliamy, E. (2019, April 6). *She loves you… Sí, Oui, Ja: How pop went multilingual*. The Guardian. Retrieved May 12, 2022, from https://www.theguardian.com/music/2019/apr/06/latin-spanish-pop-takes-over-from-english-language

Werner, V. (2018). Linguistics and pop culture: Setting the scene(s). In V. Werner (Ed.), *The language of pop culture* (pp. 3–26). Routledge.

Westermayer, L. (2019). *"What's a singer meant to sound like?" Extra- and intralinguistic influences on the singing accents of Australian indie artists*. [Unpublished MA thesis, University of Regensburg].

References

Westphal, M., & Jansen, L. (2021). English in global pop music. In B. Schneider, T. Heyd, & M. Saraceni (Eds.), *Bloomsbury World Englishes volume 1: Paradigms* (pp. 190–206). Bloomsbury Academic.

Key Readings

Gibson, A., & Bell, A. (2012). Popular music singing as referee design. In J. M. Hernández-Campoy & J. A. Cutillas-Espinosa (Eds.), *Style shifting in public: New perspectives on stylistic variation* (pp. 139–164). John Benjamins.

John, E. (2015). Zweisprachige Songs: Sprachmuster transkultureller Inszenierungen. In D. Helms & T. Phleps (Eds.), *Speaking in tongues* (pp. 157–176). transcript Verlag.

Trudgill, P. (1983). Acts of conflicting identity: The sociolinguistics of British pop-song performance. In P. Trudgill (Ed.), *On dialect: Social and geographical perspectives* (pp. 141–160). Blackwell.

Further Reading

Morrissey, F. A. (2008). Liverpool to Louisiana in one lyrical line: Style choice in British rock, pop and folk singing. In M. A. Locher & J. Strässler (Eds.), *Standards and norms in the English language* (pp. 193–216). Mouton de Gruyter.

Linguistic Landscapes

Contents

12.1 Introduction – 254

12.2 The Background to Linguistic Landscapes – 254

12.3 Types of Signs – 256

12.4 What Counts as a Sign? – 260

12.5 The Study of Linguistic Landscapes in the Context of Multilingualism and English – 261

References – 273

© The Author(s), under exclusive license to Springer Nature Switzerland AG 2023
S. Buschfeld et al., *Multilingualism*,
https://doi.org/10.1007/978-3-031-28405-2_12

12.1 Introduction

In addition to the languages that speakers hear spoken around them, speakers are also influenced by what they see and read on a daily basis. The visual presence of language in our landscape and cityscapes is often referred to as the linguistic landscape (e.g. Landry & Bourhis, 1997). In its analysis of the presence of language in society, the field of linguistic landscape study addresses concerns of language variation, sociolinguistics, discourse studies, multilingualism research, language policy research and other linguistic fields. The field also connects linguistics with other fields of research, in particular sociology, geography, or social psychology. The field evolved with the realisation that language choices in the visual landscape in general, and on signage in particular, are a relevant field of research as these are not arbitrary. Instead, they reflect language use in the community together with motives, ideologies, and decision-making processes of the creators of the signage (Shohamy & Ben-Rafael, 2015, p. 1). Thus, the language choices not only tell us what their creators consider to be most effective to reach their intended audience, but also which languages they want to be associated with themselves, or which they want to dissociate from. Such language choices are manifest in different kinds of signage: infrastructural (i.e. public) signage to provide information, regulatory signage like traffic signs, commercial signage informing customers, transgressive signs like graffiti or stickers, or commemorative signs such as memorials (Ziegler et al., 2018).

In the following chapter, we briefly outline the development of the field of linguistic landscape studies, then we move on to types of signs that are commonly distinguished before the question is asked what is in fact counted as a sign. We end the chapter by introducing three case studies based on our own research which illustrate concerns in linguistic landscape studies.

12.2 The Background to Linguistic Landscapes

The study of linguistic landscapes is a comparatively new addition to the field of multilingualism research. Pioneering research in this field has been carried out by Rosenbaum et al. (1977), who observed the foray of the English language in Keren Kayemet Street in West Jerusalem. The authors found that the English language was already used copiously in commercial signage in West Jerusalem. They further observed differences in the amount of English used in different types of signs. As the use of English was in opposition to the official language policy of the time, Rosenbaum et al. suggest this to be due to the high regard in which the English language was held. After this groundbreaking early study, it took more than a decade for the field of linguistic landscapes to attract considerably more attention from researchers. In a much-quoted study, Landry and Bourhis state that

» [t]he language of public road signs, advertising billboards, street names, place names, commercial shop signs, and public signs on government buildings combines to form the linguistic landscape of a given territory, region, or urban agglomeration. (1997, p. 25)

12.2 · The Background to Linguistic Landscapes

In their study of Francophone Canadians, Landry and Bourhis (1997) find that the linguistic landscape has an important impact on perceived language vitality and that the visual presence of a language can influence the use of this language. As a result of this, the use of minority languages in public signage can help to support language maintenance and help to counteract language shift.

Some years prior to Landry and Bourhis' (1997) study, work by Spolsky and Cooper (1991), also on Jerusalem data, introduces various taxonomies along which language of signs can be qualified. They argue that first, linguistic signs have different functions and uses, such as street signs, advertising, warnings, names of buildings, informative signs, commemorative plaques, labels of objects, or graffiti. Second, they distinguish signs according to the different materials from which they are made, for example metal, wood, stone, or paper, as well as their form, such as posters. Third, they separate signs into different levels of multilingualism, namely monolingual, bilingual, or multilingual signage. All of these factors are strongly determined by who the signs are authored by. Signs by official institutions, such as street signs, are likely to be purpose-made from materials like metal and to follow official language policies in their choice of languages used. By contrast, private messages, such as for example ad-hoc announcements or flyers on shop fronts, are likely to be made from much less permanent materials like paper, may be handwritten, and the language choice will depend on the purposes of the signs' authors. The former type of sign has been termed top-down signs, they are created by government institutions to reach the general population. As such, the top-down signs represent official language use and illustrate official language policies. The latter type of signs is known as bottom-up signs. They are created by members of the population and are representative of their language use. As a result, language use will be more varied on bottom-up signs (cf. Landry & Bourhis, 1997). A distinction between top-down and bottom-up signs can be found in many studies though it has been criticised as too simplistic: while a government notice addresses the population, a sign in a shop window does not address the government (Kallen, 2009, p. 273).

While all signs have the function to communicate something to their observers, two different core functions have been distinguished. These are the informative function and the symbolic function. In addition to communicating the intended information, the choice of language also marks the linguistic territory. In addition to the informative function of transmitting the message intended by the sign, to use a given language on a sign also symbolises that the language on the sign has currency in the particular territory where the sign is placed, thus the language use on the sign also receives a symbolic function. By using a certain language on signage, the creators of the sign invest the language with status and index this language as powerful (Landry & Bourhis, 1997, p. 29).

In fact, the choice of languages on signage is highly context-dependent. Rather than simply providing information on the presence of a language, language choice has a high symbolic value and certain 'rules' for language choice have been observed. Spolsky and Cooper (1991, pp. 81–84) argue that first, writers typically only write signs in languages that they command themselves. Yet, when languages are being used, different levels of proficiency may be represented, and this may lead to the presence of non-standard features of the languages used. Second, writers are likely to use language(s) which the intended readers can read. This rule is likely to be adhered to by businesses who want to attract clients. And finally, while the writers are likely to write in their own language, they may also choose to use a language they want to be associated with, for example because of its high prestige. By choosing a high prestige language, the authors of the signs then exploit the symbolic value of this language. This property has particularly been observed for the international use of the English language, starting with Rosenbaum et al. (1977) and various studies that have followed. As we see in the following, the English language continues to play a large role in linguistic landscape studies. With the further development of the field of linguistic landscapes, further new directions have developed that take into account in particular the connection between the choice of language and the environment in which they are used. Thus, Jaworski and Thurlow (2010) have extended the study of linguistic landscapes towards the analysis of their semiotic properties. Even more recently, the study of linguistic landscapes has broadened towards the use of ethnographic approaches. Here, especially Ethnographic Linguistic Landscape Analysis (Blommaert & Maly, 2016) has proved particularly interesting. In this approach, linguistic landscapes are used to study social action and social spaces from a perspective of super-diversity.

Research indicates that the choice of language on signage in public space is neither entirely free nor completely indicative of the languages present in the community in all cases: while discourses by authorities may honor the language rights of minorities, in many cases they do not and communicate in prestige language(s) only. Even private discourses in non-powerful languages may be suppressed, for example if a population group is prohibited for political reasons from using their language publicly.

12.3 Types of Signs

In principle, the linguistic landscape is composed of any type of written communication that language users may encounter. In order to evaluate linguistic landscapes, various taxonomies have been proposed and used. The traditional landscape approaches that have been described in ▶ Sect. 12.2 above predominantly focus on signage of various types, to be further discussed in the following. The description here follows Ziegler et al.'s (2018) taxonomy, which is based on Scollon and Scollon (2003) and Backhaus (2007).

Infrastructural discourse types are all discourses that inform the public. The information is supplied by institutions, such as town authorities, road authorities, or institutions (◘ Fig. 12.1). The signage is likely to contain, for example, names such as road names, instructions, for example on ticket machines, or opening hours. Typically, infrastructural discourse accounts for a low percentage of the written discourse; usually about a single digit of the signs found belong to this group. As infrastructural discourse is provided by authorities, it provides a clear indication of de-facto language policies in a community. A further top-down discourse type is regulatory discourse. Such signs regulate life in public spaces. This applies to all

12.3 · Types of Signs

Fig. 12.1 Multilingual infrastructural discourse: entrance sign in Vrsi, Croatia

traffic signs, prohibitions, or warnings. They are a prototypical type of governmental discourse and discourse of other authorities and thus, like infrastructural discourse, showcase official language policies. Typically, regulatory discourse also accounts for single-digit percentages of overall discourse types. A final category of top-down discourses is that of commemorative signs. These are constituted by commemorative signs and memorial plaques. As such signs often remain unaltered for long periods, they may also indicate changes in the linguistic landscape quite well. Usually, commemorative signs account for very small fractions of a percentage in public discourses.

Large proportions of visible discourse are accounted for by commercial discourses. These are shop signs, as well as signs indicating other types of businesses, or advertising. Such commercial signs are bottom-up communication, created with the intention of attracting customers, and thus they have to be understood by or kindle an interest in the customers. In a typical linguistic landscape study, this discourse type predominates by far and accounts for percentages of the discourse in high double digits (Fig. 12.2). A further bottom-up category of signs is constituted by transgressive discourse types. These are all discourses that have been added without authorisation, such as graffiti, tags, stickers, or posters (Fig. 12.3). Depending on the location in which the landscapes studies are carried out, transgressive discourse can be very highly represented, for example in high double-digit percentage points in Ziegler et al.'s (2018) study of Ruhr Valley cities. In some cases, the distinction of non-authorized, transgressive from legally produced and commissioned artistic discourse types is not entirely visible, though in most cases there is little doubt. Artistic discourse is typically rarely observed, for example in Ziegler et al.'s (2018) study it accounts for low fractions of a single percentage point.

However, even if the above division of different types of signs appears fairly neat, different, further levels of analysis can be distinguished. Kallen (2010, pp. 42–43) stresses that linguistic landscapes are multi-layered and consist of several different visual discourse frameworks. Following considerations introduced by Scollon and Scollon (2003), he uses additional categories of frames. These consid-

◘ Fig. 12.2 Multilingual commercial discourse: pseudo-Asian/English/Spanish discourse

◘ Fig. 12.3 Multilingual transgressive sign in English and German in Tübingen

erations are (1) by whom the sign was produced, (2) who the viewer is, (3) what the social situation of the sign is (in place, being installed or worked on), and (4) in which part of the material world it is found.

On the basis of Scollon and Scollon's questions, Kallen (2010, p. 43) proposes the spatial frameworks of (1) civic frames: within this frame, state authorities label territory and regulate behaviour. The frame thus comprises infrastructural and regulatory discourse types; (2) the marketplace, in which everyday competition is carried out by commerce, businesses, publications, and public and private services (◘ Fig. 12.4). This frame thus shows many overlaps with commercial discourse types introduced above; (3) portals: these provide transition places between physical and linguistic environments to other environments. They include physical portals like train stations, capital portals like banks, or electronic portals like telephone companies; (4) walls, on which graffiti, posters, or stickers can be found. Further, (5) a detritus zone, which results from products for consumption which have been discarded and form a transient feature of the environment. For example, these might be discarded newspapers, food wrappers, or cigarette boxes. Kallen (2010) suggests further possible categories, such as (6) communities, which consist of non-commercial communities of practice like sports clubs, religious groups or others, or (7) schools or other educational institutions. In this taxonomy, the inclusion of transient linguistic codes, such as litter or other types of refuse, is particularly interesting as it provides insights into people's mobility or interactions with other communities: for example, food wrappers or drink containers with writing from other countries point to personal mobilities. Thus Kallen (2010, p. 55) observes a cigarette box with Romanian writing on it, which suggests the presence of—or contacts with—Romanian speakers in the community. One might further consider other non-permanent features of the landscape, such as texts and advertisements on passing cars, information and advertisements on busses or coaches (see ▶ Sect. 12.4). While the writing on displays of busses or coaches gives information on infrastructural language choices, particularly information on private cars indexes personal language choices. ◘ Figure 12.4 illustrates a taxi-driver's choice in Dublin to use Irish language rather than English language signage.

◘ Fig. 12.4 The market place: Irish language signage on a taxi in Dublin, Ireland

12.4 What Counts as a Sign?

Linguistic landscape analyses written language on public display. This in principle allows for straightforward approaches to data collection, which collects instances of tokens from all languages found. However, the question of what counts as a token is already a more complex one. Many researchers working in linguistic landscape analyse the tokens that are on public display in streets and other public places (e.g. Landry & Bourhis, 1997; Kallen, 2009; Ziegler et al., 2018). A linguistic token is typically considered to consist of one sign (e.g. Backhaus, 2007; Kallen, 2009). Yet, if a sign is defined as a written text in a "spatially defined frame" (Backhaus, 2007, p. 66), then traffic signs or plaques provide little ambiguity as to what constitutes a sign, while a shop window or a pin board already raise the question of whether the whole window or the whole board should be considered the sign. Imagine a shop window with lettering on the window and a printed poster and a handwritten flyer. Would this window count as one sign with multiple messages or as three separate signs? Typically, each separate token with clear spatial delimitation is considered a separate sign. This would make the shop window in the example a linguistic sign or token in itself and the printed and written posters displayed on it would be additional signs. There are a number of reasons that speak for counting the shop window and the posters on it separately. For one, in this hypothetical case, the shop window and the posters on it consist of different materials: in the first case, the lettering is on glass and in the case of the posters, the writing is on paper. Further, the three tokens have different lettering (once possibly plastic on the glass, once possibly ink-printed, and once hand-written). Additionally, the emitters of the sign may be different: while the writing on the shop window will have been added by the shop owners, a printed sign or flyer might either contain additional information supplied by the shop owners, or it may advertise a community event and might have been put up by another person or company. Similar criteria can be applied to pin boards, for example in supermarkets, which also consist of a number of different signs: they are typically made of notices written by different emitters, in various printing forms. In addition, notices on a pin board are likely to be changed regularly. Notice boards thus offer a very versatile and often very vivid picture of community languages in use.

Another issue for which separate approaches exist is the question of how permanent or transient a language token is allowed to be in order to be considered part of the linguistic landscape. In the influential definition by Landry and Bourhis (1997, p. 25) referred to above, the study of linguistic landscapes focuses on road signs, advertising billboards, street names, place names, commercial shop signs, and public signs on government buildings. However, a number of more recent studies also take into account less permanent or transient signs. Thus, Sebba (2010) argues that also unfixed signs, such as on stickers, bank notes or on vehicles such as lorries, vans or busses, should be considered as they are part of the linguistic landscape around us. As seen in ▶ Sect. 12.3, also Kallen (2010), for example, includes transient linguistic items in his analysis while others only take tokens into consideration which can be expected to be in place minimally for a couple of weeks

(Scollon & Scollon, 2003). While the former approach, which also includes transient signs, gives a more comprehensive overview, the latter one is less open to chance and thus is more reproducible. However, if we include transient codes in our analysis, we obtain a better picture of the language portfolios: the writing on cars, as in ◘ Fig. 12.4 above, or the non-permanent notes in shops, as well as detritus such as the cigarette box with Romanian writing observed in Kallen (2010), give us evidence of what language preferences the language users have, which languages may be found in the community that we have not yet been aware of, and with which other speaker groups the language users may be in contact.

Thus, by expanding the analysis of the linguistic landscape from the mainly commercial, infrastructural, regulatory, and commemorative discourse types to the special framework, which includes specific contexts in which the signs are found, and which also includes the highly versatile and non-permanent transient codes, more dynamic developments are taken into consideration. It takes a comparatively long time for a road sign to be changed, but detritus, and to a certain extent also posters and stickers, are open to constant change and thus allow us to capture developments in language choice over time and through different media. By contrast, governmental and commemorative, and to a lesser degree also infrastructural discourse types, typically persist for a long period of time and can thus preserve older linguistic forms and language choices. While the governmental, commemorative, and infrastructural discourse types represent top-down language use, which may differ from the actual linguistic realities and choices of language users, the more transient codes provide a glimpse of up-to-date, current-time language use by various different speaker groups.

12.5 The Study of Linguistic Landscapes in the Context of Multilingualism and English

As seen in ► Sect. 12.2, the study of linguistic landscapes is typically concerned with visual multilingualism. Already in the early and earlier studies in the field (Rosenbaum et al., 1977; Spolsky and Cooper 1991; Landry & Bourhis, 1997), we find strong evidence of the presence of English in many different settings. Different functions of the English language have been observed: next to the informative function, in which the wide reach of English as an international lingua franca is exploited (Landry & Bourhis, 1997), its symbolic value and its connection with globalisation and innovation have also repeatedly been stressed (e.g. Landry & Bourhis, 1997; Backhaus, 2007). Thus, charting and documenting the presence and international spread of the English language has been playing a very important role in the study of linguistic landscapes. Such research is carried out from different perspectives. One perspective analyses the use of the English language in countries where English is not normally used and where its presence can be explained in terms of lingua franca use of English (e.g. Rosenbaum et al., 1977; Backhaus, 2007; Ziegler et al., 2018). Another perspective analyses the use of English from the perspective of minority language contexts. The ever-increasing spread of the

English language may increase its visual presence and causes it to makes inroads into the fragile representation of minority languages, especially those minority languages which are already in contact with English as a majority language, like Irish, Scots Gaelic or Welsh (e.g. Kallen, 2009; Ronan, 2021). In the following, potential research avenues into multilingualism in linguistic landscapes are illustrated on the basis of three case studies. The first case study illustrates the use of English and of various other languages for symbolic purposes. The second case study investigates the use of a national minority language, Irish, versus the dominant English language. The third case study illustrates commercial multilingualism in a multilingual community, the Caribbean island of St. Martin.

Data for the first case study have been collected in the German Ruhr Valley city of Dortmund. The Ruhr Valley is a formerly heavily industrialised area in which structural change towards new and innovative technologies has been underway during the last decades. Due to its industrial history, the Ruhr Valley has a long history of immigration. Already during its industrialisation in the late nineteenth century, there was supra-regional immigration to the Ruhr Valley from Poland; during the twentieth century, immigrants particularly hailed from Italy, Greece, Turkey, former Yugoslavia, Spain, and Portugal and towards the end of the twentieth century, further international migration took place from Poland and the former USSR; in the twenty-first century, international immigration mainly originated from the Near and Middle East as well as from the Maghreb and Central and Western African countries. As a result, the Ruhr Valley has considerable cultural diversity and large percentages of its population are extensively multilingual, including widespread competence in the local majority language German and the international lingua franca English. However, not all languages are represented in the linguistic landscape to the same degree. Of the non-German passport holders, in 2018, about 30% had Turkish nationality, 32% had other European nationalities, and nearly 38% came from other regions of the world (Metropole Ruhr, n.d.). In spite of this, as Ziegler et al. (2018) have already shown, Turkish and other non-European languages are less well represented in the linguistic landscapes of the Ruhr Valley than could be expected on the basis of the share that speakers have in the population. By contrast, the English language is well-represented both due to its cultural capital (i.e. its symbolic function) and due to its international understandability (informative function). Ziegler et al. further find that the extent and the distribution of visual multilingualism varies in different areas and that this depends on the population statistics of the investigated areas. The northern parts of the Ruhr Valley cities are generally more industrialised and they typically have lower average socio-economic status and larger amounts of the resident populations with a migration background. By contrast, the southern parts of the cities are more affluent, have fewer residents with a migration background and have fewer multilingual signs on display.

The influence of such social factors also becomes visible in an even more fine-grained local analysis. Hörde, which is an area in the Ruhr Valley city Dortmund, has recently undergone considerable structural change when a former steelworks site was turned into a recreational lake, surrounded by very desirable housing that reaches top price levels. As a result, around this new lake, aptly named Lake

Phoenix, various restaurants and bars have opened. Gentrification processes, with new and modern buildings replacing traditional working-class housing, are also visible throughout the area, most obviously close to Lake Phoenix itself.

In the linguistic landscape of Hörde, and especially the Lake Phoenix area, this social change can also be observed. In a survey of commercial signage in late 2021 (Ronan 2022), an area from the centre of Hörde to the shore of Lake Phoenix was surveyed and the signage of about 100 businesses (n = 107) was analysed, yielding 175 data points. Both permanent signage and semi-permanent signage, for example computer-printed or hand-written notes on shops, were taken into consideration (◘ Fig. 12.5). In this data set, the use of visual multilingualism can be shown to correspond to the social change manifesting in the urban renewal process.

The survey in ◘ Fig. 12.5 shows that German accounts for most of the 175 data points. However, English language data can also be found and is the best-represented language after German. Italian is exclusively found in restaurants, cafes, and ice-cream parlours and is likely to symbolise the authenticity of the Italian culture. These uses of Italian language data can be observed in particular directly at and close to Lake Phoenix. In the data set, the use of French is more versatile than the use of Italian. French is less concentrated in a particular area, but the data points are more likely to take a central role in the commercial discourse of the business than the Italian language does. Generally, the French language is used to advertise beauty, food, or lifestyle products. Only in one case is French the dominant language, where a French name is used for a beauty parlour, *Beauté Sensuelle*, and invokes French competence in beauty and fashion. Spanish data points are likewise centred at or close to the lake. Like Italian, the Spanish language is also mainly used in the names of restaurants and cafes. The Turkish data points equally exclusively represent either the names of restaurants or restaurant products. In contrast to Italian and Spanish, however, the Turkish data points are found in or

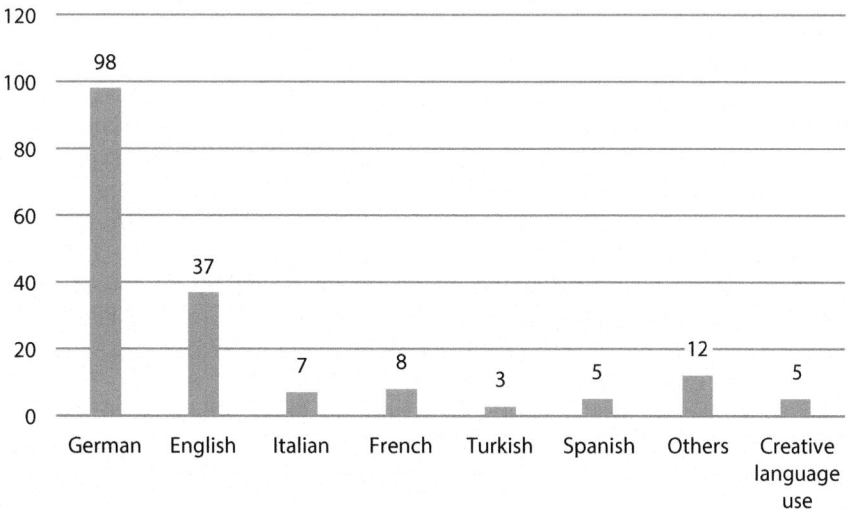

◘ Fig. 12.5 Language use in Dortmund Hörde

close to the old town centre of Hörde, where urban renewal is less in evidence. Other languages represented in the data include Polish, Latin, Japanese, and Thai. Business names with Latin components are situated close to the lake and are used for lifestyle businesses, while Japanese and Thai are used for a Sushi restaurant and a massage parlour, respectively. But also creatively created names are used, thus we find an example of a seemingly Asian name, which provides a global image (cf. ◘ Fig. 12.2: *Mu-Kii. Pan-Asian Tapas*).

Finally, English data is used in particular for clothing shops and in connection with beauty outlets. It is further frequently used in the context of restaurants and bars and telecommunication, accounting for names such as "Factory" or "My Friends" (restaurants), "Cutmaster" (a hairdresser), or "Monkey Donuts". The use of English is found both in the more modern and the more traditional parts of the area. Generally, the English language is used to exploit its indexicality of modernity and sophistication, fashion and coolness (compare Sayer 2010). It is noteworthy that though English is frequently used by some business types, it is not or hardly in evidence for some other types of business: official administration, health service providers, and bakeries typically use German only. By contrast, the German language seems to be used in contexts where tradition, dependability, and reliability are important. As a result of this linguistic distribution in our data set, regression analyses show that it is also possible to use the language of the name of a business to predict statistically which type of business uses this language.

That the English language has the potential to oust minority languages can also be observed when we investigate the linguistic landscape in an officially bilingual country, Ireland, for our second case study (Ronan, 2021). Galway, a town with a central function in the west of Ireland, is the commercial and economic centre for the population living in the mainly Irish-speaking hinterland to the west of Galway, the Connemara *Gaeltacht* ('Irish-speaking area'). Further, Galway itself has a vibrant Irish-speaking community, fueled by the presence of one of the major Irish universities in the town, which also offers Irish-medium study programs. In spite of this, the main language of the town is English and the majority of the linguistic landscape in the town, particularly the commercial signs, reflects this state. In addition to the local resident and student population, Galway is frequented by a large number of tourists, who are attracted by the town, its scenic hinterland, and its vibrant and traditional cultural scene. Naturally, these tourists are typically not Irish speakers. Expanding on a study by Kallen (2009), a more recent study has been carried out on the linguistic landscape of the commercial centre of Galway town (Ronan, 2021). The aim of that study was two-fold. First, it aimed to investigate the degree to which the Irish language was able to stand its ground against the English language in the commercial centre of Galway. Second, it asked how the visitors, to whom many of the commercial signs are addressed, perceive the use of the Irish or the English language in the linguistic landscape.

The study was carried out in the city centre of Galway in June 2019 and followed a typical tourist route from Galway's famous Eyre Square towards Quay Street and via Wolfe Tone Bridge to Raven Terrace, Lower Dominik Street, and Mainguard Street. On this walk, a total of 180 businesses were photographed. Of the 180 businesses, one, a shoe shop, had no signage. In the remaining 179 busi-

12.5 · The Study of Linguistic Landscapes in the Context...

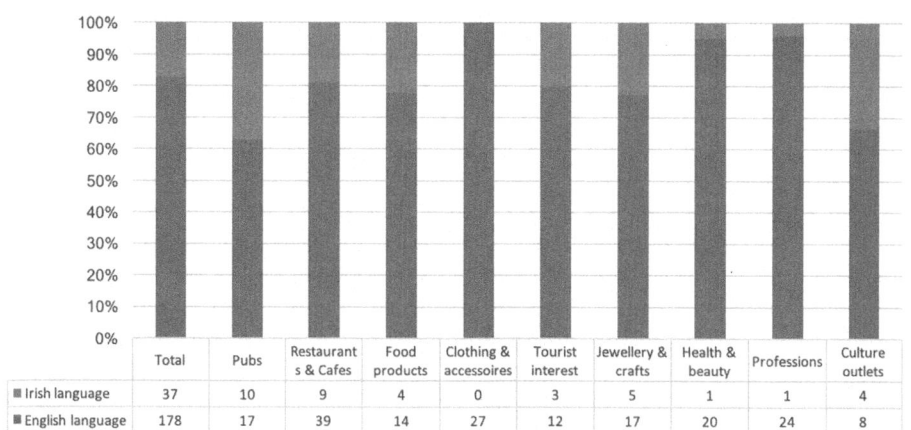

☐ **Fig. 12.6** The use of English and Irish in Galway City commercial signage

nesses, both qualitative and quantitative differences in the use of the Irish language on the respective signs can be observed (☐ Fig. 12.6). The signs were classified according to the type of business they represented and according to the languages and writing fonts that are used on them.

☐ Figure 12.6 shows that of the 179 businesses that use commercial signage, a total of 37 make use of any amount of Irish language signage, while 178 use English signage on their businesses. Only one business uses Irish language signage exclusively. However, not all types of businesses use English and Irish language signage to the same extent. We can observe that public houses (pubs) and cultural outlets (book shops, music shops, and clubs) evidence the highest use of the Irish language. By contrast, the observed clothing shops, including shoe shops and accessories shops, use no Irish language signage at all. Health and beauty outlets as well as professions (banks, lawyers, accountants, and schools) use very little Irish. There are two main exceptions to this. One is a dog-grooming business, "Hounddog", which uses an English company name but uses the same slogan both in the English language and in Irish ("It's all about the dog/*Faoin madra uilig é*"). The other one is a health store, which displays both its English language and its Irish language name on different windows ("Evergreen Health Store" / *Síorglas Sláinte Siopa*, ☐ Fig. 12.7a, b).

Some more Irish language use is found in the commercial signs of businesses which might also address tourists, namely souvenir shops, jewelers and craft shops, restaurants, and cafes and food product, with an average of about 20% of Irish language use (☐ Figs. 12.8 and 12.9). The use of Irish is most pronounced on the commercial signage of pubs and of culture-related outlets, where about one-third of the signage also features the Irish language.

Generally, we can see that the use of Irish is most pronounced in those businesses which are likely to attract tourists. It seems likely that Irish is used here for the cultural capital, that is, for the authentic Irishness that it represents.

Fig. 12.7 (**a**, **b**) Health shop with both English and Irish signage

12.5 · The Study of Linguistic Landscapes in the Context...

Fig. 12.8 Pub with English and Irish signage

Fig. 12.9 Jewelers with English and Irish signage

Fig. 12.10 Irish fonts used for English language pub name

However, it is not only the Irish language that can be found. Irish cultural capital is also likely to be conveyed by Irish-style writing fonts (cf. **◘** Figs. 12.8 and 12.9). Where Irish fonts are used for English language writing (**◘** Fig. 12.10), the businesses can draw on Irish cultural authenticity without running the risk of not being understood by the customers who they are targeting.

That cultural capital can indeed be drawn from both Irish language signage and the use of Irish language script, as could be confirmed by an interview study that was carried out at the time of data collection in one place of the route on which the survey of the linguistic landscape was carried out. At a central point of the route, at a pedestrianised intersection of three shopping streets (High Street, Shop Street, Mainguard Street), the researcher asked tourists for their attitudes to the English and Irish language shop signs. A total of 35 tourists agreed to answer the interview questions while they watched the performance of traditional dancers. The majority, 43% of the informants were German, 20% were American, and a further 20% Dutch. Single informants hailed from France, New Zealand, Brazil, Switzerland, and another Irish county, Monaghan. Of the informants, 63% identified as female and 37% as male.

This second part of the study investigated the informants' attitudes towards Irish language use on commercial signs, as well as their attitudes to Irish-style lettering on the commercial signs. The informants were asked whether they found Irish language signs of shops, restaurants, or pubs attractive. Generally, the informants had very positive attitudes both to the use of the Irish language and to the use of Irish-style lettering. On a five-point Likert scale, ranging between very attractive (1) and not-at-all-attractive (5), the attractiveness of Irish language signage received a mean value of 1.5. The use of Irish-style fonts was also considered very attractive, with a mean value of 1.6. A large number of the informants (40%) stated that the use of the Irish language was attractive because it was authentic, belonged to the country, and should be kept alive. They further stated that it looked aesthetic and attractive. However, 20% of the informants also commented on the fact that they could not understand the language and felt safer with the English

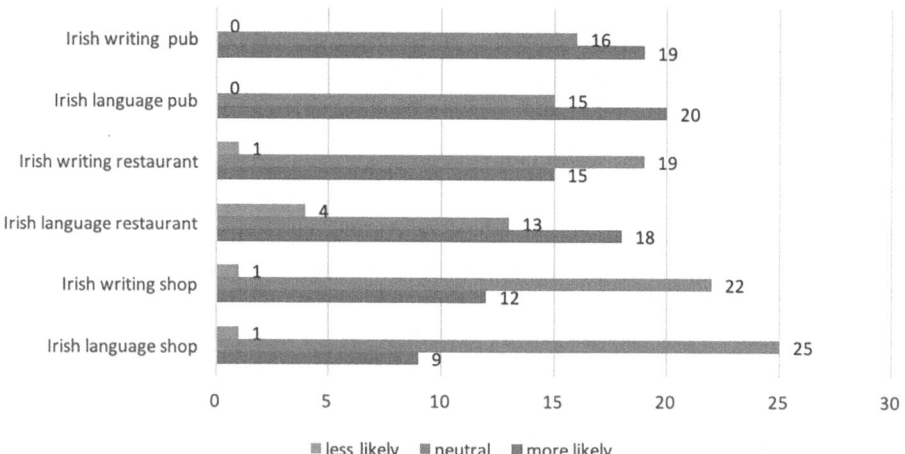

Fig. 12.11 Effect of Irish language use versus Irish-style letters on likelihood of tourists entering a business

language. However, also the use of Irish-style fonts drew favourable comments of authenticity (20%), and they were considered to be pretty (17%). Only a single informant was slightly discouraged by it, finding it hard to read.

Generally, the informants testified that there were commercial advantages for the businesses who used either the Irish language or Irish-style fonts (◘ Fig. 12.11). Informants were particularly positive about pubs with Irish language writing on them: 57% of the informants said they were more likely to go into a pub with than without Irish language signage, the remaining 43% said they had a neutral attitude. Furthermore, nobody claimed to have been discouraged by Irish language signage on a pub. The situation was similar for Irish-style fonts: Irish-style scripts were nearly as likely to attract tourists to enter a pub as Irish language use (54% were likely to be attracted and 46% were neutral).

Restaurants, too, were more likely to be frequented if they displayed the Irish language; 51% of the informants expressed a preference for the Irish language on restaurants while 37% were neutral. However, 11.5% stated they were less likely to enter a restaurant with Irish language writing. Irish-style script, again, attracted fewer tourists to restaurants than Irish language use. 43% argued they were attracted by Irish-style script, while 54% were neutral about Irish script and only one informant (3%) was less likely to go into the restaurant if it had Irish-style script. For shops, informants were slightly more likely to enter them if they had Irish-style script than if they used Irish language writing. Generally, for shops, the commercial advantage in using both Irish language and Irish-style writing to attract tourists appears to be lower than for pubs and restaurants on the basis of this data set.

This small-scale study thus suggests that the use of local minority languages not only respects the language rights of the minority language speakers but also adds cultural value for visitors who appreciate the presence of the minority language and the authenticity that it provides. However, not all informants felt comfortable about the use of the minority language: some informants indicated that they were not sure they would understand the language used in the business or be able to make themselves understood. This fear was less of an issue where Irish-style script was used for English language writing because though the cultural capital of the Irish-style script was invoked, there was no fear that the tourist might not be understood because the Irish language itself might be used in the establishment.

Finally, we turn to our third case study, multilingual signage in St. Martin (Buschfeld, Weihs, & Ronan, 2022). St. Martin is a small Eastern Caribbean island of 34 sq. mi, which was divided into two parts in 1648. Its northern part, Saint-Martin, is an overseas collectivity of the French Republic and part of the European Union. Its official language is French, but a number of other languages are spoken and used alongside French. The southern, Dutch part, St. Maarten, is one of four constituent countries of the Kingdom of the Netherlands. The official languages spoken in this part of the island are English and Dutch. English is the L1 for the majority of St. Maarteners, while Dutch is the language of the former coloniser. In general, the island is characterised by strong multilingualism, due to a long history of colonisation, strong migration movements from inside and outside the Caribbean, and due to tourism. St. Maarten is an interesting research site in two respects. First of all, we find an interesting sociolinguistic situation on the island, in particular due to the small but highly multilingual ecology shared between two nation-states. The two capitals in which the data were collected, Marigot and Philipsburg, are only a half-hour drive apart but could not be more different in their linguistic ecologies. Secondly, so far not much quantitative research has been conducted on the linguistic situation of St. Martin (for some first results on St. Maarten, see Buschfeld & Ahlers, 2022).

The research question we pursued for this study were the following: (1) Which languages dominate the linguistic landscape of St. Martin and what role does English play in this multilingual scenario? and (2) Do differences exist between the Dutch and French parts? The data to answer these questions were collected in Marigot's shopping mall and harbour area and along Philipsburg's main shopping street, Front Street, in February 2020. Pictures were taken of shop windows, street and road signs, memorials, graffiti, and any type of sign that would fall within one of the categories introduced in ▶ Sect. 12.3. Artistic signs, however, are not included in the data set and, as also discussed in ▶ Sect. 12.3, the distribution of sign types is highly skewed, with transgressive and commemorative signs being in a clear minority and commercial signs by far dominating the data set. In this study, we went for an analysis by sign, for example posters or stickers in shop windows were analysed as individual signs and not considered part of one overall shop window. Overall, we coded 373 signs for Marigot and 372 signs for Philipsburg. The study is one of the first—if not the first—which makes use of a strongly quantitative approach by means of advanced statistical modelling, which is why the signs were coded not only by type and location of the sign but according to complex and multi-layered criteria. Criteria which we employ include the exact category of sign (digital sign, street sign, road sign, graffiti, stand-up-display, shop window, etc.), their permanence, the number of languages included on the sign, the exact languages used in the signage, the exact type of multilingual language use (e.g. whether the languages are fully duplicated or complementary), and the question whether proper nouns, such as restaurant or brand names, were included. The latter question we considered important since it arguably makes a difference, whether, for example, a minority language or a language 'foreign' to the territory enters the signage as a brand name or restaurant name only, or whether it is fully productively used on the sign. In the following, we spare the reader the details of our complex analysis and simply provide a brief summary of the results and in particular those findings most interesting for the present book.

In general, the linguistic landscapes of St. Martin are characterised by strong multilingualism, with English and French as the core players (cf. ◘ Figs. 12.12 and 12.13).

A number of factors, however, influence the exact manifestations of multiple language use on public signs. Most importantly, the study by Buschfeld et al. (2022) has revealed significant differences between Philipsburg and Marigot. As ◘ Fig. 12.12 illustrates, Philipsburg is clearly dominated by English, while Marigot is dominated by French. Still, in its function as a global language and especially the language of tourism (e.g. Rosenbaum et al., 1977; Vuković-Vojnović & Nićin, 2012), English plays an important role in Marigot, too. Furthermore, even though the number of monolingual signs is similar in the two capitals, Philipsburg is multilingually more diverse than Marigot, that is, the percentage of 3 languages plus is higher (>20%) than in Marigot (~5%) (cf. ◘ Fig. 12.13). Dutch plays a dominant role in Philipsburg on official, governmental signs and is far less frequently used in Marigot overall.

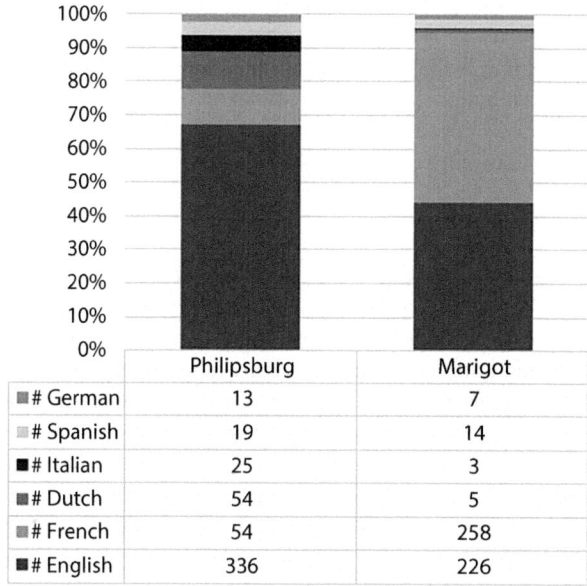

◘ **Fig. 12.12** Distribution of languages in St. Martin signage

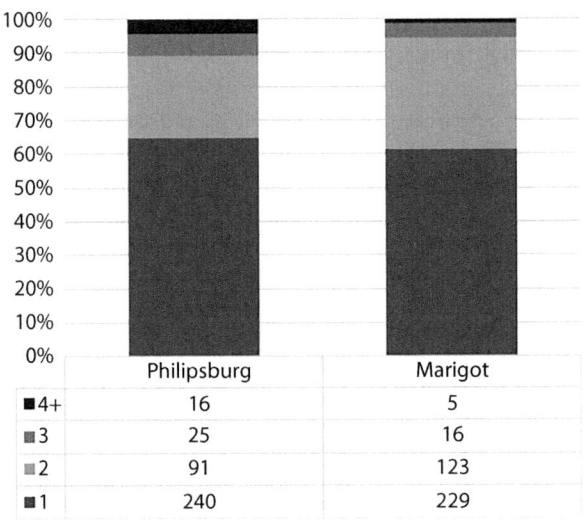

☐ **Fig. 12.13** Extent of multilingualism on St. Martin signage

❓ Exercises

1. Select an area in your town/city or in a town/city close to you and chart its visual landscape. What languages are in evidence? Why do you think particular languages are used to a larger or lesser extent? You are most likely to find strong evidence of multilingualism in the main shopping areas or in culturally diverse areas.
2. If you are using this book in the context of an educational institution, you are likely to find the use of multiple languages in your institution. Create an overview of the languages that contribute to the linguistic landscape of your institution. Which languages can you find? What is their status (majority language, minority language, lingua franca)? In what contexts and with what functions are they used (informative, symbolic)?

Summary

In this chapter, we have introduced and described the concept of linguistic landscapes. Different layers of analysis have been introduced. These include types of signs, which can be divided into official, top-down signs (infrastructural, regulatory, commemorative) and bottom-up signs (commercial, transgressive) and artistic signs taking a middle position. It has also been shown that signs can be found in different spatial frames, such as civic frames, the marketplace, portals, walls or a detritus zone. Most typically, only permanent or semi-permanent signs are considered in landscape studies, but it has been argued that studying transient features like detritus can also have benefits. We have shown that the visual multilingualism data that can be found in signage in public spaces provide valuable insights into language choices both within the community and from a top-down perspective. Our case studies illustrate that language users make deliberate language choices which are driven not only by the informative value of the chosen language. The symbolic value of languages also plays a role and the cultural capital that is associated with them. This becomes particularly obvious where minority languages are used in preference to dominant languages, and where the international lingua franca, English, is employed. English appears to be used to exploit its status of a world language either to maximise the communicative potential of the signage or to draw on the cultural capital that is conveyed by using an international language.

References

Backhaus, P. (2007). *Linguistic Landscapes: A comparative study of urban multilingualism in Tokyo*. Multilingual Matters.

Blommaert, J., & Maly, I. (2016). Ethnographic linguistic landscape analysis and social change: Case-study from Ghent. In K. Arnaut, J. Blommaert, B. Rampton, & M. Spotti (Eds.), *Language and superdiversity*. Routledge.

Buschfeld, S., & Ahlers, W. (2022). English around the World: New realities, new models, and the case of Sint Maarten. In A. Ngefac, H. -G. Wolf, & T. Hoffmann (Eds.), World Englishes and Creole languages today, vol. 1: The Schneiderian thinking and beyond. Lincom.

Buschfeld, S., Weihs, C., & Ronan, P. (2022, September 15–17). *Modeling linguistic landscapes: The case of St. Maarten* [presentation]. 9th BICLCE, Ljubljana. Retrieved from https://biclce22.ff.uni-lj.si

Jaworski, A., & Thurlow, C. (2010). *Semiotic landscapes. Language, image, space*. Continuum.

Kallen, J. L. (2009). Tourism and representation in the Irish linguistic landscape. In E. Shohamy & D. Gorter (Eds.), *Linguistic landscape: Expanding the scenery* (pp. 270–283). Routledge.

Kallen, J. L. (2010). Changing landscapes: Language, space and policy in the Dublin linguistic landscape. In A. Jaworski & C. Thurlow (Eds.), *Semiotic landscapes. Language, image, space* (pp. 41–58). Continuum.

Landry, R., & Bourhis, R. Y. (1997). Linguistic landscape and ethnolinguistic vitality: An empirical study. *Journal of Language and Social Psychology, 16*(1), 23–49.

Metropole Ruhr. (n.d.) *Statistik Analysen*. Retrieved May 13, 2018, from http://www.metropoleruhr.de/regionalverband-ruhr/statistik-analysen/statistik-trends/bevoelkerung/nationalitaeten.html

Ronan, P. (2021). Indexing Irishness in linguistic landscaping. A touristic perception of the use of Irish language and Irish style fonts. In C. Amador-Moreno & St. Lucek (Eds.), *Expanding the landscapes of Irish English: Research in honour of Jeffrey Kallen* (pp. 237–253). Routledge.

Rosenbaum, Y., Nadel, E., Cooper, R. L., & Fishmann, J. (1977). English on Keren Kayemet Street. In J. A. Fishmann, R. L. Cooper, & A. W. Conrad (Eds.), *The spread of English* (pp. 179–196). Newbury House.

Sayer, P. (2010). Using the linguistic landscape as a pedagogical resource. *ELT Journal, 64*(2), 143–154.

Scollon, R., & Scollon, S. (2003). *Discourse in place: Language in the material world*. Routledge.

Sebba, M. (2010). Discourses in transit. In A. Jaworski & C. Thurlow (Eds.), *Semiotic landscapes: Language, image, space* (pp. 59–76). Bloomsbury.

Shohamy, E., & Ben-Rafael, E. (2015). Linguistic landscape: A new journal. *Linguistic Landscape, 1*, 1–5.

Spolsky, B., & Cooper, R. L. (1991). *The languages of Jerusalem*. Clarendon.

Vuković-Vojnović, D., & Nićin, M. (2012). English as a global language in the tourism industry: A case study. In G. Rață, I. Petroman, & C. Petroman (Eds.), *The English of tourism* (pp. 3–18). Cambridge Scholars.

Ziegler, E., Schmitz, U., & Uslucan, H.-H. (2018). Attitudes towards visual multilingualism in the linguistic landscape of the Ruhr area. In M. Pütz & N. Mundt (Eds.), *Expanding the linguistic landscape. Linguistic diversity, multimodality and the use of space as a semiotic resource* (pp. 263–298). Multilingual Matters.

Key Readings

Landry, R., & Bourhis, R. Y. (1997). Linguistic landscape and ethnolinguistic vitality: An empirical study. *Journal of Language and Social Psychology, 16*, 23–49.

Scollon, R., & Scollon, S. W. (2003). *Discourses in place: Language in the material world*. Routledge.

Further Reading

Backhaus, P. (2007). *Linguistic landscapes. A comparative study of urban multilingualism in Tokyo*. Multilingual Matters.

Sebba, M. (2010). Discourses in transit. In A. Jaworski & C. Thurlow (Eds.), *Semiotic landscapes: Language, image, space* (pp. 59–76). Bloomsbury.

Methodological Perspectives

As we have seen in the preceding 12 chapters, the research field of multilingualism is rich, diverse, and utterly complex at the same time. It includes: children growing up with two or more languages simultaneously; adult second-, third-, fourth-, etc. language learners who have acquired their languages in elitist, often school-based contexts; language acquisition and use in migration contexts and the polyglot migrant; a multitude of patterns of societal multilingualism; multilingual language use on the world wide web; and the way individuals are influenced by these different patterns in their language acquisition processes. The final part of the book is devoted to presenting readers, especially students and novice researchers, with some ideas on how to conduct their own research in the field of multilingualism. To this end, we provide an in-depth but, given the multitude of possible data collection methods that exist to collect multilingual data, necessarily selective overview of some of the most relevant methodological approaches in the field.

Contents

Chapter 13   Investigating Multilingualism – 277

Chapter 14   Using Existing Data Repositories and Data Analysis – 301

Investigating Multilingualism

Contents

13.1 Introduction – 278

13.2 Multilingual Data Types and Approaches to Studying Them – 278

13.3 Before Data Collection: Getting Started on the Project – 282

13.4 Data Collection Methods – 284
13.4.1 Questionnaire Studies – 284
13.4.2 Interviews – 288
13.4.3 Ethnographic Observations – 291
13.4.4 Linguistic Landscapes – 292

13.5 Ethical Aspects of Data Collection – 293

References – 298

© The Author(s), under exclusive license to Springer Nature Switzerland AG 2023
S. Buschfeld et al., *Multilingualism*,
https://doi.org/10.1007/978-3-031-28405-2_13

13.1 Introduction

According to Tagliamonte, "fieldwork is not easy. The personal stamina required to 'stick it out' is often high" (Tagliamonte, 2006, p. 26). Tagliamonte is right, but correctly implemented, conducting fieldwork can be an extremely enriching experience, not only linguistically but also socially and personally. As we have seen in the preceding 12 chapters, the research field of multilingualism is rich, diverse, and very complex at the same time. It includes children growing up with two or more languages simultaneously, adult second-, third-, fourth-, etc. language learners who have acquired their languages in formal, often school-based contexts, as well as polyglot migrants. Furthermore, it includes a multitude of contexts, for example language acquisition and use in migration contexts, various patterns of societal multilingualism and the impact of these different patterns on individual speakers' language acquisition processes, as well as multilingual language use on the worldwide web and in popular music. To investigate these different speaker groups and contexts of language use, a variety of methodological approaches can be used. While we cannot include all of them, we present the most commonly used ones and discuss the contexts in which they are most suitable and helpful.

Ever since the linguistic turn from prescriptivism to descriptivism, linguists have been interested in describing language use as authentically and realistically as possible. To this end, linguists collect and analyse different types of data, that is, naturalistic data, reported or indirect data, and metadata, both spoken and written. These can be analysed in either quantitative or qualitative ways, with the choice mostly depending on the objectives of the individual studies and research projects. Due to the existence of such varied data types and analytical approaches, there is neither one correct way or methodology to investigate multilingualism and multilingual language use nor an agreed-upon canon of methods. The existing literature and methods are vast and it would be impossible to present them all. Consequently, we focus on a number of relevant and common approaches that originate in various fields of linguistics, that is, sociolinguistic approaches, ethnographic approaches, and corpus-linguistic approaches. Let us start with an overview of how to identify multilingual data and what to do with them.

13.2 Multilingual Data Types and Approaches to Studying Them

As mentioned before, different types of data exist. They range from naturalistic to experimental; from unguided to elicited for a concrete purpose, that is, aiming at the investigation of a specific, say, grammatical characteristic; from written to spoken and anything in between (see the brief discussion of multimedia data in ▶ Chap. 10). If we analyse linguistic characteristics such as pronunciation patterns or verbal inflections used in, for example, spontaneous oral productions, contributions to internet fora, or voice messages, we investigate naturalistic data. We assess authentic use of language, which might be more or less formal, vary more or less from the standard variety, be more or less extensive in quantity, and addressed to any or no speaker group. Naturalistic data are first-hand language use data that are often elicited without the language user knowing which aspect of language the researcher is most interested in. Such data can be particularly helpful when the researcher does not yet have any knowledge about the specific linguistic characteristics of a certain user group or context, that is, whenever researchers are charting new linguistic territory. However, naturalistic data can also be used to investigate specific linguistic phenomena and test previously formulated linguistic hypotheses. For such an approach, the researcher needs to know what they are looking for, for example which particular linguistic feature(s), and therefore needs some prior knowledge about the linguistic community they are interested in. Extensive naturalistic data that have been elicited in a specific context or a set of comparable contexts can be compiled in a corpus. Corpus data represent a collection of typically extensive data that can be used for elaborate quantitative analyses. Based on corpus data we can, for example, deduce information about the usage frequencies of particular linguistic characteristics or the lexical choices or pragmatic conversation structures of a particular group of people or of a social media phenomenon. Corpus data can be collected from spoken or written sources, and can, for example, be collected through sociolinguistic interviews eliciting specific grammatical information (cf. ▶ Sect. 13.4.2) or by compiling a corpus of newspaper or internet-based data. With respect to the latter, we can find online sources like websites or blogs, and a particularly fruitful source of data is provided by social media, such as Twitter (e.g. Dijkstra et al., 2021) or Instagram (Lee, 2018). Online data, and in particular such data taken from social media communication, are an interesting source of data, as in many respects they occupy a middle position between written and spoken data, in that they, for example, contain various features that are more typically associated with spoken than with written language (Jonsson, 2015) even though being presented in written form.

To naturalistic, first-hand data (including experimental data in the binary distinction employed here), we can add reported or second-hand data. A speaker of a language who states that a certain word was only used by older people or that they consider a specific sentence structure ungrammatical would be a provider of reported data (Sakel & Everet, 2012, p. 118). The researcher does not analyse the actual words that are uttered but the information about language use that is provided via those utterances. Therefore, the researcher's only means of deciding whether this information is correct or not is to ask many people the same question and see whether they all (or most of them) reply in a similar way. Another very common kind of reported data is answers to questionnaires, which report what speakers think they do (Sakel & Everet, 2012, p. 129). What speakers think they do does not always correspond to what they actually do. Generally, questionnaires are often used to collect information about speakers' attitudes towards languages and the contexts in which (they think) they use certain languages (cf. ▶ Sect. 13.4.1).

Finally, linguistic studies also make use of metadata, that is, data about the speakers. Their age, gender identification, or their level of education might be relevant for their use of language or their language attitudes. In longitudinal studies, that is, studies that assess the same speakers multiple times across a longer time span, the time of data elicitation can further be relevant. The same is true for intervention studies, that is, studies that manipulate participants in one of two groups by, for example, teaching them a certain learning technique that might have an influence on their language use. However, we are not aware of any linguistic studies that are based only on such metadata; they are almost always collected as complementary data to naturalistic or reported language data and are included in the subsequent analyses (see ▶ Sect. 14.3 for some more details on data analyses).

As we have seen, when assessing multilingualism, researchers might be interested in different kinds of data. Which kind of data they will choose for their research projects depends on what they would like to study or find out. Corpus-linguists might be interested in finding out how the use of pronouns has changed from Early Modern English to Modern English, while researchers with an ethnographic focus might want to find out about in what contexts or for what purpose and by whom different languages are used within a multilingual community. Other researchers might follow a sociolinguistic approach and might want to investigate how individual users use one or more languages in a conversation or during a certain activity and how language use by these speakers is influenced by sociolinguistic variables such as their age, gender, or social background and thus varies in specific communities of practice. Yet other scholars might be interested in psycholinguistics and care about how multilingual speakers learn their languages and how they store, differentiate, process, and retrieve the different languages of their multilingual repertoires at different points in time and in different situations. Although neither the different areas of linguistics (e.g., sociolinguistics, psycholinguistics, corpus linguistics) nor the respective type of research that is executed require a specific set or repertoires of methods, certain methods are often associated with a specific linguistic subfield, such as psycholinguistic experiments with the field of language acquisition. Still, we do not make such categorisations here for three interrelated reasons: first of all, data triangulation or mixed-methods approaches, that is, studies based on more than one data collection method and data type, are a current best-practice in empirical linguistic research. Secondly, crossing (sub-)discipline boundaries and employing sub-disciplinary and even interdisciplinary perspectives is currently developing into a new research standard in many linguistic areas (e.g., the edited volume "Acquisition and variation in World Englishes: Bridging paradigms and rethinking approaches" by Schmalz et al., Fc. or the new Edinburgh University Press book series "New Directions in World Englishes Research"). Thirdly, in particular the field of multilingualism research requires subdisciplinary approaches, which, for example, combine language acquisition and sociolinguistic perspectives, to understand the complex realities of the phenomenon, as we hope to have shown in the preceding 12 chapters of the textbook. Therefore, to study language use in multilingual contexts, mixed-method approaches have been understood as the gold standard as they are capable of assessing the complexity, multi-layeredness, and dynamic nature of multilingualism and multilingual speakers (e.g. Sakel & Everet, 2012, pp. 99–138; Angouri, 2018 for critical assessments of mixed methods).

However, before we move on to the specific methods, let us have a look at two further sets of approaches and terminologies often differentiated in the literature, namely inductive versus deductive and qualitative versus quantitative approaches. Even though these are more related to the overall research approach taken and the analysis of the data than to the data collection procedure or types of data as such, we briefly introduce these two notions here for reasons of comprehensibility and since data collection methods and the resulting data types are often motivated by such considerations.

The differentiation between inductive and deductive approaches is mainly concerned with our starting point of conducting research, namely what we already know about the respective speech community under observation and what our specific aims are. We would like to illustrate this by means of an example from corpus linguistics. Deductive approaches are corpus-based approaches, that is, approaches aimed towards validating a theory or hypothesis using a corpus. For pursuing such an approach, the researcher needs prior knowledge about the speech community or data they aim to investigate and on which hypothesis testing is based. Inductive approaches are corpus-driven approaches, that is, the data are used as inspiration or starting point for building a theory since the researchers have no prior knowledge about the speakers or data (cf. Lange & Leuckert, 2020, pp. 43–44). In other words, if we already know what we are looking for and/or what we would like to elicit, we follow a deductive approach; if we are interested in a specific speech community or linguistic context but do not know what we will find there, we follow an inductive approach and let the data tell us what to focus on in our investigation. In any case, we would like to advise readers to never collect data without a specific aim and, ideally, research question or hypothesis in mind, since determining the adequate approach and methodological tools would not be possible, let alone successful, without these initial considerations.

The qualitative versus quantitative distinction is mostly a question of the analytical approach to the data. In quantitative approaches, linguists count frequencies of particular linguistic phenomena or questionnaire answers, for example in form of Likert scale values (cf. ▶ Sect. 13.4.1); on their basis, linguists may measure medians, mean values, or even percentages between answer options or linguistic alternatives or model their results by means of inferential statistical approaches. As is inherent in the label, the focus of quantitative approaches is on quantifying their data and results. Qualitative approaches focus on the presentation and discussion of specific linguistic findings, that is, not on the frequencies of particular linguistic characteristics but, for example, on their precise properties, their source and emergence, and their relationship with, for example, other linguistic structures or their dependency on social factors of a particular situation or context. Some researchers have equated qualitative with inductive and quantitative with deductive approaches (e.g. Björkman, 2013, p. 65; Rasinger, 2010, p. 52, respectively) and have ascribed qualitative or quantitative characteristics to certain data types (Sakel & Everet, 2012, p. 100). And while questionnaires and psycholinguistic experiments indeed often and in the first place generate quantifiable data, and interviews, narrations, or conversations can be used for qualitative analyses, it is important to keep in mind that such assignments should not be taken as absolute. In particular, the latter set of data sources lend themselves to quantitative analysis equally well and have widely been used as databases in, for example, quantitative corpus analyses. We argue that the vast majority of data sets are neither qualitative nor quantitative *per se* but that the approaches used to assess these data might be qualitative or quantitative. Therefore, as discussed above, while the deductive versus inductive categorisation revolves around the question from where and therefore how we approach the research project, that is, what our previous knowledge is, the qualitative versus quantitative distinction is mainly a question of what exactly we do with the data. And while general relations between these approaches and some data types exist, they are never exclusive. Linguists might very well—and often do—conduct, for example, quantitative analyses following an initially inductive approach.

To sum up, today much research combines data types and kinds of approaches. In many of such mixed-methods approaches, a larger data set is assessed and analysed quantitatively and a smaller set or a subset of these data is analysed qualitatively, which means in greater depth and in more detail. The combination of qualitative and quantitative methods "offers additional benefits" (Dörnyei, 2007, p. 47) to linguistic research by making the data richer and by offering more comprehensive insights into the explored phenomenon. To find out about verbal morphology, for example, a study might combine a qualitative analysis of semi-structured interviews and a quantitative assessment of a picture-based story-retelling task. As mentioned before, the choice, combination, and accommodation of the research methods must fit the research objectives as well as the context(s) of investigation. Before we introduce a number of widely-used data collection methods, we provide a brief introduction to what needs to be considered before going into the data collection process.

13.3 Before Data Collection: Getting Started on the Project

As already mentioned, the considerations and planning prior to the actual data collection phase are most crucial for successfully conducting a research project since these considerations determine the right choice of method and data type(s) to collect. If we do not follow a specific research objective and agenda, we might be left with data that are valuable as such but not suitable for the specific research project, in other words to answer a specific research question. In this respect, Sankoff (1974) identifies three kinds of decisions about data collection a researcher should make prior to it: (1) choosing what data to collect; (2) stratifying the sample; (3) deciding how much data to collect from how many speakers. She states: "'[g]ood' data is defined as language materials of sufficient type and quantity, as well as materials which take into account the social context in which the language data is gathered. This is referred to as defining the sampling universe" (Sankoff, 1974, pp. 21–22). However, before even getting to this point, it is crucial that researchers define a research objective and formulate a clearly stated research question, hypothesis, or even more than one of both kinds. Subsequently, the researcher can start thinking about what data to collect and which method(s) of analysis would be the most suitable. If we are, for example, interested in quantifiable results on speakers' language attitudes and use, we might choose a questionnaire approach (cf. ▶ Sect. 13.4.1). If we are interested in the investigation of linguistic characteristics of a particular language variety or group of speakers, we might decide in favour of collecting spoken data by means of sociolinguistic interviews (cf. ▶ Sect. 13.4.2).

After having decided on what to investigate, in a next step, we need to find participants, which is not always an easy task. To this end, the *friend of a friend approach* has been identified as a powerful method. It assumes that "if a stranger is identified as a friend of a friend, he may easily be drawn into the network's mesh of exchange and obligation relationships. His chances of observing and participating in prolonged interaction will then be considerably increased" (Milroy, 1980, p. 53; see also Milroy, 1987, p. 66). In other words, the fieldworker should aim to become part of the investigated community, as an observer but also as a participant in the data collection process. In practice, this means that some first contacts in the community in which the research should be conducted are crucial since such contacts know further members of the community and can introduce the researcher as a trustworthy acquaintance. This approach is very fruitful, but it also entails potential risks. Firstly, social groups rarely mix. This means that if your first contacts in the community are, for example, members of the local elite, it is quite unlikely that they will get you in contact with people of another social status. This might cause your participant group to be too homogeneous so that it would not include all relevant speaker groups. Second, ethical research practices should be sustainable. When we explain how to gain access to a community and advise fieldworkers to try to become part of the community they are interested in, we do not have a 'get in—take out' strategy in mind. Ideally, fieldworkers create longstanding reciprocal relationships with the community under investigation. This, on the one hand, prevents exploitation or hierarchical relations between the researcher and their 'research objects'; on the other hand, these relationships enable a context-dependent interpretation of the research findings, which is important for an accurate representation of local realities.

Another question students and novice researchers often ask is "How much data do I need to collect?". This ultimately also depends on the objectives of the research project, which is why we cannot provide a universally valid answer to this question. For example, the compilation of very large data corpora is extremely work-intensive as these data need large amounts of time for transcription and processing (Tagliamonte, 2006, p. 33; see also Poplack, 1989). As Tagliamonte (2006, p. 33) argues: "It is better to design your sample to be smaller and better circumscribed than to end up with lots of data but not enough funds (or energy) to use it." It is indeed the case that it is better to have a small but manageable data set than not to be able to finish one's project (Feagin, 2002, p. 21). Still, researchers need to keep in mind the issue of representativeness and ask themselves whether their data really reflect the linguistic behaviour of the speech community under investigation or of just one social group or a handful of random individuals. In short, you need to find the right balance between answering your research question(s) and getting the work done. It is often advisable to pilot your study and start the analysis on a smaller data set. In this process, it will become clear whether more data or a different kind of data need to be collected.

As a final step before the actual data collection and related to the issue of representativeness, it is often necessary to sample the data. For this, two major approaches are often employed in linguistic studies, namely random and stratified random sampling. Random sampling is the random selection of participants from a larger group. When we use this approach, we may have a large data sample, but there is a risk that it may still not be representative as it overrepresents one group of a community under investigation, for example older men of higher social status, while not including other strata of society, such as younger people of lower social status. *Stratified random sampling*, also called quasi-random or judgement sampling, also uses a random sampling approach but stratifies the target data sample prior to data collection according to secondary variables (e.g., age, gender, educational background, birthplace, etc.) relevant to the actualy analysis envisaged by the researcher (Tagliamonte, 2006, p. 23). Since a pre-defined sample, and thus the knowledge of how much data to collect from what specific group, counteracts the risk of ending up with an unrepresentative data sample, stratified samples are often to be preferred over their non-stratified alternative (Biber, 1993, p. 244). Again, different projects and research questions require different sampling techniques (Tagliamonte, 2006, p. 27) and there is certainly more that needs to be considered prior to data collection, but we hope to have shown that researchers and students should not rush into a research project and data collection process without having planned the project according to its specific objectives and needs beforehand. In the following, we introduce some of the most widely used techniques of data collection and elicitation in more detail and discuss their advantages and disadvantages as well as possible fields of application.

13.4 Data Collection Methods

Presenting all possible methods to collect multilingual data for linguistic research is an impossible task and would clearly go beyond the scope of this book. To still offer readers a useful guide, we introduce some of the most widely used techniques of data collection and elicitation in more detail and discuss their advantages and disadvantages as well as possible fields of application in the following subchapters.

13.4.1 Questionnaire Studies

Questionnaires are one of the most widely and most frequently used tools to elicit data—in linguistics as well as in other areas of research. In linguistics, questionnaires are mostly used to elicit reported data, (cf. ▶ Sect. 13.2). In sociolinguistic research, for example on multilingual speakers or speech communities, questionnaires are oftentimes used to assess contexts of language use, language attitudes, or grammaticality judgments (later on referred to as acceptability judgments) (Sakel & Everet, 2012, p. 129). Furthermore, they often form the basis of quantitative

13.4 · Data Collection Methods

studies as they contain directly measurable data (e.g. Likert scale values). In general, questionnaires can be transferred into analysable codes quite easily. This is an advantage questionnaires have over interview studies since collecting and transcribing interview data is time-intensive before the data can be transferred into statistically analysable codes. Still, the exact level of ease depends on the type and number of questions used. Furthermore, questionnaires easily generate huge data sets since they can be spread online or to bigger groups of people at the same time. Of course, every questionnaire must be tailored to fit the respective purpose it is used for. Only rarely can questionnaires that have been developed for one study be reused in other studies without adaptations as differences in the precise research objectives and the peculiarities of each research context need to be taken into consideration.

Depending on the aim of the study and the respective questionnaire, the included questions might be open or closed, or a combination of these types might be used. Open questions allow participants to use their own words to answer the question and allow them to emphasise or concentrate on certain aspects of their answers. Closed questions require participants to, for example, indicate their agreement or disagreement on a numbered scale or select their answer from a set of predefined answers instead of providing it in their own words. Open questions are particularly useful for qualitative or pilot studies as the participants' answers might provide the researcher with new insights and concepts or perspectives which the researcher might not have known or thought of before. Although answers to open questions are more complex to process than those to closed questions, they are important to ensure that a study and its respective findings adequately reflect the reality of the participants and the scope of their answers. Furthermore, these insights can then be used as potential answer options in closed questions or for, for example, qualitative or quantitative thematic analyses of questionnaire data. While an extensive use of open questions may lead to extensive insights, it also extends the time it takes a participant to fill in the questionnaire which, in turn, might cause participants to lose their motivation and drop out prior to the completion of the task. Therefore, questionnaires should only include a limited number of open questions and a combination of closed and open questions is often most useful when researching multilingualism based on questionnaires.

Closed questions are questions to which potential answers of the participants are assumed beforehand and (some of) the answers the researcher is aware of or is targeting are given as options for the participant to choose from. A closed question in a questionnaire might, for example, be: "What language do you commonly use when entering a store in your hometown?". Answer options that might be suggested are: "English", "Mandarin Chinese", "French", and "other". For closed questions, not exclusively but more than for open questions, careful preparation is essential. Answer options that are not provided are likely to be lost or subsumed under the option "other". One way of trying not to lose any option is to leave a blank space after the option "other" and ask the participants to specify. Still, closed questions are faster and more convenient to answer for the participants since they often simply require ticking boxes, as, for instance, in rating scales. Furthermore, the data from such closed questions are much faster and easier to process for the researcher. In most disciplines, including linguistics, Likert scales (named after their inventor, the psychologist Rensis Likert) are the most commonly used instrument for scaling responses in survey-based studies. They are useful to avoid "yes-no" answers (Rasinger, 2010, p. 61) and offer more detailed, but still easily analysable, information. Commonly, Likert scales follow a statement that participants should rate. Consider the following statements as examples.

- Statement: "I mix my languages within a conversation with another multilingual speaker".
- Rating scales: *Never—sometimes—often—mostly—always*
- Statement: "I like using more than one language when speaking with my siblings."
- Rating scales: *I strongly disagree—I disagree—neutral—I agree—I strongly agree.*

For later analyses of the data, such statements are then translated into numbers, in our examples these would be the numbers 1–5. No fixed scale exists for such question types and answer options can have four to even six or seven levels, depending on the detail in answers required by the specific study. Furthermore, it needs to be kept in mind that these values should never be zero as meaningful statistical computations would no longer be possible.

All questionnaires should include metadata of the participants, that is, their age, gender, or other information that might be important for the respective study, while still guaranteeing the participants' anonymity. Furthermore, in order to avoid that participants who do not know the answer to a question or do not want to answer a particular question simply guess or just choose any answer, each question should include the option "not applicable" (or similar). Most importantly, however, questions must be carefully phrased to ensure that they cannot be misunderstood. In questionnaires, questions cannot be rephrased or clarified and must be understood immediately, unlike questions that are asked during interviews.

Another type of often-used questionnaire study is the *Acceptability Judgment Task* (AJT). It originates in psycholinguistic research, that is, research that investigates the psychological processes which underlie and are involved in language use, such as language comprehension, processing, and production. AJTs are often used in second-language acquisition research and ask participants to judge grammatical acceptability or unacceptability of sentences in written or oral form. AJTs contain both ungrammatical and grammatical sentences of the linguistic feature under investigation as well as distractor sentences. Participants should not find out what is being investigated, since this would lead to a focus on form and correctness and would distort the participants' spontaneous, authentic reaction towards the sentence they are presented with. Even though binary response scales ("yes/no" or "grammatical/ungrammatical") have been used in AJTs, Likert scales are more frequently used for basically two reasons. First of all, response values of more than two options allow for more nuanced ratings and thus results. Secondly, the nature of a feature as either grammatical or ungrammatical is not always clear and also depends on, for example, the raters' origin, social class, attitudes, etc. For example, while a speaker of AmE would rate a sentence such as "Did you ever try apple

13.4 · Data Collection Methods

cider?" as grammatical, a more conservative, older speaker of BrE would not, whereas a younger BrE speaker might consider it acceptable. Since these ratings are more concerned with whether speakers find linguistic elements acceptable and not their 'true' grammaticality (which probably only exists in prescriptive linguistics, i.e. linguistic approaches prescribing fixed norms of correctness), this data collection method, which was traditionally called *Grammaticality Judgment Task* (GJT), is nowadays mostly referred to as AJT (for further details on AJTs and how to design them, see Ionin, 2012; for further experimental approaches to data collection, e.g., Blom & Unsworth, 2010; De Groot & Hagoort, 2017). A large number of further psycholinguistic methods exist, such as experiments with infants and unborn babies, eye-tracking experiments, story retelling and picture naming tasks, which cannot all be covered in this chapter. The interested reader is referred to, for example, De Groot and Hagoort (2017) or Ambridge and Rowland (2013).

Even though questionnaire studies are an often-employed tool in a number of research paradigms, they come with some disadvantages which revolve around the issue that responses to, for example, questions about language attitudes and use (or any other kind of self-reported responses to linguistic and probably other matters) are not to be taken at face value. We would briefly like to point out the most important ones to raise the readers' awareness of the potential scientific inaccuracies that should be considered in the analysis and interpretation of such data.

Amongst the most prominent potential pitfalls is the so-called *social desirability bias*; according to which informants might respond in a way they regard socially most appropriate and desirable (cf. Oppenheim, 1992, p. 139). For example, in a questionnaire study on the acquisition of English as an L1 in Singapore (Buschfeld, 2020; see also Vida-Mannl, 2022 2023), parents most frequently indicated that their children acquired and spoke a standard variety of English. The actual investigation of their spoken productions, however, has revealed that this is not true in most of the cases (Buschfeld, 2020). Most likely, the parents chose this answer option since they were at least implicitly guided by the governmental stance against Singlish, the local colloquial variety of Singaporean English (cf. ▶ Sect. 5.3). Another important aspect to consider in the evaluation of questionnaire data is the so-called *acquiescence bias*, also called *agreement bias*. This postulates that respondents are more likely to agree than to disagree with items (Schuman & Presser, 1996, p. 203 on attitude surveys). Independent of the specific focus and content of the investigation, it has also been found that respondents sometimes show a tendency towards selecting or agreeing with positive rather than negative response options, even against their true preferences (Dörnyei, 2003, p. 13). A participant would therefore be much more inclined to agree with a positive statement such as "I like learning foreign languages" than with the negative counterpart "I dislike learning foreign languages"—even if the latter reflected their true attitude. The *middle-response bias* is another response bias to be found in survey research. It can be another source of inaccurate or false responses and can thus have a large impact on the validity of questionnaires or surveys. The *middle response bias* may take effect in, for example, Likert scale-based surveys which have an uneven number of answer options, for example three, five, or seven. Here, participants who do not have a particularly strong attitude or opinion about what is being asked might tend towards the middle response value (Presser and Schuman, 1980). In general, researchers should always keep in mind that Likert scales—or any other type of scaled responses—are interpreted differently by different participants. In this respect, some participants are more inclined to go for very strong statements such as *strongly agree* or *strongly disagree* than others, who would rather opt for the *agree* or *disagree* option, even though their actual sentiments or opinions might be the same. Therefore, results from questionnaire and survey data should always be taken with a pinch of salt and researchers should show awareness of such shortcomings in the interpretation of such data.

13.4.2 Interviews

In sociolinguistics, scholars are concerned with the language use of individual speakers or certain group(s) of speakers. Ultimately, they want to understand who speaks what language to whom, when, and why. Since the questionnaire approach introduced in ▶ Sect. 13.4.1 is somewhat limited in the extent of information it can elicit, linguists often conduct interviews to either learn in more detail about what people think about their language use and why they would use certain languages or dialects in certain situations or to investigate how exactly people use language, that is, the grammatical, phonological, pragmatic, or lexical characteristics of their speech. But let us start from the beginning.

The word *interview* stems from the French word *entrevue* (*s'entrevoir*; (to) see each other). Interviewing someone, hence, means to see this person and be seen by this person, that is, a reciprocal exchange of information between equals. However, a prototypical interview is often not a reciprocal exchange but creates a situation in which one party (i.e. interviewer) extracts vital information from another (i.e. interviewee). While, especially in ethnographically informed research, hierarchical interview techniques are avoided (cf. ▶ Sect. 13.4.3), linguists (and others) use interviews as "window[s] onto the mind or 'life-world' of the interviewee" (Edley & Litosseliti, 2010, p. 157). In general, three broader interview practices exist. The first is the so-called structured interview, which consists of closed questions with restricted answer options (e.g. yes/no), multiple choice questions, or rating scales. The second is the semi-structured interview, in which the interviewer follows a set of guiding questions but the conversation as such is free-flowing and indeterminate. The third is the so-called unstructured interview, in which researchers are encouraged to improvise (for further interview types and their aims, see Mason, 2002).

We further differentiate between two general types of interviews which are often used in linguistic research, namely content-based interviews and interviews geared towards eliciting linguistic structures, such as grammatical or phonological characteristics of the speech of particular people or speech groups. Content-based interviews are designed to investigate participants' general opinions and attitudes on specific topics. For example, if a researcher is interested in analysing people's opinions on a topic such as language and feminism or the use of Anglicisms in Germany, France, or any other non-Anglophone country, it can be difficult to find those topics in open, unguided conversations. Therefore, researchers have to elicit the topics they are interested in by asking direct questions or by bringing up the topic and leading the participants towards that topic. Such interviews can be conducted with single individuals, with pairs of interviewees, or in focus groups. Focus group interviews are a commonly used kind of content-based interview. A focus group constitutes a sample of the population investigated and is a selection of a number of individuals to be interviewed at the same time. Focus groups are genuinely interactive because once the researcher has introduced the topic of discussion, the participants of a focus group normally freely discuss the topic. Therefore, the focus group interview is a rather unstructured type of interview. Focus group interviews are a versatile instrument that helps the researcher to: (1) discover new information or consolidate prior knowledge; (2) gather different perspectives and voices on the topic of interest; (3) obtain information on participants' views, attitudes, beliefs, responses, motivations, and perceptions concerning the topic under investigation and discover why people think or feel the way they do; (4) investigate people's shared understanding of everyday life and their everyday use of language and culture; (5) brainstorm and generate ideas on the topic of interest; (6) gain insights into group dynamics, that is, how people are influenced by others in a group discussion; and (7) generate a sense of rapport between the researcher and the participants (Edley & Litosseliti, 2010, p. 169). Therefore, focus group interviews elicit broad opinions on different topics, coming from different speakers, and thus bring to light various more or less harmonious or conflicting opinions, which help the researcher make up their own mind and gain a lot from the interview situation. One of the major disadvantages, however, is that the researcher has only little control over the "interview 2 situation once the focus group discussion is in full swing (Edley & Litosseliti, 2010, p. 171; see Litosseliti, 2018 for an elaborate assessment of focus group interviews).

For interviews geared towards eliciting linguistic structures, the sociolinguistic interview is a prominent example, which goes back to the founding father of modern sociolinguistics, William Labov. In semi-structured interviews, of which sociolinguistic interviews are a specific type, the researcher asks open-ended questions to get insights into, for example, the language use, for example certain grammatical structures or pronunciation features, of speakers belonging to a specific speech group the researcher is interested in. Such interviews are typically conversations that have been prepared in advance, for example, by noting down questions that the researcher wants to ask their interlocutors, while still being flexible enough to go off-route in case the participant offers new information, is not interested in or willing to talk about specific topics introduced by the researcher, etc. For these interviews to be successful and as informative as possible, the researcher needs to adapt to the situation and to the participants' needs to create an atmosphere of rapport, which "means that a basic sense of trust has developed that allows for the free flow of information" (Spradley, 1979, p. 44). The sociolinguistic interview thus aims at "specific information of linguistic structures" or "data necessary for the analysis of sociolinguistic patterns" (Labov, 1984, pp. 32–33). It is considered "[t]he basic tool for recording conversation in sociolinguistic variation" (Tagliamonte, 2006, p. 37) and aims to create a relaxed, benevolent, and trusting atmosphere to elicit spontaneous, authentic speech data, that is, the speaker's vernacular, by means of "narratives of personal experiences" (Labov, 1984, p. 32). These personal experiences are accessed by using questions that are typically grouped into modules concerned with different topics of the participants' everyday lives. Topics regularly found in sociolinguistic interviews include family matters, proposals, dating, hobbies, aspirations/future plans, fights, topics of local interest, and any topic that may trigger "moral indignation" (Labov, 1984, pp. 33–35). Since the aim of sociolinguistic interviews is to trigger the vernacular, that is, the participant's colloquial, everyday language use, it is important to get the participants involved in the conversation so that they do not focus on how they say things but on what they say. So, as Tagliamonte points out, the term *interview* is actually a misnomer since "a sociolinguistic interview should be anything but an 'interview'" (Tagliamonte, 2006, p. 37) but more like an informal chat between, ideally, conversational partners on a level playing field. This, however, is not always easy to achieve since such interviews may automatically carry the burden of a hierarchical relationship in which the interviewer may be seen as being in the superior position since they are asking the questions and prompting the topics. Furthermore, the interviewer is often an outsider to the community, an observer who often does not speak the vernacular they aim for. This problem is commonly referred to as the *Observer's Paradox* (e.g. Labov, 1972, p. 113; Labov, 2006, p. 86), that is, the challenge "to observe how people speak when they are not being observed" even though they are well aware of being observed (Labov, 2006, p. 86). To overcome the Observer's Paradox and achieve rapport as well as "depth, nuance, complexity and roundedness in data" (Mason, 2002, p. 65), helpful routines and techniques have been identified over the years that researchers can draw on. We present some well-known strategies in the following. Tagliamonte (2006), for example, presents helpful and well-tried advice on how to structure, word, and conduct successful Labovian sociolinguistic interviews (cf. Labov, 1982, 1984). Most popular are her techniques on how to administer an interview. Following her advice, for a successful sociolinguistic interview in which the participants offer authentic, spontaneous, and unfiltered speech samples, researchers should:

1. Let the informant talk, that is, follow the informant's line of conversation rather than taking over too much of the conversation. This can be somewhat tricky, as the interviewer should also take over parts of the talking to create a conversation rather than a question-answer pattern. However, whenever the participants attempt to speak, the interviewer should yield to them.
2. Approximate the vernacular, that is, the interviewer should approximate the speech style of the participant to make them feel comfortable and unaware of potential formalities. In case the interviewer spoke in a very formal version of the standard variety, the participants might switch to also using formal language and would no longer be spontaneous in their language production. Of course, approximating the vernacular can be very challenging, in particular when investigating language varieties that are very different from your own. In general, researchers should at least make sure that they do not use too formal language and create a relaxed, non-formal atmosphere via their gestures, body language, and general behaviour.

3. Ask short questions since they are clearer and easier to understand and answer for the participants.
4. Take an insider's point of view, that is, the interviewer should show that they are familiar with the community they have decided to engage with. This conveys a feeling of respect for the culture and people and helps the researcher to convey a feeling of belonging to the group rather than of being an outsider.
5. Be the leaner, that is, the interviewer is not the expert but the leaner in the interview. Making this clear to the participants is likely to reduce anxiety.
(adapted from Tagliamonte, 2006, pp. 46–48)[1].

In our own experience, these are valuable pieces of advice that help, in particular, novices in the field to collect valuable speech data. As we have seen in this section, unstructured or semi-structured interviews are a great and commonly used source of naturalistic and reported data. In the next section, we turn towards more recent additions to the linguistic toolbox of data collection that are primarily used in qualitative research.

13.4.3 Ethnographic Observations

Linguistic observations might be the most multifaceted tool of data elicitation and at the core of ethnographically-informed research. Linguistic observations can take almost any possible form and are extremely rich, as researchers never 'just' observe language, but the specific contexts and/or circumstances of use tend to be considered as well. Observations can range from a word or conversation the researcher overhears while having dinner on the first evening of their research trip– these are spontaneous and unplanned insights– to planned observations, which are, for example, visits to a classroom that must be organised and aligned with school and ethics boards well in advance. Being rooted in anthropological research, the approach of linguistic observations is originally an ethnographic research tool (cf. Blommaert & Dong, 2020) and it targets language use in its complex entirety. Ideally, it includes and considers the specific cultural, social, individual, etc. aspects of the situation in which a certain utterance has been made and concatenates language with its (individual) users without the need to generalise or categorise the observed. Findings, consequently, are rarely absolute but try to paint a complex but comprehensive picture of, for example, how and why language can be used or might be used by a certain person in a specific situation. Just like, for example, sociolinguistic interviews, observations, especially when analysed open-mindedly and within their local context of use, often show aspects of language use that are new to the researcher—and might lead them to challenge what they think they know about their research focus. Observations, however, are even broader in their

---

1 Further valuable information on how to prepare and conduct sociolinguistic interviews can be found in ▶ Chaps. 2 and 3 of Tagliamonte (2006). *Analysing sociolinguistic variation*. Cambridge: Cambridge University Press.

insights: researchers might, for example, find a certain speaker to (unexpectedly) be essential for their investigation or observe certain pragmatic structures to be used across contexts, although their original focus was on only one of these contexts. This example already hints at the fact that, for practical reasons, observations typically have a certain thematic or contextual focus, target a certain location, or (a) specific speaker group(s). As observations can be made at all times, we must distinguish between planned and unplanned observations. In cases of unplanned observations, the data are often analysed qualitatively, while planned and larger-scale observations can also be compared and analysed using (descriptive) quantification. In the following, we give an example of a type of research that investigates the visual sphere of language use, the study of linguistic landscapes (see also ▶ Chap. 12).

13.4.4 Linguistic Landscapes

In addition to approaches in which human linguistic behaviour is observed, linguistic landscape approaches investigate the visual linguistic environment in public spaces. Research methods based on linguistic landscapes can be either quantitative or qualitative or combine both of these approaches. As shown in ▶ Chap. 12, a research project in linguistic landscapes traditionally determines which languages are found on particular signs in the visual landscape of a certain territory or region and may count to what extent they are used. Most typically, an urban area with many instances of publicly visible writing is selected: this could be a shopping street or town centre area, a shopping mall, or public buildings like train stations or airports. All signs, such as business signs, shop windows, restaurant names, etc., are photographed and different information on each sign, such as its precise location, the text on it, which language(s) are found on it, and what the function of the sign is, should be collected in a spreadsheet or a database programme. In order to get enough data for a quantitatively meaningful and possibly statistically relevant analysis, at least 100 signs should be collected, more would be beneficial, but this, again, also depends on the exact type of analysis and how many potentially influential variables (information such as those aspects mentioned above) are included in the analysis. The collected data might then be analysed, for example, to find out what and how many languages are used on particular types of signs. In theory, linguistic landscape studies are a quite straightforward approach, but there are certain aspects to be assessed in advance.

When carrying out the study, the basic tenet is: one sign equals one token. In most cases you will find that this rule is straightforward: a traffic sign or a commemorative plaque is clearly delimited. In other cases, it may not be so clear what constitutes a sign. A shop window, for example, can be a sign in itself, consisting of various elements such as lettering for opening hours, the name of the business itself, and other pieces of information. In addition, the shop window can host various other signs, for example, printed paper signs advertising products or services or further commercial information as well as community messages. Before starting data analysis, the researcher needs to decide what to count as one token, that is, as one sign. It also needs to be decided whether only permanent signs, like road signs, or also semi-permanent signs, like billboards, or even transient codes, like moving vehicles or refuse found in the streets, will be considered (cf. ▶ Chap. 12; see also Scollon & Scollon, 2003; Kallen, 2010). The more transient the code is, the more up-to-date our picture of language use will be. If you want to find out which processes are underway at the time of study, or if you want to know which language choices are made by language users, then investigating the less permanent codes will give you a certainly more accurate, up-to-date answer. By contrast, if you would like to get insights into official language policies, then more permanent codes, particularly on regulatory, infrastructural, or commemorative signs, will provide them. When carrying out an ethnographic linguistic landscape analysis (e.g., Blommaert & Maly, 2016), then analysing and discussing why a specific language is chosen and how the visual landscape is perceived may be the focus of your analysis. Adding ethnographic analysis methods to the observation of linguistic landscapes would, therefore, also unveil language ideologies as well as social, sociocultural, economic, and historical contexts of language use. Similar to the other methods, introduced in the preceding sections, there is no inherently right or wrong approach when investigating linguistic landscapes, but the best approach will be determined by your research question (cf. ▶ Sect. 13.3). Related to this, before setting out to research, for example, the linguistic landscape of a certain place, the parameters of the research, such as what would count as a sign, need to be clearly decided on by the researcher and, like in all (linguistic) research, must be coherently observed.

13.5 Ethical Aspects of Data Collection

As already discussed, especially when collecting naturalistic data, one of the researcher's main goals should be to avoid that the participants feel anxious, for example due to being recorded, and therefore monitor their language use. Researchers want their participants to be relaxed, spontaneous, and natural in their speech production. While there are several possibilities to achieve this so-called rapport (Spradley, 1979, p. 44), that is, to create a respectful and trusting atmosphere in which participants do not rethink their answers and the information flow is not obstructed, not telling a participant that their answers or language use are being recorded or protocolled is not an option, ever. Providing participants with informed consent is one of the cornerstones of ethical research. Every participant must be informed about the study that they are asked to participate in and must give consent to their participation and to their data being used, for example, for academic publications. In addition to their consent, researchers need to guarantee that individual participants remain anonymous throughout the analysis and publication of the research, this means that there is no possibility to identify the individual speaker based on the data published. However, gaining individual consent is not always possible. Imagine you would like to investigate how people ask for directions in a tourist information office or carry out sales interactions in a shop. First of all, you need to obtain consent from the authorities who operate the office. Then, people who could become part of the research need to be informed about the ongoing data collection process. In cases like these, many people might be present and you cannot know who will become a participant in your study, as, for example, you do not know who enters the office or shop and who will actually contribute data. Still, every potential participant must be informed about the ongoing data collection process. Consequently, it is practical to display information about your study in several, well-visible positions inside and at the entrance of the office or shop so that everybody who enters can make themselves aware of the research that is going on inside. This, of course, might lead to informants shying away from coming into the office or shop or not behaving naturally in case they do come in. The latter case would constitute another manifestation of the Observer's Paradox, as elaborated on in ▶ Sect. 13.4.2.

In addition to informed consent, research ethics assure that participants of a study are not harmed—either directly or indirectly—through their participation. One way to ensure this is by guaranteeing the participants' anonymity which must also be maintained during data storage. According to the data protection rights to be found in many countries today, the speech data collected from participants need to be stored on a secure server to which only the research team has access and separate from the meta information collected from the participants (e.g. their age, gender, etc.). As outlined above, for any participant-based study, the researcher must be given informed consent by the participants. These consent forms must be in accordance with the respective regulations of the country the researcher is based in and need to be signed by the researcher(s) and participant(s) alike. The participants should be given access to the researcher(s) and research findings and a copy of such a form should stay with the participants. In the case of minors, consent forms need to be signed by a legal guardian. Sometimes researchers collect data online, for example via online questionnaires. In such cases, the consent form can precede the online tool. ◘ Figure 13.1 is a sample consent form which has been designed for a research project on English and multilingualism in St. Maarten.

The situation is, of course, different in online research, where the data is often just culled from the internet without personal contact with the speakers. However, in using online data, like with other data sources, we have to make sure to act ethically. As a rule of thumb, publicly available data may be used for research, but data which is not publicly accessible, for example because it is taken from closed groups, can only be used with the explicit permission of the speakers. Details on up-to-date best practice in online research in general can be found on the website of The Association of Online Researchers.[2]

---

2 ▶ https://aoir.org/ethics/.

CONSENT FORM

The project: We are a team of researchers currently conducting a research project on the multilingual situation in LOCATION. This includes looking at how language(s) are used from various perspectives. Which functions do the languages have? What are typical linguistic characteristics of these languages? What do people think of these languages? And who uses which languages when?
To answer some of these questions, we are collecting several kinds of data: spoken and written speech data, interview data, as well as questionnaire data on language attitudes and use and speaker backgrounds.

How to participate: To participate, you would engage in research activities such as a word reading task or open conversations. You would also provide general information about your social background (age, gender, ethnicity, etc.).
If you agree to participate in this study, you will be asked to
- fill in a survey with general information about your age, gender, place of origin, etc. and take part in one or more of the following activities
- word reading task and reading a short text passage
- evaluate the grammatical acceptability of sentences
- engage in an open conversation about life on the island
- fill out an online questionnaire on language attitudes and use

The activities will take about 30 minutes but we would love to talk to you longer.
Your participation will be audio recorded. You can change your mind about participating at any time. It is fully voluntary and will not be compensated.

Risks and benefits: There are no foreseeable risks involved in participation. Your participation will help us better understand the multilingual situation of LOCATION. You get to have a voice in describing the linguistic reality of people living in LOCATION.

Data usage: The conversation will be written down and analyzed both with respect to the content of the conversation and linguistic features on the different levels of language organization, for example the structure of words and sentences or people's pronunciation. The findings of the project will be published in scientific journals, project reports, and other kinds of scientific publications.

Privacy and anonymity: The participants in the project will not be identified in any kind of these publications, except for general information about age, gender, etc. We guarantee that the general information will not allow conclusions about the participant's identity. Data that can lead to the identification of participants will be stored separately from the project data.

Contact Information: If you have any questions about the project, you can reach the research team via e-mail: EMAIL-ADDRESS.

Consent: If you would like to support this research project, please consent to these terms:
I am willing to participate in this project and to have my data used for linguistic analyses. I can withdraw this consent any time by writing to the researchers and asking for the deletion of my personal data. Withdrawal of consent will not have any legal or other consequences and can happen any time. This, however, only concerns the future use of the data; previous uses, e.g. in already published publications, are irreversible.

Fig. 13.1 Sample consent form for the project "Modeling English and multilingualism in St. Maarten" (conducted by S. Buschfeld, in collaboration with C. Weihs)

The researchers guarantee participants access to the data collected from them and to the general findings of the project. In case you have any questions, feel free to contact us any time.

Yes [ ]   No [ ]

1. I confirm that I have read and understand the above information for participants (and/or their parents):

Yes [ ]   No [ ]

2. I hereby indicate my consent to participate in a linguistic research project carried out by RESEARCHER 1 (AFFILIATION) and RESEARCHER 2 (AFFILIATION). I understand that this will involve one or more of the above described data collection procedures and that my participation is voluntary.

Yes [ ]   No [ ]

3. I know that I can decide to withdraw my data from future usage at any time without having to give any reason for this.

Yes [ ]   No [ ]

4. I agree that my answers may be used for linguistic research.

Yes [ ]   No [ ]

5. I understand that travelling to and from the data collection session is not covered by the insurance of the researchers.

Yes [ ]   No [ ]

6. For parents only: I agree that my/our child is allowed to participate in the research project.

Yes [ ]   No [ ]

Place, date, signature participant   *Place, date, signature researcher*

_____   _____

Place, date, signature parent(s) / legal guardian of the minor

_____

Thank you very much for your participation!

If you would like to also participate in an anonymous online survey about language attitudes and use in LOCATION, please use the link or QR code below. Consent for participation in the survey will be asked for separately on the first page of the survey.

LINK AND QR-CODE

◘ **Fig. 13.1** (continued)

❓ Exercises

1. A pilot study is commonly executed to ensure that research tools elicit the information that is supposed to be elicited. Get together in a group and think about challenges you might face during a pilot study.

13.5 · Ethical Aspects of Data Collection

2. Develop an idea for a linguistic research project.
   (a) Choose a topic and phrase a research question (RQ) that you would like to answer in your study.
   (b) Decide on which method(s) you need to employ in order to answer your RQ(s) and provide a clear rationale for your decision.
   (c) Can you think of a suitable speaker group for your research? How could these speakers be approached?
3. Get your tools ready.
   (a) Read through the consent form (◘ Fig. 13.1) and indicate how the general elaborations on ethical aspects of linguistic research find expression in the consent form and what further details it includes.
   (b) Based on Exercise 2, develop a consent form for your study. Make sure to adequately inform your participants about yourself, the purpose of your study, and the participants' part in it. Tell them whether and how their data will be anonymised, stored, etc.
   (c) Develop the data collection tool(s) for your study. These tool(s) could be a short questionnaire, some interview questions, or based on any other method introduced in ▶ Sect. 13.4.
4. Conduct your pilot study. You will learn what to do with the collected data in ▶ Chap. 14.

Summary

In this chapter, we have assessed the question of how linguistic research into multilingualism might be conducted. We have introduced different types of linguistic data, that is, first-hand data, second-hand, reported data, and metadata, which can be written, spoken, naturalistic, experimental, compiled as a corpus, etc. Furthermore, we have presented some commonly used elicitation methods, such as questionnaires, interviews, and linguistic landscapes, in greater detail and against the background of the areas of linguistics in which they are commonly used. For each, we have discussed potential pitfalls and have shown that each of these approaches and methods has their strengths and weaknesses. We conclude that the multi-method approach should be considered best practice to overcome such weaknesses and collect data and combine information of different types. Again, and as mentioned time and again throughout this chapter, what exactly is best practice depends on what one is interested in (see also Berthele, 2012; Coulmas, 2018): Do we want to conduct a case study by means of a small-scale qualitative in-depth analysis? Do we want to use large datasets that offer the analysis of representative, statistically significant linguistic patterns? Or do we want to execute experiments with selected subjects? Before any method can be implemented, the researcher has to prepare and decide what research objective exactly they want to follow. However, there is one thing, we believe, most research in multilingualism has in common: The need to make use of the extensive toolbox and the fruitful options of data assessment and analysis that are available to linguists to fully understand the complex realities their research projects have to offer.

References

Ambridge, B., & Rowland, C. F. (2013). Experimental methods in studying child language acquisition. *Cognitive Science, 4*(2), 149–168.

Angouri, J. (2018). Quantitative, qualitative, mixed or holistic research? Combining methods in linguistic research. In *Research Methods in Linguistics* (2nd ed., pp. 35–56). Bloomsbury Academic.

Berthele, R. (2012). Multiple languages and multiple methods: Qualitative and quantitative ways of tapping into the multilingual repertoire. In A. Ender, A. Lehmann, & B. Wälchli (Eds.), *Methods in contemporary linguistics* (pp. 195–218). De Gruyter.

Biber, D. (1993). Representativeness in corpus design. *Literary and Linguistic Computing, 8*, 243–257.

Björkman, B. (2013). *English as an academic lingua franca: An investigation of form and communicative effectiveness*. De Gruyter Mouton.

Blom, E., & Unsworth, S. (Eds.). (2010). *Experimental methods in language acquisition research*. John Benjamins.

Blommaert, J., & Dong, J. (2020). *Ethnographic fieldwork: A beginner's guide* (2nd ed.). Multilingual Matters.

Blommaert, J., & Maly, I. (2016). Ethnographic linguistic landscape analysis and social change: Case-study from Ghent. In K. Arnaut, J. Blommaert, B. Rampton, & M. Spotti (Eds.), *Language and superdiversity*. Routledge.

Buschfeld, S. (2020). *Children's English in Singapore: Acquisition, properties, and use*. Routledge.

Coulmas, F. (2018). *An introduction to multilingualism: Language in a changing world*. Oxford University Press.

De Groot, A. M., & Hagoort, P. (Eds.). (2017). *Research methods in psycholinguistics and the neurobiology of language: A practical guide* (Vol. 9). Wiley.

Dijkstra, J., Heeringa, W., Jongbloed-Faber, L., & Van de Velde, H. (2021). Using Twitter data for the study of language change in low-resource languages. A panel study of relative pronouns in Frisian. *Frontiers in Artificial Intelligence, 4*, 644554. https://doi.org/10.3389/frai.2021.644554

Dörnyei, Z. (2003). *Questionnaires in second language research: Construction, administration, and processing*. Lawrence Erlbaum.

Dörnyei, Z. (2007). *Research methods in applied linguistics*. Oxford University Press.

Edley, N., & Litosseliti, L. (2010). Contemplating interviews and focus groups. In L. Litosseliti (Ed.), *Research methods in linguistics* (pp. 155–179). Continuum.

Feagin, C. (2002). Entering the community: Fieldwork. In J. K. Chambers, P. Trudgill, & N. Schilling-Estes (Eds.), *The handbook of language variation and change* (pp. 20–39). Blackwell Publishers.

Ionin, T. (2012). Formal theory-based methodologies. In A. Mackey & S. M. Gass (Eds.), *Research methods in second language acquisition: A practical guide* (pp. 30–52). Wiley-Blackwell.

Jonsson, E. (2015). *Conversational writing: A multidimensional study of synchronous and supersynchronous computer-mediated communication*. Peter Lang.

Kallen, J. L. (2010). Changing landscapes: Language, space and policy in the Dublin linguistic landscape. In A. Jaworski & C. Thurlow (Eds.), *Semiotic landscapes. Language, image, space* (pp. 41–58). Continuum.

Labov, W. (1982). Building on empirical foundations. In W. Lehmann & Y. Malkiel (Eds.), *Perspectives on historical linguistics* (pp. 17–92). John Benjamins.

Labov, W. (1984). Field methods of the project on linguistic change and variation. In J. Baugh & J. Sherzer (Eds.), *Language in use. Readings in sociolinguistics* (pp. 28–53). Prentice-Hall.

Labov, W. (2006). *The social stratification of English in New York city* (2nd ed.). Cambridge University Press.

Lange, C., & Leuckert, S. (2020). *Corpus linguistics for World Englishes*. Routledge.

Lee, J. W. (2018). *The politics of translingualism—After Englishes*. Routledge.

Litosseliti, L. (2018). Critical perspectives on using interviews and focus groups. In *Research methods in linguistics* (2nd ed., pp. 195–226). Bloomsbury Academic. https://doi.org/10.5040/9781350043466.ch-009

Mason, J. (2002). Qualitative interviewing. In J. Mason (Ed.), *Qualitative researching* (2nd ed., pp. 62–83). Sage Publications.

References

Milroy, L. (1980). *Language and social networks*. University Perk Press.
Milroy, L. (1987). *Observing and analysing natural language. A critical account of sociolinguistic method*. Blackwell.
Labov, W. (1972). *Some principles of linguistic methodology*. Language in Society, 1, 97–120.
Oppenheim, A. N. (1992). *Questionnaire design, interviewing and attitude measurement*. Pinter.
Poplack, S. (1989). The care and handling of a megacorpus: The Ottawa-Hull French project. In R. Fasold & D. Schiffrin (Eds.), *Language change and variation* (pp. 411–444). John Benjamins.
Presser, S., & Schuman, H. (1980). The measurement of a middle position in attitude surveys. *Public Opinion Quarterly, 44*(1), 70–75.
Rasinger, S. M. (2010). Quantitative methods: Concepts, frameworks and issues. In L. Litosseliti (Ed.), *Research methods in linguistics* (pp. 49–67). Bloomsbury.
Sakel, J., & Everet, D. L. (2012). *Linguistic fieldwork*. Cambridge University Press.
Sankoff, G. (1974). A quantitative paradigm for the study of communicative competence. In R. Bauman & J. Sherzer (Eds.), *Explorations in the ethnography of speaking* (pp. 18–49). Cambridge University Press.
Schuman, H., & Presser, S. (1996). *Questions and answers in attitude surveys. Experiments on question form, wording, and context*. Sage Publications.
Scollon, R., & Scollon, S. (2003). *Discourse in place: Language in the material world*. Routledge.
Spradley, J. (1979). Asking descriptive questions. In M. Pogrebin (Ed.), *Qualitative approaches to criminal justice: Perspectives from the field* (pp. 44–53). Sage Publishing.
Tagliamonte, S. A. (2006). *Analysing sociolinguistic variation*. Cambridge University Press.
Vida-Mannl, M. (2022). *The value of the English language in global mobility and higher education: An investigation of higher education in Cyprus*. Bloomsbury.
Vida-Mannl, M. (Fc.) (2023). Parental language ideologies and children's language use—raising speakers of 'Standard' English? In M. Schmalz, M. Vida-Mannl, S. Buschfeld & T. Brato (Eds.), *Acquisition and variation in World Englishes: Bridging paradigms and rethinking approaches*. De Gruyter Mouton.

Key Readings

Litosseliti, L. (Ed.). (2010). *Research methods in linguistics*. Bloomsbury.
Meyerhoff, M., Schleef, E., & MacKenzie, L. (2015). *Doing sociolinguistics—a practical guide to data collection and analysis*. Routledge.
Tagliamonte, S. A. (2006). *Analysing sociolinguistic variation*. Cambridge University Press.

Further Reading

Crowley, T. (2007). *Field linguistics. A beginner's guide*. Oxford University Press.
Feagin, C. (2002). Entering the community: Fieldwork. In J. K. Chambers, P. Trudgill, & N. Schilling-Estes (Eds.), *The handbook of language variation and change* (pp. 20–39). Blackwell Publishers.
Krug, M., & Schlüter, J. (Eds.). (2013). *Research methods in language variation and change*. Cambridge University Press.
Wei, L., & Moyer, M. (2008). *Blackwell guide to research methods in bilingualism and multilingualism*. Blackwell.

Using Existing Data Repositories and Data Analysis

Contents

14.1 Introduction – 302

14.2 Making Use of Existing Data Repositories – 302
14.2.1 Collecting Data in the Multilingual Social Media Space – 302
14.2.2 Corpus Linguistics – 304

14.3 Processing and Analysing Linguistic Data – 307

References – 312

© The Author(s), under exclusive license to Springer Nature Switzerland AG 2023
S. Buschfeld et al., *Multilingualism*,
https://doi.org/10.1007/978-3-031-28405-2_14

14.1 Introduction

In ► Chap. 13, we have introduced central linguistic data collection methods used in multilingualism research and we have also pointed out that ethical concerns need to be considered in these processes. In this chapter, we turn to the use of existing data sources. To enter a speaker community and to collect one's own data is definitely an unparalleled experience and allows researchers to obtain detailed knowledge of the data and the community from which they stem. However, the use of existing data sources also comes with a number of advantages. One undeniable advantage is that using existing sources speeds up the research process as data collection times can be cut considerably. In many cases where time is an issue, be it because the time frame for graduation or post-graduate projects is restricted, or because funding or research leave will only be allocated for a short time, this is a strong point in favour of using existing resources. In addition, costs for travel, accommodation, and even compensation for informant can be avoided. During times when travelling is impossible, such as during a global pandemic, the use of existing databases may even be the best research option. In this chapter, we give an overview of some key resources, in particular social media and corpus data, and we point out how these can be harnessed for research.

14.2 Making Use of Existing Data Repositories

As we have seen in ► Chap. 13, data collection can be extremely costly and time-consuming. Researchers normally have to travel to their data collection sites, spend some time in the communities they are investigating, and, once back home, spent even more time on processing and analysing their data (for details on the latter point, see ► Sect. 14.3 below). This is why researchers often make use of existing data repositories, some of which are introduced in this chapter.

14.2.1 Collecting Data in the Multilingual Social Media Space

The first type of existing data repository that we would like to introduce here is the internet, and, more specifically, social media spaces. The data are readily available but still need to be extracted and prepared for analysis. Given the richness of this resource, research angles in the investigation of online multilingualism cover diverse perspectives and methods and use different media as sources. Due to the potentially vast database, qualitative research is frequent, but so are quantitative approaches. In recent years, mixed methods combining the observation of online data with sociolinguistic or ethnographic approaches have become more prominent. As described in Lee (2016, pp. 121–124), researchers gain valuable insights from combining their observation of online behaviour of language users with questionnaire and interview data of the same users. Analysing data that are found online is known as the analysis of *screen-based data*.

14.2 · Making Use of Existing Data Repositories

To carry out your own research project on online multilingualism, a possible research approach is to determine the different languages in any given environment (such as Facebook timelines, Instagram posts, Whatsapp chats) and determine how frequently they are used and who uses which language for what function. Additionally, particularly if you know the media users personally, you may contact them and ask for interviews or ask them to fill in questionnaires in order to find out why they were using the observed practices in the specific situation. Lee (2016) points out that researchers may conduct interviews with media users which aim to have them describe and explain their language practices and choices in the online world. This is known as the analysis of *user-based data* and for such an user-based approach, ethnographic methods are often used (cf. ▶ Sect. 13.4.3). Lee (2016, p. 124) further argues that the investigation of multilingual language practices in online media has undergone a similar development to the use of research methods in sociolinguistics (cf. ▶ Sect. 13.4): earliest research into online multilingualism offered descriptions of multilingual data found online. This was followed by increased interest in the variation that could be found in the multilingual language practices online. Finally, research has turned to incorporating ethnographic approaches which add insights into social activities and practices. Depending on the research objective, each of these may constitute a valid approach.

One possible approach of investigating online multilingual language use is to use *discourse-centred online ethnography* (Androutsopoulos, 2013; cf. Lee, 2016). In this approach, the first step is to analyse the online discourse of language users, for example on blog posts or on social media platforms. Lee (2016, p. 125) describes how, in her own research, she has investigated multilingual language use on Flickr. First, she noted the languages of profiles, captions, tags, and comments and which languages were used in different contexts and for different practices. Then, she contacted users by direct messages to arrange interviews with the users. She used these interviews to gain information on why the users chose a particular language in a particular situation, such as why English was used to comment on a picture tagged in Cantonese or the other way round. A second possible research approach that Lee uses to investigate online multilingualism is to create *technobiographies* of language users.

Technobiographies detail information on the language users' backgrounds. Added to this are the language users' interactions with media technologies on a daily basis as well as observations on the role of these technologies in the informants' lives. Lee (2016, pp. 126–127) describes how informants' use of technologies can be traced over time by determining their current media practices and the sites they contribute to. They are asked to describe their media use on a typical day, the development of their media use during their lives, as well as possible transitions in their media use. Further, informants would describe the domains in which they use the different technologies and they are asked in how far their practices might differ from those of other users or groups that they are aware of. Finally, it is determined whether they use specific online registers in writing, and which languages they use in online writing in general. Based on these technobiographies, details about individual users and their backgrounds can be related to language practices as well as to observed differences and similarities between different user groups. Lee (2016) recommends combining this approach with other methods such as questionnaires and the observation of the online sites the informants use. The practices described by Lee require the researcher to take an active, insider role in the data collection; they build a personal relationship with the informants which helps the researcher to obtain valuable insights into the motivations behind the informants' linguistic practices. For such an investigation of multilingual practices, a knowledge of the languages and cultures involved is very beneficial for the researchers.

A general advantage of using social media data is that we can draw on vast resources at our fingertips. However, when using online sources, that is social media or other, publicly available data may generally be used for research, while data which are not publicly accessible can only be used with the explicit permission of the involved parties (cf. ▶ Sect. 13.5). However, a grey area exists in the linguistic analysis of social media posts: while data have been made publicly available, the authors of the posts are not likely to have expected that their data would be scrutinised by linguists. Thus, minimally the data must be anonymised and individual cases should be carefully considered. For details on best practices consult ▶ https://aoir.org/ethics/.

14.2.2 Corpus Linguistics

A further way in which we can carry out multilingualism research in a naturalistic way is the use of corpus linguistic approaches. In linguistics, the term *corpus* (plural *corpora*) refers to (electronic) collections of naturally occurring language. Corpora may be automatically collected from internet sources and provide a large, international database on a certain domain or context, such as GloWbE (Corpus of Global Web-based English (Davies, 2013)) or other corpora belonging to the Brigham Young Corpus suite. These corpora have the advantage of providing the researcher with very large data sets: in the GloWbE corpus, 1.9 billion words from 20 different English-speaking countries are included. Next to large corpora, we typically also find a large number of smaller, purpose-built corpora which are aiming to be representative of, for example, a specific type of any language, such as English. This could either be language use in a specific context, such as corpora of the language used in front of the Old Bailey court in London (Huber et al., 2016), or corpora that represent a specific variety of a language, like the corpora belonging to the International Corpus of English (ICE) project. Such corpora that try to be representative of a language variety will aim to offer a broad spread of different language genres in order to make sure that the variety is represented in a full range of different contexts. The ICE corpora, for example, contain about 1 million words of English from a specific variety, e.g. Australian or Singaporean English. In each corpus, 60% of the data derive from transcribed spoken materials, 40% are taken from a selection of different written genres (Nelson et al., 2002). Each corpus contains data from the same or comparable speech genres and speech situations such as face-to-face communication, telephone conversations, business communication, broadcast interviews, or classroom lessons. This similarity of genres maximises the

14.2 · Making Use of Existing Data Repositories

comparability of the different data sets. In 2022, the ICE family of corpora includes corpora of British English, Canadian English, East African English, Hong Kong English, Indian English, Irish English, Jamaican English, New Zealand English, Nigerian English, Philippine English, Singapore English, and Sri Lankan English. The ICE United States only contains a written component. It is complemented by the Santa Barbara Corpus, which is a corpus of spoken American English and contains about 250,000 words. The prime objective of the ICE corpora is to offer the possibility to compare variety-specific features in the different varieties of English. In that, the ICE-corpora are geared towards analyses that focus only on English. While they mostly exclude other languages spoken in the respective locale, some of them contain speech production in languages other than English, such as instances of code-switching and -mixing; non-English words in the corpora are tagged in the majority of the corpora. This allows the user to use a corpus interface to search for the tag of the language, for example for Cantonese or Malay in ICE Singapore or for Hausa in ICE Nigeria, and determine in which contexts these languages are used in interaction with local (standard) varieties of English.

In addition to such mainly English-based and mostly monolingual corpora, we also find multilingual corpus resources. As yet, comparatively few corpora exist that really represent language users' multilingual practices and illustrate translanguaging or code-switching. A good example of such a corpus is the Childes Corpus, which contains a number of resources of young children who acquire two or more languages at young ages (▶ https://childes.talkbank.org/access/Biling/). On the Talk Bank site (▶ https://talkbank.org/), we can also find further smaller, specialised multilingual corpora. These include for example the Diaz Collazos corpus of Japanese-Spanish bilinguals in Columbia, the Gardner-Chloros corpus of Greek-English bilinguals in Israel and New York, or the Patagonia corpus with data from Welsh-Spanish bilinguals in Argentina. Many of these resources offer not only transcripts but also audio materials of the sources. Example 14.1 is taken from the bilingual Childes corpus from the TalkBank collection. It presents a conversation between a mother and her child (aged 3;7), who grows up in the predominantly French-speaking Canadian province of Montréal. It further shows that the child, while using English predominantly, also draws on French resources in the conversation. The child includes chunks of French language use: *regarde ça c'est* ('look at this, it is') and *là* ('there'). These French language items appear in the overall English-language conversation at the moment when a cousin, Laurent, is mentioned and show the fluent interaction between the two languages.

▶ **Example 14.1**

MOT: wait wait wait wait wait.
CHI: it's me.
CHI: that's us that's me that's (.) he bump in my head.
MOT: yeah.
MOT: you give your cousin Laurent a kiss ?
CHI: yeah.
MOT: yeah.
CHI: *(re)ga(rde) ça c'est* (.) Laurent kiss.

CHI: upside down.
MOT: that's how Gene stands up.
CHI: yyy.
MOT: like that ?
CHI: he <stand up> [?] like that ?
CHI: *là* he not [?] standing like that.
MOT: mmhm.
(▶ https://sla.talkbank.org/TBB/childes/Biling/GNP/gen/030709e.cha, lines 39–54) ◀

Furthermore, we also find *contrastive corpora*, which allow us to find out how the same content is expressed in different languages. For this, we typically use parallel or translation corpora. Parallel corpora typically contain one or more texts together with their translations into different languages. Here, for example, we have the United Nations Parallel Corpus (▶ https://conferences.unite.un.org/UNCorpus/), which contains United Nations records and documents with their translations into various languages. A similar corpus is provided by the Europarl Corpus (▶ https://www.statmt.org/europarl/), which consists of proceedings of the European Parliament with their translations into 21 languages of the member states. A broad range of genres is represented by the CLUVI Corpus (▶ https://ilg.usc.gal/cluvi/index.php?lang=en), which is a parallel corpus and offers a broad range of textual genres in different language combinations. A further parallel corpus that comprises one text in more than 100 languages is the Bible-corpus (Christodoulopoulos & Steedman, 2015) (▶ https://github.com/christos-c/bible-corpus). Any of these, and further parallel corpora, allow us to compare grammatical structures as well as lexicon and phraseology in the different languages in the corpus.

A further type of multilingual corpora are so-called *comparable corpora* (e.g. McEnery & Xiao, 2007). Frequent types of comparable corpora contain non-parallel texts from different languages which all deal with similar topic areas. An example of this is the Aarhus corpus of Danish, French, and English contract law (Faber & Lauridsen, 1991). Other corpora provide automated analyses of the data. For example, the HamleDT Corpus (▶ https://ufal.mff.cuni.cz/hamledt), for example, is a multi-language dependency treebank. A treebank uses a syntactic-tree structure to give a detailed overview of grammatical structures that are used in different languages and thus facilitates the comparison of dependency trees in different languages. In general, such corpora with independent text examples of different languages allow us to compare, for example, the syntactic patterns or the use of prepositions in different languages.

Data in corpora are commonly very rich and to facilitate their analysis, specifically provided corpus interfaces are used. These corpus interfaces have command lines where single or multiple words can typically be entered. Like this, we can search for particular, predefined words or phrases. In addition, we can use a specific query syntax in order to obtain more varied results. We can also look for combinations of syntactic patterns such as, for example, all combinations of any modal, auxiliary, and lexical verb, or any preposition used together with a specific noun, and many more. For such queries, specific tag sets are used. These are specific standardised short query forms based on the abbreviations of the names for parts-of-speech. Thus, looking for any modal, auxiliary, and lexical verb we could search for [v*] [v*] [vv*], where * is a wild-card, which allows you to see any example of this category, that is, any modal verb, any auxiliary, and any lexical verb. If we wanted to know whether in World Englishes you mostly are *in work* or *at work,* we can search for the verb *be* in any form [vb*] plus any preposition [i*] plus the specific noun, resulting in [vb*] [i*] work. If we look at the Corpus of Contemporary American English, COCA (Davies, 2008, ▶ https://www.english-corpora.org/COCA/), we see that in American English people are almost exclusively *at work*. If we look at the GloWbeE corpus (Davies, 2013, ▶ https://www.english-corpora.org/glowbe/), by contrast, in international varieties of English we also find examples of people being *on work* or *in work* in the same context. The full tagset that is in use for many English language corpora and allows researchers to carry out such meta-queries can be found here: ▶ https://ucrel.lancs.ac.uk/claws7tags.html.

14.3 Processing and Analysing Linguistic Data

Linguistic data can be analysed in two general ways, qualitatively and quantitatively. The general difference between the two approaches has already been discussed in ▶ Sect. 13.2. For a quantitative analysis, data must be processed, that is transcribed and coded, and/or entered into spreadsheets or a statistics programme, such as Excel sheets, the statistics programme R (R Core Team, 2019), or SPSS (IBM Corp, 2021), respectively. Whenever spoken data are concerned, more or less detailed data transcription—and this might be anything between broad orthographic to fully detailed phonetic transcriptions—usually precedes the coding process, that is the identification and markup of the linguistic or thematic features under investigation. While data transcription and coding are not necessarily key issues in this chapter, we would like to give some general information on these procedures. First of all, transcribing spoken data takes a lot of time, in particular for novice researchers, who are often neither used to the specific transcription programmes nor to transcription procedures in general. While experienced transcribers may need less time, we should typically expect to use at least one hour for transcribing 10 min of speech (Meyerhoff et al., 2015, p. 101), especially if the data that need to be transcribed are dialogue rather than monologue (Sakel & Everet, 2012, pp. 107–108). Other factors such as familiarity with the language variety being transcribed, the existence and amount of background noise, but also individual factors such as attention span and focus also play a role in the ease and speed of transcription. Researchers may also provide concrete annotations that mark, for example, grammatical features, discourse features, or lexical items. Which aspects of the data (if at all) should be annotated depends, again, on the overall aim and focus of the investigation. To aid and speed up the transcription and annotation process and facilitate the subsequent analysis of the transcribed data, transcription programmes have been developed. Widely used programmes that are also used for data transcription and annotation are ELAN (▶ https://archive.

mpi.nl/tla/elan) and CLAN (▶ https://dali.talkbank.org/clan/). Following data transcription and coding, the coded and counted data are often entered into a spreadsheet for subsequent analysis, for example to create tables and graphs. For this purpose, linguists often use programmes such as Excel (the often simplest way to start for novice researchers), R (R Core Team, 2019), SPSS (IBM Corp, 2021), or Python (Van Rossum & Drake, 2009). We return to this shortly when dealing with how to set up spreadsheets in more detail below.

Processing and analysing questionnaire data is normally less cumbersome and time-consuming than transcriptions, but—as we have seen in ▶ Sect. 13.4.1—may come with other disadvantages. Depending on the purpose and the style of the questionnaire, the researcher will have to code metric, categorical, and ordinal variables and/or enter these data into a spreadsheet for further analysis. While metric variables tend to remain in their natural form (for example the number of years the participants have spent in a country or their age/year of birth), categorical variables can be coded based on the multiplicity of provided answers. The answer to the variable *gender*, for example, can be coded as "1" for "female", "2" for "male", and "3" for "diverse", the answers to the variable L1 can be coded from "1" to "9" reflecting various individual languages and combinations of two or more languages that have been mentioned. This coding is, of course, just one option and can be replaced by any other numbers or letters or even the full answer that has been given. In case a question has not been answered this should be indicated as a missing value, which is commonly coded as "N/A". Ordinal variables, such as answers to the often-used Likert scales (see ▶ Sect. 13.4.1 for further details) can be translated into a rising numerical sequence, for example from "1" to "5", again using "N/A" for missing values.

An ideally set up spreadsheet should have one line per token, which contains the necessary information on the realisations of, say, the variable under observation, as well as, information on the speaker's background. ◘ Figure 14.1 provides an example of a rich and well-set-up spreadsheet from a project on the acquisition of English as a first language by multilingual Singaporean children.

Note that, in the Excel file excerpt (◘ Fig. 14.1), each token has its individual row. Furthermore, the file provides information on the target variable, namely whether referential subject pronouns are realised by the children or not in column I (refer = realised, pro>refer = zero), and its use. Column A provides the speaker label; the remaining columns indicate the respective extralinguistic/socio-linguis-

	A	B	C	D	E	F	G	H	I	J
1	CHILD	COUNTRY	COUNTRY_GROUP	ETHNICITY_GROUP	GENDER	LING_BACKGROUND	AGE_MONTHS	MLU_GROUP	REFER	PRN
17	1	Singapore	Singapore	S: Indian	male	multi1	29	1	refer	I
18	1	Singapore	Singapore	S: Indian	male	multi1	29	1	refer	I
19	1	Singapore	Singapore	S: Indian	male	multi1	29	1	refer	I
20	1	Singapore	Singapore	S: Indian	male	multi1	29	1	pro>refer	I
21	1	Singapore	Singapore	S: Indian	male	multi1	29	1	pro>refer	I
22	1	Singapore	Singapore	S: Indian	male	multi1	29	1	pro>refer	I
23	2	Singapore	Singapore	S: Chinese	male	multi1	30	1	refer	she
24	2	Singapore	Singapore	S: Chinese	male	multi1	30	1	refer	I
25	2	Singapore	Singapore	S: Chinese	male	multi1	30	1	refer	I

◘ **Fig. 14.1** Excerpt from an Excel file

14.3 · Processing and Analysing Linguistic Data

tic variables under observation in the study (columns B-G) as well as intralinguistic predictors included in the study (H-J). (For chapter-length treatments of data transcription, coding, and summarising, see Meyerhoff et al., 2015, pp. 99–110, 111–121.)

After data processing and coding, researchers usually continue their quantitative analyses on the basis of descriptive and/or inferential statistical approaches. Descriptive statistics help to illustrate the results by means of simple summaries of the data sample and the observations made in the study. Such summaries may be either quantitative, using numbers such as mean values, medians, standard deviations, etc., or visual, such as graphs, histograms, box plots, etc. Descriptive statistics may either form the basis of a more extensive statistical analysis or may be sufficient in themselves for a particular investigation. This, again, depends on the objectives of the overall research project. Statistical inference makes propositions about a population, using data drawn from the sample. Examples include significance testing via, e.g., t-tests, Wilcoxon-tests, F-tests; regression models (e.g. linear models, linear mixed models); classification models (e.g. ctrees, rpart trees); interdependent models (e.g. structural models, path models); Bayes models; and many more. Statistical analyses and in particular statistical inference have increasingly found their way into linguistic studies, in particular in the last 15 years. This development is summed up by Joseph (2008) stating that "[l]inguistics has always had a numerical and mathematical side [...] but the use of quantitative methods, and, relatedly, formalisations and modelling, seems to be ever on the increase; rare is the paper that does not report on some statistical analysis of relevant data or offer some model of the problem at hand" (p. 687). Evidence for what has been labelled the "quantitative turn" in linguistics is provided by a number of introductions to statistics for linguists (e.g. Gries, 2021; Levshina, 2015; Schneider 2020; Winter, 2019), as well as the numerous handbooks, textbooks, book series, and journals on quantitative corpus linguistics. In addition to that, first empirical evidence exists for this development (Buschfeld and Ahlers 2022; Kortmann, 2021; Larsson et al., 2022). We cannot go into any detail here as this would go far beyond the scope of the textbook, but the interested reader is referred to the various mentioned resources for further details and concrete methods, applications, and procedures.

A further common tool for data analysis used in, for example, sociolinguistics and corpus linguistics is AntConc (Anthony, 2021; ▶ https://www.laurenceanthony.net/software/antconc/). AntConc is a powerful freeware that offers various text analysis tools. One of the most central tools is the KWIC (Key-Word-In-Context) Tool. The tool shows the researcher in which contexts words or phrases are used in the corpora under consideration. It, for example, allows researchers to count the frequencies of particular linguistic features via the advanced search term function. ◘ Figure 14.2 shows the search query for "Singapore" (marked in blue in the tool), including three words to the right for each hit (marked in red, green, and pink, respectively).

Clicking on the hits brings the researcher to the exact position in the respective file, which can be very useful and time-saving when working with the data. However, as one can see at the top of the screenshot, AntConc offers a variety of other options as well (cf. Anthony, 2021): the plot tool displays the distribution of the

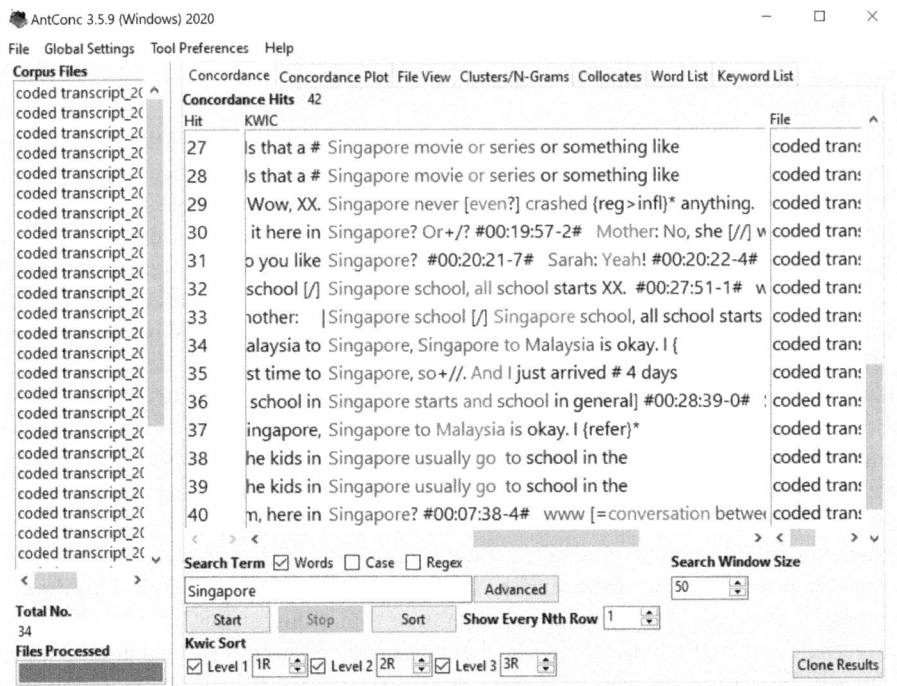

● Fig. 14.2 AntConc screenshot on a search query for "Singapore"

hits in the corpus in a barcode format. Each attestation forms a vertical line in the bar chart. This way, we can see where in the corpus the tokens are located and whether there are any specific clusters of tokens or whether they are evenly distributed. In the file tool, we can read the individual texts, which is useful if we want to see the entire context in which a token appears. Next, the cluster tool shows the most common clusters in which a word appears, and gives the rank of that cluster, its frequency and the range. The N-gram tool looks for all clusters of two, three, four, or more words that appear together and thus shows which the most frequent combinations in a corpus are. This is not only helpful in case we want to check which word combinations and which phrases are most frequent in a corpus but also when investigating how they compare between different corpora, for example between learner corpora and/or between English for Specific Purposes (ESP) corpora. If we want to find out, which word appears frequently with another specified word in a corpus, we can use the collocate tool. This tool shows those words that appear in any given distance on either side of the search term. We can also use AntConc to create a word-list of all the words in a corpus. Like this, we can find out in which order of frequency words appear in a corpus. By using the keyword list, we can find out which words are 'key', which means more frequent than elsewhere, in a given corpus. For example, we can find out which words learners overuse or underuse in comparison to non-learners. In the newest version of AntConc,

14.3 · Processing and Analysing Linguistic Data

AntConc 4.0, a corpus manager tool has also been added. This allows the corpus users to create and save databases (corpora, files, or word-lists) and also to select the corpora they want to work on in AntConc.

❓ Exercises

1. Carry out a linguistic landscapes study.
   (a) Identify a clearly defined area in your vicinity. This could, for example, be a shopping street in your town, a shopping mall, or, if you are a member of a university, a specific building or floor of your university.
   (b) Provide a systematic overview of the languages that are on visual display in this location. Before you start, decide which types of signs will be admissible and whether you want to exclude anything from consideration (non-permanent signs like flyers, detritus, etc.). Then, start your systematic collection of all the relevant signs in the area by, first, taking photographs of them and, second, adding information on location, type of sign, text on the sign, and which languages are used on the sign into a spreadsheet.
   (c) Interpret your findings: which languages do you find? Can you observe specific functions for specific languages? What can you conclude from your findings?
2. Search a corpus.
   (a) Go to the Webpage of AntConc ▶ https://www.laurenceanthony.net/software/antconc/ and download the tool onto your computer. Follow the instructions on the website and/or watch one of the video tutorials linked on the site.
   (b) Go to the Childes corpus and select one of the multilingual recordings at ▶ https://childes.talkbank.org/access/Biling/, depending on which languages you are comfortable working with. Select a transcript-only (without media) recording of the corpus data and download the data as text file(s). Load the text file(s) into AntConc.
   (c) By using the Keywords tool of AntConc, find out which words are most frequent in the data set, and, by using the N-Grams function, find out which groups of two, three, or four words appear together most frequently in the data set.
3. Build your own multilingual corpus.
   (a) Identify multilingual speakers around you and ask them if you may record them – ideally you should get their written consent that you may do so. The best results can typically be obtained if you can observe the interaction of pairs or groups of multilingual speakers who have the same linguistic background and know each other well. If you have access to such a group, ask them to discuss a topic of your choice and record the discussion.
   (b) Transcribe (parts of) the recording.
   (c) Analyse the transcription: can you find multilingual practices? Do the speakers switch languages? Under what circumstances do they do so? Can you identify any triggers for these changes?

Summary

In this chapter, we have introduced existing resources that can be used for research on multilingualism. We have shown that online and social media data can provide researchers with broad databases which offer detailed insights into the speakers and their communities, if ethnographic approaches are added to the analysis of the social media data and online users agree to provide further data. Furthermore, we have shown that existing corpora can be exploited both for research on mono- and multilingual language use and we have provided examples of extant corpora. We have further sketched how the data collected with these methods can be prepared in spreadsheets or analysed with analysis tools like AntConc. Last but not least, we have called for the use of statistical approaches to the analysis of extant data to create valid and robust insights.

References

Androutsopoulos, J. (2013). Networked multilingualism: Some language practices on Facebook and their implications. *International Journal of Bilingualism, 19*(2), 185–205.

Anthony, L. (2021). AntConc (Version 4.0.0) [Computer Software]. Waseda University. Retrieved from http://www.antlab.sci.waseda.ac.jp/

Buschfeld, S., & Ahlers, W. (2022). English around the World: New realities, new models, and the case of Sint Maarten. In A. Ngefac, H. -G. Wolf, & T. Hoffmann (Eds.), World Englishes and Creole languages today, vol. 1: The Schneiderian thinking and beyond. Lincom.

Christodoulopoulos, C., & Steedman, M., (2015). "A massively parallel corpus: the Bible in 100 languages". *Language Resources and Evaluation*, 49(2): 375–395.

Davies, M. (2008). *The Corpus of Contemporary American English (COCA)*. Retrieved November 4, 2022, from https://www.english-corpora.org/coca/

Davies, M. (2013). *Corpus of Global Web-Based English (GloWbE)*. Retrieved November 4, 2022, from https://www.english-corpora.org/glowbe/

Faber, D., & Lauridsen, K. (1991). The compilation of a Danish-English-French corpus in contract law. English Computer Corpora. *Selected Papers and Research Guide* (pp. 235–243).

Gries, S. T. (2021). *Statistics for linguistics with R*. De Gruyter Mouton.

Huber, M., Nissel, M., & Puga, K. (2016). *Old Bailey Corpus 2.0*. Retrieved June 29, 2022, from hdl:11858/00-246C-0000-0023-8CFB-2

IBM Corp. (2021). *IBM SPSS Statistics for Windows, Version 28.0*. IBM Corp.

Joseph, B. (2008). The editor's department: Last scene of all…. *Language, 84*(4), 686–690.

Kortmann, B. (2021). Reflecting on the quantitative turn in linguistics. *Linguistics, 59*(5), 1207–1226.

Larsson, T., Egbert, J., & Biber, D. (2022). On the status of statistical reporting versus linguistic description in corpus linguistics: a ten-year perspective. *Corpora, 17*(1), 137–157.

Lee, C. (2016). *Multilingualism online*. Routledge.

Levshina, N. (2015). *How to do linguistics with R*. John Benjamins.

McEnery, T., & Xiao, R. (2007). Parallel and comparable corpora: What is happening? In G. M. Anderman & M. Rogers (Eds.), *Incorporating corpora: The linguist and the translator* (pp. 18–31). Multilingual Matters.

Meyerhoff, M., Schleef, E., & MacKenzie, L. (2015). *Doing sociolinguistics—A practical guide to data collection and analysis*. Routledge.

Nelson, G., Wallis, S. & Aarts, B. (2002). Exploring natural language: Working with the British component of the International Corpus of English..

References

R Core Team. (2019). R: A language and environment for statistical computing. *R foundation for statistical computing.* https://www.R-project.org/

Sakel, J., & Everet, D. L. (2012). *Linguistic fieldwork*. Cambridge University Press.

Schneider, E. W. (2020). Calling Englishes as complex dynamic systems: Diffusion and restructuring. In A. Mauranen & S. Vetchinnikova (Eds.), *Language change: The impact of English as a Lingua Franca* (pp. 15–43). Cambridge University Press.

Van Rossum, G., & Drake, F. L. (2009). *Python 3 reference manual*. CreateSpace.

Winter, B. (2019). *Statistics for linguists: An introduction using R*. Routledge.

Key Readings

MacEnery, T., & Hardie, A. (2012). *Corpus linguistics: Method, theory and practice*. Cambridge University Press.

Winter, B. (2019). *Statistics for linguists: An introduction using R*. Routledge.

Further Reading

McEnery, T., & Xiao, R. (2007). Parallel and comparable corpora: What is happening? In G. M. Anderman & M. Rogers (Eds.), *Incorporating corpora: The linguist and the translator* (pp. 18–31). Multilingual Matters.

Supplementary Information

References – 316

Index – 339

© The Editor(s) (if applicable) and The Author(s), under exclusive licence to Springer Nature Switzerland AG 2023
S. Buschfeld et al., *Multilingualism*,
https://doi.org/10.1007/978-3-031-28405-2

References

AAAL Ethics Guidelines Task Force. (2017). *AAAL ethics guidelines*. Retrieved from http://c.ymcdn.com/sites/www.aaal.org/resource/resmgr/AAAL_Ethics_Guidelines_-_App.pdf

Ajzen, I. (1988). *Attitudes, personality, and behavior*. Dorsey Press.

Akande, A. (2012). The appropriation of African American vernacular English and Jamaican Patois by Nigerian hip hop artists. *ZAA, 60*(3), 237–254.

Alsagoff, L. (2007). Singlish: Negotiating culture, capital and identity. In V. Vaish, S. Gopinathan, & Y. Liu (Eds.), *Language, capital, culture: Critical studies and education in Singapore* (pp. 25–46). Sense Publishers.

Altarriba, J., & Heredia, R. R. (Eds.). (2018). *An introduction to bilingualism: Principles and processes* (2nd ed.). Routledge.

Altenmüller, E. (2018). *Vom Neandertal in die Philharmonie: Warum der Mensch ohne Musik nicht leben kann*. Springer.

Ambridge, B., & Rowland, C. F. (2013). Experimental methods in studying child language acquisition. *Cognitive Science, 4*(2), 149–168.

American Dialect Society. (2021). *All the words of the year, 1990 to present*. Retrieved November 4, 2022, from https://www.americandialect.org/woty/all-of-the-words-of-the-year-1990-to-present#mill

Ammon, U. (2012). Language policy in the European Union (EU). In B. Spolsky (Ed.), *The Cambridge handbook of language policy* (pp. 570–591). Cambridge University Press.

Ammon, U., & McConnell, G. (2002). *English as an Academic Language in Europe: A survey of its use in teaching*. Peter Lang.

Androutsopoulos, J. (2013). Networked multilingualism: Some language practices on Facebook and their implications. *International Journal of Bilingualism, 19*(2), 185–205.

Androutsopoulos, J., & Juffermans, K. (2014). Digital language practices in superdiversity: Introduction. *Discourse, Context and Media, 4*(5), 1–6.

Androutsopoulos, J., & Scholz, A. (2003). Spaghetti Funk: Appropriations of hip-hop culture and rap music in Europe. *Popular Music and Society, 26*(4), 463–479.

Androutsopoulos, J., & Staer, A. (2018). Moving methods online: Researching digital language practices. In A. Creese & A. Blackledge (Eds.), *The Routledge handbook of language and superdiversity* (pp. 118–132). Routledge.

Angouri, J. (2018). Quantitative, qualitative, mixed or holistic research? Combining methods in linguistic research. In *Research Methods in Linguistics* (2nd ed., pp. 35–56). Bloomsbury Academic.

Anthony, L. (2021). AntConc (Version 4.0.0) [Computer Software]. Waseda University. Retrieved from http://www.antlab.sci.waseda.ac.jp/

Antoniou, K., Grohmann, K. K., Kambanaros, M., & Katsos, N. (2014). Is bilectalism similar to bilingualism? An investigation into children's vocabulary and executive control skills. In W. Orman & M. J. Valleau (Eds.), *BUCLD 38: Proceedings of the 38th Annual Boston University Conference on Language Development, 1* (pp. 12–24).

Antoniou, K., Grohmann, K. K., Kambanaros, M., & Katsos, N. (2016). The effect of childhood bilectalism and multilingualism on executive control. *Cognition, 149*, 18–30.

Appel, R., & Muysken, P. (1987). Language contact and bilingualism. .

Arends, J., Muysken, P., & Smith, N. (1994). Pidgins and Creoles: An introduction. .

Arias, M. B., & Markos, A. (2018). Recent research on the three goals of dual language education. In M. B. Arias & M. Fee (Eds.), *Profiles of dual language education in the 21st century* (pp. 3–19). Multilingual Matters.

Armon-Lotem, S., & Meir, N. (2018). The nature of exposure and input in early bilingualism. In A. De Houwer & L. Ortega (Eds.), *The Cambridge handbook of bilingualism* (pp. 193–212). Cambridge University Press.

Aronin, L. (2019). Lecture 1: What is multilingualism? In D. Singleton & L. Aronin (Eds.), *Twelve lectures on multilingualism* (pp. 3–34). Multilingual Matters.

References

Aronin, L., & Hufeisen, B. (Eds.). (2009). *The exploration of multilingualism: development of research on L3, multilingualism and multiple language acquisition*. John Benjamins.

Aronin, L., & Jessner, U. (2015). Understanding current multilingualism: What can the butterfly tell us? In C. Kramsch & U. Jessner (Eds.), *The multilingual challenge* (pp. 271–291). De Gruyter.

Aronin, L., & Singleton, D. (2008). Multilingualism as a new linguistic dispensation. *International Journal of Multilingualism, 5*(1), 1–16.

Aronin, L., & Singleton, D. (2012). Introduction. In L. Aronin & D. Singleton (Eds.), *Multilingualism* (pp. 1–9). John Benjamins.

Aronin, L., & Singleton, D. (2019). Introduction. In D. Singleton & L. Aronin (Eds.), *Twelve lectures on multilingualism*. Multilingual Matters.

Arvaniti, A. (2006). Linguistic practices in Cyprus and the emergence of Cypriot standard Greek. *Mediterranean Language Review, 17*(2006–2010), 15–45.

Auer, P. (2005). Code-switching/mixing. In R. Wodak, B. Johnstone, & P. Kerswill (Eds.), *The SAGE handbook of sociolinguistics* (pp. 460–478). Sage.

Austin, J. L. (1962). *How to do things with words*. Harvard University Press.

BAAL. (2021). *Recommendations on good practice in applied linguistics* (4th ed.). Retrieved from November 4, 2022, from https://www.baal.org.uk/wp-content/uploads/2021/03/BAAL-Good-Practice-Guidelines-2021.pdf

Backhaus, P. (2007). *Linguistic Landscapes: A comparative study of urban multilingualism in Tokyo*. Multilingual Matters.

Bailey, A., Osipova, A., & Genesee, F. (2015). Debunking myths about multilingualism. In A. Bailey, A. Osipova, & F. Genese (Eds.), *Children's multilingual development and education: Fostering linguistic resources in home and school contexts* (pp. 24–73). Cambridge University Press.

Baker, C. (1992). *Attitudes and language*. Multilingual Matters.

Baker, C. (2006). *Foundations of bilingual education and bilingualism*. Multilingual Matters.

Baker, C. (2011). Foundations of bilingual education and bilingualism. In N. Hornberger (Ed.), *Types of bilingual education* (pp. 206–220). Multilingual Matters.

Baker, C., & Wright, W. E. (2021). *Foundations of bilingual education and bilingualism* (7th ed.).

Ball, J. (2011). *Enhancing learning of children from diverse language backgrounds: Mother tongue-based bilingual or multilingual education in the early years*. UNESCO.

Ball, P., Kelly, K., & Clegg, J. (2016). *Putting CLIL into practice*. Oxford University Press.

Ball, M., Müller, N., & Munro, S. (2001). The acquisition of the rhotic consonants by Welsh-English bilingual children. *International Journal of Bilingualism, 5*, 71–86.

Barbour, S., & Stevenson, P. (1990). *Variation in German: A critical approach to German sociolinguistics*. Cambridge University Press.

Bardovi-Harlig, K., & Sprouse, R. A. (2017). Negative versus positive transfer. In J. I. Liontas (Ed.), *The TESOL encyclopedia of english language teaching*. Wiley-Blackwell.

Barton, D., & Lee, C. (2013). *Language online: Investigating digital texts and practices*. Taylor and Francis.

Baum, S., & Titone, D. (2014). Moving toward a neuroplasticity view of bilingualism, executive control, and aging. *Applied Psycholinguistics, 35*, 857–894.

BBC. (2022). *Migrant crisis: Migration to Europe explained in seven charts*. Retrieved November 4, 2022, from https://www.bbc.com/news/world-europe-34131911

Beal, J. C. (2009). 'You're not from New York City, you're from Rotherham': Dialect and identity in British Indie music. *Journal of English Linguistics, 37*(3), 223–240.

Beal, J. C., & Faulkner, M. (2020). Language contact in the history of English. In A. P. Grant (Ed.), *The Oxford handbook of language contact* (Online ed.). Oxford Academic.

Bell, A. (1984). Language style as audience design. *Language in Society, 13*, 145–204.

Bell, A. (1992). Hit and miss: Referee design in the dialects of New Zealand television advertisements. *Language and Communication, 12*(3/4), 327–340.

Bell, A., & Gibson, A. (2011). Staging language: An introduction to the sociolinguistics of performance. *Journal of Sociolinguistics, 15*(5), 555–572.

Benson, C. (2003). Trilingualism in Guinea-Bissau and the question of instructional language. In C. Hoffmann & J. Ytsma (Eds.), *Trilingualism in family, school and community* (pp. 166–184). Multilingual Matters.

Bergelson, E., & Swingley, D. (2012). At 6–9 months, human infants know the meanings of many common nouns. *PNAS, 109*(9), 3253–3258. https://doi.org/10.1073/pnas.1113380109

Berkes, E., & Flynn, S. (2012). Enhanced L3...Ln acquisition and its implications for language teaching. In D. Gabryś-Barker (Ed.), *Cross-linguistic influences in multilingual language acquisition* (pp. 1–22). Springer.

Berns, M., & Matsuda, A. (2020). Lingua Franca and language of wider communication. In C. A. Chapelle (Ed.), *The encyclopedia of applied linguistics*. Wiley.

Berthele, R. (2012). Multiple languages and multiple methods: Qualitative and quantitative ways of tapping into the multilingual repertoire. In A. Ender, A. Lehmann, & B. Wälchli (Eds.), *Methods in contemporary linguistics* (pp. 195–218). De Gruyter.

Bhatia, T. K., & Ritchie, W. C. (1999). The bilingual child: Some issues and perspectives. In W. C. Ritchie & T. K. Bhatia (Eds.), *Handbook of child language acquisition* (pp. 569–643). Academic Press.

Bialystok, E. (2001). *Bilingualism in development. language, literacy, & cognition*. Cambridge University Press.

Bialystok, E. (2007). Introduction: Language acquisition and bilingualism. Consequences for a multilingual society. *Applied Psycholinguistics, 28*(3), 393–397.

Bialystok, E., & Kroll, J. (2018). Can the critical period be saved? A bilingual perspective. *Bilingualism: Language and Cognition, 21*(5), 908–910.

Bialystok, E., Luk, G., Peets, K., & Yang, S. (2010). Receptive vocabulary differences in monolingual and bilingual children. *Bilingualism: Language and Cognition, 13*, 525–531. https://doi.org/10.1017/S1366728909990423

Biber, D. (1993). Representativeness in corpus design. *Literary and Linguistic Computing, 8*, 243–257.

Bickerton, D. (1976). Pidgin and creole studies. *Annual Review of Anthropology, 5*, 169–193.

Biewer, C. (2011). Modal auxiliaries in second language varieties of English: A learner's perspective. In J. Mukherjee & M. Hundt (Eds.), *Exploring second-language varieties of English and learner Englishes: Bridging a paradigm gap* (pp. 7–33). John Benjamins.

Björkman, B. (2013). *English as an academic lingua franca: An investigation of form and communicative effectiveness*. De Gruyter Mouton.

Block, D. (2006). *Multilingual identities in a global city: London stories*. Palgrave.

Block, D. (2007). *Second language identities*. Bloomsbury.

Block, D. (2015). Researching language and identity. In B. Paltrage & A. Phakiti (Eds.), *Methods in applied linguistics* (pp. 527–540). Bloomsbury.

Blom, E., & Unsworth, S. (Eds.). (2010). *Experimental methods in language acquisition research*. John Benjamins.

Blommaert, J. (2010). *The sociolinguistics of globalisation*. Cambridge University Press.

Blommaert, J. (2011). The long language-ideological debate in Belgium. *Journal of Multicultural Discourses, 6*(3), 241–256.

Blommaert, J. (2014). Language: The great diversifier. In S. Vertovec (Ed.), *Routledge international handbook of diversity studies* (pp. 83–90). Routledge.

Blommaert, J., & Dong, J. (2020). *Ethnographic fieldwork: A beginner's guide* (2nd ed.). Multilingual Matters.

Blommaert, J., & Maly, I. (2016). Ethnographic linguistic landscape analysis and social change: Case-study from Ghent. In K. Arnaut, J. Blommaert, B. Rampton, & M. Spotti (Eds.), *Language and superdiversity*. Routledge.

Blommaert, J., & Verschueren, J. (1998). *Debating diversity: Analysing the discourse of tolerance*. Routledge.

Bloomfield, L. (1933). *Language*. Holt.

Böhm, M. (2003). *Deutsch in Afrika: Die Stellung der deutschen Sprache in Afrika vor dem Hintergrund der bildungs- und sprachpolitischen Gegebenheiten sowie der deutschen Auswärtigen Kulturpolitik*. Peter Lang Verlag.

References

Bokhorst-Heng, W. D., Alsagoff, L., McKay, S., & Rubdy, R. (2007). English language ownership among Singaporean Malays: going beyond the NS/NNS dichotomy. *World Englishes, 26*(4), 424–445.

Bollnow, H. (1959). Engels, Friedrich. *Neue Deutsche Biographie, 4*, 521–527. [Online-Version]. Retrieved February 17, 2022, from https://www.deutsche-biographie.de/pnd118530380.html#ndbcontent

Bosch, L., & Sebastián-Gallés, N. (2001). Evidence of early language discrimination abilities in infants from bilingual environments. *Infancy, 2*(1), 29–49.

Bosch, L., & Sebastián-Gallés, N. (2003). Simultaneous bilingualism and the perception of a language-specific vowel contrast in the first year of life. *Language and Speech, 46*(2–3), 217–243.

Bourdieu, P. (1984). *Distinction: A social critique of the judgement of taste.* Routledge.

Bremner, N. (2015). Keepin' it real? Engaging in language politics in Réunion through the juxtaposition of English and Réunionese Kreol in dancehall music. *Journal of Romance Studies, 15*(1), 111–130.

Buschfeld, S. (2013). *English in Cyprus or Cyprus English? An empirical investigation of variety status.* John Benjamins.

Buschfeld, S. (2020a). *Children's English in Singapore: Acquisition, properties, and use.* Routledge.

Buschfeld, S. (2020b). Synopsis: Fine-tuning the EIF model. In S. Buschfeld & A. Kautzsch (Eds.), *Modelling world Englishes: A joint approach to postcolonial and non-postcolonial varieties* (pp. 397–415). Edinburgh University Press.

Buschfeld, S. (2021). Grassroots English, learner English, second-language English, English as a lingua franca…: What's in a name? In C. Meierkord & E. W. Schneider (Eds.), *The growth and spread of English at the grassroots* (pp. 23–46). Edinburgh University Press.

Buschfeld, S., & Ahlers, W. (2022). English around the World: New realities, new models, and the case of Sint Maarten. In A. Ngefac, H. -G. Wolf, & T. Hoffmann (Eds.), World Englishes and Creole languages today, vol. 1: The Schneiderian thinking and beyond. Lincom.

Buschfeld, S., & Kautzsch, A. (2014). English in Namibia: A first approach. *English World-Wide, 35*(2), 121–160.

Buschfeld, S., & Kautzsch, A. (2017). Towards an integrated approach to postcolonial and non-postcolonial Englishes. *World Englishes, 36*(1), 104–126.

Buschfeld, S., Kautzsch, A., & Schneider, E. W. (2018). From colonial dynamism to current transnationalism: A unified view on postcolonial and non-postcolonial Englishes. In S. C. Deshors (Ed.), *Modelling World Englishes in the 21st century: Assessing the interplay of emancipation and globalization of ESL varieties* (pp. 15–44). John Benjamins.

Buschfeld, S., Leuckert, S., Weilinghoff, A., & Weihs, C. (2022, July 27–30). How 'real' is the quantitative turn? Investigating statistics as the 'new normal' in corpus linguistics [presentation]. ICAME 43, Cambridge. Retrieved from https://www.icame43.com

Buschfeld, S., & Schröder, A. (2020). English and German in Namibia. In R. Hickey (Ed.), *English in the German-speaking world* (pp. 334–360). Cambridge University Press.

Buschfeld, S., & Vida-Mannl, M. (Fc.) English in Cyprus. In R. Hickey (Ed.), *The new Cambridge history of the English language* (pp. page numbers), vol. 4. Cambridge University Press.

Buschfeld, S., Weihs, C., & Ronan, P. (2022, September 15–17). Modeling linguistic landscapes: The case of St. Maarten [presentation]. 9th BICLCE, Ljubljana. Retrieved from https://biclce22.ff.uni-lj.si

Byers-Heinlein, K., Burns, T. C., & Werker, J. F. (2010). The roots of bilingualism in newborns. *Psychological Science, 21*(3), 343–348. https://doi.org/10.1177/0956797609360758

Byers-Heinlein, K., & Lew-Williams, C. (2017). Language comprehension in monolingual and bilingual children. In E. M. Fernández, & H. S. Cairns (Eds.), *The handbook of psycholinguistics* (pp. 516–535).

Callies, M. (2013). Markedness. In P. Robinson (Ed.), *The Routledge encyclopedia of second language acquisition* (pp. 406–409). Routledge.

Canagarajah, S. (2013). *Translingual practice: Global Englishes and cosmopolitan relations.* Routledge.

Capstick, T. (2020). *Language and migration.* Routledge.

Carroll, S. E. (2017). Exposure and input in bilingual development. *Bilingualism: Language and Cognition, 20*, 3–16.

Cartmill, E. A., Armstrong, B. F., Gleitman, L. R., Goldin-Meadow, S., Medina, T. N., & Trueswell, J.,C. (2013). Quality of early parent input predicts child vocabulary 3 years later. *Proceedings of the National Academy of Science (PNAS)*, 1–6. Retrieved June 7, 2018, from www.pnas.org/cgi/doi/10.1073/pnas.1309518110

Castells, M. (1997). *The power of identity*. Blackwell.

Caton, S. (1991). Diglossia in North Yemen: A case of competing linguistic communities. *Southwest Journal of Linguistics, 10*, 143–159.

Cenoz, J., Hufeisen, B., & Jessner, U. (Eds.). (2001). *Looking beyond second language acquisition: Studies in tri- and multilingualism*. Stauffenburg.

Cervantes-Soon, C., Dorner, L., Palmer, D., Heiman, D., Schwerdtfeger, R., & Choi, J. (2017). Combating inequalities in two-way language immersion programs: Toward critical consciousness in bilingual education spaces. *Review of Research in Education, 41*, 403–427.

Chan, A. (2010). The Cantonese double object construction with bei2 "give" in bilingual children: The role of input. *International Journal of Bilingualism, 14*(1), 65–85.

Chaojua, T., & van Heuven, V. J. (2009). Mutual intelligibility of Chinese dialects experimentally tested. *Lingua, 119*, 709–732.

Cheshire, J., & Gardner-Chloros, P. (2018). Introduction: Multicultural youth vernaculars in Paris and urban France. *Journal of French Language Studies, 28*(Special Issue 2), 161–164.

Cheshire, J., Kerswill, P., Fox, S., & Torgersen, E. (2013). Language contact and language change in the multicultural metropolis. *Revue Francaise de Linguistique Appliquée, 18*, 63–76.

Cheshire, J., Nortier, J., & Adger, D. (2015). Emerging multiethnolects in Europe. *Queen Mary's Occasional Papers Advancing Linguistics, 33*, 1–27.

Chevalier, S. (2015). Trilingual language acquisition. Contextual factors influencing active trilingualism in early childhood. .

Chia, E., & Gerbault, J. (1991). Les nouveaux parlers urbains: le cas de Yaoundé. In E. Gouaini & N. Thiam (Eds.), *Des langues et des villes* (pp. 263–277). ACCT & Didier Erudition.

Chiswick, B. A., & Repetto, G. (2000). IZA discussion paper 177: Immigrant adjustment in Israel: Literacy and fluency in Hebrew and earnings. In S. Djajic (Ed.), *International migration: Trends, policy and economic impact* (pp. 204–228). IZA Institute of Labour and Economics. Retrieved November 4, 2022, from https://www.iza.org/de/publications/dp/177/immigrant-adjustment-in-israel-literacy-and-fluency-in-hebrew-and-earnings

Chondrogianni, V., & Marinis, T. (2011). Differential effects of internal and external factors on the development of vocabulary, morphology and complex syntax in successive bilingual children. *Linguistic Approaches to Bilingualism, 1*, 223–248. https://doi.org/10.1075/lab.1.3.05cho

CIA. (2020). *The World factbook: Namibia*. Retrieved August 27, 2021, from https://www.cia.gov/the-world-factbook/static/b5ac4db93b3379cabced51723dda44c1/WA-summary.pdf

Clark, E. V. (2016). *First language acquisition* (3rd ed.). Cambridge University Press.

Conboy, B., & Montanari, S. (2016). Early lexical development in bilingual infants and toddlers. In E. Nicoladis & S. Montanari (Eds.), *Bilingualism across the lifespan: Factors moderating language proficiency* (pp. 63–80). De Gruyter Mouton. https://doi.org/10.1515/9783110341249-006

Conboy, B. T., & Thal, D. J. (2006). Ties between the lexicon and grammar: Cross-sectional and longitudinal studies of bilingual toddlers. *Child Development, 77*(3), 712–735.

Cornips, L., & De Rooij, V. A. (2013). Selfing and othering through categories of race, place, and language among minority youths in Rotterdam, The Netherlands. In P. Siemund, I. Gogolin, J. Davydova, & M. Schulz (Eds.), *Multilingualism and language contact in urban areas: Acquisition–development–teaching–communication* (pp. 129–164). John Benjamins.

Cornips, L., & Hulk, A. (2008). Factors of success and failure in the acquisition of grammatical gender in Dutch. *Second Language Research, 28*, 267–296.

Coughlan, E. (2021). Accommodation or rejection? Teenagers' experiences of tensions between traditional and new speakers of Irish. *Journal of Sociolinguistics, 25*, 44–61.

Coulmas, F. (2018). *An introduction to multilingualism: Language in a changing world*. Oxford University Press.

Coyle, D., Hood, P., & Marsh, D. (2010). *Content and language integrated learning*. Cambridge University Press.

References

Cro (feat. Danju). (2014). Meine Gang (Bang Bang) [Song]. Retrieved June 6, 2021, from https://genius.com/Cro-meine-gang-bang-bang-lyrics
Crowley, T. (2007). *Field linguistics. A beginner's guide*. Oxford University Press.
Crystal, D. (2004). *English as a global language*. Cambridge University Press.
Cummins, J. (2000). *Language, power, and pedagogy: Bilingual children in the crossfire*. Multilingual Matters.
Cummins, J. (2001). Bilingual children's mother tongue: Why is it important for education? *Sprogforum, 19*, 15–20.
Davies, M. (2008). *The Corpus of Contemporary American English (COCA)*. Retrieved November 4, 2022, from https://www.english-corpora.org/coca/
Davies, M. (2013). *Corpus of Global Web-Based English (GloWbE)*. Retrieved November 4, 2022, from https://www.english-corpora.org/glowbe/
De Groot, A. M., & Hagoort, P. (Eds.). (2017). *Research methods in psycholinguistics and the neurobiology of language: A practical guide* (Vol. 9). Wiley.
De Groot, A. M. B., & Hagoort, P. (Eds.). (2018). *Research methods in psycholinguistics and the neurobiology of language: A practical guide*. Wiley.
De Houwer, A. (1990). *The acquisition of two languages from birth: A case study*. Cambridge University Press. https://doi.org/10.1017/CBO9780511519789
De Houwer, A. (1995). Bilingual language acquisition. In P. Fletcher & B. MacWhinney (Eds.), *The handbook of child language* (pp. 219–250). Basil Blackwell.
De Houwer, A. (2009). *Bilingual first language acquisition*. Multilingual Matters.
De Houwer, A. (2014). The absolute frequency of maternal input to bilingual and monolingual children: A first comparison. In T. Grüter & J. Paradis (Eds.), *Input and experience in bilingual development* (pp. 37–58). John Benjamins.
De Houwer, A. (2021). *Bilingual development in childhood*. Cambridge University Press.
De Houwer, A., Bornstein, M. H., & De Coster, S. (2006). Early understanding of two words for the same thing: A CDI study of lexical comprehension in infant bilinguals. *International Journal of Bilingualism, 10*(3), 331–347.
De Houwer, A., Bornstein, M. H., & Putnick, D. L. (2014). A bilingual-monolingual comparison of young children's vocabulary size: Evidence from comprehension and production. *Applied Psycholinguistics, 35*, 1189–1211. https://doi.org/10.1017/S0142716412000744
De Houwer, A., & Ortega, L. (2018a). Introduction. In A. De Houwer & L. Ortega (Eds.), *The Cambridge handbook of bilingualism* (pp. 1–12). Cambridge University Press.
De Houwer, A., & Ortega, L. (Eds.). (2018b). *The Cambridge handbook of bilingualism*. Cambridge University Press.
De Swaan, A. (2001). *The world of words: The global language system*. Polity Press.
De Winter, J. C., & Dodou, D. (2010). Five-point Likert items: t test versus Mann-Whitney-Wilcoxon. *Practical Assessment, Research & Evaluation, 15*(11), 1–12.
Delucchi Danhier, R., & Mertins, B. (2018). Psycholinguistische Grundlagen der Inklusion—Schwerpunkt Bilingualismus. In S. Hußmann & B. Welzel (Eds.), *Do Profil—Das Dortmunder Profil für inklusionsorientierte Lehrerinnen- und Lehrerbildung* (pp. 161–178). Waxmann.
Department of Statistics Singapore. (2020). *Census of population 2020. Statistical release 1: Demographic characteristics, education, language and religion*. Retrieved January 22, 2021, from https://www.singstat.gov.sg/-/media/files/publications/cop2020/sr1/cop2020sr1.pdf
Dijkstra, J., Heeringa, W., Jongbloed-Faber, L., & Van de Velde, H. (2021). Using Twitter data for the study of language change in low-resource languages. A panel study of relative pronouns in Frisian. *Frontiers in Artificial Intelligence, 4*, 644554. https://doi.org/10.3389/frai.2021.644554
Ding, H., & Yu, L. (2013). The dilemma: A study of bilingual education policy in Yi minority schools in Liangshan. *International Journal of Bilingual Education and Bilingualism, 16*(4), 451–470.
Döpke, S. (1998). Competing language structures: The acquisition of verb placement by bilingual German–English children. *Journal of Child Language, 25*, 555–584.
Dörnyei, Z. (2003). *Questionnaires in second language research: Construction, administration, and processing*. Lawrence Erlbaum.
Dörnyei, Z. (2007). *Research methods in applied linguistics*. Oxford University Press.

Doughan, D. (2021). *J.R.R Tolkien: A biographical sketch*. Retrieved May 6, 2022, from https://www.tolkiensociety.org/author/biography/

Doyle, A., Champagne, M., & Segalowitz, N. (1978). Some issues on the assessment of linguistic consequences of early bilingualism. In M. Paradis (Ed.), *Aspects of bilingualism* (pp. 13–20). Hornbeam Press.

Drummond, R. (2018). Maybe it's a grime [t]ing: th-stopping among urban British youth. *Language in Society, 47*(2), 171–196.

Duchêne, A., & Heller, M. (Eds.). (2007). *Discourses of endangerment: Ideology and interest in the defense of languages*. Continuum.

Dürmüller, U. (1997). *Changing patterns of multilingualism: From quadrilingual to multilingual Switzerland*. Pro Helvetia.

Dursteler, E. R. (2012). Speaking in tongues: language and communication in the early modern Mediterranean. *Past and Present, 217*, 47–77.

Dustman, C., & van Soest, A. (2002). Language and the earnings of immigrants. *Industrial and Labor Relations Review, 55*, 473–479.

Dutcher, N. (2004). *Expanding educational opportunity in linguistically diverse societies* (2nd ed.). Center for Applied Linguistics.

Eagleton, T. (1991). *Ideology: An introduction*. Verso.

Eberhard, D. M., Simons, G. F. & Fennig, C. D., (Eds.) (2019). Summary by country. *Ethnologue: Languages of the world* (22nd ed.). SIL International. Archived from the original on April 28, 2019.

Eberhard, D. M., Simons, G. F., & Fennig, C. D. (Eds.) (2022). *Ethnologue: Languages of the world* (25th ed.). SIL International. [Online version]. Retrieved from March 29, 2022 https://www.ethnologue.com/guides/how-many-languages

Eckert, P. (2013). Ethics of linguistic research. In R. Podesva & D. Sharma (Eds.), *Research methods in linguistics* (pp. 11–26). Cambridge University Press.

Eckert, P., & McConnell-Ginet, S. (1992). Think practically and act locally: Language and gender as community-based practice. *Annual Review of Anthropology, 21*, 461–490.

Edley, N., & Litosseliti, L. (2010). Contemplating interviews and focus groups. In L. Litosseliti (Ed.), *Research methods in linguistics* (pp. 155–179). Continuum.

Edwards, J. (2001). Multilingualism and multiculturalism in Canada. In G. Extra & D. Gorter (Eds.), *The other languages of Europe* (pp. 315–332). Multilingual Matters.

Edwards, J. (2008). Societal multilingualism: reality, recognition and response. In P. Auer & L. Wei (Eds.), *Handbook of multilingualism and multilingual communication* (pp. 447–467). De Gruyter Mouton.

Edwards, J. R. (2010). *Minority languages and group identity: Cases and categories*. John Benjamins.

Edwards, A. (2016). *English in the Netherlands: Functions, forms and attitudes*. John Benjamins.

EES. (n.d.) TV—Teaser. [Video]. Retrieved July 1, 2017, from www.youtube.com/user/eesyees (video no longer available).

EES feat. Ongoro Nomundu. (2014). *Never over* [music video]. Youtube. Retrieved June 5, 2022, from https://www.youtube.com/watch?v=9EdO4ifRJaY

EES feat. The Hunta. (2008). *Alles Beste* [music video]. Youtube. Retrieved June 5, 2022, from https://www.youtube.com/watch?v=UrhwdU7Knsk

Ellis, R. (2015). *Understanding second language acquisition* (2nd ed.). Oxford University Press.

Ellis, N. C., & Larsen-Freeman, D. (Eds.). (2009). *Language as a complex adaptive system*. Wiley.

Escamilla, K. (2006). Monolingual assessment and emerging bilinguals: A case study in the US. In O. García, T. Skutnabb-Kangas, & M. Torres-Guzmán (Eds.), *Imagining multilingual schools: Languages in education and globalisation* (pp. 184–199). Multilingual Matters.

Evans, D. (2014). The identities of language. In D. Evans (Ed.), *Language and identity: Discourse in the world* (pp. 15–35). Bloomsbury.

Faber, D., & Lauridsen, K. (1991). The compilation of a Danish-English-French corpus in contract law. English Computer Corpora. *Selected Papers and Research Guide* (pp. 235–243).

Feagin, C. (2002). Entering the community: Fieldwork. In J. K. Chambers, P. Trudgill, & N. Schilling-Estes (Eds.), *The handbook of language variation and change* (pp. 20–39). Blackwell Publishers.

References

Federal Statistical Office. (2022). *Languages*. Retrieved January 29, 2021, from https://www.bfs.admin.ch/bfs/en/home/statistics/population/languages-religions/languages.html

Ferguson, C. A. (1959). Diglossia. *Word, 15*(2), 325–340.

Ferjan Ramírez, N., Ramírez, R. R., Clarke, M., Taulu, S., & Kuhl, P. K. (2017). Speech discrimination in 11-month-old bilingual and monolingual infants: A magnetoencephalography study. *Developmental Science, 20*(1), e12427.

Fishman, J. A. (1971). National languages and languages of wider communication in the developing nations. In W. H. Whiteley (Ed.), *Language use and social change: Problems of multilingualism with special reference to Eastern Africa* (pp. 27–56). Oxford University Press for the International African Institute.

Fishman, J. A. (1989). *Language and ethnicity in minority sociolinguistic perspective*. Multilingual Matters.

Flynn, S., Foley, C., & Vinnitskaya, I. (2004). The cumulative-enhancement model for language acquisition: Comparing adults' and children's patterns of development in first, second and third language acquisition of relative clauses. *International Journal of Multilingualism, 1*(1), 3–16.

Foucault, M. (1970). The archeology of knowledge. *Social Science Information, 9*(1), 175–185.

Foucault, M. (1980). *Power/Knowledge*. Penguin.

FPI. (2021). *Global music report 2021*. Retrieved from https://www.ifpi.org/ifpi-issues-annual-global-music-report-2021/

Francis, N. (2012). *Bilingual competence and bilingual proficiency in child development*. MIT Press.

Freywald, U., Cornips, L., Ganuza, N., Nistov, I., & Opsahl, T. (2015). Beyond verb second—a matter of novel information-structural effects? Evidence from Norwegian, Swedish, German and Dutch. In J. Nortier & B. A. Svendsen (Eds.), *Language, youth and identity in the 21st century: Linguistic practices across urban spaces* (pp. 73–92). Cambridge University Press.

Gabryś-Barker, D. (2019). Lecture 2: Applied linguistics and multilingualism. In D. Singleton & L. Aronin (Eds.), *Twelve lectures on multilingualism* (pp. 35–64). Multilingual Matters.

García, O., Ibarra Johnson, S., & Seltzer, K. (2016). *The translanguaging classroom*. Caslon Publishing.

García Mayo, M. (2000). *English for specific purposes: Discourse analysis and course design*. Servicio Editorial de la Universidad del País Vasco.

García, O., & Wei, L. (2014). *Translanguaging: Language, bilingualism and education*. Palgrave Pivot.

García, O., & Wei, L. (2017). Bilingual education. In O. García, A. M. Y. Lin, & S. May (Eds.), *Encyclopedia of language and education, 5* (3rd ed.). Springer.

Garcia-Sierra, A., Ramírez-Esparza, N., & Kuhl, P. K. (2016). Relationships between quantity of language input and brain responses in bilingual and monolingual infants. *International Journal of Psychophysiology, 110*, 1–17.

Garcia-Sierra, A., Rivera-Gaxiola, M., Percaccio, C. R., Conboy, B. T., Romo, H., Klarman, L., & Kuhl, P. K. (2011). Bilingual language learning: An ERP study relating early brain responses to speech, language input, and later word production. *Journal of Phonetics, 39*(4), 546–557. https://doi.org/10.1016/j.wocn.2011.07.002

Gardner-Chloros, P. (2009a). *Code-switching*. Cambridge University Press.

Gardner-Chloros, P. (2009b). Sociolinguistic factors in code-switching. In B. Bullock & A. Toribio (Eds.), *The Cambridge handbook of linguistic code-switching* (pp. 97–113). Cambridge University Press. https://doi.org/10.1017/CBO9780511576331.007

Gardner-Chloros, P., & Secova, M. (2018). Grammatical change in Paris French: in situ question words in embedded contexts. *Journal of French Language Studies, 28*(2), 181–207.

Gass, S. M., & Selinker, L. (2008). *Second language acquisition: An introductory course* (3rd ed.). Routledge.

Gathercole, V. C. M. (1997). The linguistic mass/count noun distinction as an indicator of referent categorization in monolingual and bilingual children. *Child Development, 68*, 832–842.

Gathercole, V. C. M., & Hoff, E. (2007). Input and the acquisition of language: Three questions. In E. Hoff & M. Shatz (Eds.), *Blackwell handbook of language development* (pp. 107–127). Blackwell.

Gathercole, V. C. M., & Thomas, E. M. (2009). Bilingual first-language development: Dominant language takeover, threatened minority language take-up. *Bilingualism: Language and Cognition, 12*(2), 213–237.

Gawlitzek-Maiwald, I., & Tracy, R. (1996). Bilingual bootstrapping. *Linguistics, 34*(5), 901–926.
Gee, J. P. (2001). Identity as an analytic lens for research in education. *Review of Research in Education, 25*, 99–125.
Genesee, F. (2003). *Educating second language children: The whole child, the whole curriculum, the whole community*. Cambridge University Press.
Genesee, F., Boivin, I., & Nicoladis, E. (1996). Talking with strangers: A study of bilingual children's communicative competence. *Applied Psycholinguistics, 17*, 427–442. https://doi.org/10.1017/S0142716400008183
Genesee, F., Paradis, J., & Crago, M. B. (2008). Dual language development & disorders. In *A handbook on bilingualism & second language learning* (3rd ed.).
Gerfer, A. (2022). Authentic crossing? Jamaican Creole in African dancehall. In J. T. Farquharson, A. Hollington, & B. Jones (Eds.), *Contact languages and music*. The University of the West Indies Press.
Gibson, A., & Bell, A. (2012). Popular music singing as referee design. In J. M. Hernández-Campoy & J. A. Cutillas-Espinosa (Eds.), *Style shifting in public: New perspectives on stylistic variation* (pp. 139–164). John Benjamins.
Giles, H. (1973). Accent mobility: A model and some data. *Anthropological Linguistics, 15*, 87–105.
Giles, H., & Ogay, T. (2007). Communication accommodation theory. In B. B. Whaley & W. Samter (Eds.), *Explaining communication: Contemporary theories and exemplars* (pp. 293–310). Lawrence Erlbaum.
Giles, H., & Smith, P. (1979). Accommodation theory: Optimal levels of convergence. In H. Giles & R. St Clair (Eds.), *Language and social psychology*. Blackwell.
Gilquin, G., & Granger, S. (2011). From EFL to ESL: Evidence from the International Corpus of Learner English. In J. Mukherjee & M. Hundt (Eds.), *Exploring second-language varieties of English and learner Englishes: Bridging a paradigm gap* (pp. 55–78). John Benjamins.
Gouldner, A. (1976). *The dialectic of ideology and technology*. The Seabury Press.
Gramling, D. (2009). The new cosmopolitan monolingualism: On linguistic citizenship in twenty-first century Germany. *Die Unterrichtspraxis/Teaching German, 42*, 130–140.
Gramling, D. (2016). *The invention of monolingualism*. Bloomsbury.
Greenberg, J. H. (1956). The measurement of linguistic diversity. *Language, 32*(1), 109–115.
Greenberg, J. (1966). *Language universals*. Mouton.
Greenblatt, S. J. & Morrill, J. S. (2022, September 3). *Elizabeth I*. Encyclopedia Britannica. Retrieved October 31, 2022, from https://www.britannica.com/biography/Elizabeth-I
Gries, S. T. (2021). *Statistics for linguistics with R*. De Gruyter Mouton.
Grosjean, F. (1989). Neurolinguists, beware! The bilingual is not two monolinguals in one person. *Brain and Language, 36*, 3–15.
Grosjean, F. (1998). Studying bilinguals: Methodological and conceptual issues. *Bilingualism: Language and Cognition, 1*(2), 131–149.
Grosjean, F. (2010). *Bilingual: Life and reality*. Harvard University Press.
Grosjean, F. (2020). *How many are we? On the difficulty of counting people who are bilingual*. Psychology Today. Retrieved November 4, 2022, from https://www.psychologytoday.com/intl/blog/life-bilingual/201209/how-many-are-we
Grosjean, F. (2021). Bilingualism in the family. In *Life as a bilingual: Knowing and using two or more languages* (pp. 115–140). Cambridge University Press. https://doi.org/10.1017/9781108975490.007
Grosjean, F., & Li, P. (2013). *The psycholinguistics of bilingualism*. Wiley-Blackwell.
Gumperz, J. J. (1982). *Discourse strategies*. Cambridge University Press.
Gupta, A. F. (1994). *The step-tongue. Children's English in Singapore*. Multilingual Matters.
Gupta, A. F. (1998). The situation of English in Singapore. In J. A. Foley, T. Kandiah, Z. Bao, A. F. Gupta, L. Alsagoff, C. L. Ho, L. Wee, I. S. Talib, & W. Bokhorst-Heng (Eds.), *English in new cultural contexts: Reflections from Singapore* (pp. 106–126). Oxford University Press.
Gupta, A. F. (2000). Bilingualism in the cosmopolis. *International Journal of the Sociology of Language, 143*, 107–119.
Hackert, S. (2012). *The emergence of the English native speaker. A chapter in nineteenth-century linguistic thought*. Mouton de Gruyter.

References

Haeri, N. (2000). Form and ideology: Arabic sociolinguistics and beyond. *Annual Review of Anthropology, 29*(6), 1–87.
Hallenberg, B., Dettmar, R., & Aring, J. (2018). *Migranten, Meinungen, Milieus*. vhw-Migrantenmilieu-Survey. Retrieved April 18, 2021, from https://www.vhw.de/fileadmin/user_upload/07_presse/PDFs/ab_2015/vhw_Migrantenmilieu-Survey_2018.pdf
Hamers, J. F., & Blanc, M. H. A. (1989). *Biliguality and bilingualism*. Cambridge University Press.
Hamers, J. F., & Blanc, M. H. A. (2000). *Biliguality and bilingualism* (2nd ed.). Cambridge University Press.
Han, H. (2013). Individual grassroots multilingualism in Africa town in Guangzhou: The role of states in globalization. *International Multilingual Research Journal, 7*(1), 83–97.
Han, H. (2017). Trade migration and language. In A. Suresh Canagarajah (Ed.), *The Routledge handbook of migration and language* (pp. 258–274). Routledge.
Harrington, K. (2018). *The role of corpus linguistics in the ethnography of a closed community: Survival communication*. Routledge.
Hauser-Grüdl, N., Guerra, L. A., Witzmann, F., Leray, E., & Müller, N. (2010). Cross-linguistic influence in bilingual children: Can input frequency account for it? *Lingua, 120*, 2638–2650.
Heller, M. (2007). Bilingualism as ideology and practice. In M. Heller (Ed.), *Bilingualism: A social approach* (pp. 1–22). Palgrave Macmillan.
Herbert, R. K. (1990). The sociohistory of clicks in Southern Bantu. *Anthropological Linguistics, 32*(3/4), 295–315.
Hervé, C., & Serratrice, L. (2018). The development of determiners in the context of French-English bilingualism: a study of cross-linguistic influence. *Journal of Child Language, 45*(3), 767–787.
Heyd, T., & Mair, C. (2014). From vernacular to digital ethnolinguistic repertoire: The case of Nigerian Pidgin. In V. Lacoste, J. Leimgruber, & T. Breyer (Eds.), *Indexing authenticity. Sociolinguistic perspectives* (pp. 242–266). de Gruyter.
Hickey, R. (Ed.). (2012). *Standards of English: Codified varieties around the world*. Cambridge University Press.
Hide. (1996). *Beauty & Stupid* [music video]. YouTube. Retrieved July 6, 2022, from https://www.youtube.com/watch?v=a5sqDJGkY6Y
Higby, E., Kim, J., & Obler, L. K. (2013). Multilingualism in the brain. *Annual Review of Applied Linguistics, 33*, 68–101.
Hinton, L. (2001). Language revitalization: An overview. In L. Hinton & K. Hale (Eds.), *The Green book of language revitalization in practice* (pp. 1–18). Brill.
Hinton, L. & Hale, K. (Eds.) (2001). *The Green book of language revitalization in practice*. Brill.
Hinton, L., Huss, L., & Roche, G. (2018). *The Routledge handbook of language revitalization*. Routledge.
Hoff, E., Core, C., Place, S., Rumiche, R., Señor, M., & Parra, M. (2012). Dual language exposure and early bilingual development. *Journal of Child Language, 39*, 1–27. https://doi.org/10.1017/S0305000910000759
Hoff, E., Rumiche, R., Burridge, A., Ribot, K. M., & Welsh, S. N. (2014). Expressive vocabulary development in children from bilingual and monolingual homes: A longitudinal study from two to four years. *Early Childhood Research Quarterly, 29*(4), 433–444.
Holborow, M. (2013). Applied linguistics in the neoliberal university: Ideological keywords and social agency. *Applied Linguistics Review, 4*(2), 229–257.
Holm, J. (2000). *An introduction to Pidgins and Creoles*. Cambridge University Press.
Horner, K., & Weber, J.-J. (2018a). Introduction. In K. Horner & J.-J. Weber (Eds.), *Introducing multilingualism. A social approach* (2nd ed., pp. 3–13). Routledge.
Horner, K., & Weber, J.-J. (Eds.). (2018b). *Introducing multilingualism. A social approach*. Routledge.
House, J. (1999). Misunderstanding in intercultural communication: Interactions in English as a lingua franca and the myth of mutual intelligibility. In C. Gnutzmann (Ed.), *Teaching and learning English as a global language* (pp. 73–89). Stauffenburg.
House, J. (2003). English as a lingua franca: a threat to multilingualism? *Journal of Sociolinguistics, 7*(4), 556–578.

Howard, E. R., Lindholm-Leary, K., Rogers, D., Olague, N., Medina, J., Kennedy, B., Sugarman, J., & Christiane, D. (2018). *Guiding principles for dual language education* (3rd ed.). Center for Applied Linguistics.

Huang, Y.-T., & Su, S.-F. (2018). Motives for Instagram use and topics of interest among young adults. *Future Internet, 10*(8), 77. https://doi.org/10.3390/fi10080077

Huber, M., Nissel, M., & Puga, K. (2016). *Old Bailey Corpus 2.0*. Retrieved June 29, 2022, from hdl:11858/00-246C-0000-0023-8CFB-2

Hulk, A. C. J., & Müller, N. (2000). Bilingual first language acquisition at the interface between syntax and pragmatics. *Bilingualism: Language and Cognition, 3*, 227–244.

Hülmbauer, C., Böhringer, H., & Seidlhofer, B. (2008). Introducing English as a lingua franca (ELF): Precursor and partner in intercultural communication. *Synergies Europe, 3*, 25–36.

Hulstijn, J. (2012). The construct of language proficiency in the study of bilingualism from a cognitive perspective. *Bilingualism: Language and Cognition, 15*(2), 422–433.

Hymes, D. (1968). Linguistic problems in defining the concept of tribe. In J. Helm (Ed.), *Essays on the problem of tribe* (pp. 23–48). Washington Press for the American Ethnological Society.

IBM Corp. (2021). *IBM SPSS Statistics for Windows, Version 28.0*. IBM Corp.

Ibrahim, N. (2015). *A few more myths about speakers of multiple languages*. British Council. Retrieved April 15, 2022, from https://www.britishcouncil.org/voices-magazine/few-more-myths-about-speakers-multiple-languages

IFPI. (2021). Global music report 2021. Retrieved from https://www.ifpi.org/ifpi-issues-annual-global-music-report-2021/

Ilanguages. (2018). Retrieved February 2, 2022, from http://ilanguages.org/bilingual.php

Ionin, T. (2012). Formal theory-based methodologies. In A. Mackey & S. M. Gass (Eds.), *Research methods in second language acquisition: A practical guide* (pp. 30–52). Wiley-Blackwell.

Jakobsen, R. (1941). *Child language, aphasia, and universals of language*. Mouton.

Jansen, L. (2018). Britpop is a thing, damn it: On British attitudes toward American English and an Americanized singing style. In V. Werner (Ed.), *The language of pop culture* (pp. 116–135). Routledge.

Jansen, L., & Gerfer, A. (2022). The Arctic monkeys live at the Royal Albert Hall: Investigating Turner's "lounge singer shimmer". In V. Werner & C. Schubert (Eds.), *Stylistic approaches to pop culture*. Routledge.

Jansen, L., & Westphal, M. (2017). Rihanna works her multivocal pop persona: A morpho–syntactic and accent analysis of Rihanna's singing style. *English Today, 33*(2), 46–55.

Jansen, L., & Westphal, M. (2022). Caribbean identity in pop music: Rihanna's and Nicki Minaj's multivocal pop personas. In A. Hollington, J. T. Farquharson, & B. Jones (Eds.), *Contact languages and music*. UWI Press.

Jaworski, A., & Thurlow, C. (2010). *Semiotic landscapes. Language, image, space*. Continuum.

Jenkins, J. (2000). *The phonology of English as an international language*. Oxford University Press.

Jenkins, J. (2007). *English as a lingua franca: Attitude and identity*. Oxford University Press.

Jia, G., & Fuse, A. (2007). Acquisition of English grammatical morphology by native Mandarin speaking children and adolescents: Age-related differences. *Journal of Speech, Language and Hearing Research, 50*, 1280–1299.

John, E. (2015). Zweisprachige Songs: Sprachmuster transkultureller Inszenierungen. In D. Helms & T. Phleps (Eds.), *Speaking in tongues* (pp. 157–176). transcript-Verlag.

Jonsson, E. (2015). *Conversational writing: A multidimensional study of synchronous and supersynchronous computer-mediated communication*. Peter Lang.

Joseph, B. (2008). The editor's department: Last scene of all.... *Language, 84*(4), 686–690.

Kachru, B. B. (1985). Standards, codification and sociolinguistic realism: The English language in the outer circle. In R. Quirk & H. G. Widdowson (Eds.), *English in the world. Teaching and learning the language and literatures* (pp. 11–30). Cambridge University Press for The British Council.

Kallen, J. L. (2009). Tourism and representation in the Irish linguistic landscape. In E. Shohamy & D. Gorter (Eds.), *Linguistic landscape: Expanding the scenery* (pp. 270–283). Routledge.

Kallen, J. L. (2010). Changing landscapes: Language, space and policy in the Dublin linguistic landscape. In A. Jaworski & C. Thurlow (Eds.), *Semiotic landscapes. Language, image, space* (pp. 41–58). Continuum.

References

Kehoe, M. M. (2002). Developing vowel systems as a window to bilingual phonology. *International Journal of Bilingualism, 6*, 315–334.

Kemp, C. (2007). Strategic processing in grammar learning: Do multilinguals use more strategies? *International Journal of Multilingualism, 4*(4), 241–261.

Kennedy, C., & Bolitho, R. (1984). *English for specific purposes*. Macmillan.

Kießling, R. (2005). "Bàk mwà mè dó"—Camfranglais in Cameroon. *Lingua Posnaniensis, 47*, 87–107.

Kießling, R. (2021). Grammatical hybridity in Camfranglais? In R. Mesthrie, E. Hurst-Harosh, & H. Brookes (Eds.), *Youth language practices and urban language contact in Africa* (pp. 115–140). Cambridge University Press.

Kim, D. (2008). *English for occupational purposes. One language?* Continuum.

Kirchner, R., & Fox, S. (2021). Multicultural London English and its speakers: a corpus-informed discourse study of standard language ideology and social stereotypes. *Journal of Multilingual and Multicultural Development, 42*(9), 792–810. https://doi.org/10.1080/01434632.2019.1666856

Kortmann, B. (2021). Reflecting on the quantitative turn in linguistics. *Linguistics, 59*(5), 1207–1226.

Kosonen, K. (2005). Education in local languages: policy and practice in Southeast Asia. In *First languages first: Community-based literacy programmes for minority language contexts in Asia* (pp. 96–134). UNESCO.

Kotsinas, U. B. (2001). Pidginization, creolization and creoloids in Stockholm, Sweden. In N. Smith & T. Veenstra (Eds.), *Creolization and contact* (pp. 127–155). John Benjamins.

Koyfman, S. (2020). *When music is multilingual: 10 artists who perform in other languages*. Babbel Magazine. Retrieved May 12, 2022, from https://www.babbel.com/en/magazine/10-artists-who-perform-in-other-languages

Kretzschmar, W. A., Jr. (2015). *Language and complex systems*. Cambridge University Press.

Krug, M., & Schlüter, J. (Eds.). (2013). *Research methods in language variation and change*. Cambridge University Press.

Kulick, D. (1992). Anger, gender, language shift and the politics of revelation in a Papua New Guinean village. *Pragmatics, 2*(3), 281–296.

Kupisch, T. (2008). Dominance, mixing and cross-linguistic influence: On their relation in bilingual development. In P. Guijarro-Fuentes, P. Larrañaga, & J. Clibbens (Eds.), *First language acquisition of morphology and syntax: Perspectives across languages and learners* (pp. 209–234).

Labov, W. (1963). The social motivation of a sound change. *Word, 19*, 273–309.

Labov, W. (1968). The reflection of social processes in linguistic structures. In J. A. Fishman (Ed.), *Readings in the sociology of language* (pp. 240–251). Mouton.

Labov, W. (1982). Building on empirical foundations. In W. Lehmann & Y. Malkiel (Eds.), *Perspectives on historical linguistics* (pp. 17–92). John Benjamins.

Labov, W. (1984). Field methods of the project on linguistic change and variation. In J. Baugh & J. Sherzer (Eds.), *Language in use. Readings in sociolinguistics* (pp. 28–53). Prentice-Hall.

Labov, W. (2006). *The social stratification of English in New York city* (2nd ed.). Cambridge University Press.

Lado, R. (1957). *Linguistics across cultures*. University of Michigan Press.

Lambert, W. E., Hodgson, R. C., Gardner, R. C., & Fillenbaum, S. (1960). Evaluational reactions to spoken languages. *The Journal of Abnormal and Social Psychology, 60*(1), 44–51. https://doi.org/10.1037/h0044430

Lambert, W. E., & Tucker, G. R. (1972). *Bilingual education of children: The St. Lambert experiment*. Newbury House.

Landry, R., & Bourhis, R. Y. (1997). Linguistic landscape and ethnolinguistic vitality: An empirical study. *Journal of Language and Social Psychology, 16*(1), 23–49.

Lange, C., & Leuckert, S. (2020). *Corpus linguistics for World Englishes*. Routledge.

Larrañaga, P., & Guijarro-Fuentes, P. (2012). Clitics in L1 bilingual acquisition. *First Language, 32*, 151–175.

Larsson, T., Egbert, J., & Biber, D. (2022). On the status of statistical reporting versus linguistic description in corpus linguistics: a ten-year perspective. *Corpora, 17*(1), 137–157.

Lasagabaster, D. (2015). Language policy and language choice at European Universities: Is there really a 'choice'? *International Journal of Applied Linguistics, 3*(2), 255–276.

Le Page, R. B. (1968). Problems of description in multilingual communities. *TPS*, 189–212.
Le Page, R. B. (1975). Polarizing factors: Political, social, economic, operating on the individual's choice of identity through language use in British Honduras. In J. G. Savard & R. Vigneault (Eds.), *Les États Multilingues* (pp. 537–551). Laval University Press.
Le Page, R. B. (1978). Projection, focussing, diffusion. Society for Caribbean Linguistics Occasional Paper, 9.
Le Page, R. B., Christie, P., Jurdant, B., Weekes, A., & Tabouret-Keller, A. (1974). Further report on the sociolinguistic survey of multilingual communities. *Language in Society, 3*, 1–32.
Le Page, R. B., & Tabouret-Keller, A. (1985). *Acts of identity*. Cambridge University Press.
Lee, C. (2016). *Multilingualism online*. Routledge.
Lee, J. W. (2018). *The politics of translingualism—After Englishes*. Routledge.
Leeman, J. (2018). It's all about English: The interplay of monolingual ideologies, language policies and the U.S. census bureau's statistics on multilingualism. *International Journal of the Sociology of Language, 252*, 21–43.
Leimgruber, J. R. E. (2013). *Singapore English. Structure, variation, and usage*. Cambridge University Press.
Leimgruber, J. R. E., Siemund, P., & Terassa, L. (2018). Singaporean students' language repertoires and attitudes revisited. *World Englishes, 37*(2), 282–306.
Leslau, W. (1945). The influence of cushitic on the semitic languages of Ethiopia: A problem of substratum. *Word, 1*, 59–82.
Leslau, W. (1952). The influence of Sidamo on the Ethiopic languages of the Gurage. *Language, 28*, 63–81.
Levon, E. (2013). Ethnographic fieldwork. In C. Mallison, B. Childs, & G. Van Herk (Eds.), *Data collection in sociolinguistics* (2nd ed., pp. 71–79). Routledge.
Levshina, N. (2015). *How to do linguistics with R*. John Benjamins.
Lieberson, S. (1964). An extension of Greenberg's linguistic diversity measures. *Language, 40*(4), 526–531.
Lightbown, P., & Spada, N. (2007). *How languages are learned*. Oxford University Press.
Lightfoot, D. (2010). Language acquisition and language change. *WIREs Cognitive Science, 1*, 677–684. https://doi.org/10.1002/wcs.39
Lim, L. (Ed.). (2004). *Singapore English: A grammatical description*. John Benjamins.
Lin, Z., & Lei, L. (2020). The research trends of multilingualism in applied linguistics and education (2000–2019): A bibliometric analysis. *Sustainability, 12*(15), 6058. https://doi.org/10.3390/su12156058
Litosseliti, L. (2018). Critical perspectives on using interviews and focus groups. In *Research methods in linguistics* (2nd ed., pp. 195–226). Bloomsbury Academic. https://doi.org/10.5040/9781350043466.ch-009
Lleó, C. (2002). The role of markedness in the acquisition of complex prosodic structures by German-Spanish bilinguals. *International Journal of Bilingualism, 6*, 291–314.
Lucko, P. (2003). Is English a "killer language"? In P. Lucko, L. Peter, & H.-G. Wolf (Eds.), *Studies in African varieties of English* (pp. 151–165). Peter Lang.
Maar, R. (2021). *5 myths surrounding multilingualism*. Medium. Retrieved August 18, 2022, from https://roxanemaar.medium.com/5-myths-surrounding-multilingualism-5fcea034f01a
Mackey, W. F. (2005). Multilingual cities. In U. Ammon, N. Dittmar, K. J. Mattheier, & P. Trudgill (Eds.), *Sociolinguistics. An international handbook of the science of language and society* (Vol. 2/1, pp. 1304–1312). De Gruyter.
Macnamara, J. (1967). The bilingual's linguistic performance—A psychological overview. *Journal of Social Issues, XXIII*(2), 58–77.
MacSwan, J. (2019). Sociolinguistic and linguistic foundations of codeswitching research. In J. MacSwan & C. J. Faltis (Eds.), *Codeswitching in the classroom: Critical perspectives on teaching, learning, policy, and ideology* (1st ed., pp. 3–38). Routledge.
Maher, J. C. (2017). *Multilingualism. A very short introduction*. Oxford University Press.
Mair, C. (2002). The continuing spread of English: Anglo-American conspiracy or global grassroots movement? In D. J. Allerton, P. Skandera, & C. Tschichold (Eds.), *Perspectives on English as a world language* (pp. 159–169). Schwabe.

References

Mandus, A. (2016). *Light and shadow in Namibia. Everyday life in a dream country*. Palmato Publishing.

Maneva, B. (2004). 'Maman, je suis polyglotte!': A case study of multilingual language acquisition from 0 to 5 years. *International Journal of Multilingualism, 1*(2), 109–122.

Mansel, P. (2014). Cities of the Levant—the past for the future? *Asian Affairs, 45*(2), 220–242.

Marchman, V. A., Fernald, A., & Hurtado, N. (2010). How vocabulary size in two languages relates to efficiency in spoken word recognition by young Spanish–English bilinguals. *Journal of Child Language, 37*(4), 817–840. https://doi.org/10.1017/S0305000909990055

Marchman, V. A., Martínez-Sussman, C., & Dale, P. S. (2004). The language-specific nature of grammatical development: Evidence from bilingual language learners. *Developmental Science, 7*, 212–224.

Martin, E. (2007). "Frenglish" for sale: Multilingual discourses for addressing today's global consumer. *World Englishes, 26*, 170–190. https://doi.org/10.1111/j.1467-971X.2007.00500

Mason, J. (2002). Qualitative interviewing. In J. Mason (Ed.), *Qualitative researching* (2nd ed., pp. 62–83). Sage Publications.

May, S. (2001). *Language and minority rights: Ethnicity, nationalism, and the politics of language*. Pearson Education.

May, S. (2005). Language rights: Moving the debate forward. *Journal of Sociolinguistics, 9*(3), 319–347.

McArthur, T. (1998). *The English languages*. Cambridge University Press.

McAuley, D., & Carruthers, J. (2020). Investigating perceptions of Banlieue French: Problematising theory and methods. In C. Mar-Molina (Ed.), *Researching language in superdiverse contexts* (pp. 159–182). Multilingual Matters.

McEnery, T., & Xiao, R. (2007). Parallel and comparable corpora: What is happening? In G. M. Anderman & M. Rogers (Eds.), *Incorporating corpora: The linguist and the translator* (pp. 18–31). Multilingual Matters.

McLaughlin, B. (1978). *Second language acquisition in childhood*. Lawrence Erlbaum Associates.

McMahon, A. M. S. (1994). *Understanding language change*. Cambridge University Press.

McRae, K. D. (1983). *Conflict and compromise in multilingual societies*. Wilfried Laurier University Press.

Mehisto, P. (2012). *Excellence in bilingual education: a guide for school principals*. Cambridge University Press.

Meierkord, C. (2012). *Interactions across Englishes. Linguistic choices in local and international contact situations*. Cambridge University Press.

Meisel, J. M. (1989). Early differentiation of languages in bilingual children. In K. Hyltenstam & L. K. Obler (Eds.), *Bilingualism across the lifespan: Aspects of acquisition, maturity and loss* (pp. 13–40). Cambridge University Press.

Meisel, J. M. (1990). Grammatical development in the simultaneous acquisition of two first languages. In J. M. Meisel (Ed.), *Two first languages* (pp. 5–22). De Gruyter Mouton.

Meisel, J. M. (2001). The simultaneous acquisition of two first languages: Early differentiation and subsequent development of grammars. In J. Cenoz & F. Genesee (Eds.), *Trends in bilingual acquisition* (pp. 11–41). John Benjamins.

Meisel, J. M. (2004). The bilingual child. In T. K. Bhatia & W. C. Ritchie (Eds.), *The handbook of bilingualism* (pp. 91–113). Blackwell.

Meisel, J. M. (2011). *First and second language acquisition: Parallels and differences*. Cambridge University Press.

Meisel, J. M. (2019). *Bilingual children: A guide for parents*. Cambridge University Press.

Merriam-Webster. (1961). *Webster's third new international dictionary of the English language, unabridged*.

Mesthrie, R., & Bhatt, R. M. (2008). *World Englishes: The study of new varieties*. Cambridge University Press.

Metropole Ruhr. (n.d.) *Statistik Analysen*. Retrieved May 13, 2018, from http://www.metropoleruhr.de/regionalverband-ruhr/statistik-analysen/statistik-trends/bevoelkerung/nationalitaeten.html

Meyerhoff, M., Schleef, E., & MacKenzie, L. (2015). *Doing sociolinguistics—A practical guide to data collection and analysis*. Routledge.

Milroy, L. (1980). *Language and social networks*. University Perk Press.
Milroy, L. (1987). *Observing and analysing natural language. A critical account of sociolinguistic method*. Blackwell.
Mohanty, A. K. (2019). *The multilingual reality: Living with languages*. Multilingual Matters.
Mohanty, A., & Saikia, J. (2008). Bilingualism and intergroup relationship in tribal and non-tribal contact situations. In G. Zheng, K. Leung, & J. G. Adair (Eds.), *Perspectives and progress in contemporary cross-cultural psychology* (pp. 163–172). International Association for Cross Cultural Psychology.
Morrissey, F. A. (2008). Liverpool to Louisiana in one lyrical line: Style choice in British rock, pop and folk singing. In M. A. Locher & J. Strässler (Eds.), *Standards and norms in the English language* (pp. 193–216). Mouton de Gruyter.
Mougeon, R., & Rehner, K. (2017). The influence of classroom input and community exposure on the learning of variable grammar. *Bilingualism: Language and Cognition, 20*, 21–22.
Mufwene, S. S. (2001). *The ecology of language evolution*. Cambridge University Press.
Müller, N., & Hulk, A. C. J. (2001). Crosslinguistic influence in bilingual language acquisition: Italian and French as recipient languages. *Bilingualism: Language and Cognition, 4*, 1–21.
Musixmatch. (n.d.) *Beauty & stupid lyrics*. Retrieved July 6, 2022, from https://www.musixmatch.com/fr/paroles/hide-3/Beauty-Stupid
Myers-Scotton, C. (2002). *Contact linguistics*. Cambridge University Press.
Myhill, J. (1999). Identity, territoriality and minority language survival. *Journal of Multilingual and Multicultural Development, 20*(1), 34–50.
Nchare, A. L. (2009). *The morphosyntax of Camfranglais and the matrix language frame hypothesis*. New York University.
Nelson, G., Wallis, S. & Aarts, B. (2002). Exploring natural language: Working with the British component of the International Corpus of English. .
Newton, G. (1996). *Luxembourg and Lëtzebuergesch: Language and communication at the crossroads of Europe*. Clarendon Press.
Nicoladis, E. (2003). Cross-linguistic transfer in deverbal compounds of preschool bilingual children. *Bilingualism: Language and Cognition, 6*, 17–31.
Nicoladis, E. (2006). Cross-linguistic transfer in adjective–noun strings by preschool bilingual children. *Bilingualism: Language and Cognition, 9*, 15–32.
Nicoladis, E., Song, J., & Marentette, P. (2012). Do young bilinguals acquire past tense morphology like monolinguals, only later? Evidence from French-English and Chinese-English bilinguals. *Applied Psycholinguistics, 33*(3), 457–479.
Niedzielski, N., & Giles, H. (2008). Linguistic accommodation. In H. Goebl, P. H. Nelde, Z. Starý, & W. Wölck (Eds.), *1. Halbband: Ein internationales Handbuch zeitgenössischer Forschung* (pp. 332–342). De Gruyter Mouton.
O'Rourke, B., & Brennan, S. C. (2019). Regimenting the Gaeltacht: Authenticity, anonymity, and expectation in contemporary Ireland. *Language & Communication, 66*, 20–28.
Odlin, T. (1989). *Language transfer: Cross-linguistic influence in language learning*. Cambridge University Press.
Odlin, T. (2016). Was there really ever a contrastive analysis hypothesis? In R. Alonso Alonso (Ed.), *Crosslinguistic influence in second language acquisition* (pp. 1–23). Multilingual Matters.
Office for National Statistics. (2020). Population of the UK by country of birth and nationality: 2020. Retrieved March 10, 2022, from https://www.ons.gov.uk/peoplepopulationandcommunity/populationandmigration/internationalmigration/bulletins/ukpopulationbycountryofbirthandnationality/2020
Oiarzabal, P. J. (2012). Diaspora Basques and online social networks: An analysis of users of Basque institutional diaspora groups on Facebook. *Journal of Ethnic and Migration Studies, 38*(9), 1469–1485. https://doi.org/10.1080/1369183X.2012.698216
Oppenheim, A. N. (1992). *Questionnaire design, interviewing and attitude measurement*. Pinter.
Opsahl, T., & Nistov, I. (2010). On some structural aspects of Norwegian spoken among adolescents in multilingual settings in Oslo. In P. Quist & B. A. Svendsen (Eds.), *Multilingual urban Scandinavia. New linguistic practices* (pp. 49–63). Multilingual Matters.
Ortega, L. (2009). *Understanding second language acquisition*. Hodder Education.

References

Ortega, L. (2014). Ways forward for a bi/multilingual turn in SLA. In S. May (Ed.), *The multilingual turn: Implications for SLA, TESOL, and bilingual education* (pp. 32–53). Routledge.
Otsuji, E., & Pennycook, A. (2010). Metrolingualism: Fixity, fluidity and language in flux. *International Journal of Multilingualism, 7*, 240–254.
Oxford Lexico. (2022). *Bilingualism*. Retrieved October 18, 2022, from https://www.lexico.com/definition/bilingualism
Ozóg, C., & Marsh, D. (2009). CLIL: An interview with Professor David Marsh. *International House Journal of Education and Development, 26*.
Pakenham, T. (1991). *The scramble for Africa: White man's conquest of the dark continent from 1876 to 1912*. Avon Books.
Paradis, J. (2001). Do bilingual two-year-olds have separate phonological systems? *International Journal of Bilingualism, 5*, 19–38.
Paradis, J. (2007). Early bilingual and multilingual acquisition. In P. Auer & L. Wei (Eds.), *Handbook of multilingualism and multilingual communication* (pp. 15–44). Mouton de Gruyter.
Paradis, J. (2011). Individual differences in child English second language acquisition: Comparing child-internal and child-external factors. *Linguistic Approaches to Bilingualism, 1*(3), 213–237.
Paradis, J. (2017). Parent report data on input and experience reliably predict bilingual development and this is not trivial. *Bilingualism: Language and Cognition, 20*, 27–28.
Paradis, J., & Genesee, F. (1996). Syntactic acquisition in bilingual children: Autonomous or interdependent? *Studies in Second Language Acquisition, 18*, 1–25.
Paradis, J., Genesee, F., & Crago, M. (2010). *Dual language development & disorders: A handbook on bilingualism & second language learning* (2nd ed.). Paul Brookes.
Paradis, J., & Navarro, S. (2003). Subject realization and crosslinguistic interference in the bilingual acquisition of Spanish and English: What is the role of the input? *Journal of Child Language, 30*(2), 371–393.
Parsons, T. (1959). The social structure of the family. In R. N. Anshen (Ed.), *The family: Its functions and destiny* (pp. 173–201). Harper and Row.
Patsko, L. (2013, November 21). *What is the Lingua Franca core?* ELF Pronunciation. Retrieved June 27, 2022, from https://elfpron.wordpress.com/2013/11/21/what-is-the-lfc/
Pavlenko, A. (2002). 'We have room but for one language here': Language and national identity at the turn of the twentieth century. *Multilingua, 21*, 163–196.
Pavlenko, A., & Blackledge, A. (2004). Introduction. New theoretical approaches to the study of negotiation of identities in multilingual contexts. In A. Pavlenko & A. Blackledge (Eds.), *Negotiation of identities in multilingual contexts* (pp. 1–33). Multilingual Matters.
Pearson, B. Z. (2009). Children with two languages. In E. L. Bavin (Ed.), *The Cambridge handbook of child language* (pp. 379–397). Cambridge University Press.
Pearson, B. Z. (2013). Distinguishing the bilingual as a late talker from the late talker who is bilingual. In L. A. Rescorla & P. S. Dale (Eds.), *Late talkers: language development, interventions, and outcomes* (pp. 67–87). Brookes.
Pearson, B. Z., Fernández, S., Lewedeg, V., & Oller, D. K. (1997). The relation of input factors to lexical learning by bilingual infants. *Applied Psycholinguistics, 18*, 41–58. https://doi.org/10.1017/S0142716400009863
Pennycook, A. (2016). Mobile times, mobile terms: The trans-super-poly-metro movement. In N. Coupland (Ed.), *Sociolinguistics: theoretical debates* (pp. 201–216). Oxford University Press.
Pichler, H. (2016). Uncovering discourse-pragmatic innovations: Innit in Multicultural London English. In H. Pichler (Ed.), *Discourse-pragmatic variation and change in English. New methods and insights* (pp. 59–85). Cambridge University Press.
Pierce, L. J., Genesee, F., Delcenserie, A., & Morgan, G. (2017). Variations in phonological working memory: Linking early language experiences and language learning outcomes. *Applied Psycholinguistics, 38*, 1265–1300.
Place, S., & Hoff, E. (2011). Properties of dual language exposure that influence two-year-olds' bilingual proficiency. *Child Development, 82*, 1834–1849.
Ponzanesi, S. (2020). Digital diasporas: Postcoloniality, media and affect. *International Journal of Postcolonial Studies, 22*(8), 977–993. https://doi.org/10.1080/1369801X.2020.1718537

Poplack, S. (1989). The care and handling of a megacorpus: The Ottawa-Hull French project. In R. Fasold & D. Schiffrin (Eds.), *Language change and variation* (pp. 411–444). John Benjamins.

Poplack, S., & Meechan, M. (1995). Patterns of language mixture: Nominal structure in Wolof-French and Fongbe-French bilingual discourse. In P. Muysken & L. Milroy (Eds.), *One speaker, two languages* (pp. 199–232). Cambridge University Press.

Presser, S., & Schuman, H. (1980). The measurement of a middle position in attitude surveys. *Public Opinion Quarterly, 44*(1), 70–75.

Quirk, R., Greenbaum, S., Leech, G., & Svartvik, J. (1972). *A grammar of contemporary English*. Longman.

Quirk, R., Greenbaum, S., Leech, G., & Svartvik, J. (1985). *A comprehensive grammar of the English language*. Longman.

Quiroz, B. G., Snow, C. E., & Zhao, J. (2010). Vocabulary skills of Spanish–English bilinguals: Impact of mother–child language interactions and home language and literacy support. *International Journal of Bilingualism, 14*(4), 379–399.

Quist, P. (2008). Sociolinguistic approaches to multiethnolect: Language variety and stylistic practice. *International Journal of Bilingualism, 12*, 43–61.

R Core Team. (2019). R: A language and environment for statistical computing. *R foundation for statistical computing*. https://www.R-project.org/

Rampton, B. (1995). *Crossing: Language and ethnicity among adolescents*. Longman.

Rasinger, S. M. (2010). Quantitative methods: Concepts, frameworks and issues. In L. Litosseliti (Ed.), *Research methods in linguistics* (pp. 49–67). Bloomsbury.

Research Centre on Multilingualism. (2004). *Euromosaic III—Cyprus*. Retrieved December 10, 2022, from https://publications.europa.eu/en/publication-detail/-/publication/4dc487cf-3c39-40ac-9b97-c55110263a56

Rivera-Gaxiola, M., Silva Pereyra, J., & Kuhl, P. K. (2005). Brain potentials to native and non-native speech contrasts in 7 and 11 month old American infants. *Developmental Science, 8*(2), 162–172.

Robinson, P. C. (1991). *ESP today: A practitioner's guide*. Prentice Hall.

Romaine, S. (1995). *Bilingualism* (2nd ed.).

Romaine, S. (2004). The bilingual and multilingual community. In T. Bhatia & W. C. Ritchie (Eds.), *The handbook of bilingualism* (pp. 385–406). Blackwell.

Ronan, P. (2016). Perspectives on English in Switzerland. *Cahiers de l'ILSL, 48*, 9–26.

Ronan, P. (2020). English in Ireland: Intra-territorial perspectives on language contact. In S. Buschfeld & A. Kautzsch (Eds.), *Modelling current linguistic realities of English world-wide: The extra and intra-territorial forces model put to the test* (pp. 322–346). Edinburgh University Press.

Ronan, P. (2021). Indexing Irishness in linguistic landscaping. A touristic perception of the use of Irish language and Irish style fonts. In C. Amador-Moreno & St. Lucek (Eds.), *Expanding the landscapes of Irish English: Research in honour of Jeffrey Kallen* (pp. 237–253). Routledge.

Ronan, P. (2022a). Sprachliche Landschaft im Wandel. Ein Beispiel aus Dortmund Hörde. In S. Hübscher & C. Kreutchen (Eds.), *verorten* (pp. 33–44). Athena.

Ronan, P. (2022b). Linguistic inclusion of school-age immigrants in Ruhr valley schools from a teacher's perspective. In A. Auer & J. Thorburn (Eds.), *Approaches to migration, language and identity* (pp. 199–222). Peter Lang.

Ronan, P. (Fc). English in Switzerland. In K. Bolton (Ed.), *The Wiley Blackwell encyclopedia of World Englishes*. Wiley Blackwell.

Ronan, P., & Buschfeld, S. (Fc 2023). From second to first language: Language shift in Singapore and Ireland. In M. Schmalz, M. Vida-Mannl, S. Buschfeld, & T. Brato (Eds.), *Acquisition and variation in world Englishes: Bridging paradigms and rethinking approaches*. De Gruyter Mouton.

Ronan, P., & Melles, W. (2022). Linguistic inclusion of school age immigrants in Ruhr valley schools: A translanguaging perspective. In P. Ronan & E. Ziegler (Eds.), *Language and identity in migration contexts* (pp. 277–296). Peter Lang.

Rosenbaum, Y., Nadel, E., Cooper, R. L., & Fishmann, J. (1977). English on Keren Kayemet Street. In J. A. Fishmann, R. L. Cooper, & A. W. Conrad (Eds.), *The spread of English* (pp. 179–196). Newbury House.

Rowe, C., & Grohmann, K. K. (2013). Discrete bilectalism: Towards co-overt prestige and diglossic shift in Cyprus. *International Journal of the Sociology of Language, 224*, 119–142.

References

Rubín, J. (1968). *National bilingualism in Paraguay*. Mouton.
Safont-Jordà, P. (2013). Early stages of trilingual pragmatic development: A longitudinal study of requests in Catalan, Spanish and English. *Journal of Pragmatics, 59*, 68–80.
Sakel, J., & Everet, D. L. (2012). *Linguistic fieldwork*. Cambridge University Press.
Sankoff, G. (1974). A quantitative paradigm for the study of communicative competence. In R. Bauman & J. Sherzer (Eds.), *Explorations in the ethnography of speaking* (pp. 18–49). Cambridge University Press.
Sarpeah, A. (2017, August 21). *The fake patois used by Shatta Wale, Stonebwoy, others can't be labeled as Dancehall*. Ghbase.com. Retrieved March 10, 2019, from https://www.ghbase.com/fake-patois-used-shatta-wale-stonebwoy-others-cant-labeled-dancehall-root-eye/
Sayer, P. (2010). Using the linguistic landscape as a pedagogical resource. *ELT Journal, 64*(2), 143–154.
Scheele, A., Leseman, P., & Mayo, A. (2010). The home language environment of monolingual and bilingual children and their language proficiency. *Applied Psycholinguistics, 31*, 117–140. https://doi.org/10.1017/S014271640999019
Schieffelin, B. B., Woolard, K., & Kroskrity, A. (Eds.). (1998). *Language ideologies: Practice and theory*. Oxford University Press.
Schmalz, M., Vida-Mannl, M., Buschfeld, S., & Brato, T. (Eds.) (Fc. 2023). *Acquisition and variation in World Englishes: Bridging paradigms and rethinking approaches*. De Gruyter Mouton.
Schmid, M. (2011). *Language attrition*. Cambridge University Press.
Schneider, E. W. (2007). *Postcolonial English. Varieties around the World*. Cambridge University Press.
Schneider, E. W. (2012). Exploring the interface between World Englishes and second language acquisition–and implications for English as a lingua franca. *Journal of English as a Lingua Franca, 1*(1), 57–91.
Schneider, E. W. (2013). Leisure-activity ESP as a special case of ELF: The example of scuba diving English. *English Today, 29*(3), 47–57.
Schneider, E. W. (2016a). Grassroots Englishes in tourism interactions. *English Today, 32*(3), 2–10.
Schneider, E. W. (2016b). Hybrid Englishes: An exploratory survey. *World Englishes, 35*(3), 339–354.
Schneider, E. W. (2016c). World Englishes on YouTube: Treasure trove or nightmare? In E. Seoane & C. Suárez-Gómez (Eds.), *World Englishes: New theoretical and methodological considerations* (pp. 253–282). John Benjamins.
Schneider, E. W. (2016d). World Englishes and English as a lingua franca: Relationships and interfaces. In M.-L. Pitzl & R. Osimk-Teasdale (Eds.), *English as a Lingua Franca: Perspectives and prospects* (pp. 105–114). Walter de Gruyter Inc.
Schneider, E. W. (2020). Calling Englishes as complex dynamic systems: Diffusion and restructuring. In A. Mauranen & S. Vetchinnikova (Eds.), *Language change: The impact of English as a Lingua Franca* (pp. 15–43). Cambridge University Press.
Schneider, E. W., & Buschfeld, S. (2022). The geographical and demographic expansion of English. In S. S. Mufwene & A. M. Escobar (Eds.), *The Cambridge handbook of language contact* (Population movement and language change) (Vol. 1, pp. 583–610). Cambridge University Press.
Schneider, G., & Lauber, M. (2019). *Statistics for linguists: A patient, slow-paced introduction to statistics and to the programming language R*. Digitale Lehre und Forschung UZH. https://doi.org/10.5167/uzh-183632
Schröder, A. (2007). Camfranglais: a language with several (sur)faces and important sociolinguistic functions. In A. Bartels & E. Wiemann (Eds.), *Global fragments. (Dis)orientation in the new world order* (pp. 281–298).
Schuman, H., & Presser, S. (1996). *Questions and answers in attitude surveys. Experiments on question form, wording, and context*. Sage Publications.
Scollon, R., & Scollon, S. (2003). *Discourse in place: Language in the material world*. Routledge.
Sebba, M. (2010). Discourses in transit. In A. Jaworski & C. Thurlow (Eds.), *Semiotic landscapes: Language, image, space* (pp. 59–76). Bloomsbury.
Seidlhofer, B. (2011). *Understanding English as a Lingua Franca*. Oxford University Press.
Serratrice, L. (2013a). The bilingual child. In T. K. Bhatia & W. C. Ritchie (Eds.), *The handbook of bilingualism and multilingualism* (2nd ed., pp. 87–108). Wiley-Blackwell.

Serratrice, L. (2013b). Cross-linguistic influence in bilingual development: Determinants and mechanisms. *Linguistic Approaches to Bilingualism, 3*(1), 3–25.
Serratrice, L. (2018). Becoming bilingual in early childhood. In A. De Houwer & L. Ortega (Eds.), *The Cambridge handbook of bilingualism* (pp. 15–35). Cambridge University Press.
Serratrice, L., & Hervé, C. (2015). Referential expressions in bilingual acquisition. In L. Serratrice & S. Allen (Eds.), *The acquisition of reference* (pp. 311–333). John Benjamins.
Shahidullah, S., & Hepper, P. G. (1994). Frequency discrimination by the foetus. *Early Human Development, 36*(1), 13–26.
Sharma, B. K. (2014). On high horses: Transnational Nepalis and language ideologies on YouTube. *Discourse, Context and Media, 4*(5), 19–28.
Shohamy, E., & Ben-Rafael, E. (2015). Linguistic landscape: A new journal. *Linguistic Landscape, 1*, 1–5.
SIL International. (2022). *How many languages are there in the world?* Retrieved July 2, 2022, from https://www.ethnologue.com/guides/how-many-languages
Silvén, M., Voeten, M., Kouvo, A., & Lundén, M. (2014). Speech perception and vocabulary growth: A longitudinal study of Finnish–Russian bilinguals and Finnish monolinguals from infancy to three years. *International Journal of Behavioral Development, 38*(4), 323–332.
Silverstein, M. (1985). Language and the culture of gender: At the intersection of structure, usage, antideology. In E. Mertz & R. J. Parmentier (Eds.), *Semiotic meditation: Sociocultural and psychological perspectives* (pp. 219–259). Academic Press.
Simon-Cereijido, G., & Gutiérrez-Clellen, V. F. (2009). A cross-linguistic and bilingual evaluation of the interdependence between lexical and grammatical domains. *Applied Psycholinguistics, 30*(2), 315–337.
Simpson, P. (1999). Language, culture and identity: With (another) look at accents in pop and rock singing. *Multilingua—Journal of Cross-Cultural and Interlanguage Communication, 18*(4), 343–368.
Singleton, D., & Aronin, L. (Eds.). (2019). *Twelve lectures on multilingualism*. Multilingual Matters.
Skutnabb-Kangas, T. (2000). *Linguistic genocide in education—or worldwide diversity and human rights?* Erlbaum.
Smith, G. P., & Siegel, J. (2013). Tok Pisin. In S. M. Michaelis, P. Maurer, M. Haspelmath, & M. Huber (Eds.), *The survey of Pidgin and Creole languages* (English-based and Dutch-based languages) (Vol. I, pp. 214–222). Oxford University Press.
Speech by Prime Minister Lee Kuan Yew. (1984). Retrieved April 22, 2018, from www.nas.gov.sg/archivesonline/data/pdfdoc/lky19840921a.pdf
Spolsky, B. (2004). *Language policy*. Cambridge University Press.
Spolsky, B. (2005). Language policy. In J. Cohen, K. T. McAlister, K. Rolstad, & J. MacSwan (Eds.), *ISB4: Proceedings of the 4th international symposium on bilingualism* (pp. 2152–2164). Cascadilla Press.
Spolsky, B. (Ed.). (2012a). *The Cambridge handbook of language policy*. Cambridge University Press.
Spolsky, B. (2012b). What is language policy? In B. Spolsky (Ed.), *The Cambridge handbook of language policy* (pp. 3–15). Cambridge University Press.
Spolsky, B., & Cooper, R. L. (1991). *The languages of Jerusalem*. Clarendon.
Spradley, J. (1979). Asking descriptive questions. In M. Pogrebin (Ed.), *Qualitative approaches to criminal justice: Perspectives from the field* (pp. 44–53). Sage Publishing.
Stavans, A., & Hoffmann, C. (2015). *Multilingualism*. Cambridge University Press.
Stewart, W. A. (1968). A sociolinguistic typology for describing national multilingualism. In J. A. Fishman (Ed.), *Readings in the sociology of language* (pp. 531–545). Mouton.
Stockwell, R., Bowen, J., & Martin, J. (1965). *The grammatical structures of English and Spanish*. University of Chicago Press.
Strang, B. M. H. (1970). *A history of English*. Methuen.
Strauss, J. (2011). Linguistic diversity and everyday life in the Ottoman cities of the Eastern Mediterranean and the Balkans (late 19th–early 20th century). *The History of the Family, 16*(2), 126–141.
Stringer, D. (2013). Attrition. In P. Robinson (Ed.), *The Routledge encyclopedia of second language acquisition* (pp. 48–51). Routledge.

References

Stroud, C. (2003). Postmodernist perspectives on local languages: African mother tongue education in times of globalisation. *International Journal of Bilingual Education and Bilingualism, 6*(1), 17–36.

Sundara, M., & Scutellaro, A. (2011). Rhythmic distance between languages affects the development of speech perception in bilingual infants. *Journal of Phonetics, 39*(4), 505–513.

Sundara, M., Ward, N., Conboy, B., & Kuhl, P. K. (2020). Exposure to a second language in infancy alters speech production. *Bilingualism: Language and Cognition, 23*(5), 978–991. https://doi.org/10.1017/S1366728919000853

Tabouret-Keller, A. (1998). Language and identity. In F. Coulmas (Ed.), *The handbook of sociolinguistics* (pp. 315–326). Blackwell.

Tagliamonte, S. A. (2006). *Analysing sociolinguistic variation*. Cambridge University Press.

Tan, Y.-Y. (2014). English as a 'mother tongue' in Singapore. *World Englishes, 33*(3), 319–339.

Taxitari, L., Kambanaros, M., Floros, G., & Grohmann, K. (2017). Early language development in a bilectal context: The Cypriot adaptation of the Macarthur-Bates CDI. In E. Babatsouli, D. Ingram, & N. Müller (Eds.), *Crosslinguistic encounters in language acquisition: Typical and atypical development* (pp. 145–171). Multilingual Matters.

The Official Website of Berlin. (2022). *35 percent of Berliners with foreign roots*. Retrieved March 25, 2022, from https://www.berlin.de/en/news/6092347-5559700-berlin-inhabitants-with-foreign-roots.en.html

Thomas, M. (2006). Robert Lado, 1915–1995. In K. Brown (Ed.), *Encyclopedia of language and linguistics* (Vol. 6, pp. 301–302). Elsevier.

Thomason, S. G. (2001). *Language contact. An introduction*. Edinburgh University Press.

Tickoo, M. L. (1996). Fifty years of English in Singapore: All gains, (a) few losses? In J. A. Fishman, A. W. Conrad, & A. Rubal-Lopez (Eds.), *Post-Imperial English: Status change in former British and American colonies, 1940-1990* (pp. 431–455). Mouton de Gruyter.

Todd, L. (1990). *Pidgins and Creoles* (2nd ed.). Routledge.

Tollefson, J. W., & Tsui, A. B. (2014). Language diversity and language policy in educational access and equity. *Review of Research in Education, 38*, 189–214.

Treffers-Daller, J. (2018). The measurement of bilingual abilities. In A. De Houwer & L. Ortega (Eds.), *The Cambridge handbook of bilingualism* (pp. 289–306). Cambridge University Press.

Trudgill, P. (1983). Acts of conflicting identity: The sociolinguistics of British pop-song performance. In P. Trudgill (Ed.), *On dialect—social and geographical perspectives* (pp. 141–160). New York University Press.

Trust for London. (2022). *London's non-UK born population by country of birth (2010 and 2020)*. Retrieved March 10, 2022, from https://www.trustforlondon.org.uk/data/country-of-birth-population/

Turell, M. T. (Ed.). (2001). *Multilingualism in Spain: Sociolinguistic and psycholinguistic aspects of linguistic minority groups*. Multilingual Matters.

UIS (UNESCO Institute for Statistics). (2017). *Fact sheet no. 45*. Retrieved November 4, 2022, from http://uis.unesco.org/sites/default/files/documents/fs45-literacy-rates-continue-rise-generation-to-next-en-2017_0.pdf

United States Census Bureau. (2019). *DP02—Selected social characteristics in the United States: Miami City, Florida. 2019: American Community Survey 1-year estimates*. Retrieved March 10, 2022, from https://data.census.gov/cedsci/table?g=1600000US1245000&tid=ACSDP1Y2019.DP02

Unsworth, S. (2013). Current issues in multilingual first language acquisition. *Annual Review of Applied Linguistics, 33*, 21–50.

Valdés, G. (2001). Heritage language students: Profiles and possibilities. In J. K. Peyton, D. A. Ranard, & S. McGinnis (Eds.), *Heritage languages in America: Preserving a national resource*. Center for Applied Linguistics.

Van Dijk, C., Van Wonderen, E., Koutamanisi, E., Kootstra, G. J., Dijkstra, T., & Unsworth, S. (2022). Cross-linguistic influence in simultaneous and early sequential bilingual children: A meta-analysis. *Journal of Child Language, 49*(5), 897–929. https://doi.org/10.1017/S0305000921000337

Van Rossum, G., & Drake, F. L. (2009). *Python 3 reference manual*. CreateSpace.

VanPatten, B., & Benati, A. G. (2015). *Key terms in second language acquisition*. Bloomsbury Academic.

Velupillai, V. (2015). Pidgins, Creoles and mixed languages. An introduction. .

Vertovic, S. (2007). Super-diversity and its implications. *Ethnic and Racial Studies, 30*(6), 1024–1054.

Vida-Mannl, M. (2022). *The value of the English language in global mobility and higher education: An investigation of higher education in Cyprus*. Bloomsbury.

Vida-Mannl, M. (Fc. 2023). Parental language ideologies and children's language use in Singapore—raising speakers of 'Standard' English? In M. Schmalz, M. Vida-Mannl, S. Buschfeld & T. Brato (Eds.), Acquisition and variation in World Englishes: Bridging paradigms and rethinking approaches. De Gruyter Mouton.

Vogel, S., & García, O. (2017). *Translanguaging. Oxford research encyclopedia of education*. https://doi.org/10.1093/acrefore/9780190264093.013.181

Volterra, V., & Taeschner, T. (1978). The acquisition and development of language by bilingual children. *Journal of Child Language, 5*(2), 311–326.

Vuković-Vojnović, D., & Nićin, M. (2012). English as a global language in the tourism industry: A case study. In G. Rață, I. Petroman, & C. Petroman (Eds.), *The English of tourism* (pp. 3–18). Cambridge Scholars.

Vulliamy, E. (2019, April 6). *She loves you… Sí, Oui, Ja: How pop went multilingual*. The Guardian. Retrieved May 12, 2022, from https://www.theguardian.com/music/2019/apr/06/latin-spanish-pop-takes-over-from-english-language

Walsh, O. (2014). 'Les anglicismes polluent la langue française'. Purist attitudes in France and Quebec. *Journal of French Language Studies, 24*(3), 423–449. https://doi.org/10.1017/S0959269513000227

Wardhaugh, R. (2002). *An introduction to sociolinguistics* (4th ed.).

Watts, R. J. (2011). *Language myths and the history of English*. Oxford University Press.

Wechsler, A. (2017, June 5). *The international-school surge*. The Atlantic. Retrieved November 4, 2022, from https://www.theatlantic.com/education/archive/2017/06/the-international-school-surge/528792/

Wei, L. (2018). Translanguaging as a practical theory of language. *Applied Linguistics, 39*(1), 9–30.

Wei, L., & Moyer, M. (2008). *Blackwell guide to research methods in bilingualism and multilingualism*. Blackwell.

Weikum, W. M., Vouloumanos, A., Navarra, J., Soto-Faraco, S., Sebastián-Gallés, N., & Werker, J. F. (2007). Visual language discrimination in infancy. *Science, 316*(5828), 1159. https://doi.org/10.1126/science.1137486

Werker, J. (2012). Perceptual foundations of bilingual acquisition in infancy. *Annals of the New York Academy of Sciences, 1251*(1), 50–61. https://doi.org/10.1111/j.1749-6632.2012.06484.x

Werner, V. (2018). Linguistics and pop culture: Setting the scene(s). In V. Werner (Ed.), *The language of pop culture* (pp. 3–26). Routledge.

Westermayer, L. (2019). *"What's a singer meant to sound like?" Extra- and intralinguistic influences on the singing accents of Australian indie artists*. [Unpublished MA thesis, University of Regensburg].

Westphal, M., & Jansen, L. (2021). English in global pop music. In B. Schneider, T. Heyd, & M. Saraceni (Eds.), *Bloomsbury World Englishes volume 1: Paradigms* (pp. 190–206). Bloomsbury Academic.

Wiegel, M. (2013, May 21). Regierung will Englisch an Universitäten erlauben. *FAZ*. Retrieved November 4, 2022, from https://www.faz.net/aktuell/politik/ausland/frankreich-regierung-will-englisch-an-universitaeten-erlauben-12189945.html

Wiese, H. (2009). Grammatical innovation in multiethnic urban Europe: New linguistic practices among adolescents. *Lingua, 119*, 782–780.

Wiese, H. (2012). Kiezdeutsch. *Ein neuer Dialekt entsteht*. C. H. Beck.

Wiese, H. (2020). Contact in the city. In R. Hickey (Ed.), *Wiley handbook of language contact* (pp. 261–279). Wiley-Blackwell.

Wiley, T. G. (2014). Diversity, super-diversity, and monolingual language ideology in the United States: Tolerance or intolerance? *Review of Research in Education, 38*, 1–32.

References

Wilkinson, R. (2013). English-medium instruction at a Dutch university: Challenges and pitfalls. In A. Doiz, D. Lasagabaster, & J. M. Sierra (Eds.), *English-medium instruction at universities: Global challenges* (pp. 3–24). Multilingual Matters.

Wilson, G. (2021). Language use among Syrian refugees in Germany. In C. Meierkord & E. W. Schneider (Eds.), *World Englishes at the grassroots* (pp. 211–232). Edinburgh University Press.

Winter, B. (2019). *Statistics for linguists: An introduction using R*. Routledge.

Wolf, G. (2019). Studying dialect spelling in its own right. Suggestions from a case study. In B. Birte & C. Claridge (Eds.), *Norms and conventions in the history of English* (pp. 191–212).

Wolff, M. (2010). China's English mystery—the views of a China 'foreign expert'. *English Today, 104*(26), 53–56.

Woolard, K. A. (1998). Introduction. In B. B. Schieffelin, K. A. Woolard, & P. V. Kroskrity (Eds.), *Language ideologies: Practice and theory* (pp. 3–20). Oxford University Press.

World Population Review. (2022a). *World city populations 2022*. Retrieved March 25, 2022, from https://worldpopulationreview.com/world-cities

World Population Review. (2022b). *Immigration by country 2022*. Retrieved March 10, 2022, from https://worldpopulationreview.com/country-rankings/immigration-by-country

Wright, L. (Ed.). (2000). *The development of standard English 1300–1800: Theories, descriptions, conflicts*. Cambridge University Press.

Yiakoumetti, A. (2014). Language education in our globalised classrooms: Recommendations on providing for equal language rights. In M. Solly & E. Esch (Eds.), *Language education and the challenges of globalisation: Sociolinguistic issues* (pp. 13–31). Cambridge University Press.

Ziegler, E., Schmitz, U., & Uslucan, H.-H. (2018). Attitudes towards visual multilingualism in the linguistic landscape of the Ruhr area. In M. Pütz & N. Mundt (Eds.), *Expanding the linguistic landscape. Linguistic diversity, multimodality and the use of space as a semiotic resource* (pp. 263–298). Multilingual Matters.

Zsombok, G. (2021). Prescribing French: A corpus-linguistic approach to official terminology in French newspapers. *Journal of French Language Studies, 31*(3), 270–293. https://doi.org/10.1017/S0959269520000204

Zwanziger, E. E., Allen, S. E. M., & Genesee, F. (2005). Crosslinguistic influence in bilingual acquisition: Subject omission in learners of Inuktitut and English. *Journal of Child Language, 32*(4), 893–909.

Index

A

Acceptability Judgment Task (AJT) 286
Accommodation theory 79, 155, 238
Achieved bilingual 10
Acquisitional processes 52
Addition of features 91
Additive bilingual 10
Advantages 51
Age 60
Age effect 79
Age of onset of acquisition 78
Ambilingual 10
American English 237
Amount and quality 61
Annotations 307
AntConc 309
Artistic 257
Ascendant bilingual 10
Ascribed bilingual 10
Asymmetrical bilingual 10
Attitudes 157
Authenticity 263, 268

B

Balanced bilingual 10
Balanced multilinguals 183
Bengali 229
Bilingual 8
Bilingual first language acquisition 46–47, 51
Bilingualism 47
Bilingual second language acquisition 46
Borrowing 84, 89
Bottom-up signs 255

C

Canada 184
Child-external factors 60
Child-internal factors 60
Closed questions 285
Code alternation 89
Code-mixing 88, 228, 246
Coding 307
Commemorative signs 254
Commercial discourses 257
Communities of practice 4, 151, 218
Community language 32
Comparable corpora 305
Complex Dynamic System 115
Compound bilingual 10
Consciousness 78
Consecutive bilingual 10
Consent 293
Construction of identities 150
Contact-induced language change 77, 82, 95
Content and Language Integrated Learning (CLIL) 185
Content-based interviews 288
Contexts of language use 284
Contrastive corpora 305
Convergence 80, 94
Coordinate bilingual 10
Corpus data 279
Corpus linguistics 304
Covert bilingual 10
Creoles 25
Cross-linguistic influence 38, 63, 79
Cross-linguistic interactions 8
Cultural capital 262, 268
Cyprus 138, 140

D

Data collection 282
Data transcription 307
Degree of use 130
Descriptive statistics 309
Diagonal bilingual 10
Dialects 49
Diasporas 210
Digital diasporas 211
Disadvantage 35–37, 55
Discrimination on linguistic 162
Diverge 80
Domains of language use 62
Dominant 38
Dominant bilingual 10
Dormant bilingual 10
Dortmund 262
Dual system hypothesis 60, 63
Dutch 270

340 Index

E

Early bilingual 10
Educational 129, 177
Elite/elective multilingualism 12
Emergent bilingual 10
Emojis 231
Endangered 4
English as a Foreign Language (EFL) 103, 114
English as a Lingua Franca (ELF) 106
English as a Native Language (ENL) 103
English as a Second Language (ESL) 103, 114
English for Specific Purposes (ESP) 106, 107
English-medium study programmes 189
Equilingual 10
Ethical research 293
Ethnographic research 291
Ethnography 303
Exploitation colonies 28
Extra- and Intra-territorial Forces 114
Extrinsic motivation 12

F

Facebook 222
Feature loss without replacement 91
Fieldwork 278
Focus group interviews 289
French 270
Friend of a friend-approach 283
Functional bilingual 10

G

Globalisation 133
Glocalisation 221
Grammaticality judgments 284
Grammaticality Judgment Task (GJT) 287
Grassroots Englishes 106, 108, 114
Grassroots multilingualism 12
Guest workers 25, 196

H

Heritage language 132
Heritage language education 184
Heritage/folk/immigrant multilingualism 12
Hindi 227
Hip hop 246
Home language 32
Horizontal bilingual 10
Human capital 199

Hybrid identity 245
Hybrid languages 109

I

Identity 150
– construction 13, 152
– problems 38, 39
Ideologies 158
Immigrants 197, 198
Incipient bilingual 11
Incomplete 78
Incomplete acquisition 37
Index of communication 126
Indexicality 161
Indexical order 202
Individual multilingualism 12
Inductive and deductive approaches 281
Informative function 255
Informed consent 294
Infrastructural discourse 256
Input 79
Instagram 230
Interference 38
International 129
International Corpus of English (ICE) corpora 304
Internationalisation 188
International schools 181
Intersentential code-switching 88
Interview 288
Intrasentential changes 88
Intrinsic 12
Ireland 163, 264
Irish 264

L

L1-medium education 178
L1-medium instructions 181
L2 acquisition 78
Language acquisition 7
Language attitudes 157, 284
Language attrition 9, 75
Language change 81
Language contact 24, 74, 162
– in educational contexts 26
– intensity 82
Language death 75
Language dominance 62, 184
Language exposure 60
Language hierarchies 75

Index

Language immersion 182
Language innovation 209
Language maintenance 161
Language mixture 76
Language planning 165
Language policies 76, 162, 164, 169
Language revitalisation 134
Language rights 168
Language shift 161
Late bilingual 11
Learner Englishes 114
Lexicon 55
Likert scales 281, 285
Lingua franca 26, 131
Linguistic discrimination 154
Linguistic diversity 124
Linguistic factors 81
Linguistic heterogeneity 237
Linguistic identity 154, 155
Linguistic landscape 292
Linguistic minorities 132
Linguistic observations 291
Linguistic repertoire 91, 186
Linguistic sign 260

M

Mainstream education 181
Mainstream majority language education 177
Maintenance of minority languages 225
Markedness 82
Matched guise technique 158
Maximal bilingual 11
Messaging apps 218
Metadata 279, 286
Metalinguistic awareness 8
Middle response bias 287
Migration/immigration 25, 132, 196
Minimal bilingual 11
Minority language 32, 131
Minority language education 179
Mixed code 111
Mixed languages 110
Mixed-method approaches 280
Mixing of language 37
Mobility 201
Monolingual 7
Monolingual approaches to education 178
Monolingual bias 50
Monolingual education 179
Monolingualism is the norm 35
Monolingual national ideologies 31
Monolingual policies 167

Morphosyntactic 59
Multicultural London English 205
Multicultural Paris French 205
Multi-ethnic 205
Multi-ethnic varieties 208
Multiethnolects 205
Multilinguals 7, 8
– corpus 305
– education 179
– first language acquisition 51
– hierarchies 141
– identities 236
– practices 233
– signage 255
– songs 241
Multilingualism in a state 31
Multilingualism is a recent phenomenon 33, 34
Multiliteracy 182

N

Namibia 135
National languages 32, 131
National multilingualism 128
Native speakers 50
Nativisation 104
Natural bilingual 11
Naturalistic data 278
Negative transfer 64
Negotiation of identities 156, 242
New media 220

O

Observer's Paradox 290
Official language 129, 131, 167
One nation—one language 161
One nation-one language ideology 35, 159
Online data 279
Online multilingualism 303
Online research 294
Open questions 285
Orders of indexicality 202
Overgeneralisation 80
Overregularisation 80

P

Participants 283
Participants' anonymity 294
Passive bilingual 11
Personality principle 143

Pidgin and creole 104
Pidgins 25, 76
Polyglot 8
Pop music 236
Power relations 75, 131
Primary bilingual 11
Process of language acquisition 36
Productive bilingual 11
Proximity 25
Public signage 254
Purist ideology 164

Q

Qualitative versus quantitative 281
Questionnaires 284

R

Random sampling 284
Rap 239
Receptive bilingual 11
Recessive bilingual 11
Refugees 196
Regulatory discourse 256
Regulatory signage 254
Relative linguistic diversity 128
Relexification 94
Reported data 279
Representativeness 283

S

Screen-based data 302
Script 268
Secondary bilingual 11
Semibilingual 11
Semilingual 11
Semi-structured interview 288
Separate systems 52
Sequential multilingual acquisition 78
Settlement colonies 28
Sheltered immersion 177
Signage 254
Simplification 80
Simultaneous bilingual 11
Singapore 137, 143
Singlish 110, 143
Social desirability bias 287
Social factor 81
Social media 218, 302
Social status 142

Societal multilingualism 12
Sociolinguistic interview 289
Sociolinguistic scales 201
Sound discrimination 53
Sound perception 54
Sound system(s) 53–55
Spatial 259
Speaker fluency 83
Speakers' attitudes 86
St. Martin 137, 270
Standard 131
Standard language ideology 159, 164
State 168
Statistical inference 309
Stratified random sampling 284
Strong multilingual approaches 182
Structured interview 288
Subordinate bilingual 11
Substratum interference 85
Subtractive bilingual 11
Successive bilingual 11
Super-diversity 198
Symbolic function 255
Symmetrical bilingual 11

T

Technobiographies 303
Territoriality principle 142
Tertiary education 188
Token 292
Top-down signs 255
Tourists 265
Trade colonisation 28
Transfer 79
Transfer of grammatical features 81
Transgressive discourse 257
Transgressive signs 254
Translanguaging 90
Translanguaging pedagogy 186
Translation equivalents 58
Trilingual 7
Types of data 278

U

Ultimate attainment 78
Une langue 31
Une nation 31
Unitary System Hypothesis 60
Unstructured interview 288
User-based data 303

V

Vertical bilingual 11
Vocabulary size 57

W

Weak multilingual approaches 180
Web 2.0 219

Y

YouTube 224

Printed by Printforce, United Kingdom